ENGL

REACHING THE HIGHEST LEVEL

LEARNERS

OF ENGLISH LITERACY

GILBERT G. GARCIA

ROWLAND HEIGHTS, CALIFORNIA, USA

EDITOR

INTERNATIONAL
Reading Association
800 Barksdale Road, PO Box 8139
Newark, Delaware 19714-8139, USA
www.reading.org

KH

The International Reading Association attempts, through its publications, to provide a forum for a wide spectrum of opinions on reading. This policy permits divergent viewpoints without implying the endorsement of the Association.

Director of Publications   Joan M. Irwin
Editorial Director, Books and Special Projects   Matthew W. Baker
Senior Editor, Books and Special Projects   Tori M. Bachman
Production Editor   Shannon Benner
Permissions Editor   Janet S. Parrack
Acquisitions and Communications Coordinator   Corinne M. Mooney
Assistant Editor   Charlene M. Nichols
Administrative Assistant   Michele Jester
Editorial Assistant   Tyanna L. Collins
Production Department Manager   Iona Sauscermen
Supervisor, Electronic Publishing   Anette Schütz
Senior Electronic Publishing Specialist   Cheryl J. Strum
Electronic Publishing Specialist   R. Lynn Harrison

Project Editor   Shannon Benner

Cover   Design: Linda Steere
Photographs: left, Getty Images; right, PhotoDisc

Proofreading   Peggy Mason

Library of Congress Cataloging-in-Publication Data
English learners : reaching the highest level of English literacy / Gilbert G. Garcia, editor.
        p.   cm.
    ISBN 0-87207-455-2
1. English language—Study and teaching—Foreign speakers.   2. Literacy.
3. Reading.   I. Garcia, Gilbert G.
    PE1128.A2 E544 2002
    428'.0071--dc21

                                                                        2002008716

Fourth Printing, May 2004

12/21/04

CONTENTS

FOREWORD   vi

PREFACE   ix

CONTRIBUTORS   xii

SECTION I
Teaching English Learners to Read: Current Policy and Best Instructional Practice

CHAPTER 1   2
Reading and the Bilingual Student: Fact and Friction
Jim Cummins

CHAPTER 2   34
Teaching English Learners to Read: Learning or Acquisition?
David Freeman and Yvonne Freeman

CHAPTER 3   55
Three Roles for Reading for Minority-Language Children
Stephen Krashen

CHAPTER 4   71
Orthographic Development and Learning to Read in Different Languages
Donald R. Bear, Shane Templeton, Lori A. Helman, and Tamara Baren

CHAPTER 5   96
Scaffolding Reading Experiences for Multilingual Classrooms
Michael F. Graves and Jill Fitzgerald

CHAPTER 6   125
Making Content Instruction Accessible for English
Language Learners
Ana Hernández

SECTION II
**Teaching English Language Development:
Rethinking and Redesigning Curriculum**

CHAPTER 7   152
Communicative Approaches to Second-Language Acquisition:
The Bridge to Second-Language Literacy
Alan N. Crawford

CHAPTER 8   182
Meeting the Needs of English Learners in All-English
Classrooms: Sharing the Responsibility
Julie M. Coppola

CHAPTER 9   197
Revisioning the Blueprint: Building for the Academic
Success of English Learners
Gilbert G. García and Dolores Beltrán

CHAPTER 10   227
Rethinking English Language Instruction: An Architectural
Approach
Susana Dutro and Carrol Moran

CHAPTER 11   259
Multilevel Collaboration for English Learners:
An Asian American Perspective
Ji-Mei Chang

CHAPTER 12   286
Standards-Based Instruction for English Language Learners
Joseph Laturnau

SECTION III
Optimizing Culture as a Bridge to Literacy Learning

CHAPTER 13   308
Connecting Children, Culture, Curriculum, and Text
MariAnne George, Taffy E. Raphael, and Susan Florio-Ruane

CHAPTER 14   333
Reading With a Hero: A Mediated and Literate Experience
Paul Boyd-Batstone

CHAPTER 15   357
Access to Books and Beyond: Creating and Learning From
a Book Lending Program for Latino Families in the Inner City
David B. Yaden, Jr., Patricia Madrigal, and Anamarie Tam

CHAPTER 16   387
Mediating Language and Literacy: Lessons From
an After-School Setting
Margaret A. Gallego, Robert Rueda, and Luis C. Moll

AUTHOR INDEX   409

SUBJECT INDEX   419

The government agents gathered the children.
They took the children to boarding schools
far from their homes and families.
The children from the West
were taken to the East.
The children from the East
were taken to the West.
The People's children were scattered
like leaves torn from a tree.
At schools far from home,
the children were taught to become Americans.
They learned to be ashamed of their People.

(Ortiz, 1994, p. 17)

The preceding excerpt from the picture storybook *The People Shall Continue* by Simon Ortiz, a poet of Acoma heritage, focuses on the boarding school experience that was inflicted on many young Native Americans in years past as part of their public education in the United States. Whenever I teach an early childhood literacy course for undergraduates, I read and display segments from this book-length narrative poem to stimulate class discussion about language and literacy policies in schools and the United States at large. The overall intent is to get prospective teachers to examine societal and school perspectives on language and cultural diversity, and specifically, policy orientations to literacy instruction for children from diverse backgrounds. Class members are encouraged to ponder and debate how far the U.S. public school system has moved from simplistic approaches that view language and cultural differences as problems to be eradicated, toward more humane and effective responses to the literacy needs of children whose home language is not English.

In recent semesters, this class activity has become a timely endeavor for teachers-to-be—and *The People Shall Continue* has become a compelling text—due to ongoing school policy developments at national, state, and local levels. Once again, educational policymakers appear to be instituting simple and myopic, if not oppressive, ways to educate the children of diverse peoples in the United States, this time justifying "reforms" with the rhetoric of accountability, standards, scientifically based research, research-based practice, and the like.

At a national educational conference that I attended last year, a high-ranking government education official devoted several minutes of his featured address to extolling the virtues of a commercial English language basal reading series currently enjoying success in a number of states with large numbers of English language learners. The speaker even touted the reading series over a competitor series that he also named, and anointed the former as an exemplar for appropriate reading instruction in the primary grades, particularly for culturally and linguistically diverse children having difficulty learning to read.

For many of us who have committed our professional lives to helping advance the language and literacy education of culturally and linguistically diverse children, these are some of the worst of times in recent educational history. Efforts by educational policymakers to reduce the complexities of literacy teaching and learning to a mere matter of reading methods, to homogenize the cultural and linguistic characteristics of children, and to ignore inequitable schooling conditions hearken back to a less enlightened era that some of us experienced firsthand with less than positive effects. Ironically, these may also be the best of times for those of us who currently are teaching or conducting research in multilingual classrooms in which exciting pluralistic communities of young readers and writers are being forged, challenging pernicious stereotypes of "poor," "at risk," or "minority" learners.

For example, during the past two years, I have engaged in collaborative research with an early childhood teacher committed to capitalizing on the cultural and linguistic backgrounds of her students. She transforms her classroom into a multilingual environment that invites everyone there to learn in, through, and about the different home languages of the children. In the recent past, these have included English, Spanish, Vietnamese, Japanese, Russian, and American Sign Language. In no way can her teaching effectiveness or the children's language and literacy learning, documented by quantitative and qualitative measures, be attributed simply to instructional methods, materials, or tests. A more realistic explanation must take into account the professional knowledge and disposition of the teacher, her relationship with the children's families, her interactions with the children, the children's innate abilities and desires to grow in oral and written language, their social relations with one another in literacy events, and the teacher's resourcefulness to bring multilingual resources into the classroom, among other factors. The upshot of this example is that literacy teaching and learning cannot be captured by a simple formula.

In *English Learners: Reaching the Highest Level of English Literacy*, readers will be duly informed and/or reminded of the multifaceted and complex nature of educating children from linguistically diverse backgrounds in today's politicized educational arena. In the preface, editor Gilbert G. García provides a sobering thumbnail sketch of the current educational state of affairs for this growing population, which the contributors then fill in with deeper scrutiny and finer detail. Collectively, these scholars and researchers address policy, theory, research, and practice, sometimes drawing from the international literature to buttress their arguments and explanations. All question explicitly and implicitly the wisdom of literacy teaching, curriculum, and assessment for English language learners that does not take into account students' cultural and linguistic backgrounds. The literacy contexts considered are not confined to the classroom; they include home and community, most involving English language learners in the elementary and middle grades, which are critical periods for educational support.

This volume provides a real service to the educational field at a pivotal point by amplifying the ongoing conversation on literacy teaching and achievement to include attention to an oft-neglected segment of the school enrollment. The overall tone of the volume is serious and concerned, yet marked by a firmness of purpose to continue to improve literacy opportunities for children in the process of learning the school language. Given the significant demographic change that is occurring in U.S. schools, the potential readership for *English Learners* is expansive, encompassing inservice and preservice teachers, school administrators, teacher educators, researchers, and educational policymakers affiliated with multilingual, bilingual, and monolingual schools. It is hoped that this volume will help to incite among all its readers a shared responsibility to create the best school literacy programs for English language learners, now and in the future. As the epic poem by Ortiz (1994) expresses, shared responsibility is critical in these matters.

> We must take great care with each other.
> We must share our concern with each other.
> Nothing is separate from us.
> We are all one body of People. (p. 23)

Rosalinda B. Barrera
University of Illinois at Urbana-Champaign
Champaign, Illinois, USA

REFERENCE

Ortiz, S.J. (1994). *The people shall continue*. Emeryville, CA: Children's Book Press.

PREFACE

This book grew out of the initial efforts of the International Reading Association's Multilingual Classroom Committee during the 2000–2001 committee year. The Association has taken a proactive role in addressing important literacy issues that confront English learners and their dedicated teachers. The creation of the Multilingual Classroom Committee, the publication of journal articles and books pertinent to English learners, and the publication of this volume are all testaments to IRA's resolve to provide significant resources that embrace theory, critical pedagogy, and praxis. This volume will inform those concerned with English learner literacy issues and help them meet the very complex literacy needs of this burgeoning population.

English Learners: Reaching the Highest Level of English Literacy examines three important English learner issues: (1) current policy and best practice for English reading instruction in an immersion setting, (2) rethinking and redesigning curriculum to improve teaching of English language development, and (3) cultural issues as they pertain to English learners in and out of the classroom. This compilation was originally conceived of as the third coming of a seminal work on English learners titled *Schooling and Language Minority Students: A Theoretical Framework* (California State Department of Education, 1981). This book was a progress report on bilingual education that served as the initial research-based theoretical framework designed to assist educators in defining, planning, and improving their bilingual programs. It focused on linguistic, academic, and sociocultural factors that affect schooling for English learners. Bilingual education was identified as the vehicle for improving the schooling of these students.

Most of the thinking in this original volume has withstood the test of time; indeed, the majority of today's teachers are more committed to the theories Jim Cummins and Stephen Krashen proposed in that volume than were most teachers at the time of its publication. These theories were relatively new at the time, and so were many of the teachers. Most of these same teachers have now successfully applied these theories for many years. Their professional growth has coincided with the growth of the English learner population and bilingual education.

The second edition of *Schooling and Language Minority Students* (1994) was a second progress report that identified instructional elements of successful bilingual education programs. This edition has remained in print and is still held in high regard by all who believe in employing the best teaching practices for students whose first language is not English.

The ideas put forth in those two editions laid a firm foundation for educational practice for English learners over the years. Primary language was the heart and soul of the five chapters in both editions. The books were published in an era when bilingual education was growing and attempting to flourish, but growing antibilingual sentiment grew to such proportions as to practically outlaw bilingual education and the use of primary language in some states. The focus has switched from a focus on using primary language to reach an English literacy goal for English learners, to an English language development focus to achieve the same goal. This switch accounts for the focus of this new volume; however, this book still advances the importance of the primary language in the literacy development of English learners.

This book takes a critical look at the status quo, through the eyes of a combination of original theorists and current practitioners. Some of the topics and instructional strategies that were discussed in the aforementioned editions also will be discussed here, because three of the original seven authors have contributed to this new volume; times have changed, however, and so has educational practice for a growing number of English learners. Primary language instruction is no longer the norm in many of our schools. Immersion is now the rule in many quarters, and English learners must become literate in English via methodologies and programs that ignore much of what we have learned in the last 30-plus years of practice. This book offers a fresh look at what we have learned. It proposes new ways of looking at practice in the context of what we are presently doing in our English literacy instruction for English learners. It suggests why we need to reexamine our current practices, and it also suggests what we can do to change them. It examines reading and English literacy instruction for English learners in a political and educational context in which simultaneous achievement of both English language acquisition and English language arts standards is required. This is the main difference in the focus of this volume when compared to the other two aforementioned books. This book takes a close look at essential components of English language development and recommends specific practices for successful implementation. Finally, it suggests the importance of our cultural roots and celebrates the polyphony of voices that our English learners represent.

Currently, both theory and practice have been usurped by policy. All of our legislative bodies seem to know what is best for English literacy development, including what is best for English learners. Policy has even come directly from voters themselves, in the form of initiatives that dictate educational practice. The voices of the practitioners, and even of the most revered sages of educational theory and practice, are largely ignored in most of these legislative mandates. Politics now shape the nature of the English literacy instruction that will prepare our current generation of English learners. Bilingual education is struggling to survive in this English-only environment. We cannot abandon what we believe. We must not allow this policy shift to force us into silence. English learners are often unattended, invisible, and hidden under an umbrella of misleading research that results in misguided policy. We must avert what may become metaphorically and literally the instructional dark ages for English learners. We must act on what we know, and generate the research that we need to prevent this from happening.

The majority of U.S. teachers who have spent their career implementing the bilingual education theories of the 1960s and 1970s are rapidly approaching retirement. They know what works, but policy often prevents them from doing what they know works. Additionally, we are now hiring a whole new generation of teachers without that same experience. The burgeoning numbers of English learners who also are failing academically in alarming numbers force us to review, rethink, and revise what we have been doing instructionally. English learners cannot be left behind. This book suggests that a renaissance of instructional practice based on sound theory and pedagogy is much needed. The authors offer valuable guidance to all educators who are seeking to implement the very best instructional practices to promote the academic success of English learners. Our hope is that the wisdom offered by the original contributors to those seminal works and by the new contributors to this volume will make our educational community more resolute in its efforts to succeed and help English learners succeed. To fail is unacceptable.

—GGG

REFERENCES

California State Department of Education. (Ed.). (1981). *Schooling and language minority students: A theoretical framework*. Los Angeles: Evaluation, Dissemination, and Assessment Center, California State University.

California State Department of Education. (Ed.). (1994). *Schooling and language minority students: A theoretical framework* (2nd ed.). Los Angeles: Evaluation, Dissemination, and Assessment Center, California State University.

Tamara H. Baren
Nevada Early Literacy Intervention
    Program Coordinator
Nevada State Regional Professional
    Development Program
Reno, Nevada, USA

Donald R. Bear
Director and Professor
E.L. Cord Foundation Center
    for Learning and Literacy
University of Nevada, Reno
Reno, Nevada, USA

Dolores Beltrán
English Learner Specialist
Los Angeles County Office
    of Education
Downey, California, USA

Paul Boyd-Batstone
Assistant Professor of Language
    and Literacy
California State University, Long
    Beach
Long Beach, California, USA

Ji-Mei Chang
Professor of Special Education
San Jose State University
San Jose, California, USA

Julie M. Coppola
Assistant Professor of Education
Boston University
Boston, Massachusetts, USA

Alan N. Crawford
Professor Emeritus of Education
California State University, Los
    Angeles
Los Angeles, California, USA

Jim Cummins
Professor of Education
University of Toronto
Toronto, Ontario, Canada

Susana Dutro
Director of English Language
    Development, California
    Reading and Literature Project
Biliteracy Coordinator, Monterey
    County Office of Education
Santa Cruz, California, USA

Jill Fitzgerald
Professor of Literacy and Assistant
    Dean
The University of North Carolina at
    Chapel Hill
Chapel Hill, North Carolina, USA

Susan Florio-Ruane
Professor of Teacher Education
Michigan State University
East Lansing, Michigan, USA

David E. Freeman
Professor of Reading
University of Texas, Pan American
Edinburg, Texas, USA

Yvonne S. Freeman
Professor of Bilingual Education
University of Texas, Pan American
Edinburg, Texas, USA

Margaret A. Gallego
Associate Professor of Education
San Diego State University
San Diego, California, USA

Gilbert G. García
Educational Representative
Houghton Mifflin Company
San Jose, California, USA

MariAnne George
Learning Consultant, Rochester
    Community Schools
Oakland University Doctoral
    Student
Rochester, Michigan, USA

Michael F. Graves
Professor of Literacy Education
    and Guy Bond Fellow
    in Reading
University of Minnesota
Minneapolis, Minnesota, USA

Lori A. Helman
Nevada Reading Excellence Act
    Lecturer and Coordinator
University of Nevada, Reno
Reno, Nevada, USA

Ana Hernández
Teacher
Valley Center – Pauma Unified
    School District
Valley Center, California, USA

Stephen Krashen
Professor Emeritus of Education
University of Southern California
Los Angeles, California, USA

Joseph Laturnau
Program Specialist, Pacific
    Comprehensive Assistance
    Center
Pacific Resources for Education
    and Learning
Honolulu, Hawaii, USA

Patricia Madrigal
Project Coordinator, Development
    of English Language and
    Literacy in Spanish-Speaking
    Students
California State University, Long
    Beach
Long Beach, California, USA

Luis C. Moll
Professor of Education
University of Arizona
Tucson, Arizona, USA

Carrol Moran
Director, UC Santa Cruz
    Educational Partnership Center
University of California Santa Cruz
Santa Cruz, California, USA

Taffy E. Raphael
Professor of Literacy Education
University of Illinois at Chicago
Chicago, Illinois, USA

Robert Rueda
Professor of Education
University of Southern California
Los Angeles, California, USA

Anamarie Tam
Teacher Specialist
Glendale Unified School District
Glendale, California, USA

Shane Templeton
Foundation Professor
 of Curriculum and Instruction
University of Nevada, Reno
Reno, Nevada, USA

David B. Yaden, Jr.
Associate Professor of Learning
 and Instruction
University of Southern California
Los Angeles, California, USA

Teaching English Learners to Read: Current Policy and Best Instructional Practice

CHAPTER 1

Reading and the Bilingual Student: Fact and Friction

Jim Cummins

Perhaps the two most volatile issues in contemporary educational debate in North America are (1) appropriate ways of teaching reading to both English first language (L1) and English language learning (ELL) students and (2) appropriate ways of promoting academic achievement among bilingual/ELL students. This chapter addresses both of these concerns. I attempt to outline the current state of theory and research related to these issues and to synthesize this theory and research in such a way that false oppositions are resolved and implications for effective practice are highlighted.

The Policy Context

In many areas across the curriculum, last year's doctrine has become today's heresy. Fashions in the teaching of reading, math, and science have changed radically in the space of the last decade. For example, in the new orthodoxy of the 1990s, whole language and literature-based approaches to the teaching of reading are out; phonics and phonemic awareness are in. The pendulum has similarly swung back and forth in the teaching of math and science, between experiential/constructivist orientations and more teacher-centered, didactic approaches. In teaching ELL students, bilingual education, once hailed by many educators as the bridge between home and school, is now virtually outlawed in Arizona and California and viewed with suspicion in many other states.

In short, across this highly contested curricular landscape, what many educators learned as effective instruction in teacher education courses is now berated by policymakers and media pundits as the ruination of the next generation.

State-mandated standardized assessments add to the pressure. Many educators fear that such assessments constrict the curriculum and force us to "teach to the test," thereby reducing the quality of instruction rather than enhancing it. The empirical data suggest that such fears may be well founded (McNeil, 2000). Standardized tests, such as the SAT-9 in California, also pressure educators to reduce the emphasis on L1 literacy in bilingual programs, because assessment is conducted only in English (Gándara et al., 2000).

In this cacophony of conflicting ideologies and prescriptions, what can we say with any degree of confidence about effective reading instruction for bilingual/ELL students? Surprisingly, we can say quite a lot. There is actually far more coherence in the research and theory about what works and what constitutes effective literacy instruction for ELL students than we might assume from the volatile controversies about the topic.

I argue that if we understand the relation of vocabulary knowledge to reading comprehension (and to academic achievement generally), then there really should be no controversy as to how to teach reading. I suggest that *how* we teach phonics and phonemic awareness is not particularly important so long as we ensure that students *do* acquire decoding skills and relevant knowledge about how the sounds of the language relate to the written code. What determines reading achievement in the long term is how effectively we develop students' reading comprehension—and reading comprehension is overwhelmingly related to the extent to which students engage in extensive reading. Simply put, books are virtually the only place where students get access to the low-frequency Greco-Latin lexicon of English. Thus, a diet of engaging books works much better than a diet of worksheets and drills in developing reading comprehension and academic language (see Krashen, chapter 3 in this volume).

In order to interpret the research on reading development among bilingual/ELL students, it is important to elucidate the nature of proficiency in a language and to consider how language proficiency relates to reading achievement. Specifically, three dimensions of language proficiency must be distinguished (Cummins, 2001).

Three Dimensions of Language Proficiency

Misconceptions about language proficiency are at the root of some of the most controversial policy initiatives in the areas of both reading instruction and the education of bilingual/ELL students. Proposition 227 in California, for example, claimed that one year of specific instructional support was sufficient for students to acquire English and integrate successfully into the mainstream classroom. The research data, however, overwhelmingly suggest that one to two years may be sufficient for the acquisition of conversational fluency in English but that at least five years (and frequently more) are required for students to bridge the gap in academic English between them and their native English-speaking peers (Cummins, 2001; Klesmer, 1994; Thomas & Collier, 1997).

Similarly, the fact that second-language learners can learn phonological awareness and decoding skills in English when these are explicitly taught in the early grades has been taken as evidence that students can catch up rapidly to grade norms in academic skills. In fact, the evidence shows minimal transfer from the acquisition of these discrete language skills to more general academic language proficiency (Kwan & Willows, 1998; Lambert & Tucker, 1972). Frequently, low-income students who have acquired discrete language skills in the early grades experience what has been termed "the grade 4 slump." This phenomenon refers to the sudden drop in reading achievement between grades 4 and 6 among low-income students who appear to have been making good progress in the early grades. Chall, Jacobs, and Baldwin (1990), who highlighted the phenomenon, point out that

> the reading task changes around grade 4 from a focus on reading familiar texts where the task is one of recognizing and decoding words to one of comprehension of harder texts that use more difficult, abstract, specialized, and technical words. (p. 49)

Thus, students who have developed fluent decoding skills can still experience a sharp drop in reading comprehension scores when the instructional focus changes from learning to read (grades 1–3) to using reading as a tool for learning (grades 4 and up).

The three dimensions of language proficiency—conversational fluency, discrete language skills, and academic language proficiency—are described below. It is important to note that these dimensions are not totally independent of one other: They develop concurrently, and at various stages of development will correlate with one other. However, they also behave differently from one other—with respect to when they reach a developmental plateau, to the kinds of experiences and instruction that promote each dimension, to the communicative contexts in which they are likely to be exhibited, and to the components of language on which they rely.

Conversational fluency is the ability to carry on a conversation in familiar face-to-face situations. This is the kind of proficiency that the vast majority of native speakers of English have developed by the time they enter school at age 5. It involves use of high-frequency words and simple grammatical constructions. Communication of meaning is typically supported by cues such as facial expressions, gestures, intonation, and the like. ELL students generally develop fluency in conversational aspects of English within a year or two of exposure to the language either in school or in the out-of-school environment.

Discrete language skills reflect specific phonological, literacy, and grammatical knowledge that students acquire as a result of direct instruction and both formal and informal practice (e.g., reading). Some of these discrete language skills are acquired early in schooling; some continue to be acquired throughout schooling. The discrete language skills acquired early include knowledge of the letters of the alphabet and of the sounds represented by individual letters and combinations of letters, along with the ability to decode written words into appropriate sounds. ELL students can learn these specific language skills at a relatively early stage in their acquisition of English; in fact, these skills can be learned concurrently with their development of basic vocabulary and conversational proficiency.

As students progress through the grades, they also will learn conventions of spelling, capitalization, and punctuation as well as information about grammatical rules (e.g., the fact that pluralization in English generally involves adding -*s* or -*es* to words) and exceptions to these rules (e.g., the fact that *took*, rather than *taked*, is the past tense of the verb *take*).

Academic language proficiency includes knowledge of the less-frequent vocabulary of English as well as the ability to interpret and produce increasingly complex written (and oral) language. As students progress through the grades, they encounter far more low-frequency words (primarily from Greek and Latin sources), complex syntax (e.g., passive voice), and abstract expressions that are virtually never heard in everyday conversation. Students are required to understand linguistically and conceptually demanding texts in various content areas (e.g., literature, social studies, science, mathematics) and to use this language in an accurate and coherent way in their own writing.

All three aspects of language proficiency are important. There is an enormous amount of confusion, however, about the relation among these three aspects of proficiency. As noted above, many ELL students who have acquired fluent conversational skills in their second language (L2) are still a long way from grade-level performance in academic language proficiency (as measured, for example, by reading comprehension tests). Similarly, when the focus is on intensive phonics instruction in the early grades, discrete language skills can sometimes be learned in virtual isolation from the development of academic language proficiency. ELL (and native-speaking) students who can "read" English fluently may have only a very limited understanding of the words they can decode.

Reading Development in L1 and L2 Contexts

Part of the confusion regarding the reading research derives, as we have seen, from the failure of many policymakers and media warriors to distinguish the process of acquiring decoding skills from the process of developing reading comprehension abilities. Confusion also results from the distortion of opposing views that almost inevitably occurs when issues are hotly debated. For example, phonics advocates have erroneously tended to depict whole language as an approach to reading that paid no attention to phonics, while some whole language theorists appeared to argue so strenuously against phonics in isolation that they contributed to the impression that what defined whole language was its opposition to the teaching of phonics. In fact, good whole language teaching develops phonemic awareness and phonological skills in a variety of ways (e.g., through some direct instruction and through writing activities in which students make hypotheses about sound-symbol relationships [invented spelling]). By the same token, a focus on explicit systematic phonics teaching is not in any way incompatible with a concurrent or later focus on encouraging extensive reading for meaning.

At this time, whole language teaching has fallen very much from favor in states such as California and Texas, where phonics has been constructed by some policymakers as the solution for all the problems of academic underachievement. It is unfortunate that the central message of whole language teaching regarding the importance of focusing on meaningful engagement with text and encouraging extensive reading of a wide variety of linguistic genres has gotten lost in the ideological conflicts over reading. All the research supports the fact that extensive reading and immersion in a literate environment are strongly related to the development of reading comprehension (e.g., Postlethwaite & Ross, 1992; Tizard, Schofield, & Hewison, 1982). The research is also clear, however, that for many students some explicit teaching of phonemic awareness and the "alphabetic principle" (the relationship of sounds to letters) is useful in developing word decoding skills.

As noted earlier, part of the confusion derives from the failure to clearly distinguish what the research is saying with respect to decoding, on the one hand, and with respect to reading comprehension, on the other. These are considered separately in the following sections.

Decoding

PHONICS AND READING: THE ALTERNATIVE POSITIONS. The California Department of Education (1996) points out that "research has shown repeatedly that phonemic awareness is a powerful predictor of success in learning to read" (p. 4). Phonemic awareness is the awareness that spoken words are made up of sounds, and it includes the ability to segment a word into its constituent sounds. The California report advocates systematic explicit phonics instruction "where letter-sound correspondences for letters and letter clusters are directly taught; blended; practiced in words, word lists, and word families; and practiced initially in text with a high percentage of decodable words linked to the phonics lesson." Teachers should provide "prompt and explicit feedback" (p. 6). This perspective emphasizes the use of decodable texts as the most appropriate initial reading materials:

> Research strongly asserts that from the beginning of first grade and in tandem with basic phonics instruction, the most appropriate materials for independent reading are decodable texts. Toward creating a solid foundation for learning to read, most new words in these texts should be wholly decodable on the basis of the phonics that students have been taught. Sight words should be familiarized ahead of time so that they will not divert this purpose. As soon as children can read such basic decodable texts with reasonable comfort and fluency, they can move on to less controlled texts such as trade books. Some students will be ready to do so sooner than others. (p. 12)

Despite its emphasis on a rigid instructional sequence, from phonemic awareness to phonics to decodable texts, this report does acknowledge a crucial role for extensive reading in developing reading comprehension:

> Even so, the single most valuable activity for developing children's comprehension is reading itself. The amount of reading that children do is shown to predict the growth in reading comprehension across the elementary school years even after controlling for entry-level differences. It predicts the quantity as well as the language, vocabulary, and structure of students' writing. It also predicts the richness of their oral storytelling. Among older students and adults, it predicts receptive vocabulary, verbal fluency, content-area achievement, and all manner of general knowledge even when measures of school ability, general intelligence, age, education, and reading comprehension itself are taken into account.... Through reading, students encounter new words, new language, and

new facts. Beyond that, however, they encounter thoughts and modes of thinking that might never arise in their face-to-face worlds. (p. 11)

This perspective with respect to the importance of extensive reading for the development of reading comprehension is identical to that emphasized by whole language theorists. However, Coles (2000), Krashen (1996a), McQuillan (1998), and other whole language theorists strongly dispute the emphasis placed on explicit sequential skills instruction by policymakers and many reading researchers (e.g., Foorman, Fletcher, Francis, & Schatschneider, 2000; Mathes & Torgeson, 2000; Stanovich & Stanovich, 1998). They acknowledge that phonemic awareness and phonological knowledge are correlated with reading development but argue that this knowledge can develop without explicit instruction and is a *consequence* of reading experience and print exposure rather than a direct causal factor in explaining either decoding or reading comprehension development. In Coles's words, "phonological awareness, although important in early literacy development, needs to be seen as a 'marker' of access to extensive literacy opportunities" (2000, p. 90). These theorists acknowledge a role for some explicit phonics instruction but argue that the teaching of more complex aspects of phonics and phonemic awareness is unnecessary and rapidly reaches a point of diminishing returns.

PHONICS AND READING: THE RESEARCH. My reading of the research is that there is general acknowledgment that phonemic awareness is a significant predictor of word recognition (decoding) skills and that instruction in phonemic awareness can increase performance both on tests of phonemic awareness and on some skills related to decoding (Ehri, Nunes, Stahl, & Willows, 2001; Foorman et al., 2000; Krashen, 1999; Stanovich & Stanovich, 1998). The link between phonics/phonemic awareness instruction and reading comprehension is much more tentative. There is minimal evidence, in fact, that such training, by itself, has any significant or long-lasting effects on the development of reading comprehension (e.g., Allington & Woodside-Jiron, 1999; Coles, 2000; Ehri et al., 2001; Krashen, 1999; McQuillan, 1998; Taylor, Anderson, Au, & Raphael, 2000). The evidence does suggest that the development of reading comprehension is best promoted by a broadly based program that combines extensive exposure to meaningful and varied texts with (a) some explicit phonemic awareness and phonics instruction and (b) instruction that encourages students to develop effective learning strategies for both decoding and comprehending text—to increase both metalinguistic and metacognitive awareness (Cunningham, 1990; Iverson & Tunmer, 1993; Muñiz-Swicegood, 1994; Tunmer & Chapman, 1999).

It is instructive to go back to an earlier influential report that was written at a time when the polemics about reading were less intense. Anderson, Hiebert, Scott, and Wilkinson (1985), in *Becoming a Nation of Readers*—cited positively by both sides of this issue—expressed the importance of phonics instruction in a less definitive way than is typical of current phonics advocates:

> Phonics is instruction in the relationship between letters and speech sounds. The goal of phonics is not that children be able to state the "rules" governing letter-sound relationships. Rather the purpose is to get across the alphabetic principle, the principle that there are systematic relationships between letters and sounds. Phonics ought to be conceived as a technique for getting children off to a fast start in mapping the relationships between letters and sounds.
>
> It follows that phonics instruction should aim to teach only the most important and regular of letter-to-sound relationships because this is the sort of instruction that will most directly lay bare the alphabetic principle. Once the basic relationships have been taught, the best way to get children to refine and extend their knowledge of letter-sound correspondences is through repeated opportunities to read. If this position is correct, then much phonics instruction is overly subtle and probably unproductive. (p. 38)

The authors go on to suggest that a number of reading programs try to teach too many letter-sound relationships and that phonics instruction drags out over too many years. They suggest that phonics instruction should be done early and kept simple. Except in cases of diagnosed individual need, there should be little need for phonics instruction beyond the second grade.

In a similar vein, Krashen's 1996 report *Every Person a Reader: An Alternative to the California Task Force Report on Reading* acknowledges that some phonics instruction can contribute to reading development: "Some knowledge of the more straight-forward sound-spelling correspondences is certainly useful" (p. 12), particularly initial consonants. However, he suggests, there is a point of diminishing returns with phonics: "Many phonics rules are not useful...they are very complex, and have numerous exceptions" (p. 13).

Keith Stanovich, a strong advocate of explicit, systematic phonics instruction, has endorsed what appears to be a similar position. He distinguishes a continuum of phonological sensitivity ranging from shallow to deep sensitivity (Stanovich, 1992). At a deeper level of sensitivity, a child would be able to distinguish explicitly small sound units, such as phonemes, whereas at a shallower level of sensitivity the child may be able to distinguish larger sound units, such as syllables, or basic letter-sound regularity. Stanovich suggests that only shallow phonological sensitivity is required for the process of reading acquisition to begin. Krashen (1996a) also has quoted Share and

Stanovich's (1995) view that "a minimal level of phonological sensitivity and letter-sound knowledge skill may enable a child to acquire rudimentary self-teaching skill" (p. 22). However, Stanovich is also very clear about the importance of "explicit analytic instruction in word decoding in the early years of schooling" (Stanovich & Stanovich, 1998, p. 54; see also Juel & Minden-Cupp, 2000). The difference between Stanovich's position and that of whole language theorists with respect to the role of explicit phonics instruction appears to be primarily a matter of emphasis.

What does this all mean for reading instruction with bilingual/ELL students? Some of what we know can be expressed in these three overlapping statements:

1. The most effective approaches to developing initial reading skills are those that combine extensive and varied exposure to meaningful print with explicit and systematic instruction in phonemic awareness and letter-sound correspondences.

2. Just as immersion in a literate environment in the home enables most children to acquire initial reading skills with minimal explicit phonics instruction, immersion in a literate environment in school is a crucial supplement to phonics instruction in order for strong literacy (and biliteracy) skills to develop (see Krashen, chapter 3 in this volume).

3. Systematic phonics instruction can enable second-language learners to acquire word recognition and decoding skills in their second language to a relatively high level, despite the fact that their knowledge of the second language is still limited. These decoding skills, however, do not automatically generalize to reading comprehension or other aspects of second-language proficiency.

Each of these positions is considered in more detail below:

1. Virtually all researchers endorse some variant of a "balanced" view of reading instruction that incorporates varying amounts of explicit phonics instruction together with an emphasis on extensive reading as students progress through the grades. The instructional programs that work best for promoting reading comprehension (as compared to individual word decoding) are those that (a) emphasize extensive and varied exposure to meaningful print; (b) provide, in the early grades, some explicit and systematic instruction in phonemic awareness and letter-sound correspondences; and (c) provide instruction designed to help students develop metacognitive strategies for recognizing words and improving

their own reading abilities. Programs that provide primarily explicit and systematic phonics instruction in the early grades, without extensive exposure to print, work relatively well in developing phonemic awareness and some word recognition skills. However, there is little evidence of generalization of these decoding skills to long-term growth in reading comprehension.

The pattern of findings can be illustrated with reference to Cunningham's 1990 study in which the author compared three instructional approaches used with kindergarten and grade 1 students. The first involved isolated phonics instruction in which children learned phonemic segmentation and blending and related skills but were not encouraged to apply their knowledge to real reading tasks. This was a typical "skill-and-drill" program that proceeded in a sequential way to teach phonics skills in isolation. The second group also received instruction in phonemic awareness; in addition, they were directed to try to identify unknown words through sound-symbol relationships and contextual cues. The instruction also encouraged children to think about the story and to reflect on and refine their own strategies for decoding and understanding words (i.e., to develop metacognitive awareness). A third group (the control group) only listened to stories and answered questions about them during the time the other two groups were engaged in their specific instructional program. All children received reading instruction in grade 1 from a basal reading program. The second group, which was taught to reflect on and apply their evolving literacy knowledge, performed significantly better than either of the other groups on a reading achievement test, whereas the isolated phonics group was found to have scores similar to the control group. This study suggests the importance of a balanced approach that combines explicit demystification of written language with opportunities to actively engage with meaningful text.

Tunmer and Chapman (1999) also reviewed research supportive of metacognitive approaches to teaching initial reading. The authors note that

> in general, metacognitive approaches to instruction are in sharp contrast to skill-and-drill approaches in which word-level skills are taught in an isolated, piecemeal fashion with little or no emphasis placed on developing within beginning readers an understanding of how and when to apply such knowledge. (p. 89)

Hatcher, Hulme, and Ellis's (1994) study also reported superior results from a "reading with phonology" group in comparison with a "phonology training alone" group and a "reading alone" group. The "phonology training alone" students were taught word segmentation, rhyming words, sound synthesis into words, and other phonemic awareness skills. The "reading with phonology" group completed about half this program but also devoted time to reading and rereading books, writing stories, and engaging in phonological activities related to the stories. The "reading alone" group performed reading and writing activities similar to the "reading with phonology" group, but there was no explicit focus on phonology or letter-sound relationships.

A year after these instructional approaches were completed, the "reading with phonology" group was found to exhibit significantly superior perform-ance in reading comprehension, word identification, and spelling than either of the other two groups. The "phonology training alone" group made signifi-cantly more progress in phonological skills, but this did not translate into bet-ter reading or writing performance. Thus, there was no direct path from acquiring phonological skills to developing reading skills (see also Freeman & Freeman, chapter 2 in this volume).

Coles (2000) interprets these studies as supportive of whole language ap-proaches and assumptions, because they show the centrality of engagement with text to students' reading progress. He notes that

> researchers have moved toward recognizing that phonological abilities are learned best when they are related to reading and writing activities rather than as a singular skill. This shift has moved the phonological awareness paradigm closer to rather than away from whole language theory and practice. (p. 89)

Nevertheless, most advocates of explicit phonics instruction interpret this same research as *refuting* whole language approaches and assumptions. Stanovich and Stanovich (1998), for example, acknowledge the criticism that most studies supporting explicit systematic teaching of phonics have focused on decoding skills rather than reading comprehension. However, they cite Cunningham (1990), Hatcher et al. (1994), and Iverson and Tunmer (1993), among others, to show that "children given training in phonological sensitivi-ty and/or alphabetic coding show superior outcomes on measures of compre-hension and text reading as well as word recognition" (p. 53). In other words, they claim that phonics training *does* benefit reading comprehension in addi-tion to decoding, and they suggest that the "way now seems clear for whole language advocates to reconstitute their position in a scientifically respectable way" (p. 54).

Clearly, these conflicts have reached a profoundly unproductive stage. There is room in the inn both for ensuring that all children are developing word-analysis skills (some may require more systematic instruction than others) and for providing ample opportunities for all children to engage with meaningful print and relate the wonder of books to their own lives. Researchers and theorists on both sides of the reading debate agree with this basic position—but both sides have set up straw horses in an attempt to prove the other side wrong. Phonics advocates have characterized whole language classrooms as focusing on reading only, with minimal attempt to demystify how sounds and symbols relate; whole language advocates have characterized phonics-oriented classrooms as focusing on isolated skill-and-drill instruction, with no attention paid to applying these skills to authentic texts. The research appears clear that neither of these extremes is as effective as instruction that focuses on *both* immersion of students in a literate environment *and* demystification of how the language works.

Unfortunately, the combination of high-stakes standardized testing (e.g., the SAT-9 in California) and the demonization of whole language has resulted in precisely the wrong type of phonics instruction being implemented in many schools. The research cited above is very clear that isolated phonics instruction that teaches complex subskills in a rigid sequential manner involving minimal engagement with meaningful texts is not effective in developing reading comprehension. Yet, this is precisely what appears to be happening in many California schools as a result of that state's three-pronged quick fix for underachievement: Proposition 227, the elimination of heretical whole language approaches in favor of phonics instruction, and the policing of schools and teachers by means of the SAT-9 (Gándara et al., 2000). Teachers observed and interviewed in the Gándara et al. study felt compelled to teach to the test, placing much greater emphasis on "English word recognition or phonics, bereft of meaning or context" (p. 19):

> Teachers also worried greatly that if they spent time orienting the children to broader literacy activities like story telling, story sequencing activities, reading for meaning or writing and vocabulary development in the primary language, that their students would not be gaining the skills that would be tested on the standardized test in English. They feared that this could result in the school and the students suffering sanctions imposed by the law.... Heavy emphasis was placed on decoding skills (phonics) and vocabulary development rather than developing broader literacy skills such as reading for meaning, or writing. (pp. 19–21)

Thus, there is considerable merit to the concerns of Taylor et al. (2000) that the almost exclusive emphasis in recent research (e.g., Foorman, Francis, Fletcher, Schatschneider, & Mehta, 1998) on the importance of teaching the alphabetic principle, to the exclusion of other central components of the reading process, will have the effect of narrowing the curriculum for students from diverse backgrounds. As one illustration, the requirement in the 1999/2000 Texas reading adoption that there be at least 80% decodable words in reading texts in the early grades suggests that this version of a "balanced approach" is actually quite unbalanced. As pointed out by Allington and Woodside-Jiron (1999), there is no direct research support for emphasizing "decodable" text over "predictable" text in early reading materials. In response, Mathes and Torgeson (2000) acknowledge the lack of direct research on this issue but argue that what we know about transfer and generalization indirectly supports the use of decodable text.

2. Children who are immersed in a literate environment in the home can usually pick up decoding skills with minimal formal instruction in phonics. By the same token, immersion in a literate environment in school is a crucial supplement to phonics instruction in order for strong literacy (and biliteracy) skills to develop.

Children immersed in a literate home environment usually need some initial help to "break the code," but once they have done so they make rapid progress on their own by relating their knowledge of oral language and their concepts about print to the written text. They know that there is a payoff for comprehending print so they are highly motivated to become independent readers. With the exception of children who experience some form of reading disability or dyslexia, middle-class children rarely experience failure in learning to read, regardless of what type of instructional program they receive in the early grades (along a continuum from phonics-oriented to whole language–oriented).

An example of this phenomenon comes from students in Canadian French immersion programs and English background students in dual-language or two-way bilingual immersion programs. These students are typically introduced to reading instruction through their L2 (French or Spanish)—in which, at the beginning of grade 1, they have minimal fluency. English reading in these programs is not formally introduced until grade 2, grade 3, or sometimes even grade 4. It is almost invariably observed that shortly after students have developed some decoding skills in French (or Spanish), they spontaneously start decoding in English (their L1). By the end of grade 1, these students are usually much more fluent readers in English than in their L2 (see Cashion & Eagan, 1990). They have had no formal phonics instruction in English, but because of their immersion in a literate home environment and the support for literacy provided in school they typically become very fluent readers. This shows clearly that direct instruction in the complex phonics rules for English is not always necessary in order for students to develop strong decoding and comprehension skills in English.

This is further illustrated by Reyes (2000) in a longitudinal case study of the "spontaneous biliteracy" of four low-income working-class Mexicano/Latino children in a bilingual program, two of whom were taught to read initially only in Spanish and two only in English, according to their language dominance on entry into the program. The children received structured phonics instruction (in English or Spanish) in kindergarten, but in first and second grade only minimal phonics was taught. All four children spontaneously transferred their literacy skills from their initial language to their second language without formal instruction. Their "natural, spontaneous, and uncomplicated approach to bilingualism and biliteracy" was supported by their interest in writing in both languages and also by their social play, wherein they challenged each other to read in the language in which they had received no formal reading instruction. This process of spontaneous transfer of literacy across languages parallels what is typically observed in French immersion programs and again illustrates the fact that the goal of phonics instruction should be to get students started on the process of working out the code and to support them in that process. It is certainly not necessary, and in many cases probably counterproductive, to teach the more complex, exception-ridden phonics rules; children's time would be much better spent (a) applying their basic phonological awareness to reading engaging texts, with adult support, and (b) beginning to express their identities through personal writing. The centrality of these affective dimensions related to students' identity tends to be omitted from current "phonics as panacea" dogma. Reyes has strongly emphasized the importance of issues related to identity in the process of spontaneous biliteracy development, noting that the bilingual program

> legitimated children's bicultural identity, unleashing their potential for bilingualism and biliteracy rather than forcing them to choose between their two cultures.... There is no doubt that these students felt their languages and their culture affirmed.... Although each of the girls received instruction in only one language, all their learning from kindergarten to second grade took place in classrooms where the teachers supported and nurtured their cultural and linguistic resources. Each day they heard their teachers and peers use Spanish and English. Their teachers also made great efforts to treat English and Spanish as equally as possible, valuing both languages for personal, social, and academic purposes. (p. 116)

The centrality of identity negotiation to the process of literacy and biliteracy development has been neglected in the current controversies about reading. Creating contexts where bilingual children can invest their identities in the process of becoming literate is probably far more important to ultimate success than the extent to which the instructional focus is predominantly on form versus meaning (Cummins, 2001). Reyes concludes that Latino/Latina children's cognitive and linguistic abilities continue to be underestimated in most schools where bilingualism is still construed as a problem (as illustrated by Propositions 227 and 203 in California and Arizona, respectively). She notes that although "many Latinos come to school with the natural potential to become biliterate, that potential frequently is undermined, dismissed, and ignored" (p. 119), resulting in a process whereby children are permitted to develop only half their potential.

Reyes's study shows that school and home can combine to create socioculturally supportive conditions for biliteracy development in working-class contexts in a very similar way to what is typically observed in middle-class contexts. A key element is immersion in a literate environment that enables children to engage their identities with reading and writing.

3. Students instructed through a second language can acquire word-recognition and decoding skills in their second language to a relatively high level, despite the fact that their knowledge of the second language is still limited. These decoding skills, however, do not automatically generalize to reading comprehension or other aspects of second-language proficiency.

The evidence regarding the acquisition of decoding skills in a second language comes from two sources. The first is research on French immersion programs in Canada (e.g., Lambert & Tucker, 1972). In the original St. Lambert program near Montreal, English L1 students in grades 1 and 2 who were instructed exclusively through French in kindergarten and grade 1 and introduced to reading through French performed either better (grade 1) or at the same level (grade 2) on a French word discrimination measure than did native French-speaking control students. In other words, they learned very specific decoding skills in their second language to a level equivalent to that of native speakers.

There were major differences in virtually all other aspects of their French proficiency, however. For example, on a French picture vocabulary measure at grade 2, the French immersion (English L1) students obtained a score of 53.85 compared to 63.48 for the French L1 control group, a difference that was highly significant ($F = 27.45$, $p < 01$). However, on word discrimination, the groups obtained almost identical scores (immersion 25.28, controls 25.60). Students in French immersion programs usually require the entire elementary school period to catch up with French L1 speakers in French reading comprehension despite the fact that they rapidly catch up in French decoding skills.

The second source of data is research conducted on ELL students acquiring English reading skills in all-English programs. Kwan and Willows (1998), for example, examined the effects of the Jolly Phonics program among a sample of 240 English L1 and ELL kindergarten students in Toronto, Canada. This program (Lloyd, 1992) is described as a systematic training program aimed at developing phonemic awareness and teaching letter/sound correspondences. The program is playful and multimodal and designed to appeal to the younger child. It requires minimal teacher training and can be easily integrated into a regular kindergarten program as it requires only about 15 minutes per day (Kwan & Willows, 1998). The study found that exposure to the Jolly Phonics program resulted in superior performance on a variety of phonological measures among both English L1 and ELL students. No effects of the program were observed with respect to a broader array of linguistic proficiency measures that assessed linguistic concepts, vocabulary, sentence memory, and word memory. Despite the fact that ELL students performed more poorly than their English L1 counterparts on all the linguistic proficiency measures and on one of the four phonological processing measures (within treatment groups), they still benefited in phonological processing from participating in the Jolly Phonics program. They also outperformed English L1 students in the control group who received no training in phonological awareness. Kwan and Willows summarize the implications of their findings as follows:

> These results call into question the prevailing assumptions that require second-language instructional methods to by-pass perceived acoustic-based processing weaknesses in L2 children and focus solely on native language literacy development. Indeed, instructional methods that provide explicit and systematic training in English alphabetic coding skills and phonemic awareness are beneficial to L2 learners in that the goal of instruction is tied more to the development, rather than the by-pass, of English phonology and early literacy skills. (Abstract)

These results are clearly consistent with those of Lambert and Tucker (1972) in showing that L2 phonics skills can be taught to second-language students in the early stages of schooling. The findings are also consistent with the very positive results obtained in 50:50 (half-time L1 and L2) dual-language programs that introduce L1 and L2 reading either simultaneously or in quick succession. *There is thus no need to delay the introduction of English reading instruction within a bilingual program* (see Cummins, 2000). Furthermore, despite the assumptions of both advocates and opponents of bilingual education, the order in which reading instruction is introduced in a bilingual program is not, in itself, a significant variable.

However, the Kwan and Willows study is also consistent with other results considered in this chapter in showing that phonics/phonemic awareness training is no panacea—insofar as it does not, by itself, benefit broader aspects of language proficiency that are strongly related to the development of reading comprehension (e.g., vocabulary). The data also in no way contradict the fact that a period of at least five years is typically required for ELL students to catch up in academic aspects of L2 proficiency (e.g., reading comprehension). As noted, neither conversational fluency nor discrete language skills transfer directly to the development of academic language proficiency.

Students vary widely, then, in the extent to which they require and will benefit from an explicit focus on phonics as they develop adequate decoding skills. Some who have been immersed in a literate environment in the home may require minimal formal instruction to start decoding, whereas others who have experienced less exposure to print in the home may require much more direct and explicit instruction—focused on phonics but also on many other features of language. The purpose of phonics instruction should be to facilitate access to and comprehension of meaningful print. When children start to engage with print in a motivated way they will begin to figure out on their own, and with adult help, how letters, sounds, and meaning relate to each other. This is why phonemic awareness instruction succeeds much better when it is integrated with authentic reading activities than when it is implemented in isolation. In addition, it should not be forgotten that it is not only phonemic sensitivity that is related to early reading development but also the wider spectrum of language awareness that Marie Clay has termed *concepts about print* and that is assessed by the test of that name. Demonstration of this awareness in both L1 and L2 has been found to be strongly related to English reading development among Portuguese background students in Toronto (Cummins, 1991).

In short, for ELL students who do not come from a highly literate home environment, initial instruction should focus on (a) developing awareness of how the language works (phonics and beyond) and (b) inducting students into the excitement of books both in school and, to the extent possible, at home. What this might look like in practice is illustrated by Goldenberg's (1998) description of a successful school change project, involving bilingual education for Latino/Latina students, wherein both "bottom-up" and "top-down" processes were applied. Among the former for kindergarten and grade 1 students were naming and recognizing letters, recognizing beginning sounds of words, hearing and discriminating rhymes, writing letters and words from dictation, and "estimating" the spellings of words when they wrote (i.e., in whole language parlance, "invented spelling"). Top-down strategies included reading or "pseudoreading" for pleasure, talking about books, and encouraging attempts at communicative writing.

It is pointless and counterproductive for whole language advocates to argue against the use of programs such as Jolly Phonics, which succeed well in demystifying important aspects of language among kindergarten children, require only about 15 minutes a day to implement, and are fun for children and teachers alike. A more appropriate target is the dogmatic insistence among some phonics advocates and policymakers that the vast majority of early reading materials consist of "decodable text" to the exclusion of more authentic reading material. Some use of decodable text is nonproblematic, particularly if the texts have been imaginatively constructed to minimize their contrived nature; to insist on near-exclusive use of decodable texts, however, reflects an extreme and antiquated behaviorist learning philosophy that ignores what cognitive science has discovered about the importance of encouraging children to engage in hypothesis testing and knowledge construction in interaction with supportive adults within what Vygotsky (1978) termed the Zone of Proximal Development. This construct refers to the distance between the level of development or problem-solving children are capable of on their own, without adult guidance, and the level of development that children can potentially attain under the influence of, or in collaboration with, more capable adults and peers (see Graves & Fitzgerald, chapter 5 in this volume).

The crucial contribution of whole language theory relates more to the development of reading comprehension than to the development of initial decoding skills. Unfortunately, this contribution risks being ignored despite massive empirical evidence in support of whole language principles regarding the development of reading comprehension.

Reading Comprehension

The limitations of viewing phonics as a panacea are immediately apparent from what is probably the largest study of reading achievement and instruction ever conducted. Postlethwaite and Ross (1992), in an evaluation of reading achievement in 32 systems of education around the world, showed that the amount of time students reported spending in voluntary reading activities was the second strongest predictor of a school's overall reading performance. More than 50 variables were ranked in order of importance with respect to reading comprehension at grade 4 and grade 8 levels. The first-ranked indicator was the school's perception of the degree of parent cooperation. This variable is probably a reflection of socioeconomic status. The significance of reading frequency in promoting reading development is also evident from the high rankings of variables such as reading in class (3), amount of reading materials in the school (8), having a classroom library (11), and frequency of borrowing books from a library (12). With respect to teaching methods, a focus on comprehension instruction was ranked 9 and emphasis on literature was ranked 17, both considerably more significant than whether or not the school engaged in explicit phonics teaching (41). The ranking of relevant variables in this study from home, school, and classroom spheres is outlined in Figure 1.1.

The low ranking of explicit phonics instruction in predicting reading comprehension does not, of course, mean that phonics instruction is not

FIGURE 1.1 Indicators predicting reading comprehension (grade 4)

Home
02. Amount of free voluntary reading
12. Frequency of borrowing books from library

School Resources
08. Amount of reading materials in the school
14. School resources (school library, reading room for students, student/school newspaper)
19. School library books per student

School Initiatives
16. Sponsoring of reading initiatives

Classroom Conditions and Teacher Practices
03. Reading in class
11. Having a classroom library
18. Frequency of visiting school library

Teacher Methods
09. Comprehension instruction (deliberate emphasis on text understanding)
17. Emphasis on literature (encouragement of silent reading, listened to student reading, focus on library skills, etc.)
41. Phonics teaching

from Postlethwaite & Ross (1992)

important in the early stages of learning to read. As indicated above, for many students it may be a crucial component. At higher levels of reading proficiency, however, phonics plays a lesser role in comparison with the amount of reading that students engage in and the amount of instruction they receive that is specifically focused on comprehension.

Virtually identical trends emerge from analyses of the 1994 National Assessment of Educational Progress (NAEP) data within the United States. The direct relation between reading performance and the amount of reading fourth graders report is evident in the fact that those who reported they read almost every day obtained a score of 221, compared with 217 for those who reported they read one or two times a week and 198 for those who report never or hardly ever reading (McQuillan, 1998). Ken Goodman (1997) also points to the fact that, in the 1994 NAEP data,

> in most cases, kids who read silently [in school] almost everyday score better than those who read silently at least weekly. But the sharp disadvantage is for kids who rarely read silently in school. They scored about thirty points lower on average in both years than daily silent readers. (p. 54)

Treadway (1997), in response to Goodman, acknowledges the importance of extensive reading for the development of reading comprehension but insists that systematic instruction in decoding is a necessary means to achieve that end. He notes that the three strongest predictors of student success in early reading are phonemic awareness, letter knowledge (meaning almost any knowledge about letters), and concepts about print. He disputes the claims by Goodman, Krashen, and other whole language theorists that children learn to read by reading, arguing instead that

> children that have phonemic awareness learn to decode. Those that learn to decode, learn to read, enjoy reading, and continue to do it. Those that do not learn to read by the end of first grade find reading frustrating and often quite trying. (1997, p. 58)

Treadway's argument appears convincing if it is interpreted as claiming that phonemic awareness is important in learning how to decode and that decoding ability is a necessary condition for strong development of reading comprehension. It is much less convincing, however, if it is interpreted as claiming that phonemic awareness in isolation is a major causal factor in the development of decoding and reading comprehension. This claim is problematic on two counts: (1) Research findings cast doubt on the simple theory that there is a direct causal path from phonological skills to reading skills (e.g., Hatcher et al., 1994), and (2) those who come to school with advanced phonemic awareness, letter knowledge, and concepts about print are those who have been immersed in a literate environment at home and have been read to extensively. These students generally require only minimal explicit phonics instruction to learn how to break the code. Thus, phonemic awareness can be promoted through immersion in a literate environment as well as through explicit instruction.

Treadway's causal sequence could be reformulated as follows:

- Children who are immersed in a literate environment develop phonemic awareness.
- Those who have phonemic awareness learn to decode with appropriate instruction.
- Those who do not come to school with phonemic awareness already developed will benefit from immersion in a rich literate environment together with explicit instruction designed to develop concepts about print, including phonemic awareness and the alphabetic principle.
- Those who learn to decode will apply and extend their decoding skills to independent reading when they are provided with extensive exposure to varied and meaningful texts.

As noted earlier, from my perspective it does not ultimately matter *how* children develop phonemic awareness, letter knowledge, and general concepts about print. However, it *is* important for them to develop this knowledge about language. It seems reasonable to advocate that there is an important place for both immersion in a literate environment in the early years of school (e.g., reading Big Books to children, encouragement of writing, etc.) and explicit demystification of how sounds and symbols relate to each other. This appears to be a position that advocates at opposite poles of the whole language/phonics debate (e.g., Coles and Treadway) can endorse, albeit grudgingly.

Both of these instructional emphases—a focus on extensive reading and writing for self-expression and the development of explicit awareness of how the language works—are also important for reading comprehension instruction. The danger in states that have adopted the phonics-as-panacea mantra is that the importance of immersion in a literate environment gets omitted from both the decoding and comprehension equations. The so-called "balanced" reading approach can easily become a very *un*balanced focus on skills, drills, and worksheets, with minimal reading of stories and other authentic text and minimal creative writing. In order to emphasize just how overwhelming the data are regarding the importance of extensive reading for the development of reading comprehension, consider some additional evidence.

Consistent with the Postlethwaite and Ross results and the "whole language" arguments of Coles, Goodman, Krashen, and McQuillan, Fielding and Pearson's (1994) review of research in this area highlights four components of a reading program that are strongly supported by the research data:

1. Large amounts of time for actual text reading;
2. Teacher-directed instruction in comprehension strategies;
3. Opportunities for peer and collaborative learning; and
4. Occasions for students to talk to a teacher and one another about their responses to reading. (p. 62)

The power of extensive reading in a second language to promote knowledge of this language is supported in a wide variety of studies. Elley and Mangubhai (1983), for example, demonstrated that fourth- and fifth-grade students in Fiji exposed to a "book flood" program during their 30-minute daily English (L2) class—in which they simply read books, either alone or with the guidance of their teacher—performed significantly better after two years than students taught through more traditional methods. Elley (1991) similarly documented the superiority of book-based English-language teaching programs among primary school students in a variety of other contexts (see also Krashen, 1993, 1999, and McQuillan, 1998, for comprehensive reviews).

How does extensive reading promote the growth of reading comprehension ability and overall second-language proficiency? A simple answer is that it is only through reading that children get access to the low-frequency vocabulary and grammatical structures that constitute the language of academic success. This becomes clear when we understand the nature of the English lexicon and the ways in which vocabulary knowledge is related to reading comprehension.

VOCABULARY KNOWLEDGE AND READING. The English lexicon derives from two main sources. The Anglo-Saxon language (of Germanic origin and related to other languages of northern Europe) had established itself as the major language in England from about the 5th century AD. In the 11th century the Normans invaded, and their language (derived from Old French, Greek, and Latin) became the high-status language of the society, used among the nobility and in the courts. The Anglo-Saxon language continued to be spoken among peasants and those in lower status positions in the society. From the 12th through 16th centuries the two languages merged with each other to form the core of what we now call "English." The lexicon of each language did not blend evenly across all domains and functions of language, however. The Anglo-Saxon lexicon continued to be used predominantly in everyday conversation; the Greco-Latin lexicon became the language of literacy and governed the more formal functions of the society (e.g., legal transactions).

Corson's (1993, 1995, 1997) detailed analysis of this process highlights the fact that today the academic language of texts continues to draw heavily on Greco-Latin words, whereas everyday conversation relies more on an Anglo-Saxon–based lexicon. Greco-Latin words tend to be three or four syllables long, whereas the high-frequency words of the Anglo-Saxon lexicon tend to be one or two syllables in length. Corson (1997) points out that

> academic Graeco-Latin words are mainly literary in their use. Most native speakers of English begin to encounter these words in quantity in their upper primary school reading and in the formal secondary school setting. So the words' introduction in literature or textbooks, rather than in conversation, restricts people's access to them. Certainly, exposure to specialist Graeco-Latin words happens much more often while reading than while talking or watching television.... Printed texts provided much more exposure to [Graeco-Latin] words than oral ones. For example, even children's books contained 50% more rare words than either adult prime-time television or the conversations of university graduates; popular magazines had three times as many rare words as television and informal conversation. (p. 677)

Among the highest frequency Anglo-Saxon nouns are *time*, *people*, *years*, *work*, *something*, *world*, and *children* (Corson, 1997). A listing of 570 word families that are commonly found in academic texts in English but that are not among the most frequent 2,000 words of the language is provided by Coxhead (2000). Some of the words from Coxhead's list are *analyze*, *benefit*, *concept*, *context*, *establish*, *identify*, and *interpret*. Coxhead notes that "more than 82% of the words in the AWL [Academic Word List] are of Greek or Latin origin, indicating that the study of prefixes, suffixes, and stems may be one way to study this vocabulary" (pp. 228–229). The Latin and Greek origins of academic vocabulary in English also means that there are many cognates between this vocabulary and the vocabulary of Spanish and other Romance languages. This reality opens many possibilities for cross-linguistic language exploration. Coxhead cautions, however, that direct study of the vocabulary in isolation is insufficient for effective learning. Direct study "needs to be balanced with opportunities to meet the vocabulary in message-focused reading and listening and to use the vocabulary in speaking and writing" (p. 228).

Paul Nation (1990, 1993) and his colleagues have carried out the most comprehensive research on the nature and learning of English vocabulary. Like Corson, he points out that most low-frequency vocabulary comes to English from Latin or Greek. He estimates that about two thirds of the low-frequency words in English derive from these linguistic origins. Nation (1990) further points out that

> high frequency vocabulary consists mainly of short words which cannot be broken into meaningful parts. Low frequency vocabulary, on the other hand, while it consists of many thousands of words, is made from a much smaller number of word parts. The word, *impose*, for example, is made of two parts, *im-* and *-pose*, which occur in hundreds of other words—*imply*, *infer*, *compose*, *expose*, *position*. This has clear implications for teaching and learning vocabulary. (p. 18)

Nation (1993) suggests that for pedagogical purposes the vocabulary of a language can be classified into four groups:

1. *High-frequency words.* In English these consist of around 2,000 word families that cover more than 80% of most written text. These word families include words such as *put*, *end*, *difficult*, and *come*.

2. *General academic vocabulary.* This group of words consists of about 800 word families (527 in Coxhead's more recent research) that cover about 8–10% of academic text.

3. *Technical or specialized vocabulary.* This usually comprises about 2,000 words for a particular subject area. These words are proportionately much more frequently encountered in a specialized area than they are in the language as a whole, and mastery of this vocabulary develops as a result of mastery of the field. They account for about 4–5% of academic text.

4. *Low-frequency words.* Nation estimates that there remain at least 123,000 low-frequency word families. He notes that adult native speakers of English with a postsecondary education have a vocabulary size of about 20,000 word families. Most of this vocabulary is made up of low-frequency words that "are learned through diverse and wide-ranging contact with the language" (1993, p. 125). Nation reviews research showing that "informal spoken language does not provide much opportunity for growth in knowledge of low frequency words" (p. 129). This vocabulary grows slowly and "requires

substantial amounts of reading or listening to language that contains more low frequency words than colloquial language does" (p. 129).

Nation emphasizes that learners must be given the opportunity to use the language if vocabulary is to develop to its full potential: "If learners have a sufficiently large vocabulary but they are not given the opportunity to put this vocabulary to use and develop skill in using it, their growth in knowledge and further vocabulary growth will not be achieved" (1993, p. 132).

Commenting on the relation between vocabulary and reading, Nation and Coady (1988) point out that "vocabulary difficulty has consistently been found to be the most significant predictor of overall readability" (p. 108). Once the effect of vocabulary difficulty (usually estimated by word frequency and/or familiarity and word length) is taken into account, other linguistic variables, such as sentence structure, account for little incremental variance in the readability of a text. They summarize their review as follows: "In general the research leaves us in little doubt about the importance of vocabulary knowledge for reading, and the value of reading as a means of increasing vocabulary" (p. 108).

One example of the research illustrating the extent to which vocabulary can be acquired from context is Nagy, Herman, and Anderson's (1985) demonstration that the probability of learning a word from context after just one exposure is between 10% and 15%. As learners read more in their second language, repeated exposure to unfamiliar words will exert an incremental effect on vocabulary learning. There are limits to inferencing unknown words, however. Laufer (1992) has shown that learners need 95% "lexical coverage" of the words in a text before they can readily infer from context the meanings of the remaining, unknown words. When the proportion of words in a text known by the reader falls below this 95% threshold, the possibility of inferring the unknown words decreases significantly. A Spanish speaker who can supplement the use of context by drawing on cognate connections between Spanish and academic English words (e.g., *encounter-encontrar*; *predict-predecir*) has an important advantage in the reading process (see Bear et al., chapter 4 in this volume). Similarly, instruction that enables students from all backgrounds to develop strategies for analysis of the morphological structure of words (prefixes, suffixes, and roots) can significantly increase their power to infer the meaning of unknown words (Biemiller, 1999; White, Power, & White, 1989; White, Sowell, & Yanagihara, 1989).

In short, all the research evidence suggests that reading extensively in a wide variety of genres is essential for developing high levels of both vocabulary knowledge and reading comprehension. This is particularly the case for

ELL students, because they are attempting to catch up to students who are continuing to develop their English (L1) academic language proficiency.

The important role that extensive reading itself plays in fueling reading development does not mean that teacher-directed instruction is unimportant. On the contrary, students will become more effective readers if they acquire efficient strategies for text interpretation and analysis and if the teacher directs their attention to how the language of text works (e.g., the role of transitional words such as *however*, *although*, etc.). This is illustrated by the strong showing of comprehension instruction in the Postlethwaite and Ross (1992) study. Fielding and Pearson (1994) similarly rank "teacher-directed instruction in comprehension strategies" second to "large amounts of time for actual text reading" in their review of the implications of reading research for instruction (see Chamot, Barnhardt, El-Dinary, & Robbins, 1999, and Chamot & O'Malley, 1994, for comprehensive reviews of the significance of learning strategies for ELL students' academic learning).

Fillmore (1997) has articulated the role that teachers should play in making texts work as input for language learning:

- Provide the support learners need to make sense of the text.
- Call attention to the way language is used in the text.
- Discuss with learners the meaning and interpretation of sentences and phrases within the text.
- Point out that words in one text may have been encountered or used in other places.
- Help learners discover the grammatical cues that indicate relationships such as cause and effect, antecedence and consequence, comparison and contrast, and so on.

In short, teachers help written texts become usable input not only by helping children make sense of the text but by drawing their attention to how language is used in the materials they read. If this is done consistently enough, the learners themselves will soon come to notice the way language is used in the materials they read. When they do that, everything they read will be input for learning. (p. 4)

Conclusions

The volatile debates on how to teach reading that continue to occupy researchers, policymakers, and educators are largely a waste of everybody's time. There is actually a considerable degree of consensus hidden behind the cacophony of ideological debate. For example, almost everybody agrees that

- immersion in a literate environment either in home or in school (and preferably in both) is a strong predictor of success in both decoding and reading comprehension;

- the development of phonemic awareness, letter knowledge, and concepts about print is an important component of the development of initial decoding skills;

- an explicit instructional focus on developing phonemic awareness, letter knowledge, and concepts about print, *together with a significant instructional focus on actual reading*, contributes to the development of decoding skills and early reading comprehension skills. A combined focus on the code *and* the meaning works significantly better for most children than instruction that focuses primarily on isolated sequential phonics drills alone or on exposure to authentic text alone; and

- the amount of access to print and the amount of actual reading that students carry out is by far the major determinant of reading comprehension development as students progress through the grades.

The most significant point of contention appears to be the extent to which tight control should be exercised over students' access to authentic text (i.e., text that would not be classified as "decodable"). Those in the phonics advocacy camp emphasize that decodable text should predominate in initial reading materials, with only limited access being provided to "nondecodable" text (e.g., children's literature). Mathes and Torgeson (2000), for example, express this perspective as follows:

> Likewise, to ask children to read text that they cannot decode using the alphabetic elements and skills that they have been taught is to communicate to them that the alphabetic knowledge and skill they have spent effort learning is not really relevant to reading, and that they must rely heavily on guessing the identity of words from context. (p. 12)

In other words, it is seen as problematic for children to encounter words in reading materials for which the letter-sound correspondences have not been previously taught in an explicit and systematic way.

By contrast, those who emphasize the importance of phonics skills as a starting point for getting into reading generally have little problem with some use of decodable texts but also would encourage students to use the totality of their concepts about print (including knowledge of phonics, contextual clues, and knowledge of the world) to engage with books and other texts that they are motivated to read. When students are motivated to read, and their identities are invested in the process, they will try their evolving decoding skills on environmental print, stories, and other texts. In doing so, they will receive feedback and scaffolding from teachers, parents, and older siblings and use this feedback to infer more complex letter-sound correspondences, which may not have been taught explicitly.

Essentially, the contrast here is between a behaviorist and sociocultural (Vygotskian) approach to learning. The evidence reviewed in this chapter clearly shows that in a culturally responsive learning environment, guided or scaffolded by supportive adults, children are very capable of developing more complex phonological and decoding skills than they have been taught explicitly.

The orientation of this chapter is much more consistent with a Vygotskian approach to learning than with the more mechanistic behaviorist approach. Conceptualizing learning as occurring within the interpersonal space of teacher-student interactions (the Zone of Proximal Development) enables us to reflect on how learning to read is affected by identity negotiation rooted in societal power relationships in addition to specific instructional strategies or content. Within a Vygotskian framework, there is scope for discussing the centrality for children's reading development of notions such as cognitive engagement and identity investment rather than simply the technical characteristics of instruction (e.g., how many phonics rules should be taught explicitly and in what sequence).

At one level, the differences in the opposing positions are profound, insofar as they reflect very different notions of what it means to learn. As noted above, however, these differences can also be seen as a matter of emphasis. At a practical level, what this means is, *avoid the extremes*. A similar perspective is expressed by Celia Genishi and Dorothy Strickland (1999):

> In practice, teachers who advocate holistic approaches are apt to include strong word-recognition programs with phonics as a key tool for word recognition; and teachers who support intensive, systematic phonics often employ instructional strategies such as reading aloud to children and the encouragement of invented spelling. Although the matter of emphasis is not to be taken lightly, it is unlikely that you will find classrooms that reflect polar ends of an instructional continuum. (p. viii)

I am less confident than Genishi and Strickland, however, that most classrooms are balanced in their approach. The phonics-as-panacea movement has influenced policymakers in states such as California and Texas to such an extent that what is being implemented in many classrooms is isolated phonics drills (often combined with exposure to decodable text) to the exclusion of any significant emphasis on extensive reading of authentic text (Gándara et al., 2000). Even worse, in some behavioristically oriented programs teachers are expected to read scripts that dictate exactly what they should say to students in order to develop their phonics skills. Deviation from the script is strongly discouraged. There is certainly nothing inappropriate with providing illustrative scripts to *guide* instruction; new or inexperienced teachers may benefit from initially following the script until they gain more confidence (see García & Beltrán, chapter 9 in this volume). But the top-down imposition of scripts on all teachers represents an attempt to "teacher-proof" the curriculum. It reflects a profound distrust of teachers and an extremely narrow interpretation of the teaching-learning process. Nowhere in this anemic instructional vision is there room for really connecting with culturally diverse students, affirming their identities, or generating any intrinsic motivation to learn and engage cognitively with the instruction. Teachers and students alike are construed as programmable robots. This kind of programming reduces instruction to a technical exercise; neither teachers nor students are encouraged to invest their identities in the teaching-learning process. Linda McNeil of Rice University in Houston commented astutely in *Time* magazine that this kind of programming will "drive out the best teachers and give the weakest a place to hide" (Morse, 2000, p. 61).

REFERENCES

Allington, R.L., & Woodside-Jiron, H. (1999). The politics of literacy teaching: How "research" shaped educational policy. *Educational Researcher, 28*(8), 4–13.

Anderson, R.C., Hiebert, E.H., Scott, J.A., & Wilkinson, I.A.G. (1985). *Becoming a nation of readers: The report of the Commission on Reading.* Washington, DC: National Institute of Education.

Biemiller, A. (1999). *Language and reading success.* Cambridge, MA: Brookline Books.

California Department of Education. (1996). *Teaching reading: A balanced, comprehensive approach to teaching reading in prekindergarten through grade three.* Sacramento, CA: California State Board of Education.

Cashion, M., & Eagan, R. (1990). Spontaneous reading and writing in English by students in total French immersion: Summary of final report. *English Quarterly, 22*(1–2), 30–44.

Chall, J.S., Jacobs, V.A., & Baldwin, L.E. (1990). *The reading crisis: Why poor children fall behind.* Cambridge, MA: Harvard University Press.

Chamot, A.U., Barnhardt, S., El-Dinary, P.B., & Robbins, J. (1999). *The learning strategies handbook.* White Plains, NY: Longman.

Chamot, A.U., & O'Malley, J.M. (1994). *The CALLA handbook: Implementing the cognitive academic language learning approach*. Reading, MA: Addison-Wesley.

Coles, G. (2000). *Misreading reading: The bad science that hurts children*. Portsmouth, NH: Heinemann.

Corson, D. (1993). *Language, minority education and gender: Linking social justice and power*. Clevedon, UK: Multilingual Matters.

Corson, D. (1995). *Using English words*. New York: Kluwer.

Corson, D. (1997). The learning and use of academic English words. *Language Learning, 47*(4), 671–718.

Coxhead, A. (2000). A new academic word list. *TESOL Quarterly, 34*(2), 213–238.

Cummins, J. (1991). The development of bilingual proficiency from home to school: A longitudinal study of Portuguese-speaking children. *Journal of Education, 173*, 85–98.

Cummins, J. (2000). *Language, power and pedagogy: Bilingual children in the crossfire*. Clevedon, UK: Multilingual Matters.

Cummins, J. (2001). *Negotiating identities: Education for empowerment in a diverse society* (2nd ed.). Los Angeles: California Association for Bilingual Education.

Cunningham, A. (1990). Explicit versus implicit instruction in phonemic awareness. *Journal of Experimental Child Psychology, 50*, 429–444.

Ehri, L.C., Nunes, S., Stahl, S., & Willows, D. (2001). Systematic phonics instruction helps students learn to read: Evidence from the National Reading Panel's meta-analysis. *Review of Educational Research, 71*(3), 393–447.

Elley, W.B. (1991). Acquiring literacy in a second language: The effect of book-based programs. *Language Learning, 41*, 375–411.

Elley, W.B., & Mangubhai, F. (1983). The impact of reading on second language learning. *Reading Research Quarterly, 19*, 53–67.

Fielding, L.G., & Pearson, P.D. (1994). Reading comprehension: What works. *Educational Leadership, 51*(5), 62–68.

Fillmore, L.W. (1997). *Authentic literature in ESL instruction*. Glenview, IL: Scott Foresman.

Foorman, B.R., Fletcher, J.M., Francis, D.J., & Schatschneider, C.S. (2000). Response: Misrepresentation of research by other researchers. *Educational Researcher, 29*(6), 27–37.

Foorman, B.R., Francis, D.J., Fletcher, J.M., Schatschneider, C.S., & Mehta, P. (1998). The role of instruction in learning to read: Preventing reading failure in at-risk children. *Journal of Educational Psychology, 90*(1), 37–55.

Gándara, P., Maxwell-Jolly, J., García, E., Asato, J., Gutiérrez, K., Stritikus, T., et al. (2000). *The initial impact of Proposition 227 on the instruction of English learners*. Davis, CA: University of California Linguistic Minority Research Institute.

Genishi, C., & Strickland, D. (1999). Foreword. In G.B. Thompson & T. Nicholson (Eds.), *Learning to read: Beyond phonics and whole language* (pp. vii–ix). New York: Teachers College Press; Newark, DE: International Reading Association.

Geva, E. (2000). Issues in the assessment of reading disabilities in L2 children: Beliefs and research evidence. *Dyslexia, 6*, 13–28.

Goldenberg, C. (1998). A balanced approach to early Spanish literacy instruction. In R.M. Gersten & R.T. Jiménez (Eds.), *Promoting learning for culturally and linguistically diverse students: Classroom applications from contemporary research*. Belmont, CA: Wadsworth.

Goodman, K. (1997). California, whole language, and the NAEP. *CLIPS: A Journal of the California Reading & Literature Project, 3*(1), 53–56.

Hatcher, P., Hulme, C., & Ellis, A. (1994). Ameliorating early reading failure by integrating the teaching of reading and phonological skills: The phonological linkage hypothesis. *Child Development, 65*, 41–57.

Iverson, S., & Tunmer, W.E. (1993). Phonological processing skills and the Reading Recovery program. *Journal of Educational Psychology, 85*, 112–126.

Juel, C., & Minden-Cupp, C. (2000). Learning to read words: Linguistic units and instructional strategies. *Reading Research Quarterly, 35*(4), 458–492.

Klesmer, H. (1994). Assessment and teacher perceptions of ESL student achievement. *English Quarterly, 26*(3), 8–11.

Krashen, S.D. (1993). *The power of reading*. Englewood, CO: Libraries Unlimited.

Krashen, S.D. (1996a). *Every person a reader: An alternative to the California Task Force Report on Reading*. Culver City, CA: Language Education Associates.

Krashen, S.D. (1996b). *Under attack: The case against bilingual education*. Culver City, CA: Language Education Associates.

Krashen, S.D. (1999). *Three arguments against whole language and why they are wrong*. Portsmouth, NH: Heinemann.

Kwan, A.B., & Willows, D.M. (1998, December). *Impact of early phonics instruction on children learning English as a second language*. Paper presented at the 48th annual meeting of the National Reading Conference, Austin, TX.

Lambert, W.E., & Tucker, G.R. (1972). *Bilingual education of children: The St. Lambert experiment*. Rowley, MA: Newbury House.

Laufer, B. (1992). How much lexis is necessary for reading comprehension? In H. Bejoint & P. Arnaud (Eds.), *Vocabulary and applied linguistics* (pp. 126–132). London: Macmillan.

Lloyd, S. (1992). *The phonics handbook*. Essex, UK: Jolly Learning.

Mathes, P.G., & Torgesen, J.K. (2000). A call for equity in reading instruction for all students: A response to Allington and Woodside-Jiron. *Educational Researcher, 29*(6), 4–14.

McNeil, L.M. (2000). *Contradictions of school reform: Economic costs of standardized testing*. New York: Routledge.

McQuillan, J. (1998). *The literacy crisis: False claims, real solutions*. Portsmouth, NH: Heinemann.

Morse, J. (2000, March 6). Sticking to the script. *Time*, 60–61.

Muñiz-Swicegood, M. (1994). The effects of metacognitive reading strategy training on the reading performance and student reading analysis strategies of third grade bilingual students. *The Bilingual Research Journal, 18*(1&2), 83–97.

Nagy, W.E., Herman, P.A., & Anderson, R.C. (1985). Learning words from context. *Reading Research Quarterly, 20*, 233–253.

Nation, P. (1990). *Teaching and learning vocabulary*. Boston: Heinle & Heinle.

Nation, P. (1993). Vocabulary size, growth, and use. In R. Schreuder & B. Weltens (Eds.), *The bilingual lexicon* (pp. 115–134). Amsterdam: John Benjamins.

Nation, P., & Coady, J. (1988). Vocabulary and reading. In R. Carter & M. McCarthy (Eds.), *Vocabulary and language teaching* (pp. 97–110). London: Longman.

Postlethwaite, T.N., & Ross, K.N. (1992). *Effective schools in reading: Implications for educational planners. An exploratory study*. The Hague, The Netherlands: The International Association for the Evaluation of Educational Achievement.

Reyes, M.d.l.L. (2000). Unleashing possibilities: Biliteracy in the primary grades. In M.d.l.L. Reyes & J. Halcón (Eds.), *The best for our children: Critical perspectives on literacy for Latino students* (pp. 96–121). New York: Teachers College Press.

Share, D., & Stanovich, K.E. (1995). Cognitive processes in early reading development: Accommodating individual differences into a model of acquisition. *Issues in Education: Contributions from* Educational Psychology, *1*(1), 1–57.

Stanovich, K.E. (1992). Speculations on the causes and consequences of individual differences in early reading acquisition. In P.B. Gough, L.C. Ehri, & R. Treiman (Eds.), *Reading acquisition* (pp. 307–342). Hillsdale, NJ: Erlbaum.

Stanovich, K.E., & Stanovich, P.J. (1998). Ending the reading wars. *Orbit, 28*(4), 49–55.

Taylor, B.M., Anderson, R.C., Au, K.H., & Raphael, T.E. (2000). Discretion in the translation of research to policy: A case from beginning reading. *Educational Researcher, 29*(6), 16–26.

Thomas, W.P., & Collier, V.P. (1997). *School effectiveness for language minority students.* Washington, DC: National Clearinghouse for Bilingual Education.

Tizard, J., Schofield, W.N., & Hewison, J. (1982). Collaboration between teachers and parents in assisting children's reading. *British Journal of Educational Psychology, 52*, 1–15.

Treadway, J. (1997). Response to Ken Goodman's critique of the NAEP Report. *CLIPS: A Journal of the California Reading & Literature Project, 3*(1), 57–58.

Tunmer, W.E., & Chapman, J.W. (1999). Teaching strategies for word identification. In G.B. Thompson & T. Nicholson (Eds.), *Learning to read: Beyond phonics and whole language* (pp. 74–102). New York: Teachers College Press; Newark, DE: International Reading Association.

Vygotsky, L.S. (1978). *Mind in society: The development of higher psychological processes* (M. Cole, V. John-Steiner, S. Scribner, & E. Souberman, Eds. and Trans.). Cambridge, MA: Harvard University Press. (Original work published 1934)

White, T.G., Power, M.A., & White, S. (1989). Morphological analysis: Implications for teaching and understanding vocabulary growth. *Reading Research Quarterly, 24*, 283–304.

White, T.G., Sowell, J., & Yanagihara, A. (1989). Teaching elementary students to use word-part clues. *The Reading Teacher, 42*, 302–308.

CHAPTER 2

Teaching English Learners to Read: Learning or Acquisition?

David Freeman and Yvonne Freeman

Teaching reading in public schools has always posed a challenge, but two recent developments have made it more difficult: (1) an increase in the number of English learners in classes across the country and (2) an increased emphasis on accountability. More teachers than ever before are being asked to teach reading in classes with English learners. At the same time, these teachers are being held ever more accountable for students' reading test scores.

The demographic shift has been dramatic. In the last decade, the number of English learners more than doubled. In 1989–1990, 2.1 million students in grades K–12 were identified as limited English proficient (LEP); the number of LEP students for the academic year 1999–2000 was 4.4 million. This represents a 105% rise during a period in which the overall increase in students was only 24.2%. Not only are there more English learners in classes across the United States, but these learners come from a greater variety of language and educational backgrounds. In addition, many English learners move from one area to another, so schools that previously had many Hispanic students might now have students from Bosnia or the Sudan.

At the same time that the student population has undergone a dramatic change, teachers are being asked to teach every student to read, regardless of the student's English proficiency. Teachers are being held accountable for student progress. States and school districts have developed new standards, and all students are expected to demonstrate competence in these standards by scoring at appropriate levels on designated exams. In many cases, teachers are evaluated based on their students' performance on such tests. Standards are being developed in all academic areas—but in most schools, the first area being assessed is reading.

Teachers, then, are being asked to bring all their students to high levels of reading proficiency, including students who are just beginning to learn English. How can teachers succeed under these trying conditions? Many school districts have looked to new materials or new reading programs developed for native speakers of English as the answer, and many of these new reading programs emphasize phonics and decoding skills. In this chapter, we argue that attempts to teach English learners to read using programs that emphasize phonics and decoding skills will not succeed with the majority of English learners. We develop this argument by contrasting two views of second-language development, two views of reading, and two views of reading proficiency.

Two Views of Second-Language Development

How do we become proficient in a second language? Do we learn languages in the same way we learn other school subjects, like math or social studies, or do we acquire a second language the same way we acquired our first language? Most current research in second-language acquisition suggests that we *acquire* a second language—and that learning plays only a minor role in the process (Krashen, 1982).

If you studied a foreign language in high school or college, you probably experienced *learning*. We learn a language in formal contexts, like classrooms, as the result of direct teaching. We study rules and memorize vocabulary. Learning is a conscious process that usually involves presentation of the parts of the language, practice using those parts, and testing to determine mastery.

On the other hand, if you picked up some Spanish when you went to Mexico on vacation, you *acquired* the language. Acquisition often occurs in informal situations. It is a subconscious process that occurs as you use language to do things: order a meal, shop for souvenirs, or ask for directions. Table 2.1 highlights some of the differences between learning and acquisition.

TABLE 2.1 Learning and acquisition

Learning	Acquisition
Conscious	Subconscious
Occurs in formal situations	Occurs in informal situations
Results from direct teaching	Results from trying to communicate
Involves learning rules	Involves learning to use language for real purposes
Can be tested	Can be used

Unfortunately, most of us who studied a second language in a high school or college classroom are not very proficient. David's four years of French did not prepare him to travel to France and carry on daily activities in French. In contrast, David lived in Colombia, Mexico, and Venezuela at different times, and during these stays he acquired enough Spanish to function reasonably well in that language. Most teachers can see the results of language acquisition in their classrooms. Students who come to school speaking languages other than English acquire the English needed for basic communication fairly quickly without formal instruction. However, extensive research (e.g., Collier, 1992; Cummins, 1996) has shown that it takes much longer to acquire the academic language needed for school success.

The key to acquisition is receiving messages we understand—what Krashen (1982) calls *comprehensible input*. This is what happens when we understand directions in a foreign country and actually get where we hoped to go. Every time we understand a message, we acquire a bit more of the new language. Comprehensible input leads to language development.

Two Views of Reading

In the same way that there are two views of how people develop a second language, there are also two views of how people learn to read. The word recognition view is similar to learning in language development. Current phonics-based approaches to teaching reading are based on the idea that reading is primarily a process of recognizing words. The sociopsycholinguistic view is similar to acquisition and emphasizes that reading is a process of constructing meaning. This view holds that readers acquire literacy in the same way they acquire oral language, by focusing on meaning.

Krashen (1993, 1996, 1999) has extended his theory of acquisition to include literacy. He argues that we acquire the ability to read and write in the same way that we acquire a second language. In the case of reading, the input comes from written language; teachers make the input comprehensible when they read to students from Big Books or poetry charts. As students follow along, they begin to make connections between this oral reading and print. Eventually, they acquire enough knowledge of written language to read on their own.

Those who hold a word recognition view believe that the main task during reading is to identify words. Readers develop a set of skills that allows them to make a connection between the black marks on the page and words in their oral vocabulary. Teaching reading involves helping students develop the necessary skills to make this connection. For example, students might learn to sound out letters and then blend the sounds to pronounce and identify words.

Those who hold a sociopsycholinguistic view believe that the main task during reading is to construct meaning. Readers use their background knowledge and cues from the text to make sense of print. Teaching reading involves helping students understand the functions and purposes of reading as well as helping them develop the strategies they need to construct meaning. If a class is studying the solar system, the teacher might start by having students raise questions that they would like to investigate. Then students would conduct research in small groups to answer their questions. In this process, they would read charts and maps of the solar system along with stories and content materials about space. They would talk together about their questions, complete projects, and write reports to communicate the results of their investigations.

Both those who hold a word recognition view of reading and those who hold a sociopsycholinguistic view would probably agree that good readers comprehend texts. The two views might be seen simply as different routes to this common end. These different routes translate into very different classroom practices, however. As Table 2.2 shows, they involve different goals; different approaches to vocabulary, word study, and phonics; and different classroom reading activities for both students and teachers. In the following sections we look in more detail at how the two views differ in each of these areas.

TABLE 2.2 Two views of reading

Word Recognition View	Sociopsycholinguistic View
Goal: Identify words to get to meaning of text.	Goal: Use background knowledge and cues from three systems to construct meaning from text.
Learn vocabulary through preteaching activities.	Acquire vocabulary by encountering words in context.
Learn to break words into parts to identify them.	Study word parts only during linguistic investigations.
Build a bank of sight words and use phonics rules to sound out words to identify them.	Use graphophonics as just one of three cueing systems.
Activity: Read orally so the teacher can help students learn to identify words and can supply words students do not know.	Activity: Read silently using the strategies the teacher has helped students internalize to construct meaning from a text.

Word Recognition View of Reading

GOALS.   The goal for a teacher who takes a word recognition view of reading is to help students identify the marks on the paper as words they already know in their oral vocabulary. In this view, written language builds on an oral language base. This perspective gives rise to several concerns, especially with respect to English learners:

- The idea that written language develops only after oral language is mastered can result in delaying the teaching of reading. In early grades, teachers who believe that reading is based solely on identifying and saying aloud words in a child's oral vocabulary work first with students on readiness activities helping students "get their sounds," and building their oral vocabulary before introducing print. In classes with English language learners, teachers often work on vocabulary and pronunciation of English words. In some cases, nonnative English speakers are not introduced to reading until they can pronounce words without a foreign accent and may even be referred to speech therapy.

- Pronouncing a word and apprehending its meaning are not the same thing. Languages contain many homonyms, words that look and sound the same but have different meanings. For example, *leaf* could be part of a table or a tree. In a story with a sentence such as "Mother told her, 'Get the leaf for the table,'" a young reader might pronounce *leaf* correctly but miss the meaning by connecting *leaf* to the meaning associated with a tree. For teachers working in multilingual contexts, this is a real concern. English language learners often have not developed the multiple meanings of many words, and this makes it more difficult for them to comprehend texts. Thus, teachers who have studied a foreign language know how difficult it can be to get a joke. That is because jokes are often based on double meanings. In the same way, readers may not know the different meanings of the words they encounter.

- The assumption is that if students can identify words, they can put the meanings of the individual words together to make sense of a whole text. This is a common-sense view, one that seems logical, but it does not always work. There are times we all have tried to read passages in which we "knew" all the words but still did not end up understanding what we read. The context can help shape the meaning, but readers also may need background knowledge that cannot be derived from the text itself. For example, David reads the bridge column in the newspaper most mornings. He knows that *East* and *North* refer to players sitting at certain positions around a table, not to compass points. He also knows what it means for players to *bid* during an *auction* that results in a *contract*. Those three words have specialized meanings in bridge. And he knows that North ends up as the *dummy* every time even though he may be of average intelligence. Comprehending the bridge column requires a reader to bring certain background knowledge to the text, not simply to add up the meanings of the words in the text.

■ Teachers know that just listening to students read is not enough. If David gave the bridge column to someone who did not play bridge, he could not tell just by listening to that friend read whether or not he or she had comprehended the text. In the same way, there is a danger in assuming that a child who pronounces words easily is comprehending. This is particularly true with English language learners (see Cummins, chapter 1 in this volume). These students may think that if they can say the words, they are good readers. Teachers have commented to us that they were surprised that their second language students were not able to answer questions about a story they had "read" fluently. Actually, the teachers should not have been surprised. It is quite possible to separate pronunciation from meaning. We all have heard famous musicians sing beautifully in a language they cannot speak or understand.

The goal from the word recognition viewpoint is to identify individual words and to put those word meanings together to get to the meaning of the text. We have outlined the problems with this approach to constructing meaning. Teachers may delay introducing reading until students reach a certain level of oral language proficiency. Students may connect a word in a text to a meaning in their oral vocabulary that does not fit the text. A focus on identifying individual words may mean that students do not use context cues or develop the background knowledge needed to comprehend a text. Finally, teachers cannot tell from listening to students, even when they pronounce words correctly, whether or not they have understood a text.

VOCABULARY.   Teachers who hold a word recognition view of reading know that there will be some words in any text that most of the students will not know. Even if students succeed in sounding out these words, they have nothing in their oral vocabulary to attach the sounds to. For that reason, teachers may choose some words to preteach. For example, they might pick a list of words from a story and ask students to look up the words and write definitions. Many teachers have tried this, but a key problem with students' choosing definitions from a dictionary is that the definition they choose often does not fit the story. The word *circulation*, for example, might refer in one reading to how blood travels through the body but in another to traffic movement, and in still another to newspaper sales.

Teachers can avoid this problem by giving students both the words and their definitions. Providing words and definitions is still not the best approach to vocabulary, however. It is difficult to predict which words all the students will have problems with. Some students know all or almost all the words in any story; studying the words before reading is not a good use of their time. For other students, so many words are new that any list just scratches the surface.

Often, teachers combine vocabulary study with spelling practice. On a test, teachers dictate the words, and students have to spell them correctly and define them as well. Students who already know the words will score high on a test even without studying, whereas struggling students study to learn lots of words and still score low on a test. This may appear an efficient way to cover certain language arts objectives, but it takes lots of class time, time that could be spent in actual reading.

What about English language learners? Don't they need more work on vocabulary? In fact, many second language students say they like spelling and vocabulary exercises, and they often do well on such tests. They study hard to memorize definitions and spellings. Our experience, though, is that students have trouble applying the knowledge they gain in studying these isolated word lists to the stories and content texts they read. In the same way that students can spell words correctly on a test and then misspell them in an essay, students can define words correctly on a test and then have trouble applying that knowledge as they read. Again, we would prefer to see students spending more time in reading activities than in prereading activities like vocabulary study.

One other concern with vocabulary is the relation between concepts and the words we use to label those concepts. Take the *circulation* example used above. If we are talking about how blood travels through the body, this is an important concept in science. If a teacher chooses *circulation* as a vocabulary item to preteach before assigning a chapter from a science text, students may be able to memorize a definition without really learning the concept. Teachers know that students need lots of hands-on work to comprehend scientific concepts. In the same way that a teacher might be misled into thinking that a student understands a word he or she can pronounce, a teacher may also be misled into thinking that a student understands a scientific concept if he or she can define the relevant vocabulary term.

Preteaching vocabulary, then, is an attempt to make reading easier by preparing students for difficult words before assigning a story or a content text. Difficulties involved with preteaching vocabulary include deciding which words to teach, deciding whether to have the students look up the meanings or giving them the definitions, and determining whether vocabulary knowledge transfers into actual reading. There is also the danger that students may learn the vocabulary—the labels—without acquiring the underlying content area concepts. Finally, time spent on preteaching vocabulary is time taken away from other activities, including reading.

WORD PARTS.   In addition to teaching whole words when preteaching vocabulary, teachers who follow a word recognition view also teach word parts, or morphology. They show students how to break a large word into smaller, more recognizable parts. For example, a student who has trouble identifying a word like *unimaginable* might figure it out by dividing it into its basic meaning units or morphemes. This could produce *un+imagine+able*. The student can then see the little word *imagine* inside the big word, and get at the meaning "not able to be imagined." This process can be applied to many different words, and it overcomes some of the problems with concentrating on one vocabulary word at a time. It allows students to use the vocabulary they have to recognize new words built out of that vocabulary.

Being able to recognize roots, prefixes, and suffixes is especially helpful during multiple-choice tests. If students can discern the base word, they often can pick out the right definition. This skill is more difficult, but not impossible, to apply during reading. Some difficult words can be identified quickly by using knowledge of word parts. This should be a strategy students know how to use.

This strategy has limitations, however. These include deciding *how* to break the word into its parts, recognizing assimilated prefixes, recognizing roots that change their spelling when a suffix is added, and knowing which meaning of a prefix to use. In addition, many English words have Latin or Greek bases, and students would not know the meaning of those bases. (See Cummins, chapter 1 in this volume, for a discussion of Latin and Greek roots and their relation to academic language.)

The first task is to break the word into its parts. This is not difficult with a word like *unimaginable*, but it is more difficult with a word like *cognate*. Is it *cogn* plus *ate*, or is it *co* plus *gnate*? This example also highlights the difficulty of understanding words with Latin and Greek bases. Most students do not know the meanings of roots such as *cogn* or *gnatus*. Teachers have to decide if it is more efficient to teach the word parts or just teach the words.

Prefixes like *un* seem quite stable. The spelling does not change when it is added to different roots. It generally means "not" when added to adjectives, such as *unusual*. However, when we add *un* to a verb, it has a different meaning: If we say we will untie our shoelaces, we do not mean that we will *not* tie them. Other prefixes also change their meaning. *In* can either mean "in," as in *inside*, or "not," as in *inarticulate*. This prefix also changes its spelling to match the first letter of the root word. *In*, meaning "not," changes to *il* in *illogical*, to *ir* in *irreplaceable*, and to *im* in *immature*. Many other common prefixes are similarly hard to recognize.

Roots also change their spelling. In our previous example of *unimaginable*, students have to realize that *imagine* loses an *e* before *able*. In fact, a better analysis of the word would break it down even further into *un+image+ine+able*, but students might have trouble building the meaning of the whole from these parts.

Finding small words inside big words and using the meaning of the smaller, known word to get at the meaning of the larger word is a useful strategy. Nevertheless, using word parts to get at meaning can be difficult, for the reasons we have pointed out here. And if native English speakers encounter problems with finding word meanings by looking at the parts, the task becomes even more complex for nonnative speakers of English. Teachers must decide how much time to spend in teaching morphology, because any time spent teaching students how to break words into parts and then determine meaning is time taken away from actual reading.

SIGHT WORDS AND PHONICS.   Although teachers may preteach some vocabulary and may show students how to use word parts to unlock the meanings of complex words, most teachers who take a word recognition view of reading spend the most instructional time on sight words and phonics rules. Earlier debates over reading centered on whether to teach whole words through a "look-say" approach or to use phonics. Many teachers recognize the importance of using both visual cues *and* sound cues; they combine sight words with sounding out.

Some common words in English violate normal phonics rules. For example, it is fairly difficult to sound out words like *one*, *the*, or *of*. For this reason, teachers who hold a word recognition view of reading teach some sight words. For most other words, they teach students to use phonics. We discuss both phonics and phonemic awareness in more detail below. At this point, let us just note that many of the phonics rules found in teachers' guides work only some of the time, and this can frustrate students. For example, according to Weaver (1996), the old rule "When two vowels go walking, the first one does the talking" is true only about two thirds of the time. For English language learners, phonics is an even bigger problem, because their pronunciation is seldom conventional. Finally, we should note once again that time spent on learning a set of sight words or on learning phonics rules is time taken away from actual reading.

PHONEMIC AWARENESS.   Recently, researchers have argued that students need phonemic awareness in order to succeed at phonics. Phonemic awareness (PA) is the ability to perceive and manipulate the phonemes that make up words. Children with PA can look at a word like *fan* and recognize that it consists of three sounds. Phonemic awareness also includes the ability to manipulate those sounds. For example, students might be asked to delete a sound, add a sound, substitute one sound for another, blend individual sounds, or break a word into its component sounds. Some typical PA exercises, arranged from easiest to most difficult, are

- Sound matching: Which word starts with /s/? Think of a word that starts with /s/.
- Sound isolation: What sound do you hear at the beginning (middle, end) of *dog*?
- Blending: Combine the sounds of /p/, /u/, and /t/. What word do you get?
- Sound addition or substitution: Add a sound to a word (*b+and=band*), or substitute one sound for another (*rat, cat, sat*).
- Segmentation: Break the word *dog* into its phonemes and say each one separately.

The claim is that students need to develop PA to a certain level before they can benefit from instruction in phonics. As Honig (1996) writes, "Students need to be assessed early for their phonemic awareness level and then an organized support system should be provided for those who score below the levels necessary to profit by phonics instruction" (p. 50).

We have several concerns with reading programs in which PA is taught directly:

■ Exercises like the ones listed above are not meaning centered. A great deal of language arts time in many classes, even classes for older students, is now being devoted to helping students develop PA to prepare them for phonics lessons which, in turn, may also not be meaningful.

■ The students most likely to fail screening tests for PA are English language learners. If PA tests are administered in English, students not proficient in English will score poorly. Students who are not proficient in PA are given many PA exercises (followed by phonics exercises) and few opportunities for meaningful reading. Some English language learners may decide that reading, at least reading in English, is not meaningful.

■ The exercises are presented as though they were simple when, in fact, they are quite complex, because phonemes are complex. Phonemes are units that speakers of a language perceive because they are the sounds that make a difference in meaning in that language. In English, we know that /p/ and /b/ are two distinct phonemes because we have words like *pat* and *bat* that only differ by the /p/ and /b/ sounds.

What allows us to hear /p/ and /b/ as different sounds? They are each produced by stopping the airflow with the lips. They differ in that with /p/ our vocal cords do not vibrate, but with /b/ they do. This is referred to as a difference in *voicing*. Speakers of English perceive /p/ and /b/ as different phonemes because they notice this difference in voicing. There are other differences between /p/ and /b/: In a word like *pat*, /p/ gets a puff of air, called *aspiration*, but in *bat*, /b/ is not aspirated. Aspiration does not signal a difference in meaning in English, so native speakers can ignore that physical difference. However, English learners have to figure out which physical differences to attend to and which they can ignore because they do not make a difference in meaning.

Not only are phonemes complex, they change in different contexts. These variations on phonemes are called *allophones*. For example, /t/ sounds quite different in *tan*, *cat*, *kitten*, and *letter*. Or try saying "Cape Cod." Feel where your tongue is for the two *k* sounds. The /k/ in *Cape* is pronounced with the tongue further forward than the /k/ in *Cod*. Native speakers of English can ignore these physical differences in production, because the sound changes do not mark a change in meaning. Young children, however, are much more aware of the physical aspects of sound. The concept of phonemes as meaningful sounds is an abstract idea, and young children may be confused when they are told that two sounds that are physically different are "the same sound."

Of course, English language learners face a similar problem: They have to decide which sound differences to pay attention to and which ones to ignore. Phonemes are the meaningful sounds within one language; a sound that is a phoneme in one language may not be a phoneme in another. For example, in English the sound of *th* in *the* is a phoneme, but in Spanish it is not. Spanish speakers do make this sound, but in Spanish it is an allophone of *d*. Because phonemes and their allophones vary from one language to another, English language learners often have trouble with PA tests in English.

■ The research on PA is not compelling. Byrne and Fielding-Barnsley (1989), for example, found that differences in students' ability to do PA tasks diminishes over time. Kindergarten students trained in PA did better when tested in kindergarten on isolated word identification, spelling, and nonsense word reading than students who received no PA training. In first grade, however, "there were no differences between the trained and untrained groups on word identification or spelling, and only a small advantage for the trained group in nonsense word reading" (p. 319). This study suggests that PA is acquired naturally as long as children are read to and have opportunities to read. It is a *result* of reading, not a prerequisite for it (see also Cummins, chapter 1 in this volume).

Even when students show a difference in ability to complete PA tasks, they show little difference in comprehension. McQuillan (1998) reports on a study conducted by Torgesen and Hecht, in which 200 children were identified by low scores on phoneme deletion and letter-naming tasks in kindergarten. The children were given 80 minutes of one-on-one tutorial assistance in kindergarten and first grade. At the end of this time, the groups that received training in PA and phonics did much better than the group that received no assistance in the area of "word attack," which is the ability to pronounce an unfamiliar word or a nonsense word. The trained group also did somewhat better on PA tasks such as phoneme blending, but the trained group did not score significantly higher on measures of reading comprehension than the group that received no one-on-one tutoring. These and other studies suggest that students develop PA as a result of reading and being read to. They fail to show that PA training leads to better reading comprehension.

We question the value of teaching phonemic awareness and phonics directly. We believe that these aspects of language can only be acquired. Knowledge of graphophonics is acquired naturally as children learn how to write (Freeman & Freeman, 1997, 2000). As children move toward more conventional spelling, they work out the connections between sounds and spellings. Knowledge gained in writing transfers to reading, and reading and writing activities mutually reinforce students' development of graphophonics (Goodman, 1993).

ROUND-ROBIN READING. In classes where teachers take a word recognition view, round-robin reading is a common activity. Teachers sit with small groups of students, having them read aloud. When a student has difficulty with a word, the teacher might supply the word or might help the student sound it out. Often, other students will say the word.

Small-group instruction allows a teacher to coach individual children, but most teachers recognize the problems that come with this kind of oral reading exercise. Students get restless. Some are bored because the reading is easy for them and their classmates' oral reading is too slow. Others are frustrated because the reading is too difficult. While teachers read with a group, the other students have to work quietly on independent activities. Teachers struggle as they monitor a whole class and, at the same time, try to give individual attention to the students in the reading groups. Taking turns reading aloud is a school activity that is not characteristic of the normal reading behavior outside school, so it does not provide an appropriate model for learning how to read (Lindfors, 1989).

Many teachers have been trained to use programs consistent with a word recognition view of reading. They are taught to help students develop the skills needed to identify and pronounce individual words. They work with students on vocabulary, on word parts, on sight words, and on phonics skills. Their training assumes that students can put the meanings of the words together to construct a meaning for a text. If some of the students do not learn to read, these teachers give students more exercises and drills to help them develop the needed skills. If this does not work, teachers may blame themselves, thinking they are not planning or directing the activities correctly. Because program promoters claim that their materials can teach all students to read, teachers or unmotivated students become the scapegoats. Seldom is it considered that it is the view of reading that may be the problem. In the next section, we describe an alternative view consistent with an acquisition theory of language development.

Sociopsycholinguistic View of Reading

GOALS.   Earlier we noted that according to a sociopsycholinguistic view of reading, the main task during reading is the construction of meaning. That is, readers are focused on getting the meaning, not on getting the words. When we say that meaning is "constructed," we refer to a process that involves using cues from the printed text and from background knowledge to build understanding. This idea of constructing meaning may seem abstract, so let's consider an example. In the previous section, we discussed reading a bridge column. When David starts to read, he looks at the distribution of cards in the hand being discussed, and then he goes over the bidding. There really are no words in this section of the text, but David is reading nonetheless. He is making a prediction based on past readings of bridge columns, and he is bringing his knowledge of bridge to this task. The marks on the page have no meaning in themselves, but they represent possible meanings. Thus, when David sees S 2D in the bidding sequence, he decides that the player sitting in the South position bid two diamonds.

How about other texts? A young Jewish reader who has lived all his life in New York City constructs a different meaning from a Jan Karon novel about an aging Episcopal priest's adventures in a small southern town than a middle-aged, lifelong Episcopalian who was raised in a small community. Ads are texts, too. What meaning can you construct from the phrase "double coupons"? Is this a command to multiply the number of coupons by two? That is the meaning you might construct if you have not previously read shopping ads. What is an "early bird special"? Can you imagine the confusion this can cause an English language learner trying to read a menu? And are "early birds" the same as "snow birds"? They might be, in Arizona. In fact, we predict that readers with different backgrounds might construct quite different meanings from this paragraph. After all, the marks we made on the page only have a meaning *potential*, not a fixed meaning.

The reader's previous experiences play an important role in meaning construction: Background knowledge is crucial to building meaning. The other source of meaning is the text itself. Readers use three kinds of text cues: graphophonic, syntactic, and semantic. Proficient readers make a balanced use of cues from these three sources along with their background knowledge in order to construct meaning.

The term *graphophonic* comes from Goodman (1996) and refers to the combination of visual and sound information readers use as they scan a text. Any written language has limits on the possible combinations of letters and sounds that make up words. Readers acquire a knowledge of these combinations and use this knowledge to confirm the predictions they make as they read. English speakers, for example, know that if the first letter of a word is *b* and a consonant follows, it might be *l* or *r* but never *g*.

Good readers rely on more than letters and sounds, though. They also use their knowledge of how words go together. This is the *syntax* of the language. By using syntax cues, readers can predict what will come next. For example, if a sentence begins "She put..." students who are proficient in English will predict that the sentence will continue by telling what she put and where she put it. In English, we cannot simply say, "She put the pen," and we cannot say "She put on the table." English speakers would never predict those structures, because they know how English syntax works. Proficient readers notice the words (they use graphophonics), but they also see how the words work in longer stretches of text. They use syntactic cues to make sense of phrases, clauses, and sentences.

The third cueing system is *semantics*. Semantic cues help readers predict what words will occur in a given context. For example, in an article about baseball, a reader might expect to see words such as *batter*, *inning*, or *pitch*. Individual words take on meaning in certain contexts, like a sports story. Context will tell the reader that *batter* has a baseball meaning in this text and not a cooking meaning, or that *pitch* has a baseball meaning rather than a musical meaning. Semantics has to do with meaning, but semantic cues by themselves do not provide the meaning for a text. Rather, semantics is one of three cue sources, along with background knowledge, that enable a reader to construct meaning from a text. Reading is complex, and teachers who take a sociopsycholinguistic view help students use what they already know as well as the cues a text provides to construct meaning. The focus is always on the meaning, not on individual words.

VOCABULARY.   Teachers who take a sociopsycholinguistic view engage students in reading with the expectation that students will develop vocabulary knowledge as a result of seeing words in context. Vocabulary knowledge is thus viewed as a *result of* reading rather than a *prerequisite for* reading. It is only as they see words in a variety of contexts that students gain word knowledge.

When teachers preteach vocabulary, they often assume that knowing a word means knowing a definition for the word. But in addition to recognizing a word, being able to pronounce it, and attaching some meaning to it, students need to know how the word functions in a sentence (the syntax), what other words occur with it (the semantics), and the level of formality. Vocabulary knowledge relies on all the cueing systems of reading.

We remember our daughter, Mary, struggling through a typical vocabulary exercise for homework. She had to look up 20 words and write a sentence with each one. When she came to *condolences*, her sentence read, "She said her condolences to her sick friend." Did she know this vocabulary item? She had the right basic meaning, but although we can "offer" or "send" our condolences, we cannot "say" them. Mary's sentence does not sound like English. She needed more experience with this term, experience that can come only from seeing the word in print (or hearing it in conversation) repeatedly. This would allow her to *acquire* the conventional use of *condolences*.

WORD PARTS.   Teachers who take a sociopsycholinguistic view of reading may point out that large words are often composed of meaningful parts; taking note of those parts is a strategy readers can use to make sense of a text. But such teachers do not allocate much time to teaching word parts, because they prefer to spend time reading to students or having students read.

There are limitations to the usefulness of studying word parts, or morphology, in helping identify words, as we noted earlier. Nevertheless, there are real benefits in engaging students in word study for its own sake as part of a linguistic investigation. An important part of language arts is the study of language (Freeman, 1996). Students are interested in words, including their structure and formation. For example, students might work in small groups to investigate "scribe" words (see Bear et al., chapter 4 in this volume). The class could discuss what a scribe does, and they could look up the history of the word. Then they might list all the words they can think of that contain *scribe*, and they could try to connect the meaning of each complete word to the meaning of the root. Students could also figure out sound and spelling shifts that change *scribe* to *script* in words such as *description*. If each small group investigates a different word and then shares its results with the class, all students can increase their word knowledge. With the teacher's help, they also can begin to develop a scientific approach to word study, and this knowledge can help in their own reading and spelling. When students begin to study words closely, they become interested in words and in how they are formed.

PHONICS AND GRAPHOPHONICS.   We have already pointed out that graphophonics is one of three cueing systems that readers use to construct meaning. Graphophonics is an important cueing system that is a combination of visual and sound information that readers use as they scan a text. If meaning is constructed through a transaction between a reader and a text, we certainly cannot ignore the marks on the page. Some beginning readers do not pay enough attention to the words, relying on their knowledge of the story and the pictures, but proficient readers use all the available cues.

It is important to recognize that graphophonics is only one of three cueing systems. The word recognition view makes graphophonics the premier system. After all, if the goal is to identify and pronounce words, it is natural to elevate the graphophonic system to a position of highest importance. But the sociopsycholinguistic view insists that all three cueing systems are equally useful, because the goal of reading is to use all the systems to make sense of a text.

Graphophonics is different from phonics (see Table 2.3). Teachers who use phonics to teach reading present lessons that focus on specific rules that connect sound and spelling. Students are asked to *learn* these rules and apply them as the major means of decoding texts; phonics knowledge is seen as a prerequisite for reading. Phonics knowledge can be tested by using individual words or word lists.

In contrast, graphophonics is knowledge that is *acquired*. Such knowledge is not conscious, and students can seldom state the rules they use to pronounce words. However, they can use their knowledge of the relation between sounds and letters to pronounce new words. Graphophonics develops as students read. Readers use graphophonic cues, along with syntactic and semantic cues and their background knowledge, to construct meaning from texts. To determine how well a reader is using graphophonic knowledge, a teacher asks the student to read a story and uses a procedure such as miscue analysis to assess how well the reader is using each of the three cueing systems.

TABLE 2.3 Phonics and graphophonics

Phonics	Graphophonics
Conscious: learned, as a result of direct, systematic, explicit teaching	Subconscious: acquired, in the process of reading
The primary source of information used in decoding words	One of three sources of information used in constructing meaning
A prerequisite *for* reading	A result *of* reading
Can be tested independently of meaningful reading	Can be assessed only in the context of meaningful reading

SILENT READING.   Teachers who take a sociopsycholinguistic view set aside time for silent reading rather than having students do round-robin oral reading. Most of us read silently more often than we read aloud. It is helpful for teachers to read to students, even older students, but most reading that students do should be silent reading. We should qualify "silent" to include some vocalization that occurs as beginning readers read by themselves. And often children may read with a buddy or read along with a taped recording of a story. It is important that students are working at transacting with a text—at constructing meaning—not at trying to pronounce words correctly (see Graves & Fitzgerald, chapter 5 in this volume).

In many schools, time is set aside for Sustained Silent Reading (SSR) or for DEAR (Drop Everything and Read) time. This is a time when students can enjoy a good story or content area text. Smith (1973) has pointed out that we learn to read by reading, so time for reading is crucial. During reading time, students should employ the strategies they have learned while working with the teacher and with classmates. These might include sounding out a word, but they could also include rereading or skipping a word. If students have selected appropriate books, they can benefit greatly from reading, because this is the time that they refine their strategies, increase their repertoire of strategies, and expand their vocabulary. Above all, they begin to *enjoy* reading when they get involved with a good book.

Oral reading does occur in classes in which teachers take a sociopsycholinguistic view of reading. Teachers can engage students in many different authentic oral reading activities. For example, students might write and perform a Readers Theatre. Opitz and Rasinski (1998) describe many useful oral reading activities that teachers of English learners can use to improve students' English proficiency as well as their reading ability.

Both the word recognition view of reading and the sociopsycholinguistic view have the ultimate goal of meaning construction. Teachers who adopt a word recognition view believe that students must get the words first and the meaning will come later. The focus of their classes is to help students *learn* the skills needed to recognize and pronounce words. In contrast, teachers who take a sociopsycholinguistic view keep the focus on meaning. They help students *acquire* the strategies they need to use their background knowledge and cues from the text to construct meaning. Above all, these teachers provide students with many opportunities to read, because they believe that the abilities that proficient readers develop can be acquired only in the process of reading.

TABLE 2.4 Two views of reading proficiency

Proficiency	Word Recognition	Sociopsycholinguistic
Defined as:	accuracy + fluency	effectiveness + efficiency
Achieved by:	sounding out; recognizing sight words	balanced, minimal use of three cueing systems
Attitude toward errors:	all errors equally bad	errors differ in importance
Response to errors:	give correct form; provide extra practice	improve readers' use of cueing systems; help readers keep focus on comprehension

Two Views of Reading Proficiency

The two views of reading we have described are based on two different views of reading proficiency (see Table 2.4).

From a word recognition perspective, proficiency is defined as accurate, fluent reading. A good reader reads rapidly without making errors. Proficiency is achieved by using knowledge of phonics and sight words. Those holding a word recognition view treat all errors as problems to be corrected through correction and practice. The problem with this approach to reading proficiency is that students may become good "word callers" and still not comprehend what they are reading. English learners in particular may focus so much on reading accurately and rapidly that they fail to construct meaning.

On the other hand, those who take a sociopsycholinguistic view of reading define proficiency as a combination of effectiveness and efficiency. Good readers are *effective* because they make a balanced use of all three cueing systems. At the same time, they are *efficient* because they use just the cues they need to construct meaning. From this perspective, all errors are not the same; only those errors that cause readers to lose meaning are problematic. Teachers respond to errors with strategy lessons designed to strengthen students' use of the cueing systems while keeping them focused on comprehension.

Conclusions

In the past, at many schools it was the ESL or bilingual teacher who worked with English learners; most teachers did not have English learners in their classes. In most schools, teachers were given latitude in their approach to teaching reading. If the school required teachers to administer a standardized reading test, the results reflected primarily on the students, not on the teacher. Test results were not widely publicized. English learners were generally excluded from the testing process.

Times have changed. Now, most teachers find one or several English learners in their classes. In some states, the majority in many classes may be limited English proficient. At the same time, teachers often are required to follow the district-adopted reading program, using only approved materials and methods. All students are tested, and test results are distributed widely. Teachers may be rewarded (with merit pay) or punished (by not having their contract renewed) based on their students' reading test scores.

The approach that many schools have adopted is based on a word recognition view of reading consistent with what second-language theorists call learning. This approach is not supported by second-language acquisition research and is not the most effective way to teach English learners to read. Instead, as we have argued, a sociopsycholinguistic approach, which is consistent with an acquisition view of language development, is more effective. English learners develop both English proficiency and reading ability in classes in which teachers present reading as a meaning-making activity.

Teachers are under great pressure to produce results. Reading instruction based on a word recognition view provides students with the ability to translate the written symbols on a page into oral language—but then students, and particularly English learners, may come to regard reading as oral performance. Their early apparent success vanishes when reading tests shift to comprehension. And students who cannot comprehend what they read will not succeed academically. For that reason, we encourage teachers to resist quick-fix solutions to reading problems and instead help all their students, including their English learners, become proficient at constructing meaning from texts.

REFERENCES

Byrne, B., & Fielding-Barnsley, R. (1989). Phonemic awareness and letter knowledge in the child's acquisition of the alphabetic principle. *Journal of Educational Psychology, 81*(3), 313–321.

Collier, V. (1992). A synthesis of studies examining long-term language-minority student data on academic achievement. *Bilingual Research Journal, 16*(1 & 2), 187–212.

Cummins, J. (1996). *Negotiating identities: Education for empowerment in a diverse society.* Ontario, CA: Association of Bilingual Education.

Freeman, D.E. (1996). Putting language back into language arts: A linguistics course for teachers. In K. Whitmore & Y. Goodman (Eds.), *Whole language voices in teacher education* (pp. 205–213). York, ME: Stenhouse.

Freeman, D.E., & Freeman, Y.S. (2000). *Teaching reading in multilingual classrooms.* Portsmouth, NH: Heinemann.

Freeman, Y.S., & Freeman, D.E. (1997). *Teaching reading and writing in Spanish in the bilingual classroom.* Portsmouth, NH: Heinemann.

Goodman, K.S. (1993). *Phonics phacts.* Portsmouth, NH: Heinemann.

Goodman, K.S. (1996). *On reading.* Portsmouth, NH: Heinemann.

Honig, B. (1996). *How should we teach our children to read?* San Francisco: Far West Laboratory.

Krashen, S.D. (1992). *Principles and practices in second language acquisition.* New York: Pergamon.

Krashen, S.D. (1993). *The power of reading.* Englewood, CO: Libraries Unlimited.

Krashen, S.D. (1996). *Every person a reader: An alternative to the California Task Force Report on Reading.* Culver City, CA: Language Education Associates.

Krashen, S.D. (1999). *Condemned without a trial: Bogus arguments against bilingual education.* Portsmouth, NH: Heinemann.

Lindfors, J. (1989). The classroom: A good environment for language learning. In P. Rigg & V. Allen (Eds.), *When they don't all speak English: Integrating the ESL student into the regular classroom* (pp. 39–50). Urbana, IL: National Council of Teachers of English.

McQuillan, J. (1998). *The literacy crisis: False claims, real solutions.* Portsmouth, NH: Heinemann.

Opitz, M., & Rasinski, T. (1998). *Good-bye round robin reading: 25 effective oral reading strategies.* Portsmouth, NH: Heinemann.

Smith, F. (1973). *Psycholinguistics and reading.* New York: Holt, Rinehart and Winston.

Weaver, C. (1996). *Teaching grammar in context.* Portsmouth, NH: Boynton/Cook.

CHAPTER 3

Three Roles for Reading for Minority-Language Children

Stephen Krashen

will argue here that reading can play three major roles in language development for minority-language children:

1. In early stages of English-language development, developing literacy in the primary language is a shortcut to English literacy.

2. Once some proficiency in English is achieved, free voluntary reading in English is a clear route to English literacy and the development of academic English.

3. There is no reason to stop reading in the primary language once English is acquired. Continued reading is an important means of developing advanced proficiency in the heritage language.

Early Stages: First-Language Reading and Second-Language Literacy

There is very good reason to believe that learning to read in the primary language facilitates learning to read in a second language. The argument in favor of this proposition has three steps:

1. We learn to read by reading, by understanding what is on the page. (This is the Smith-Goodman hypothesis, considered to be the foundation of the whole language approach. Despite recent attacks on this hypothesis, there is, in my view, still overwhelming evidence supporting it, as well as good reason to doubt the correctness of the attacks [Krashen, 1999; McQuillan, 1998a].)

2. It is easier to understand text in a language you already know.

3. Once you can read, you can read; reading ability transfers across languages.

Correlational Studies

Support for step 3 comes from several sources (for a review, see Krashen, 1996), and includes studies showing a clear correlation between reading in primary and second languages: Those who read better in their primary language also tend to read better in English. In Table 3.1, I review some of these studies.

Inspection of the fourth column, "*r* with L1 RC" (correlation of scores on tests of reading comprehension in first and second languages), shows that although most correlations are positive, there is some variation.

TABLE 3.1 Relation between first- and second-language literacy

Study	L1	Grade	*r* with L1 RC	*r* with oral L2
Escamilla (1987)	Spanish	4	0.48	0.19
Saville-Troike (1984)	various	2–6		0.26
Tregar & Wong (1984)	Spanish	elementary school (3–5)	0.95	0.1
Tregar & Wong (1984)	Chinese	elementary school	0.4	-0.17
Cummins et al. (1984)	Japanese	2–6	0.23	
Hacquebord (in Bosser, 1991)	Turkish	age 13.9	0.4	
Gonzales (1989)	Spanish	6	0.48	0.44
Garcia-Vazquez et al. (1997)	Spanish	8	0.24	0.74
Hacquebord (in Bosser, 1991)	Turkish	age 15.9	0.09	
Tregar & Wong (1984)	Spanish	middle school (6–8)	0.26	0.42
Tregar & Wong (1984)	Chinese	middle school	-0.14	-0.59
Cummins et al. (1984)	Vietnamese	age 13.2 *	.41, .51	
Oketani (1997)	Japanese	age 20	0.21	
Nguyen et al. (2000)	Vietnamese	5–8	0.06	
Cobo-Lewis et al. (2002)	Spanish	2 and 5	0.55	
Okamura-Bichard (1985)	Japanese	6	0.09	

* *low length of residence (LOR) (5–22 months)*

Some of this variation is due to age; the correlation between age and the relation of L1 to L2 reading ability is -.32 (correlation between average grade level, at times estimated from age, and L1–L2 reading comprehension correlations; based on 14 studies). In other words, correlations between reading ability across languages are higher for younger children. For those studies using only Spanish speakers, the relation was strong ($r = -.801$, $n = 6$ studies). This result suggests that reading ability in the primary language has its strongest effect in the early stages of second-language literacy development. An especially clear case of this is Hacquebord (cited in Bosser, 1991), who tested the same subjects at age 13.9 and again at 15.9. The correlation between their ability to read in their first language (Turkish) and their second (Dutch) declined from .4 at age 13.9 to .09 at age 15.9.

In the early stages of second-language literacy acquisition, the influence of fluency in the primary language appears to be stronger than the influence of spoken second-language competence (Escamilla, 1987; Tregar & Wong, 1984). This is, of course, the essence of Cummins's important distinction between conversational and academic language and his hypothesis of a strong relation between academic language proficiency in first and second languages (Cummins, 1981; see also Cummins, chapter 1 in this volume).

Saville-Troike's (1984) study of 19 children, grades 2–6, deserves special mention. She reported low correlations between English reading ability and measures of oral fluency ($r = .26$), and even lower correlations between English reading ability and the amount of interaction children had with other children or adults in English ($r = -.057$ and .131, respectively). Because of the variety of first languages involved, no measure of L1 literacy was available, but Saville-Troike notes that

> in almost all cases bilingual instructors' judgments of students' relative competence in native language studies coincided with the same students' relative achievement in English...[a] Japanese girl who scored highest in reading English, for instance, was reported to read several years above grade level in Japanese, and her Japanese vocabulary and grammar were considered "exceptional" for a child her age. (p. 214)

(There were, however, two exceptions—two students who read very well in their first language but made little progress in English reading that year.)

August, Calderon, and Carlo (2001) examined the relation between reading ability in the first language at the end of second grade and reading ability in English at the end of third grade, a design that makes a great deal of sense: One would expect the impact of first-language literacy to have a greater impact on subsequent second-language literacy than on current second-language literacy. Controlling for oral ability and general intelligence, the authors reported that performance on a test of word identification at grade 2 in Spanish predicted word identification competence in English one year later, but only for those who received early instruction in Spanish.

Cobo-Lewis, Eilers, Pearson, and Umbel (2002) reported that for second- and fifth-grade acquirers of English as a second language who spoke Spanish as a first language, performance on tests involving reading and writing (Word Attack, Letter-Word, Passage Comprehension, Proofing and Diction) were highly intercorrelated, regardless of the language of the test. Performance on tests involving oral language (verbal analogies, oral vocabulary), however, intercorrelated only with other oral tests given in the same language. These results are consistent with the hypothesis that literacy transfers across languages.

These correlational studies are consistent with other areas of research: Comparisons of bilingual and all-English alternatives for limited–English-proficient (LEP) children consistently show that those in bilingual education programs that are set up correctly, that include reading in the primary language as well as subject matter taught in English, read in English as well as or better than those in all-English programs (Krashen, 1996; Krashen & Biber, 1988; Oller & Eilers, 2002).

Reports From Teachers

In addition, reports from teachers confirm that transfer of reading ability from the first to the second language occurs. In Krashen (1996), I published a case history showing that children who learned to read in Spanish found it easy to transfer this knowledge to English (pp. 28–29). Here is a synopsis:

Lorraine Ruiz taught a second-grade class of Spanish speakers, all LEP or non-English speakers. The children had aural comprehensible input in English, but much of the curriculum was in Spanish and reading was taught in Spanish done with whole language teaching "with a little dab of phonics." Ms. Ruiz had a classroom library with books in both English and Spanish. At the beginning of the year the children could not read the English books, but by the end of the year they could. The children themselves were amazed. One child asked Ms. Ruiz, "When did you teach us to read in English?" My conclusion was that Ms. Ruiz helped them learn to read in Spanish—and once you can read, you can read. I also claimed that this experience was not an isolated one.

In a personal communication by e-mail, a reporter for the *Santa Cruz Sentinel*, then in the process of preparing a series of articles on bilingual education, questioned the generality of this phenomenon. She said that this case study was "interesting," but "perhaps it is the exception to the rule." To see if this case was an exception I posted a request on several listservs, asking whether Ruiz's case was indeed an exception, or whether according to educators' experience it really was true that once children read very well in their first language, and have some aural competence in English, they pick up English reading quickly.

Lorraine Ruiz herself was among those who responded, and she confirmed that the event was not an isolated one: "The same thing happened in other classes that I have taught as well. As research indicates, once you can read you can read. It is just a matter of transferring the skills to another language." Here are some of the other testimonials I received:

"Transition was 'a piece of cake'" (sent by Yolanda Garcia, Redwood City, California):

I was an assistant in a 1st grade Bilingual class at Selby Lane School...about 11 years ago. I taught the Spanish speakers reading, writing, and arithmetic and the teacher taught the English speakers (30 students per class). Two of the three groups were on or near grade level. After that year I left assisting and went to graduate school for my teaching credential. As part of an independent study I returned to track that group of students (and had them perform a play that I converted from one of their literature books). Then in third grade, their teacher told me that their transition had been a piece of cake. They were reading with the fluency of their English-only counterparts, had the comprehension, and their test scores were high! They were also in a strong ESL program. Then a few years later, while taking a CLAD [Crosscultural, Language, and Academic Development certificate] preparation course, I met a teacher who taught Junior High. She was raving about a group of students that she had and their high level of English fluency and excellent test scores. To my surprise she was talking about my same group of students!

I do not believe they were the exceptions to the rule. We had a good program with continuity and a positive transition program.... I have been an employee in the bilingual program with the Redwood City School District for 25 years. I have seen it roller coaster, both functioning and faltering. At one point the program was unstable due to lack of parent education, or support. There were also many changes in staff and an administration causing discontinuity. When these factors became stable, students gained a strong development of their native language. This ability to dominate their native language enabled them to dominate English (and other Romance Languages). Our students end up prepared to live in a global world with the advantage of speaking/knowing multiple languages, and more importantly, having a strong sense of self.

"They transition themselves" (sent by Ginny Kalish, selected as teacher of the year by the Arizona Educational Foundation):

I teach a bilingual second grade. My best readers in Spanish who have had a great deal of exposure to oral English just pick up English books and start reading. I have one girl who is writing in her journal in English (her choice) everyday. The monolingual English teachers say her entries rival their top students' entries. When their skills are strong in their first language, and they have had lots of exposure listening to English it seems that they transition themselves. I have had students pick up English books and read them fluently the first time they saw them. I do no "formal" English reading or writing instruction.

"The top five readers in English were also the top five readers in Spanish" (sent by Fay Shin, California State University, Long Beach):

I have done many observations and student teacher supervisions—some in bilingual classes or transitioning bilingual classes. I observed one class in Montebello Unified School District. They were fourth graders who were transitioned from a K–3 Spanish bilingual program to fourth-grade English instruction. The top five readers in English were also the top five readers in Spanish (from third grade). I particularly observed a fourth-grade girl who was reading very well in English (she was at the top of her class), and I was told by her teacher that she was also an excellent reader in Spanish.

Also, I observed Korean bilingual students in a third-grade class in LAUSD [Los Angeles Unified School District], Wilton Elementary. The students were actually reading and writing in Korean very well, and I was amazed at how well they read in English also. Of course it is easy to argue that they would have done well in an English-only class, but I was very impressed at how well they did in language arts in both English and Korean.

"The rule, not the exception" (sent by Francisco Ramos, LAUSD [now at Florida International University, Miami]):

In my experience (eight years in elementary school) [transfer of literacy from the first language] has been the rule, not the exception. In addition I have constantly been asking friends and teachers at my school and they all agree: good skills in the first language almost for sure guarantee no problems in English. In my class at (Cal State) Fullerton (teaching middle school and high school teachers) even people who don't support bilingual education also agree.

More: In my own experience learning English as a Foreign Language, I was never taught the English phonetic system. I learned to read in English by reading simple words and simple sentences first, and proceeding to more complicated sentences later. My wife...came from Cuba at 11, very literate in Spanish. She was translating for her family six months later. She holds an MA in Speech and Language, she reads in both languages, writes in both languages, and never lost her Spanish.

"The more proficient the Spanish reading, the more easily English reading is achieved" (sent by Kerry Anne Dees, Redwood City, California):

As second and third grade aged students grow from beginning to more fluent readers I see this change occur annually. In the beginning of the year they don't themselves believe that they can read in English and I have never forced the issue. But having a library such as the one named above [Ruiz's classroom library], the students eventually find the courage and take on the challenge to read out of those English books. They share with their peers and attack the text with all of the reading strategies they have learned: decoding, contextual clues, pictures, etc. They have at this point, NEVER been instructed to read in English. And it is true, the more proficient the Spanish reading, the more easily English reading is achieved.

"Students who have a good background in L1 reading generally teach themselves to read in English" (sent by Pam Isaacs, San Diego Unified School District):

I frequently have the opportunity to notice this very phenomenon. I have been a bilingual teacher for the last 16 of my 30 years of teaching. I currently provide literacy support for students in the general education population. Therefore, I see and work with a large number of students, many of them English language learners, many of them in bilingual education. Students who have a good background in L1 reading generally teach themselves to read in English. They are guided by the teacher, but most of it occurs very quickly. Of course, direct instruction in English phonics, spelling and further oral vocabulary development helps the process along. Since I know some students well over a period of years (second through fifth grade), I have been able to make many observations. First, the specific skills or lack of skills that a student has carries directly over into second language reading. For instance, a student who was taught only to decode in Spanish will carry this imbalance into English language, and not use meaning as a cue, a severe handicap in English reading. Students who have learned to monitor themselves and self-correct often in Spanish, will carry this skill into English reading.... Students who learn to think carefully about what they read, the story line and abstract concepts, will carry this comprehension skill into their second language reading.... I have absolutely no question that primary language instruction assists in the acquisition of English literacy.

(For additional reports, see Krashen, 2002).

Taken alone, these reports provide, at best, suggestive evidence; a critic could claim that they were reported by dedicated supporters of bilingual education and may not represent what occurs in all cases. They are, however, consistent with the research and confirm that Ruiz's case is not a rare exception.

I sent these and other reports to the *Sentinel* reporter, as well as a copy of my book *Under Attack* (Krashen, 1996), which includes a review of some of the published research. Here is what appeared in the *Sentinel* on February 6, 2000:

> Some experts such as Stephen Krashen, a professor of education at the University of Southern California, say that students who can speak English and read Spanish should be able to read in English without much formal instruction. But practice doesn't always reflect theory. Educators agree that in Santa Cruz County, as in other areas, some immigrant students have been hampered by untrained teachers and a watered-down curriculum. Taught to read in Spanish, they seemed to do well. When they started reading in English, however, they fell behind. At most schools, less than 10 percent became fluent in English by fifth or sixth grade. Often they gave up in frustration.

The reporter clearly ignored the case histories I sent, as well as the empirical data in *Under Attack*. She also provides no additional details about the students who apparently failed to transfer their reading knowledge to English. We do not know how many cases there were like this, and how many cases there were in which transfer was successful. We also do not know what the "untrained teachers" did wrong, what "fluent in English" means, the level of reading achieved in the first language, or the availability of print in either language.

As noted earlier, the evidence suggests that the transfer effect from the first language appears to decline as children get older. The most obvious reasons for this decline include the loss in first-language literacy competence that typically occurs as children get older, owing to lack of access to print (see discussion that follows). A second is that other factors become stronger, especially one that is rarely considered in studies of this kind: reading in English.

Reading in the Second Language

There is overwhelming evidence that reading in a second language, especially free voluntary reading or pleasure reading, makes a powerful contribution to the development of academic proficiency in a second language. The evidence comes from several sources: correlational studies, studies of in-school free reading, and case histories.

In-School Free Reading

I focus here on one of these sources of evidence, in-school free reading. In-school free reading studies include evaluations of several kinds of programs;

in the most common, Sustained Silent Reading (SSR), students read whatever they please (within reason) for a short time each day and there is no accountability required (see Cummins, chapter 1, and Freeman & Freeman, chapter 2, in this volume).

I have reviewed the available research on in-school free reading in several places (Krashen, 1993, 2001b). In my most recent summary (Krashen, 2001b), I found that students who participated in these programs did as well as or better than comparison students in traditional language arts or second-language programs on tests of reading comprehension in 51 of 54 comparisons. The results were even more impressive when one considers only studies lasting one academic year or longer: In 8 of 10 cases, participants in in-school reading programs outperformed comparisons, and in two cases there was no difference.

The National Reading Panel (National Institute of Child Health and Human Development, 2000), supported by the U.S. government, also reviewed studies of in-school reading—and reached the startling conclusion that there is no clear evidence supporting this practice. They were, however, able to find only 14 comparisons, all lasting less than one academic year, between students in in-school free reading programs and comparison children, and devoted only 6 pages of their report to this topic (as compared to approximately 120 pages devoted to research on phonemic awareness and phonics).

Interestingly, in-school reading did not fare badly even in the limited analysis done by the panel, with in-school readers doing better in four cases and never doing worse. Note that even a finding of "no difference" suggests that free reading is just as good as traditional instruction, an important theoretical and practical point. Because free reading is so much more pleasant than regular instruction, and because it provides readers with valuable information, a finding of no difference provides strong evidence in favor of free reading in classrooms.

I have also argued (Krashen, 2001b) that the National Reading Panel not only missed many studies, they also misinterpreted some of the ones they included. I present here a discussion of some recent studies that have particular relevance to second-language acquisition in children.

In Elley and Mangubhai (1983), fourth- and fifth-grade students of English as a foreign language were divided into three groups for their 30-minute daily English class. One group had traditional audiolingual method instruction, a second did only free reading, and a third did "shared reading."

Shared reading

> is a method of sharing a good book with a class, several times, in such a way that the students are read to by the teacher, as in a bedtime story. They then talk about the book, they read it together, they act out the story, they draw parts of it and write their own caption, they rewrite the story with different characters or events. (Elley, 1998, pp. 1–2)

After two years, the free reading group and the shared reading group were far superior to the traditional group in tests of reading comprehension, writing, and grammar. Similar results were obtained by Elley (1991) in a large-scale study of second-language acquirers ages 6 through 9 in Singapore.

Elley's most recent data (1998) come from South Africa and Sri Lanka. In all cases, children who were encouraged to read for pleasure outperformed traditionally taught students on standardized tests of reading comprehension and other measures of literacy. Table 3.2 presents the data from South Africa. In this study, EFL students who lived in print-poor environments were given access to sets of 60 high-interest books, which were placed in classrooms, with another 60 made available in sets of six identical titles. The books were used for read-alouds by the teacher, for shared reading, and for silent reading. Table 3.2 presents data from different provinces; in every case the readers outperformed those in comparison classes, and the gap widened with each year of reading.

Shin (2001) examined the impact of a six-week self-selected reading experience among 200 sixth and seventh graders who had to attend summer school because of low reading proficiency. Students attended class four hours per day; during this time, approximately two hours were devoted to SSR, including 25 minutes in the school library. The district invested $25 per student on popular paperbacks and magazines, with most books purchased from the Goosebumps series. In addition, about 45 minutes per day were devoted to reading and discussing novels such as *Holes* (Sachar, 2000) and *Island of the*

TABLE 3.2 In-school reading in South Africa

Reading Test Scores						
Province	**Std 3**		**Std 4**		**Std 5**	
	Readers	Nonreaders	Readers	Nonreaders	Readers	Nonreaders
Eastern Cape	32.5	25.6	44	32.5	58.1	39
Western Cape	36.2	30.2	40.4	34.3	53	40.4
Free State	32.3	30.1	44.3	37.1	47.2	40.5
Natal	39.5	28.3	47	32.3	63.1	35.1

from Elley (1998)

Blue Dolphins (O'Dell, 1987). Comparison children ($n = 160$) followed a standard language arts curriculum during the summer. Attrition was high for both groups but similar (class size dropped from 20 to 14.3 among readers, and from 20 to 13.2 among comparisons), as was the percentage of limited–English-proficient children (31% in the reading group, 27% in the comparison group). The readers gained approximately five months on the Altos test of reading comprehension and vocabulary over the six-week period, while comparisons declined. On the Nelson-Denny reading comprehension test, the summer readers grew a spectacular 1.3 years (from grade 4.0 to grade 5.3). On the vocabulary section, however, the groups showed equivalent gains.

First-Language Reading and Heritage-Language Proficiency

Continuing development of the heritage language after English has been acquired has several advantages, including cognitive benefits, career-related benefits, and the attainment of true biculturalism (Tse's [1998] "ethnic identity incorporation stage"). It is, however, extremely difficult to develop and maintain high levels of competence in the heritage language (Krashen, Tse, & McQuillan, 1998). There is some evidence that pleasure reading in the heritage language can contribute to heritage language development.

Correlational evidence comes from Cho and Krashen (2000), a study of 114 Korean Americans, ages 18–30, who were either born in the United States or arrived at a very early age. As indicated in Table 3.3, free reading in Korean was a significant and independent predictor, along with several other significant variables, of self-reported Korean-language competence.

Tse (2001) examined a group of 10 bilinguals who developed high levels of competence in their heritage language. All were born in the United States or had arrived in the U.S. before age 6, none had studied for longer than two weeks in the country where the heritage language is used, all were fluent in English, and all could read the heritage language at a level typical of native-speaking adolescents in the heritage language. Tse found that a number of factors were present in each case: They had input from parents, a peer group that valued the use of the heritage language, and formal instruction in the heritage language (not always a positive experience). In addition, all subjects had literacy experience in the heritage language at home and in the community. Of interest to us, Tse notes that "the most frequently mentioned activity the participants engaged in independently was reading for pleasure" (p. 692). Two subjects were dedicated comic book readers in the heritage language

TABLE 3.3 Predictors of competence in Korean as a heritage language

Predictor	beta	t	p
Parental use of Korean	0.37	4.02	0
Visiting Korea	0.22	2.31	0.023
Watching Korean TV	0.245	2.67	0.01
Reading in Korean	0.22	2.49	0.014
Attending HL classes	0.072	0.85	0.4
Age	-0.103	-0.756	0.451
Length of residence (LOR)	0.162	1.06	0.293
r2 = .398			

from Cho and Krashen (2000)

(Japanese) in junior high school, two others reported heavy magazine reading in Spanish, and one other was a devoted nonfiction reader on a variety of topics in her heritage language.

Kondo (1998) also noted that one of her subjects who was successful at maintaining the heritage language was an enthusiastic reader of comic books ("manga" in Japanese).

McQuillan (1998b) reviewed several experimental studies of university students confirming the value of free reading in developing the heritage language, including one SSR study and two studies of Spanish for Native Speaker classes that focused on popular literature and literature circles (see also McQuillan & Rodrigo, 1998). Results included clear gains in Spanish vocabulary and improved attitudes toward reading in Spanish.

McQuillan also notes that heritage-language reading may not work in all cases. In Schon, Hopkins, and Vojir (1984), immigrant heritage-language students were more enthusiastic about reading in Spanish than were those born in the United States. McQuillan notes that those in the second group may have been in the "ethnic avoidance/ambivalence" stage, a time in which there is little interest in, or even disdain for, the heritage language and culture (Tse, 1998). This typically occurs during high school, the age of the subjects in this study.

Conclusions

There is good evidence for each of the following three roles for reading:

1. In early stages, reading in the primary language is of great help in promoting second-language literacy.

2. Free reading in the second language makes a strong contribution to advanced second-language development.

3. Free reading in the heritage language appears to make a strong contribution to continued heritage-language development.

In addition to demonstrating that reading has a positive impact on literacy development, research also shows what every reader of this chapter already knows: Free voluntary reading is also extremely pleasant (Krashen, 1994; Nell, 1988). The major problem in making sure that reading happens is access to books, and this problem is extremely serious.

There is very good evidence that providing access to interesting reading is the crucial factor in encouraging reading. In many cases, it is all that is necessary (Ramos & Krashen, 1998; Von Sprecken & Krashen, 1998).

For many children, especially those in high-poverty areas, there is little to read outside of school (Neuman & Celano, 2001). For children acquiring English as a second language, print resources outside of school in the heritage language are also seriously lacking. The average U.S. family owns about 137 books (Purves & Elley, 1994), but the average Hispanic family with limited–English-proficient children owns only about 26 (Ramirez, Yuen, Ramey, & Pasta, 1991).

It is therefore of great concern that school libraries, the only source of reading material for many children, are so inadequate in so many places. Current studies show that better libraries are associated with better reading (Krashen, 1995, 2001a; Lance, 1994; McQuillan, 1998a). The sad state of school libraries has been documented in several publications (Allington, Guice, Baker, Michaelson, & Li, 1995; Krashen, 1996, 1999; McQuillan, 1998a), and the situation is particularly grim with respect to books in Spanish (Pucci, 1994). Here is an additional report, focusing on the lack of books in the primary language.

Pucci and Ulanoff (1996) surveyed four school libraries in the greater Los Angeles area, focusing on schools with 90% or more Spanish-speaking children. Data were available only from two of the four libraries. The authors reported that three of the four libraries did not have regular hours or regular staff, and one was "periodically used as a storeroom." In the two libraries studied, only 15 to 22% of the books were in Spanish; of these, about two thirds were at the K–2 level and about 3% were at the grade 5–6 level. Pucci and Ulanoff also surveyed 32 school librarians: Fifty-four percent said that books written in Spanish were difficult to obtain and 70% said that their cost was "prohibitive." Of 5,000 books on an approved reading list for purchase for libraries, only 300 were in Spanish. Pucci and Ulanoff note that "even if these books were age appropriate, a child reading two books per week would finish every Spanish volume in the library before entering fourth grade" (p. 114).

Children of poverty have little to read, in school or outside of school. If their primary language is Spanish, the problem is even more serious. There have been no formal studies of availability of books in other heritage languages, but we can be sure that the situation is even worse than it is in Spanish. (See Yaden et al., chapter 15 in this volume.)

All this gives us reason to be optimistic. As noted earlier, bilingual programs have been shown to be successful. If we add a healthy supply of books in both languages, they have the potential of being much more successful.

REFERENCES

Allington, R., Guice, S., Baker, K., Michaelson, N., & Li, S. (1995). Access to books: Variations in schools and classrooms. *The Language and Literacy Spectrum, 5*, 23–25.

August, D., Calderon, M., & Carbo, M. (2001). Transfer of skills from Spanish to English: A study of young learners. *NABE News, 24*(4), 11–12, 42.

Bosser, B. (1991). On thresholds, ceilings, and short-circuits: The relation between L1 reading, L2 reading and L2 knowledge. *AILA Review, 8*, 45–60.

Cho, G., & Krashen, S. (2000). The role of voluntary factors in heritage language development: How speakers can develop the heritage language on their own. *ITL: Review of Applied Linguistics, 127/128*, 127–140.

Cobo-Lewis, A., Eilers, R., Pearson, B., & Umbel, V. (2002). Interdependence of Spanish and English knowledge. In D.K. Oller & R.E. Eilers (Eds.), *Language and literacy in bilingual children* (pp. 64–97). Clevedon, UK: Multilingual Matters.

Cummins, J. (1981). The role of primary language development in promoting educational success for language minority students. In California State Department of Education (Ed.), *Schooling and language minority students: A theoretical framework* (pp. 3–49). Los Angeles: Evaluation, Dissemination, and Assessment Center, California State University.

Cummins, J., Swain, M., Nakakjima, K., Handscombe, J., Green, D., & Tran, C. (1984). Linguistic interdependence among Japanese and Vietnamese immigrant students. In C. Rivera (Ed.), *Communicative competence approaches to language proficiency: Research and application* (pp. 60–81). Clevedon, UK: Multilingual Matters.

Elley, W. (1991). Acquiring literacy in a second language: The effect of book-based programs. *Language Learning, 41*(3), 375–411.

Elley, W. (1998). *Raising literacy levels in Third World countries: A method that works.* Culver City, CA: Language Education Associates.

Elley, W., & Mangubhai, F. (1983). The impact of reading on second language learning. *Reading Research Quarterly, 19*, 53–67.

Escamilla, K. (1987). *The relationship of native language reading achievement and oral English proficiency to future achievement in reading English as a second language.* Unpublished doctoral dissertation, University of California, Los Angeles.

Garcia-Vazquez, E., Vazquez, L., Lopez, I., & Ward, W. (1997). Language proficiency and academic success: Relationship between proficiency in two languages and achievement among Mexican American students. *Bilingual Research Journal, 21*(4), 395–408.

Gonzales, L. (1989). Native language education: The key to English literacy skills. In D. Bixler-Marquez, J. Ornstein-Glaicia, & G. Green (Eds.), *Mexican-American Spanish in its societal and cultural contexts* (Rio Grande Series in Languages and Linguistics 3, pp. 209–224). Brownsville, TX: University of Texas–Pan American.

Kondo, K. (1998). Social-psychological factors affecting language maintenance: Interviews with Shin Nisei university students in Hawaii. *Linguistics and Education, 9*(4), 369–408.

Krashen, S. (1993). *The power of reading.* Englewood, CO: Libraries Unlimited.

Krashen, S. (1994). The pleasure hypothesis. In J. Alatis (Ed.), *Georgetown University Round Table on Languages and Linguistics* (pp. 299–322). Washington, DC: Georgetown University Press.

Krashen, S. (1995). School libraries, public libraries, and the NAEP reading scores. *School Library Media Quarterly, 23*, 235–238.

Krashen, S. (1996). *Under attack: The case against bilingual education.* Culver City, CA: Language Education Associates.

Krashen, S. (1997). Does free voluntary reading lead to academic English? *Journal of Intensive English Studies, 11*, 1–18.

Krashen, S. (1999). *Three arguments against whole language and why they are wrong.* Portsmouth, NH: Heinemann.

Krashen, S. (2001a). Current research: The positive impact of libraries. *California School Library Journal, 25*(1), 21–24.

Krashen, S. (2001b). More smoke and mirrors: A critique of the National Reading Panel (NRP) report on "fluency." *Phi Delta Kappan, 83*(2), 119–123.

Krashen, S. (2002). Does transition really happen? Some case histories. *The Multilingual Educator, 3*(1), 50–54.

Krashen, S., & Biber, D. (1988). *On course: Bilingual education's success in California.* Ontario, CA: California Association for Bilingual Education.

Krashen, S., Tse, L., & McQuillan, J. (Eds.). (1998). *Heritage language development.* Culver City, CA: Language Education Associates.

Lance, K. (1994). The impact of school library media centers on academic achievement. In C. Kuhlthau (Ed.), *School library media annual* (Vol. 12, pp. 188–197). Englewood, CO: Libraries Unlimited.

Mangubhai, F., & Elley, W. (1982). The role of reading in promoting ESL. *Language Learning and Communication, 1*, 151–60.

McQuillan, J. (1998a). *The literacy crisis: False claims and real solutions.* Portsmouth, NH: Heinemann.

McQuillan, J. (1998b). The use of self-selected and free voluntary reading in heritage language programs: A review of research. In S. Krashen, L. Tse, & J. McQuillan (Eds.), *Heritage language development* (pp. 73–87). Culver City, CA: Language Education Associates.

McQuillan, J., & Rodrigo, V. (1998). Literature based programs for first language development: Giving native bilinguals access to books. In R. Constantino (Ed.), *Literacy, access, and libraries among the language minority population* (pp. 209–224). Lanham, MD: Scarecrow Press.

National Institute of Child Health and Human Development. (2000). *Report of the National Reading Panel. Teaching children to read: An evidence-based assessment of the scientific research literature on reading and its implications for reading instruction* (NIH Publication No. 00-4769). Washington, DC: U.S. Government Printing Office.

Nell, V. (1988). *Lost in a book*. New Haven, CT: Yale University Press.

Neuman, S., & Celano, D. (2001). Access to print in low-income and middle-income communities. *Reading Research Quarterly, 36*, 8–26.

Nguyen, A., Shin, F., & Krashen, S. (2000). Development of the first language is not a barrier to second language acquisition: Evidence from Vietnamese immigrants to the United States. *International Journal of Bilingual Education and Bilingualism, 4*(3), 159–164.

Okamura-Bichard, F. (1985). Mother-tongue maintenance and second language learning: A case of Japanese children. *Language Learning, 35*(1), 63–89.

Oketani, H. (1997). Additive bilinguals: The case of post-war second generation Japanese Canadian youths. *Bilingual Research Journal, 21*(4), 359–379.

Oller, D.K., & Eilers, R.E. (Eds.). (2002). *Language and literacy in bilingual children*. Clevedon, UK: Multilingual Matters.

Pucci, S. (1994). Supporting Spanish language literacy: Latino children and free reading resources in the schools. *Bilingual Research Journal, 18*, 67–82.

Pucci, S., & Ulanoff, S. (1996). Where are the books? *The CATESOL Journal, 9*(2), 111–116.

Purves, A., & Elley, W. (1994). The role of the home and students' differences in reading performance. In W. Elley (Ed.), *The IEA Study of Reading Literacy: Achievement and instruction in thirty-two school systems* (pp. 89–121). Oxford, UK: Pergamon.

Ramirez, D., Yuen, S., Ramey, D., & Pasta, D. (1991). *Final report: Longitudinal study of structured English immersion strategy, early-exit and late-exit bilingual education programs for language minority students, Vol. I*. San Mateo, CA: Aguirre International.

Ramos, F., & Krashen, S. (1998). The impact of one trip to the public library: Making books available may be the best incentive for reading. *The Reading Teacher, 51*, 614–615.

Saville-Troike, M. (1984). What really matters in second language learning for academic achievement? *TESOL Quarterly, 18*(2), 199–219.

Schon, I., Hopkins, K., & Vojir, C. (1984). The effects of Spanish reading emphasis on the English and Spanish reading abilities of Hispanic high school students. *The Bilingual Review/La Revista Bilingue, 11*, 33–39.

Shin, F. (2001). Motivating students with Goosebumps and other popular books. *CSLA Journal (California School Library Association), 25*(1), 15–19.

Tregar, B., & Wong, B.F. (1984). The relationship between native and second language reading comprehension and second language oral ability. In C. Rivera (Ed.), *Communicative competence approaches to language proficiency: Education and policy issues* (pp. 152–164). Clevedon, UK: Multilingual Matters.

Tse, L. (1998). Ethnic identity formation and its implications for heritage language development. In S. Krashen, L. Tse, & J. McQuillan (Eds.), *Heritage language development* (pp. 15–29). Culver City, CA: Language Education Associates.

Tse, L. (2001). Resisting and reversing language shift: Heritage-language resilience among U.S. native biliterates. *Harvard Educational Review, 71*(4), 676–706.

Von Sprecken, D., & Krashen, S. (1998). Do students read during sustained silent reading? *California Reader, 32*(1), 11–13.

CHILDREN'S LITERATURE CITED

O'Dell, S. (1987). *Island of the blue dolphins*. Glenview, IL: Scott Foresman.

Sachar, L. (2000). *Holes*. New York: Yearling Books.

CHAPTER 4

Orthographic Development and Learning to Read in Different Languages

Donald R. Bear, Shane Templeton, Lori A. Helman, and Tamara Baren

Eight-year-old Alicia, a native Spanish speaker, looks up quizzically when she gets to the word *crane* in her reading. "Crah-nay? Cran? Crane?" she asks. Her teacher nods patiently, but inside she is wondering, "Why is Alicia still confusing vowel sounds? We moved beyond short vowels a long time ago, and she memorized the long vowel words in spelling. I don't understand what the problem is."

Alicia is part of a growing population of English language learners learning to read in English in schools in the United States. The latest census data reveal an increase of almost 50% in the Latino population alone in the United States during the last 10 years. The teaching force, on the other hand, is made up predominantly of women who come from English-only households and whose cultural and economic backgrounds often differ significantly from those of students like Alicia.

What is it that Alicia's teachers need to understand about spelling or orthography and word-study practices in English, and what do these educators need to know about Alicia's native language, Spanish, to support her growth in reading and spelling? In this chapter we explore orthographic development across languages and literacies, the use of spelling to assess development, and the nature and specifics of supporting English language learning students across the developmental continuum as they study words in English.

Word study is an integrated way to teach phonics, spelling, and vocabulary that is based on a developmental model of word knowledge (Bear, Invernizzi, Templeton, & Johnston, 2000). Word-study activities are chosen based on our understanding of students' development, and these activities are important to their progress in learning to read and spell (Bear & Templeton, 2000). How do we conduct word study with students when they are learning English as a new language? Following the lead of Edmund Henderson at the University of Virginia, under whom a number of researchers in the area of orthographic development studied in the 1970s and 1980s, we conduct spelling assessments to reveal students' orthographic knowledge—what they know about words and how they are spelled (Henderson, 1992; Templeton & Bear, 1992). At first glance, it may seem odd to look at what students spell as a means of understanding their reading. This view of spelling as a window into literacy processes reflects Henderson's original insight (Henderson, 1981), and it highlights the reciprocal relation between learning to read and learning to spell (Bear, 1992; Ehri, 1997; Ellis, 1997; Vernon & Ferreiro, 1999). Why is the consideration of orthographic knowledge so important in planning literacy instruction? It is important because orthographic knowledge is a powerful engine that propels reading development (Henderson, 1992; Perfetti, 1985). In this chapter, we share ways in which word-study instruction—the exploration of orthography—can take into account the languages and literacies students know and are learning.

The Nature and Course of Orthographic Development

Most orthographies are composed of three organic and evolving layers or levels of information: *sound*, *pattern*, and *meaning*. Each written language offers learners a unique configuration and combination of these layers. Accordingly, an orthography that is highly regular in its sound-symbol correspondences is described as a *shallow*, *transparent*, or *translucent* orthography. Spelling in Spanish and Italian, for example, is highly regular; written words are easy to decode because there are fewer sounds and a more direct correspondence between sounds and letters. French and English, on the other hand, are examples of *deep* or *opaque* orthographies; for a number of reasons, the correspondence between letters and sounds in those languages is often much less direct. In English, the many possible combinations of letters representing long and short vowels are testimony to the history and complexity of even single-syllable words. Chinese is a deep orthography composed of characters that represent morphemes, and though Chinese writing is not alphabet-based beyond the primary grades, the characters contain sound, pattern, and meaning layers. Orthographies are also described as *semitranslucent* or *semitransparent*; German is an example of a semitransparent orthography that lies somewhere between the shallow and deep orthographies.

Observation and study of students' writing and orthographic development—their knowledge of the structure of words—reveals a progression across these three layers. Using English as the focus language, the developmental progression in Figure 4.1 is illustrated by the arrows that show a developmental continuum beginning with the sound layer.

In many languages, students' progression along a continuum of literacy learning may be described in terms of stages or "phases of dominance" in spelling and reading (Rieben, Saada-Robert, & Moro, 1997). Though students' word knowledge as revealed through spelling at any point along a developmental continuum may reflect aspects of more than one layer of orthographic

FIGURE 4.1 Three layers of orthographic knowledge and the relation between the stages of reading and spelling

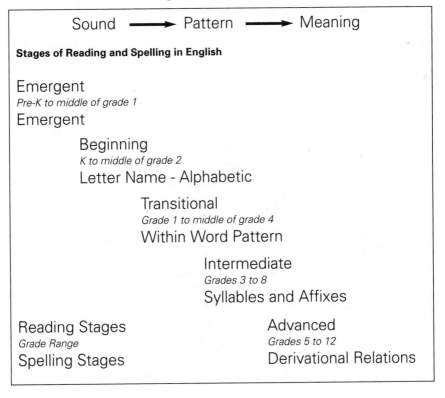

information, one of these three layers will usually predominate and guide students' strategies in spelling and reading words. As Figure 4.1 illustrates, in English, the stages or phases of reading and spelling correspond to the three levels of orthographic knowledge (Henderson, 1981). Different phases of this developmental progression have been studied in a variety of languages, including English (Ellis, 1997; Henderson & Beers, 1980), Finnish (Korkeamäki & Dreher, 2000), French (Gill, 1980; Rieben et al., 1997), German (Wimmer & Hummer, 1990), Greek (Porpodas, 1989), Hebrew (Geva, Wade-Woodley, & Shany, 1993), Portuguese (Pinheiro, 1995), and Spanish (Cuetos, 1993; Fashola, Drum, Mayer, & Kang, 1996; Ferroli & Krajenta, 1990; Temple, 1978; Zutell & Allen, 1988)—and even in character-based orthographies like Chinese (Perfetti & Zhang, 1991; Shen & Bear, 2000; Shu & Anderson, 1999).

As students progress through the sound layer of orthography, they master the basic sound-symbol correspondences for that orthography while acquiring a sight vocabulary of up to 250 words by the end of this stage. The next level involves an examination of single-word (or multicharacter) patterns most relevant to that orthography. At this *pattern* level, students move beyond a simple sound analysis to a more abstract level of analysis in which they make generalizations about orthographic patterns. The development of patterns takes place with a store of 250 to 400 sight words or characters. Because English is a more opaque orthography, patterns are examined earlier and for a longer period of time than in more transparent orthographies like Spanish. In English, students learn to differentiate patterns within single-syllable words through comparisons between the consonant-vowel-consonant (CVC) short-vowel pattern and the many long-vowel patterns (CVCe, CVVC, CVV, CV). The meaning layer comes into focus as students acquire a strong knowledge of the orthographic patterns of single-syllable words. At this level students recognize the consistent spelling of morphemes among related words. This is a general trend that we have observed across languages (see Freeman & Freeman, chapter 2 in this volume).

To develop a word-study program for students learning a new language, educators need to know a good deal about the spoken and written languages of their students. They should understand that at the level of sound, the interaction between spoken languages influences what students hear and how they pronounce words. For example, the short *i* a teacher hears in *bit* may sound more like a long *e* (as in *beat*) to her students.

Even in the case of a character-based orthography, children follow a developmental sequence that can be related to the model of orthographic development outlined here for English. In an analysis of 7,000 spelling errors from the writing of 1,200 children in grades 1 through 6 in the People's Republic of China, nearly 80% of the spelling errors had some phonological base, decreasing from 96% in first grade to 53% in sixth grade. Pattern errors, on the other hand, increased from 4% in first grade to 33% in sixth grade. Likewise, meaning errors jumped from .3% in first grade to 11% in sixth grade (Shen & Bear, 2000).

For younger children, the process of learning to read in two or more languages involves some mental gymnastics that can occur at a tacit level. In comparative studies of orthographic knowledge, bilingual learners negotiate between languages and literacies (Tolchinsky & Teberosky, 1998). Yet a learner's dominant language has significant influence on the first round of strategies the learner will set in motion. Rather than being confused by differences in orthographies, students apply what they know about spelling and reading in one language to their learning of others. There can be linguistic and cognitive advantages to bilingualism, and when students learn multiple languages and literacies their knowledge base with respect to these individual languages often grows stronger (Guion, Flege, Liu, & Yeni-Komshian, 2000; Lieberman, 1991; Ransdell, Arecco, & Levy, 2001; Schmitt & McCarthy, 1997; see also Cummins, chapter 1, and Krashen, chapter 3, in this volume).

The relative complexity of orthographies was illustrated in a recent study that compared Italian and English word reading, a measure of orthographic knowledge, and found that reading difficulties were more prevalent among English readers (Paulesu et al., 2001). It is likely that word reading difficulties are more apparent earlier for students learning a writing system like English, a deep orthography. In contrast, in a more shallow, phonemically based writing system like Italian, students may have fewer difficulties learning to read words, as there are fewer vowel sounds, fewer vowel changes, and more regular sound-symbol correspondences.

Are different processes involved in reading and writing in different languages? Perhaps we can examine this question best through another, related, query: To what degree is a reader's processing defined by the weight that the language's orthography places on each of the three layers? We explore this fundamental question in the remainder of this chapter through a discussion of the assessment process and the application of this information to word-study instruction, paying particular attention to the relative importance of the sound, pattern, and meaning layers of different languages.

Assessments of Orthographic Knowledge

The selection and organization of word-study activities is based on informed assessment of students' orthographic knowledge. There are many ways to assess such knowledge. Word recognition tasks in which students read words on graded lists have been used commonly to see what words students can read and what their strategies are when they read unknown words. Students' spelling has been used in a similar way for many years. The way students spell words they do not know shows us what they are experimenting with in their learning about words and suggests how they apply this knowledge when they read (Henderson, 1990; Russell, 1844).

In recent years, spelling inventories have been designed so as to include words carefully selected to assess salient features of the relevant orthography (Schlagal, 1992); the words are sequenced to reflect increasing levels of orthographic complexity across sound, pattern, and meaning. For example, words that begin with *dr*, an alveolar affricate, are often included because beginning readers in the letter-name alphabetic stage often substitute a palatal affricate (JRIV for *drive*). Students in the transitional stage of reading and the within word-pattern stage of spelling are exploring long vowel patterns; for example, they may spell *wait* as WATE. Spelling assessments indicate what words students can read easily—for what they can spell, we know they can read. Spelling provides a conservative measure of students' decoding or reading of words. Students' spelling errors show us the edge of their learning, and these spelling inventories show us where to begin word-study instruction (Bear & Templeton, 2000).

For students acquiring English as a new language, spelling inventories in English and in the students' primary language are suggested to teachers in order to learn what students know about English orthography, what they know about their primary language, and how they apply this understanding to written English. After writing the correct words next to the errors, the teacher determines a spelling stage for each student. A number of scoring guides have been developed to help teachers to determine stages for students (Bear et al., 2000; Ganske, 1999); experienced teachers are often able to "eyeball" students' writing to determine a stage.

A number of spelling inventories have been created in several languages, including Spanish (California Reading and Literature Project, 1999; Consortium on Reading Excellence, 1999; Estes, 1998; Ferroli & Krajenta, 1993), Chinese (Shen & Bear, 2000), and English (Bear et al., 2000). A spelling inventory in a student's home language provides valuable information about that student's pool of orthographic knowledge and may be examined to find common features that would transfer positively to English spelling. Likewise, sound and spelling features that are *not* consistent with English spelling can be directly compared and taught. For example, a first grader's spelling of PLAHA for *plancha* in Spanish gives a teacher important background information for word study in English: In addition to omitting the preconsonantal nasal (*n*), the student used a letter-name strategy to write *h* (pronounced *ah-chay*) to represent the *ch* sound. This information about a student's understanding of Spanish spelling points to the need to clarify the differences in sound-spelling correspondence between the *h* in Spanish and in English. This logical substitution of *h* for *ch* would also be expected to appear in English writing assignments.

The Three Layers of Orthographies (Sound, Pattern, Meaning): Principles, Assessment, and Instruction

In this discussion of the layers of orthography, we illustrate basic principles of orthographic development across languages through comparisons of several orthographies. Critical points in a word-study program for English language learners are presented in the context of instructional-level word-study activities. Throughout, the word-study lessons presented are constructed within a classroom flow from whole group to small group so as to provide interactive structures for all students, and an especially low-risk setting for English language learners within which to explore ideas, pose questions, and internalize information. Greater coverage is given to the discussion of the first two layers, sound and pattern, as these layers form the stable base on which students expand to understand derivations in word roots and bases.

Sound Layer

Sound, the first layer, corresponds to the first two stages of reading and spelling development in Figure 4.1 (see page 73). In alphabet-based orthographies, this layer is usually called the *alphabetic* layer.

EMERGENT SPELLING AND READING.   Children in the emergent phase experience spoken and written language in many ways, from the sound play of a poem or nursery rhyme to hearing the rhythm in repetitive stories and connecting text to oral language. In the early part of the emergent stage, young children's orientation to sound is in terms of its rhythmic and syllabic aspects. Numerous rhyming activities can be presented in conjunction with songs, stories, dances, and movement games similar to those that the children experience at home. Writing during this stage begins with what seem to be random scribbles. As children are read to and the directionality of the writing system is modeled, they scribble in the conventional direction for the orthography. As they increasingly attend to written symbols, they begin to use graphs that look more and more like letters.

In a sense, children are our finest linguists, and they make quite subtle sound discriminations (Read & Schreiber, 1982). English-speaking learners in the emergent stage play with sound at the syllabic level, but they are unable to reread familiar text accurately; their fingerpointing or tracking, for example, does not accurately follow their recitation of a rhyme or dictation that they try to read (Morris, 1992). Toward the end of this phase, as Read's (1971) landmark study of the spelling of 32 preschoolers demonstrated, children use orthography to categorize sounds phonetically.

In orthographies like Chinese, this ability to track may be learned earlier. When each character represents a single syllable, as is the case in Chinese, children may make the match between the sound and writing systems early, at around 4 years of age (Lee, 1990); their ability to match speech to print may occur a year earlier than for English-speaking children (Cathey, 1993; Templeton & Spivey, 1980). Emergent readers and spellers learning a shallow orthography may appear more advanced than students learning a deep orthography: They may be able to track a text and make a few sound-symbol correspondences, but we would not expect them to build an extensive sight vocabulary or represent more than the most prominent sounds when they spell (Treiman & Zukowski, 1991).

During the emergent phase, exploring and making distinctions among concepts is very important. In our instruction, we facilitate this through concept sorts in which children sort or categorize objects and pictures such as plastic animals, buttons, and macaroni according to different criteria. Children learn the names of the letters through song and recognition sorts including the "Concentration"-type format and name matching using uppercase and lowercase letters of students' names. Pictures and objects used in concept sorts also are used to sort by sound. Students begin to sort by the way the names of pictured objects sound at the beginning. The beauty of concept sorts is that students are not limited by vocabulary, and this makes it possible for students to work with partners and share ideas. Importantly, concept sorts also help students learn basic vocabulary, such as common objects, color words, and comparative terms (for example, *larger/largest, smaller/smallest*).

LETTER-NAME–ALPHABETIC/PHONETIC SPELLING AND BEGINNING READING. Beginning conventional readers are able to reread familiar texts with some support and develop a stable sight vocabulary. Beginning readers are disfluent and unexpressive in their reading, and they tend to read aloud to themselves and fingerpoint as they read (Bear, 1992). In English, at the beginning of this phase readers may have as few as 10 sight words. In other, more shallow, orthographies, it is easier to read more words accurately at this phase. This is why we see faster reading rates among primary children learning to read in Spanish. Reading with expression, however, is another matter and is more complicated and difficult for a beginning reader to manage on first reading, even in a translucent (transparent) orthography like Spanish.

As beginning readers learn the alphabetic principle of English, they rely primarily on a letter-name strategy to spell. In English and other orthographies, the letter names themselves are clues to spelling both consonants and vowels. Letter-name–alphabetic spellers in English represent the beginning, end, and usually medial vowels in single-syllable words. For students learning to speak, read, and write in two or more languages, we want to emphasize the *phonetic* or *sound* quality of their spelling during this stage. Universally, at this time, learners examine sound-symbol regularities, particularly where there is a linear, one-to-one relation between letters and sounds.

Students who can spell in this way are more ready than emergent learners for formal word-study instruction. As we know from extensive research conducted during the last 15 years, developing an awareness of the phonological segments in words is an important prerequisite to understanding how an alphabetic transcription represents speech (Ball & Blachman, 1991). Written language wraps to oral language, and when readers begin to organize letters into words, the orthographic information they possess activates their knowledge of other language systems. As a universal principle across languages, phonological processes are activated quickly in reading (Morita & Matsuda, 2000; Perfetti & Tan, 1999; Spinks, Liu, Perfetti, & Tan, 2000); this rapid processing is a foundation for advanced reading.

How does the sound layer being explored by beginning readers relate to character-based scripts? Let's look at Chinese as an example. Chinese is a monosyllabic spoken language, and each syllable contains three sounds: an initial sound, a final sound, and usually a tone. There are 21 initial and 38 final sounds that combine to form 440 basic syllables. Any of these syllables can be spoken with one of the four tones. There are many syllables that sound the same in Chinese except in tone. Characters are meaningful units like English morphemes. The number of characters that constitute a word (or the equivalent of a word) may range from one to six, but is usually two.

In character-based writing systems, learners match the characters with the oral sound system. Homophones are not homographs in Chinese, as they are written with different characters. By the end of first grade, students have learned approximately 430 characters, and by this time they are toward the end of the beginning stage of reading (Shen & Bear, 2000). Interestingly, in mainland China, students learn "Pinyin," an alphabetic orthography that teaches them how to pronounce the characters in Mandarin, the written language used throughout mainland China and Taiwan. The Pinyin letters accompany the characters as they are introduced. This alphabet is also what children use in their beginning writing until they learn enough characters to express their ideas in characters.

In English-language instruction, knowledge of the similarities and differences between the sound systems of English and students' home languages is essential. We will illustrate this importance for beginning readers and writers by considering Spanish as we aim to answer this question: What do teachers need to know about Spanish to understand Spanish-speaking children's spelling development as they learn English?

An important first step is to learn what sounds the two languages have in common. To understand what Spanish-speaking students reading in English will know about consonants, we need to know what consonants Spanish and English share and what sounds are unique to each language. Although there may be slight regional variations in pronunciation, the following consonants of English exist in Spanish: /b/, /k/, /s/, /f/, /g/, /h/, /l/, /m/, /n/, /p/, /t/, /x/, /y/, and /ch/.

Spanish-speaking students may have difficulty producing the sounds /d/, /j/, /r/, /v/, /z/, /sh/, /th/ (as in *thin*), /zh/, and /ng/; beginning and ending blends with *s*, and ending blends with *r*. Table 4.1 highlights sounds in English that may be difficult for Spanish speakers, and some common sound substitutions that may be made.

Our observations of students' spelling as they learn sounds in English reveals logical spelling errors that are based on the fundamental principles characteristic of the letter-name–alphabetic stage. For example, students spell *bug* as VUG and *van* as BAN. The /sh/ sound is often spelled CH, as in CHIP for *ship*. It is common to add an *e* in front of a word beginning with an *s* blend (ESTAMP for *stamp*) or not to include the final consonant in a word that ends in a blend (RES for *rest*).

TABLE 4.1 Difficult English consonant sounds for Spanish speakers learning English

Difficult consonant sounds	May be pronounced
d as in *dog*	<u>th</u>og
j as in *jump*	<u>ch</u>ump
r as in *race*	(rolled r) <u>r</u>ace
v as in *very*	<u>b</u>ery
z as in *zoo*	<u>s</u>oo
sh as in *shine*	<u>ch</u>ine
th as in *think*	<u>t</u>ink
zh as in *measure*	mea<u>ch</u>ure
Beginning s blends *st-, sp-, sc-, sk-, sm-, sn-, scr-, squ-, str-, spr-, spl-*	espace, esquirt, esplash
Ending blends with *r*: -rd, -rt, -rl, -rp, -rs	har (hard), cur (curl), tar (tarp)
-ng as in *sing*	sin (g)
Ending blends with *s*: -sp, -st, -sk	was (wasp), pos (post), as (ask)

Vowel sounds add another layer of complexity for the English learner attempting to work from his or her knowledge of Spanish. Table 4.2 outlines vowel sounds from English that exist orally in Spanish; Table 4.3 delineates vowel sounds in English that are *not* part of spoken Spanish and are thus more difficult for students to discriminate, speak, and write.

Beginning readers and writers use a letter-name strategy when they spell. For English-only students, the search for the letters to spell short vowels relies on an analysis of how the sound is articulated in the mouth. Beginning writers often misspell *bed* as BAD because the letter name *a* is closest to the short *e* sound. Spanish-speaking students use the same strategies to spell vowels, but their misspellings may seem unusual because they are influenced by a Spanish pronunciation of English. In addition, many bilingual learners bring substantial knowledge of Spanish orthography to the writing process in English. Based on their knowledge of Spanish spelling, they attach the closest letter name in Spanish to the unknown vowel sound, and the results look different than they would for English-only letter-name spellers. Where an English-only letter-name speller may try to spell *bake* as BAK, a bilingual Spanish speaker may write the same word as BEK.

TABLE 4.2 Vowel sounds present in both English and Spanish

English letter and word		Spanish letter and word	
a *as in*	cake	e *as in*	hecho
e	bean	i	ido
i	like	ai	aire
o	hope	o	ocho
o	top	a	ajo
u	June	u	usted
oy	toy	oy	voy

TABLE 4.3 Some English vowel sounds not present in Spanish

English letter and word	
a *as in*	man
e	pen
i	tip
u	cup
ou	could

Students who bring Spanish literacy to an English reading and writing program may write something like the following: DA MEN RANS FES (*The man runs fast*). At first glance, the spelling in this sentence may seem illogical. After a deeper analysis, however, we see that this student is using linguistic knowledge based on Spanish orthography to translate spoken language into print. These differences highlight the need to spend more time with short vowel sounds and patterns in order to give students time to unravel the confusions among vowels in orthographies and sound systems.

Literacy instruction with Alicia, the child we introduced at the beginning of this chapter, illustrates the word study we present to many students who are English language learners. Alicia's teacher wondered why she had difficulty reading *crane* after they had already covered short and long vowels. When Alicia began to meet with a reading specialist, she had spent two years of reading instruction organized by grade level alone, and as a third-grade English language learner she was unable to accurately and reliably read or write—except for (in a rote, memorized fashion) single-syllable CVC and CVCe words. Her reading and writing were hesitant. Her reading strategies showed a mixture of graphic errors based on initial and final consonants, and her reading of vowels in unfamiliar words seemed to be a blend of guesswork and contextual support.

Alicia worked in a small group with her school's reading specialist four times a week. Instruction was based on her development, and over several months, Alicia grew in her understanding of English orthography. She became automatic enough in word recognition with appropriate materials to feel success as a reader, and she experienced sufficient fluency in written expression to feel success as a writer. At first, her instructional level was with rhythmic and predictable texts coupled with daily word study of short-vowel word families, activities suited for students in the letter-name–alphabetic stage of spelling. Her knowledge of word families such as -*at*, -*ot*, and -*am* grew through many sorting activities, word-study game playing, and word hunts. She gradually expanded her knowledge of consonant blends and digraphs with these word family structures, and she began to examine and read with ease more difficult words, such as *scratch*, *trick*, and *stretch*. Five minutes of daily practice selecting these types of words from her reading and breaking them down into their component parts was a regular element of her word study.

Alicia also learned to look for meaning connections among words. In weekly poetry sessions that included an "interesting word" activity, Alicia chose "interesting words" related to her word knowledge. For example, while studying one poem she observed that *do*, *doing*, *does*, and *doesn't* were related by meaning and had a spelling "chunk," or base, that could be identified within each word. She noticed that *frost* was related to *frosty*, *frosting*, *frosted*, and *frosts*. Searching for related words shows students that knowing one word in English enables them to know many. The combination of this systematic sorting, breaking-down activities during reading, and looking for relationships between words helped Alicia to accelerate her understanding of the structure of words and begin to pose important questions about word meaning. These multiple layers of engagement with words, tying the words to her reading and writing experiences and focusing study on words at her developmental level, helped Alicia clarify and solidify her understanding of ideas and vocabulary (see Freeman & Freeman, chapter 2 in this volume).

Pattern Layer

Exploration of pattern occurs during several spelling stages. Across orthographies, what is common about this stage is the focus on graphic similarities. Students begin to make generalizations about words and characters that are no longer just sound- or phonetically based. Understanding the pattern layer requires abstraction in students' understanding of the orthography, moving beyond a simple one-to-one correspondence between the sound and symbol. In English, in the middle to late part of the letter-name–alphabetic stage and throughout the within-word pattern stage, students examine and learn the patterns of single-syllable words; in the intermediate phase of reading, students examine the syllable patterns that characterize polysyllabic words.

LETTER-NAME–ALPHABETIC/PHONETIC SPELLING AND BEGINNING READING. At this phase, students learn the fundamental and beginning patterns of their orthography. In English, the most basic pattern is the consonant-vowel-consonant (CVC) pattern. This is a closed syllable, and in the most common CVC patterns there is a one-to-one correspondence between the letters and sounds. These are the word families or *rimes* of English (*-at*, *-ed*). Shallow orthographies have *closed* and *open* syllable patterns, and these few patterns alone take readers into polysyllabic words. In Spanish word study at this level, students examine word families of two-syllable words, as in a word family sort contrasting *-apa*, *-asa*, *-ama*, and *-ana* sorts (Bear, Invernizzi, Templeton, & Johnston, 2001). It has been suggested that primary grade children reading German, also a transparent orthography, may not develop patterns or strategies that focus on graphic similarities as they learn to read (Wimmer & Hummer, 1990). The orthographic landscape is more complex in English. In many single-syllable words there are double letters and consonant digraphs and blends at the beginning and end of syllables that need to be understood as a single unit, as part of the consonant element. Words such as *ball*, *talk*, and *church* stretch the principle of one-to-one correspondence between letters and sounds. Toward the end of the letter-name–alphabetic/phonetic stage, students learn to read more single-syllable words, and they make accommodations and expand their concept of CVC words to include these doublets and consonant clusters.

WITHIN-WORD PATTERN SPELLING AND TRANSITIONAL READING. Transitional readers and writers who examine the orthography at the pattern layer are able to "chunk" these groups of letters as single perceptual units; this ability, together with their greater store of sight words or characters, allows them to read more fluently. At this phase, reading words and characters, or decoding, runs ahead of spelling words or characters in writing. Students experiment with the spelling of long-vowel patterns (Bear & Templeton, 2000) and explore the less frequent and more ambiguous consonant blends and digraphs. The within-word pattern stage is also a time when dialectical differences are sorted out. With a greater understanding of orthographic patterns, students rely less on the sound layer to spell, and differences in pronunciation become less important in reading and spelling most words. In fact, the inverse may be the case at this time, as orthographic knowledge influences students' pronunciation changes. In an interesting study of reading and pronunciation, children shifted pronunciation as they learned more about vowel patterns (Cantrell, 2001). In discussing the impact of orthography on the way children changed their pronunciation of vowels, Cantrell observed,

> Words in a child's lexicon that were first related tacitly in a phonological, semantic, and syntactic way appear to begin to be related to one another symbolically through the orthography. Therefore, as children internalize certain vowel patterns, the mediational nature of the orthography may play an increasingly interactive role as the degree of abstractness (i.e., long vowel spelling patterns) of the orthography increases. (p. 19)

Across languages, homophones and homographs are also sorted out at this time. Single-syllable English homophones (*soar/sore*, *made/maid*) and homographs (*read/read*, *dove/dove*) are studied toward the end of this stage. As we shall see, this study involves a relatively complex examination of patterns that extend into the meaning layer, where higher linguistic levels of semantics and syntax may be more explicitly involved. In the case of homophones, for example, the distinction between different spellings for the same pronunciation is based on a difference in meaning.

Transitional learners in shallow orthographies experiment with and examine polysyllabic words and more complex characters. Considerations of Spanish at this time involve two-syllable word patterns, stress assignment, the silent *h*, the soft and hard *g* and *c*, and simple prefixes and suffixes. Figure 4.2 illustrates a word-study activity in Spanish at this level. In this sort students begin to examine the more abstract nature of stress assignment in Spanish and the reasons why some words begin with *ha-* and *he-*.

In Chinese, the analysis of patterns occurs some time around second grade, when different tones and characters distinguish syllables with the same phonemes. During this stage, students learn approximately 700 more of the 3,000 high-frequency characters. Within characters, students learn about the 214 radicals in modern Chinese. Radicals are fundamental units within characters that usually describe the "member-set relationship" of the character (Shu & Anderson, 1999, p. 3). Spelling errors in Chinese at this stage are not solely phonetic or exclusively semantic, and many of the errors have a graphic component that is related to the pattern within and among characters. As in

FIGURE 4.2 Word sort contrasting words that begin with *ha-* and *he-* with words that begin with *a* and *e*. / Contraste de palabras que empiezan con *ha-* y *he-* con palabras que empiezan con *a* y *e*.

Contrast words that begin with ha- and he- with words that begin with a and e / Contraste palabras que empiezan con ha- y he- con palabras que empiezan con a y e	estufa	hábil
elefante	haba	enfermera
hambre	ángel	araña
anillo	abeja	hacha
habitación	hecho	helado
hecha	escalones	habitante
hacienda	estrella	escalera
elote	avión	animal

from Bear, Invernizzi, Templeton, & Johnston (2001); reprinted with permission

English, homophones among characters are studied, as they denote distinctions in meaning (Shen & Bear, 2000).

SYLLABLES AND AFFIXES, SPELLING, AND INTERMEDIATE READING.   Students examine a number of patterns as they move to the next stages of spelling and reading. These patterns include plurals, consonant doubling, compound words, basic syllabication, and accent. Even as the meaning connections become evident in word-study activities, students continue to examine patterns. For example, the consonant doubling exploration leads students to a study of how syllables combine (vowel-consonant-vowel or VCV juncture pattern, as in *label*, compared to a vowel-consonant-consonant-vowel or VCCV juncture between syllables, as in *napkin*).

At this pattern level, there is as much an analysis of the syntactic aspects of language as there is of the semantic aspects. For example, at this spelling stage in English, students examine -ed endings. (For some English language learners, learning to pronounce the -ed sound is a goal as well.) Part of the -ed word study will show that -ed is a past tense ending in English. This simple example highlights a fundamental principle of word study at this time: Grammar studies are combined with word-study and spelling activities.

INSTRUCTIONAL ACTIVITIES THAT EXPLORE PATTERN AND FACILITATE VOCABULARY DEVELOPMENT. *Sorting activities* may continue to be applied across the curriculum. At first, with the teacher guiding the students on an overhead and then independently, older students sort word cards of the states geographically as part of a fifth-grade social studies lesson. The categories may start with north/south/east/west and be broken down into specific regions later. Sorts in science reach numerous levels of complexity; for example, students may start a picture or object sort with a two-category "rock/nonrock" sort and then move to a three-category "smooth/bumpy/complex surfaces" sort. Subsequent sorts may be based on, for example, degree of sparkle, or hardness and density, or the object's past or morphology (igneous/metamorphic/sedimentary).

Students are actively involved in *charting activities* beginning with examination of the pattern layer. Charting is a way to guide students' explorations and also a way for students to work as partners, in small groups, or independently. Teachers model charting; they build webs with what students share as they talk about what they know about a topic. In the process of charting, and watching the teacher and other students write on charts, students learn to listen to syllables, think about word parts, and use analogies to spell.

An easy beginning chart is a chart of words we know from around the world. Word study of other languages is important to monolingual English-speaking students, because it furthers an understanding of the languages they hear and affords them the opportunity to notice, share, and explore common roots and ideas across languages. Vocabulary studies across languages deepen and broaden students' vocabulary in English, their conceptual development, and their appreciation of other languages—and students enjoy seeing these collections of words grow into full charts.

Older English language learning students may collaborate in discussing and writing down unfamiliar words; in small groups, this is an excellent way for students to wrestle with the vocabulary surrounding new concepts. For example, the words boldfaced in content materials are often the important conceptual vocabulary and are good choices for word study.

English language learners are supported by instructional practices that use oral language to bridge to an understanding of the written. As we discussed earlier with respect to Alicia's instruction, *"interesting word" activities* invite students to select words they find challenging, beautiful, puzzling, or unknown to examine, discuss, and investigate. As students read, they focus on words they find interesting and they bring these words to class to discuss.

English language learners need a low-risk forum in which to begin to pose questions about words. Charting interesting words is a way to display and document how students can collect words. The chart in Figure 4.3 is an example of an "interesting word" hunt by a small literature group reading *Tooter*

FIGURE 4.3 Word chart for the novel *Tooter Pepperday*

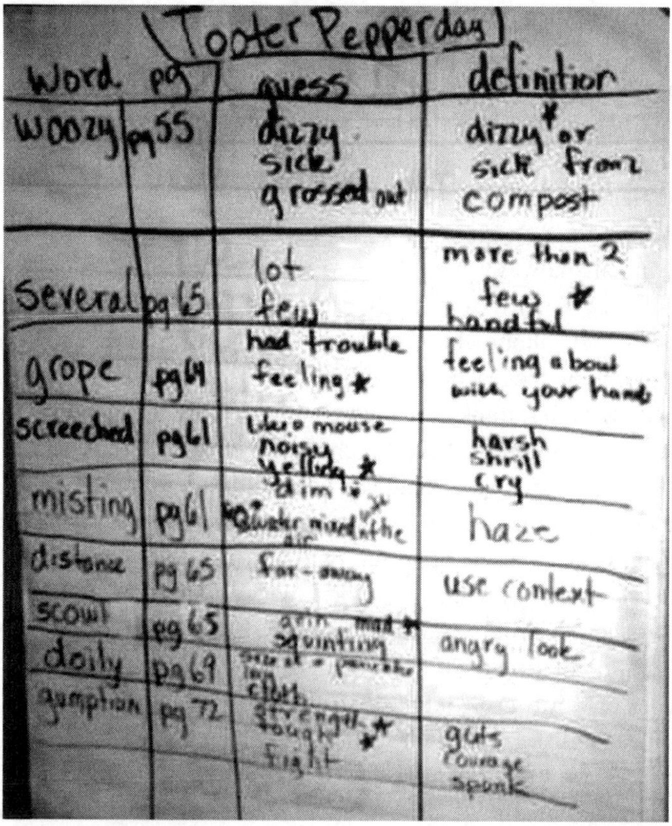

Pepperday by Jerry Spinelli (1995). Students collected interesting words as they read silently, guessed meaning based on context, and then used other students, the teacher, class dictionaries, and thesauruses to clarify meaning. In the first entry, students investigate the meaning of *woozy*. Students demonstrate their comprehension as they discuss getting sick from compost. The entry of such a basic word as *several* may be a surprise; yet such a common word to a native speaker may be new to an English language learner. Small-group charting is just the type of forum that makes it easier for English language learners to explore vocabulary.

Meaning Layer

When students examine the meaning level of English orthography they examine the relations between spelling and meaning, and they come to understand that words related in meaning are often related in spelling, despite changes in sound. Across languages, this period of orthographic development is linked closely to significant, extensive vocabulary development. As we noted earlier, the foundation for understanding the role that meaning plays in the spelling system is laid toward the end of the within-word pattern stage. At that phase, students examine less frequent abstract vowel patterns and bring meaning into focus as they learn homophones and further solidify their knowledge of single-syllable words. In character-based languages, the meaning units are found in the basic construction of the characters. In Chinese, there are 214 radicals that are morphemes within characters. In one study of children learning to read Chinese, by third grade, students understood that the radicals within characters represented meaningful units (Shu & Anderson, 1999).

SYLLABLES AND AFFIXES, SPELLING, AND INTERMEDIATE READING.   Students at this level still examine patterns, and they learn common prefixes and suffixes. They learn to look deeper than sound—at pattern, and now at meaning. And though -ed may be pronounced like /t/ as in *stopped*, they see that spelling is linked to meaning differences. Silent reading rates up to 250 words per minute are common among intermediate readers. They explore new genres, and the vocabulary they learn is also related to new concepts.

Students in the Syllables and Affixes spelling stage can spell a relatively easy word like *fortunate*, but now, as they examine the meaning layer, they understand how *fortune* and *fortunate* are related. The suffix -ate lends the sense of "having the quality of" to the base, *fortune*, and serves the same function in many other words that end in -ate. Comparisons among words like *donor/donate*, *liberty/liberate*, and *remedy/remediate* are rich for spelling and vocabulary study (see Freeman & Freeman, chapter 2 in this volume).

DERIVATIONAL RELATIONS, SPELLING, AND ADVANCED READING.   For English language learners who are at this phase, teachers have a prime opportunity to build on connections between students' home languages and English. For native Spanish speakers, a multitude of cognates can be found that bridge English spelling and vocabulary with Spanish (see Cummins, chapter 1 in this volume). As students examine word roots and their derivations (e.g., *therm/thermal/thermometer/thermos*), connections also can be made to Spanish vocabulary (e.g., *termómetro*). Affixes also can be compared in English and Spanish (e.g., *-tion/-ación* in *consideration/consideración*, or *-ing/-ando/-iendo* in *walking/caminando/comiendo*). These activities help students understand orthographic features conceptually in addition to building vocabulary and self-esteem.

Secondhand dictionaries in Spanish, French, and German are resources for students who want to explore similarities among languages. In addition, with good access to the Internet, students can find dictionaries for nearly all written languages, including online dictionaries that pronounce the words. A number of websites offer translations; though they vary in the degree to which they capture the sense of one language when translated to another, they are quite reliable at the level of the individual word. (Thus, entering *consideration* would yield *consideración*.) Examining cognates at this level is an excellent way for students to expand their vocabularies. The directions in Figure 4.4 are placed at a word-study center or word-study table for a small group in which students hunt through Spanish and English dictionaries. The students' examples, as illustrated in Figure 4.4, are discussed in small groups with the teacher; and as extension activities, students enter their work in their word-study notebooks and develop and post a chart of cognates and related words.

Conclusions

Throughout this discussion of the layers of orthographic knowledge and related developmental stages, examples of effective word-study practices have been highlighted. The following key ideas and instructional practices have emerged.

Orthographic knowledge is developmental; word study requires ongoing assessment to guide instruction. An initial spelling inventory assesses a student's stage of development; we find the level at which students are "using

FIGURE 4.4 Directions and examples of a word study activity to find cognates

From Spanish to English–A Dictionary Word Hunt

Purpose: Expand vocabularies through finding relations among languages.

Directions:

1. With a Spanish-English dictionary, find words in Spanish that remind you of words in English. Briefly note the definition or synonym.
2. With an English dictionary, find words that share the same root or affix. Write these related words into your word-study notebooks.
3. Use a Spanish dictionary to find related words with the same meaning: *night–noche*.

Here are some sample entries on a class chart of related words that students collected in this activity:

Spanish (Translation)	English Relations	Spanish Relations
presumir (boast)	presume, presumption, presumptuous	presumido, presunción
extenso (extensive)	extend, extension	extensivo, extender
nocturno (nightly)	nocturnal, nocturne	noche, noctámbulo
polvo (powder)	pulverize (from Latin, pulvis, dust)	polvillo, polvorear

but confusing" orthographic concepts (Invernizzi, Abouzeid, & Gill, 1994). Ongoing activities and student writing samples provide opportunities to assess student progress informally and prescribe successive steps for word work. Assessing each student's orthographic knowledge and providing instruction to match that level supports English language learners by providing comprehensible input and simplifying the complexities of the English writing system.

Learning is a social interaction; word study involves discussions and interactions between teacher and students and conversations, sorts, and games among students. In word-study activities, teachers present learning opportunities, such as word sorts, and ask students, "What do you notice about these words?" Teachers also dialogue with students as they express their growing orthographic understandings. Social dialogue among students as they engage in word-study activities supports English language learners by relating language to new learning, enlarging and clarifying vocabulary, and providing many opportunities for developing interpersonal connections.

New knowledge connects to previous knowledge; word study builds on oral language resources, background experiences, and literacy in other languages. Word-study activities build on students' oral language reserves and extend their understanding of the orthographic system. Similarities between primary and second languages are highlighted, and differences between language systems are studied explicitly. After examining words through sorts and activities, students return to meaningful texts to apply their learning and search for additional examples of patterns. The connection of new learning to previous knowledge supports English language learners by pointing out relationships and helping new ideas fit into a larger conceptual picture.

Learning is the construction and application of new understandings; word study provides hands-on opportunities to examine words and discover patterns in their structure. Word study is an interactive, manipulative process in which students are constantly comparing words, noticing common features, and exploring relationships among words, often across different languages. Obvious contrasts of words that *do* versus words that *don't* are addressed before finer distinctions are made (Invernizzi et al., 1994). In word study, "rules" are not declared; rather, patterns are discovered. This active construction of knowledge supports English language learners by taking instruction beyond the verbal level; learning comes from opportunities to physically sort and manipulate words into and within different categories, and practice leads to automaticity.

Importantly, systematic word study builds a foundation for increased sophistication in spelling and reading. It draws attention to words and meanings, and provides opportunities to use and apply these in interactive learning situations. Word study helps English language learning students build bridges between the known language and the new one, thus honoring their strengths and making the most of their abilities.

In this chapter we have shown how the three layers of orthography are in focus at different points developmentally. Throughout, principles of orthographic development across written languages have been presented, and instructional-level word-study activities useful to English language learners have been suggested. Literacy teachers at all grade levels can support their English language learning students by understanding the development of orthographic knowledge across languages and providing appropriate word-study activities. These initial insights, together with the practices of many conscientious educators, add to our knowledge base in the constantly evolving global teaching context.

REFERENCES

Ball, E.W., & Blachman, B. (1991). Does phoneme awareness training in kindergarten make a difference in early word recognition and developmental spelling? *Reading Research Quarterly*, *26*, 49–66.

Bear, D. (1992). The prosody of oral reading and stage of word knowledge. In S. Templeton & D.R. Bear (Eds.), *Development of orthographic knowledge and the foundations of literacy: A memorial festschrift for Edmund H. Henderson* (pp. 137–189). Hillsdale, NJ: Erlbaum.

Bear, D.R., Invernizzi, M., Templeton, S., & Johnston, F.R. (2000). *Words their way: Word study for phonics, vocabulary, and spelling instruction* (2nd ed.). Upper Saddle River, NJ: Prentice Hall.

Bear, D.R., Invernizzi, M., Templeton, S., & Johnston, F.R. (2001). *Words their way: An interactive resource* [Computer software]. Columbus, OH: Merrill/Prentice Hall.

Bear, D.R., & Templeton, S. (2000). Matching development and instruction. In N. Padak & T. Rasinski et al. (Eds.), *Distinguished educators on reading: Contributions that have shaped effective literacy instruction* (pp. 334–376). Newark, DE: International Reading Association.

California Reading and Literature Project. (1999). Spanish spelling inventory. In *Reading professional development institute: Focusing on results, pre-K–3.* (Available from the CA Reading and Literature Project, University of California at San Diego, 9500 Gilman Drive 0415, La Jolla, CA 92093-0415)

Cantrell, R.J. (2001). Exploring the relationship between dialect and spelling for specific vocalic features in Appalachian first-grade children. *Linguistics and Education, 12,* 1–23.

Cathey, S.S. (1993). *Emerging concept of word: Exploring young children's abilities to read rhythmic text.* Unpublished doctoral dissertation, University of Nevada, Reno.

Consortium on Reading Excellence. (1999). ESL spelling inventory. In *Assessing reading: Multiple measures for kindergarten through eighth grade.* Novato, CA: Arena Press.

Cuetos, F. (1993). Writing processes in a shallow orthography. *Reading and Writing, 5,* 17–28.

Ehri, L.C. (1997). Learning to read and learning to spell are one and the same, almost. In C.A. Perfetti, L. Rieben, & M. Fayol (Eds.), *Learning to spell: Research, theory, and practice across languages* (pp. 237–269). Mawah, NJ: Erlbaum.

Ellis, N. (1997). Interactions in the development of reading and spelling: Stages, strategies, and exchange of knowledge. In C.A. Perfetti, L. Rieben, & M. Fayol (Eds.), *Learning to spell: Research, theory, and practice across languages* (pp. 271–294). Mawah, NJ: Erlbaum.

Estes, T.H. (1998, April). *Bilingual children's knowledge of orthographic features of Spanish.* Paper presented at the annual meeting of the American Educational Research Association, San Diego, CA.

Fashola, O.S., Drum, P.A., Mayer, R.E., & Kang, S. (1996). A cognitive theory of orthographic transitioning: Predictable errors in how Spanish-speaking children spell English words. *American Educational Research Journal, 33,* 825–843.

Ferroli, L., & Krajenta, M. (1990). Validating a Spanish developmental spelling test. *The Journal of the National Association for Bilingual Education, 14,* 41–61.

Ganske, K. (1999). *Word journeys.* New York: Guilford.

Geva, E., Wade-Woodley, L., & Shany, M. (1993). The concurrent development of spelling and decoding in two different orthographies. *Journal of Reading Behavior, 25,* 383–406.

Gill, C.E. (1980). An analysis of spelling errors in French (Doctoral dissertation, University of Virginia, 1980). *Dissertation Abstracts International, 41-09A,* 3924.

Guion, S.G., Flege, J.E., Liu, S.H., & Yeni-Komshian, G.H. (2000). Age of learning effects on the duration of sentence produced in a second language. *Applied Psycholinguistics, 21,* 205–228.

Henderson, E.H. (1981). *Learning to read and spell: The child's knowledge of words.* DeKalb, IL: Northern Illinois University Press.

Henderson, E.H. (1990). *Teaching spelling* (2nd ed.). Boston: Houghton Mifflin.

Henderson, E.H. (1992). The interface of lexical competence and knowledge of written words. In S. Templeton & D.R. Bear (Eds.), *Development of orthographic knowledge and the foundations of literacy: A memorial festschrift for Edmund H. Henderson* (pp. 1–30). Hillsdale, NJ: Erlbaum.

Henderson, E.H., & Beers, J. (1980). *Developmental and cognitive aspects of learning to spell: A reflection of word knowledge.* Newark, DE: International Reading Association.

Invernizzi, M., Abouzeid, M., & Gill, J.T. (1994). Using students' invented spelling as a guide for spelling instruction that emphasizes word study. *The Elementary School Journal, 95,* 155–167.

Korkeamäki, R.L., & Dreher, M.J. (2000). Finnish kindergartners' literacy development in contextualized literacy episodes: A focus on spelling. *Journal of Literacy Research, 32,* 349–393.

Lee, L.-J. (1990). *Emergent literacy in Chinese: Print awareness of young children in Taiwan.* Unpublished doctoral dissertation, University of Arizona, Tucson.

Lieberman, P. (1991). *Uniquely human: The evolution of speech, thought, and selfless behavior.* Cambridge, MA: Harvard University Press.

Morita, A., & Matsuda, F. (2000). Phonological and semantic activation in reading two-kanji compound words. *Applied Psycholinguistics, 21,* 487–503.

Morris, D. (1992). Concept of word: A pivotal understanding in the learning to read process. In S. Templeton & D.R. Bear (Eds.), *Development of orthographic knowledge and the foundations of literacy: A memorial festschrift for Edmund H. Henderson* (pp. 53–77). Hillsdale, NJ: Erlbaum.

Paulesu, E., Demonet, J.-F., Fazio, F., McCrory, E., Chanoine, V., Brunswick, N., et al. (2001). Dyslexia: Cultural diversity and biological unity. *Science, 291,* 2165–2167.

Perfetti, C.A. (1985). *Reading ability.* New York: Oxford University Press.

Perfetti, C.A., & Tan, L.H. (1999). The constituency model of Chinese word identification. In J. Wang, A.W. Inhoff, & H.-C. Chen (Eds.), *Reading Chinese script: A cognitive analysis* (pp. 115–134). Mahwah, NJ: Erlbaum.

Perfetti, C.A., & Zhang, S. (1991). Phonological processes in reading Chinese. *Journal of Experimental Psychology, 17,* 633–643.

Pinheiro, Â.M.V. (1995). Reading and spelling development in Brazilian Portuguese. *Reading and Writing: An Interdisciplinary Journal, 7,* 111–138.

Porpodas, C.D. (1989). The phonological factor in reading and spelling of Greek. In P.G. Aaron & R.M. Joshi (Eds.), *Reading and writing disorders in different orthographic systems* (pp. 177–190). Norwell, MA: Kluwer Academic.

Ransdell, S., Arecco, M.R., & Levy, C.M. (2001). Bilingual long-term working memory: The effects of working memory loads on writing quality and fluency. *Applied Psycholinguistics, 22,* 113–128.

Read, C. (1971). Preschool children's knowledge of English phonology. *Harvard Educational Review, 41,* 1–34.

Read, C., & Schreiber, P. (1982). Why short subjects are harder to find than long ones. In E. Wanner & L. Gleitman (Eds.), *Language acquisition: The state of the art* (pp. 78–101). New York: Cambridge University Press.

Rieben, L., Saada-Robert, M., & Moro, C. (1997). Word search strategies and stages of word recognition. *Learning and Instruction, 7,* 137–159.

Russell, W. (1844). *Spelling-book, or second course of lessons in spelling and reading.* Boston: Charles Tappan.

Schlagal, R.C. (1992). Patterns of orthographic development into the intermediate grades. In S. Templeton & D.R. Bear (Eds.), *Development of orthographic knowledge and the foundations of literacy: A memorial festschrift for Edmund H. Henderson* (pp. 31–52). Hillsdale, NJ: Erlbaum.

Schmitt, N., & McCarthy, M. (1997). *Vocabulary: Description, acquisition and pedagogy.* Cambridge, UK: Cambridge University Press.

Shen, H., & Bear, D.R. (2000). The development of orthographic skills in Chinese children. *Reading and Writing: An Interdisciplinary Journal, 13,* 197–236.

Shu, H., & Anderson, R. (1999). Learning to read Chinese: The development of metalinguistic awareness. In J. Wang, A.W. Inhoff, & C.-H. Chen (Eds.), *Reading Chinese script: A cognitive analysis* (pp. 1–18). Mahwah, NJ: Erlbaum.

Spinelli, J. (1995). *Tooter Pepperday.* New York: Random House.

Spinks, J.A., Liu, Y., Perfetti, C.A., & Tan, L.H. (2000). Reading Chinese characters for meaning: The role of phonological information. *Cognition, 76,* B1–B11.

Temple, C.A. (1978). An analysis of spelling errors in Spanish (Doctoral dissertation, University of Virginia, 1978). *Dissertation Abstracts International, 40-02A,* 0721.

Templeton, S., & Bear, D.R. (1992). Summary and synthesis: "Teaching the lexicon to read and spell." In S. Templeton & D.R. Bear (Eds.), *Development of orthographic knowledge and the foundations of literacy: A memorial festschrift for Edmund Henderson* (pp. 333–352). Hillsdale, NJ: Erlbaum.

Templeton, S., & Spivey, E.M. (1980). The concept of "word" in young children as a function of level of cognitive development. *Research in the Teaching of English, 14,* 265–278.

Tolchinsky, L., & Teberosky, A. (1998). The development of word segmentation and writing in two scripts. *Cognitive Development, 13,* 1–24.

Treiman, R., & Zukowski, A. (1991). Levels of phonological awareness. In S.A. Brady & D.P. Shankweiler (Eds.), *Phonological process in literacy: A tribute to Isabelle Y. Liberman* (pp. 67–83). Hillsdale, NJ: Erlbaum.

Vernon, S.A., & Ferreiro, E. (1999). Writing development: A neglected variable in the consideration of phonological awareness. *Harvard Educational Review, 69,* 395–415.

Wimmer, H., & Hummer, P. (1990). How German-speaking first graders read and spell: Doubts on the importance of the logographic stage. *Applied Psycholinguistics, 11,* 349–368.

Zutell, J., & Allen, J. (1988). The English spelling strategies of Spanish-speaking bilingual children. *TESOL Quarterly, 22,* 333–340.

CHAPTER 5

Scaffolding Reading Experiences for Multilingual Classrooms

Michael F. Graves and Jill Fitzgerald

Each year, hundreds of thousands of teachers in the United States and many other countries enter multilingual classrooms and begin teaching students with diverse language backgrounds, diverse language skills, and diverse reading proficiency. Although teaching in multilingual classrooms is by no means a recent phenomenon, it is an experience new to many teachers; and while it presents teachers with significant opportunities, such as examining diverse perspectives and preparing students to live in a diverse world, it also presents significant challenges. One of those challenges is, of course, that of teaching reading to students whose proficiency in reading—often in both their native language and the language of instruction—differs markedly. Meeting these challenges requires powerful, multifaceted approaches—approaches that involve many facets of the classroom, extend beyond individual classrooms into the school as a whole, and extend beyond the school into children's homes and neighborhoods.

The approach described here addresses only one aspect of reading instruction; it is by no means meant to be a comprehensive reading program. However, we believe that it is an important part of a comprehensive reading program. With all the approaches used and wherever children learn and practice their reading skills, one factor is crucial to their becoming able and avid readers. We must do everything possible to make children's reading experiences *successful*. It is extremely important that children understand what they read, enjoy the experience of reading, learn from what they read, and realize that they *have* learned from and understood what they read.

In this chapter, we discuss one approach to assisting students in multilingual classrooms to read, understand, learn from, and enjoy—and feel successful about reading—the texts they read in the classroom: the scaffolded reading experience (SRE) (Fitzgerald & Graves, in press; Graves & Graves, 2003; Tierney & Readence, 2000). We first describe some central concepts underlying the SRE; we next describe the SRE framework, explaining what an SRE is and reviewing in some detail the characteristic components of an SRE. We then present examples of SREs that might be used in multilingual classrooms, and we conclude the chapter with a reminder of what SREs are and a note on what they are not—along with some consideration of how often to construct SREs in multilingual classrooms and how much scaffolding to provide.

Concepts Underlying the Scaffolded Reading Experience

Not surprisingly, the central concept underlying the scaffolded reading experience is that of scaffolding. The term *scaffolding* was first used in its educational sense by Wood, Bruner, and Ross (1976), who used it to characterize mothers' verbal interaction when reading to their young children. For example, in sharing a picture book with a child and attempting to assist the child in reading the words that identify the pictures, a mother might at first simply page through the book, familiarizing the child with the pictures and the general content of the book. Then she might focus on a single picture and ask the child what it is. After this, she might point to the word below the picture, tell the child that the word names the picture, ask the child what the word is, and provide him or her with feedback on the correctness of the answer. The important point is that the mother has neither simply told the child the word nor simply asked him or her to say it. Instead, she has built an instructional structure, a scaffold, that assists the student in learning.

Scaffolding, as Wood and his colleagues (1976) aptly put it, is "a process that enables a child or novice to solve a problem, carry out a task, or achieve a goal which would be beyond his [or her] unassisted efforts" (p. 90). Or, to use Anderson's (1989) words, a scaffold is "a temporary and adjustable support that enables the accomplishment of a task that would be impossible without the scaffold's support" (p. 106). As applied to the thinking behind SREs, we would extend Anderson's definition and say that scaffolding enables students to accomplish a task that would be impossible without the scaffold or enables them to accomplish a task more fully or more easily than they could without the scaffold. Thus, for example, without a scaffold a child might laboriously read a text and gain a rudimentary understanding of it, while with a scaffold he or she might be able to more readily read it and gain a fuller understanding of it.

Since its introduction 25 years ago, the concept of instructional scaffolding has been investigated, elaborated, related to other instructional concepts, and strongly endorsed by a host of educators. Among those supporting scaffolding are Anderson (1989), Anderson and Armbruster (1990), Applebee and Langer (1983), Brown and Palincsar (1989), Cazden (1992), Pearson (1996), Pressley (1998), Raphael (2000), Routman (2000), Snow (Snow, Burns, & Griffin, 1998), and Taylor (Taylor, Pearson, Clark, & Walpole, 2000). Moreover, studies have shown that scaffolding students' reading can be a powerful instructional technique in classrooms (Cooke, 2002; Fournier & Graves, in press; Graves & Liang, in press; Taylor et al., 2000; Warton-McDonald, Pressley, & Hampston, 1998), small groups (Brown & Palincsar, 1989; Palincsar, 1986), and one-to-one tutoring sessions (Beed, Hawkins, & Roller, 1991).

Although different authors define scaffolding slightly differently, three closely related features are essential attributes of effective scaffolding. First, there is the scaffold itself, the temporary and supportive structure that helps a student or group of students accomplish a task they could not accomplish—or could not accomplish as well or as readily—without the scaffold.

Second, the scaffold must place the learner in what Vygotsky (1978) has termed the Zone of Proximal Development. As explained by Vygotsky, at any particular point in time, children have a circumscribed zone of development, a range within which they can learn. At one end of this range are learning tasks that children can complete independently; at the other end are learning tasks that they cannot complete, even with assistance. Between these two extremes is the zone most productive for learning, the range of tasks children can succeed at if they are assisted by some more knowledgeable or more competent other.

And third, over time, the teacher must gradually dismantle the scaffold and transfer the responsibility for completing tasks to students. As Pearson and Gallagher (1983) have explained, effective instruction often follows a progression in which teachers gradually do less of the work and students gradually assume increased responsibility for their learning. It is through this process of gradually assuming more and more responsibility for their learning that students become competent, independent learners.

These concepts and a number of others that we have discussed elsewhere (Fitzgerald & Graves, in press; Graves & Graves, 2003) underlie the SRE framework, which we now describe.

The Scaffolded Reading Experience Framework

A scaffolded reading experience is a set of prereading, during-reading, and postreading activities specifically designed to assist a particular group of students in successfully reading, understanding, learning from, and enjoying a particular selection. As such, an SRE is somewhat similar to traditional instructional plans such as Betts's Directed Reading Activity (1946) and Stauffer's Directed Reading-Thinking Activity (1969), and to more recent plans such as Fountas and Pinnell's Guided Reading (1996). Tierney and Readence (2000) classify all these plans as "lesson frameworks," and this is an appropriate classification for the SRE.

However, the SRE framework differs markedly from these other instructional frameworks in that an SRE is not a preset plan for dealing with whatever reading situation you face. Instead, an SRE is a flexible plan that you tailor to a specific situation. The SRE framework is derived from the powerful insights Jenkins (1976) captured in his tetrahedral model of reading and is consistent with the model of comprehension adopted by the RAND Reading Study Group (2002). As Jenkins explained, the outcome of any learning situation will be influenced by at least four different factors: characteristics of the learner, the nature of the materials, the learning activities, and the criterial tasks. The SRE framework shows teachers in multilingual classrooms ways to manipulate these factors so that students get the most they can out of each and every reading experience. The framework, which is shown in Figure 5.1, has two parts or phases.

The first phase of the SRE is the planning phase, during which you plan and create the entire experience. The second phase is the implementation phase, comprising the activities you and your students engage in as a result of your planning. This two-phase process is a vital feature of the SRE approach, in that the planning phase allows you to tailor each SRE you create to the specific situation you face in that particular reading experience. Different situations call for different SREs.

Planning takes into account the students, the reading selection, and the reading purpose. Suppose you are working with sixth graders in a multilingual classroom that includes five students whose native language is Spanish and two students whose native language is Korean. Assume also that the seven English language learners in your class read English reasonably well but are not as proficient in reading English as most of your other students. Finally, assume that you want all students in the class to develop a fairly deep

FIGURE 5.1 Two phases of a scaffolded reading experience for English language learners

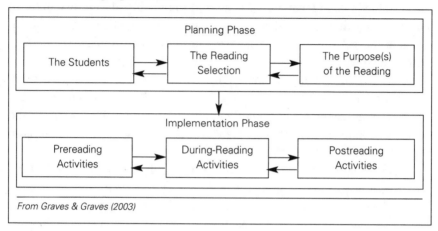

From Graves & Graves (2003)

understanding about the migration of whales and that the text you have chosen is fairly demanding.

Or consider a very different situation. Suppose you are working with these same sixth graders, your purpose is to have them read a humorous short story for the pure enjoyment of it, and you have chosen a fairly easy reading selection.

In both these situations, your planning leads to the creation of the SRE itself and to your implementing it; but the SRE for the whale migration text will be quite different than that for the short story. As shown in the lower half of Figure 5.1, the components of the implementation phase are prereading, during-reading, and postreading activities. With the whale migration text, we have already suggested that you want students to develop some fairly deep knowledge and to retain much of what they learn. This means that your SRE for the whale migration text is likely to be a substantial one, with prereading activities that thoroughly prepare students to read the difficult text, during-reading activities that lead them to interact and grapple with the text in ways that help them understand and learn from it, and postreading activities that give them opportunities to check their understanding of the text and solidify their learning. Consequently, the class might spend four or five days reading the chapter and completing the learning activities you have assembled. Your English language learners, however, are likely to need more scaffolding with this text than your other students. You might begin working with them on the migration text a day or two before you begin working with the class as a whole, perhaps previewing the text for them, going over the major concepts, and letting them get a head start on reading it.

As we just noted, your SRE for the humorous short study is likely to be quite different. Given a fairly easy short story and the major goal of students' simply enjoying the reading experience, your SRE is likely to be minimal. Prereading might consist of a brief motivational activity; students might read the story silently to themselves; and postreading might consist of an optional discussion. Moreover, because the reading presents few problems and because it is generally desirable to have your English language learners engage in the same reading experiences as your other students so long as they can do so successfully, you would not expect to have any separate activities for them. All in all, the class might spend only a day or so reading and responding to the short story.

In addition to recognizing that the SRE framework results in very different SREs for different situations, it is important to recognize that the components of each phase of the SRE are interrelated. Consider the three components of the planning phase—the students, the text, and your purposes. Once you decide which students you are going to work with, there are only some texts you can use and only some purposes you can expect to accomplish. Once you decide which text you are going to use, there are only some students who will be able to read it and only some purposes you can achieve with it. And once you decide what your purposes are, there are only some texts you can use to accomplish those purposes and only some students who will be able to achieve them. The same sort of interdependency holds with respect to the three components of the implementation phase. For example, if you decide you are going to have some very challenging postreading tasks, you will want to include prereading activities and during-reading activities that thoroughly prepare students to accomplish those challenging tasks.

The possible prereading, during-reading, and postreading components of an SRE are listed in Figure 5.2. As you can see, the list includes ten types of prereading activities, five types of during-reading activities, and eight types of postreading activities. On the following pages, we say a few words about prereading, during-reading, and postreading activities generally and then describe each of the types of activities that you might use before students read, as they are reading, and after they read.

Several issues are important to keep in mind as you consider the SRE framework and the component activities. First, the framework presents a list of options. No single SRE will contain all of these activities. Second, the purpose of the list is to suggest a wide variety of activities. It is certainly not the only

FIGURE 5.2 Possible components of a scaffolded reading experience for English language learners

Prereading Activities
    Motivating
    Activating or building background knowledge
    Providing text-specific knowledge
    Relating the reading to students' lives
    Preteaching vocabulary
    Preteaching concepts
    Prequestioning, predicting, and direction setting
    Using students' native language
    Engaging students and community people as resources
    Suggesting strategies

During-Reading Activities
    Silent reading
    Reading to students
    Guided reading
    Oral reading by students
    Modifying the text

Postreading Activities
    Questioning
    Discussion
    Building connections
    Writing
    Drama
    Artistic, graphic, and nonverbal activities
    Application and outreach activities
    Reteaching

way to classify activities, and it is not intended to limit the activities you might use or to suggest that you need to rigidly classify activities into one category or another. Moreover, activities listed in one part of the framework can sometimes be useful in other parts. For example, Relating the Reading to Students' Lives (activity names have been capitalized) could be something you do after students read a selection as well as before they read it. Similarly, although we list Writing as a postreading activity, it can also be used as a prereading or during-reading activity—as, for example, when students write a list of what they know about a topic *before* reading, or take notes *while* reading. Additionally, two of the activities listed as prereading activities—Using Students' Native Language and Engaging Students and Community People as

Resources—are every bit as appropriate when used as during-reading or postreading activities. We do not list them again in those sections simply to avoid redundancy.

Prereading Activities

Prereading activities prepare students to read the upcoming selection. They can serve a number of functions, including getting students interested in reading the selection, reminding students of things they already know that will help them understand and enjoy the selection, and preteaching aspects of the selection that may be difficult. Prereading activities are important for all students, but they are particularly important for many English language learners, both because these children are often not experienced with typical topics in texts used in United States schools and because the vocabulary and idioms in the materials they encounter may be new to them. Providing adequate preparation is the best way to ensure English learners the most enjoyable, rewarding, and successful reading experience possible.

Prereading activities are recommended widely (see, for example, Aebersold & Field, 1997; Ciborowski, 1992; Fountas & Pinnell, 1996; Readence, Moore, & Rickelman, 2000; Schoenbach, Greenleaf, Cziko, & Hurwitz, 1999; Yopp & Yopp, 1992), and a number of different types of prereading activities have been suggested. In creating a list of possible prereading activities for SREs, we have attempted to propose a relatively small set of categories that suggest a large number of useful activities in which teachers and students can engage.

By Motivating we refer to any activity designed to interest students in a selection and entice them to read it. For example, in order to motivate students in an eighth-grade civics class about to read a section of a chapter titled something like "The Media and the Road to the Presidency," a teacher might make statements and pose questions such as these:

> One of the most important things people in the United States do is elect a president, because the president of the United States plays a huge role in what happens in the country and that affects all of us. As you know, each adult in the United States gets a vote, and so it is important for anyone running for president to get the message he or she wants voters to hear out to everyone. Suppose you were running for president. What are some ways that you would try to get your message out to all the people? Jot some of these down before you read.

Then the teacher might ask students to read the selection to find out how the approaches they suggested compare with those discussed in the chapter.

In many cases, motivational materials can accomplish some other purpose besides motivating students. As in the above example, questions may serve both to motivate students and to focus their attention as they read. We list Motivating as a separate activity, however, because we believe that motivating should be a very frequent part of an SRE. Motivating activities are particularly important when introducing material to English language learners because English learners frequently have to devote so much attention to understanding new concepts and vocabulary, as well as to general language processing, that a learning and reading activity can seem daunting to them. By using motivational activities teachers can spark interest in students, and this interest can sustain them when the reading is challenging.

Activating or Building Background Knowledge is often necessary for students to get the most from what they read. When you *activate* background knowledge, you prompt students to bring to consciousness already known information that will help them in understanding a text. For example, let's say a group of your sixth graders is researching the plight of migrant workers. Before these students read a story you have recommended from *The Circuit: Stories From the Life of a Migrant Child* (1999), Francisco Jimenez's award-winning collection of stories based on his own experiences as a child migrant worker in California, you might encourage them to discuss what they have already learned about migrant workers from their previous reading or experience.

In addition to activating background knowledge, it is sometimes necessary to *build* background knowledge—knowledge that the author, usually tacitly, has presupposed that readers already possess. For example, in reading the stories in *The Circuit*, you might find that Jimenez presupposes some specific knowledge of California geography, knowledge that you are pretty sure your English language learners lack. In this case, supplying the information would make good sense.

In contrast to activities that activate or build background knowledge, activities such as Providing Text-Specific Knowledge give students information that is contained in the reading selection. Providing students with advance information on aspects of the content of a selection is certainly justified if the selection is difficult or densely packed with information. For many English language learners, even materials that you might normally consider reader friendly may present many unfamiliar concepts. For these children, providing the concepts orally or visually in advance of the reading is not only justified; it may be imperative.

Many English language learners will not automatically see the relevance of the selections they read to their lives. Therefore, Relating the Reading to Students' Lives can be extremely important. Thus, for example, if you are in California and your newly arrived Asian students are reading Betsy Byers's "Sam's Storm"—which deals with a boy's bravery when a tornado hits his home in the Midwest—you might point out to your students that, though they are unlikely to experience tornadoes, they may have to deal with earthquakes or floods.

Preteaching Vocabulary and Preteaching Concepts are activities that are related and can be conveniently considered together. We list these two as different activities to contrast two quite different instructional tasks: teaching words that are merely new labels for concepts that students already know versus teaching words that represent new and potentially difficult concepts. With English language learners, it is often difficult for teachers to know when words are new labels for concepts already known and when the concept itself must be taught. For example, a fourth-grade teacher can just about always assume that all her students, including her English language learners, understand the concept of "red," and so teaching the word *crimson* would be giving a new label to a known concept. However, suppose the three English language learners in her class recently arrived from a small pueblo in Guatemala, where they attended two years of school and lived with no running water or electricity. She would probably assume that the word *igloo* represents a known concept for her other fourth graders, but she could reasonably wonder if her English learners would understand that concept, or even those of "snow" and "ice."

When the basic concepts are known, up to half a dozen or so new words can easily and quickly be presented before students read an upcoming selection. When the basic concepts are not known, however, teaching them usually takes a significant amount of time and requires powerful instruction. This generally means that only two or three words representing new concepts can be taught before students read a selection.

We have listed Prequestioning, Predicting, and Direction Setting together because we see them as three methods of accomplishing the same task. With any of them, you are focusing students' attention and telling them what is important to look for as they read. Such focusing is often necessary, because without it students, especially English language learners, may not know what to attend to.

One category of activities that is unique to multilingual classrooms is that of Using Students' Native Language. When the going gets tough—when the gulf between students' proficiency in English and the task posed by the reading becomes wide and deep—one extremely helpful alternative is to switch to students' native language. You might, for example, present a preview of a book such as Seymour Simon's *Earthquakes* in Spanish. Or you might give your Spanish-speaking students directions for reading *Earthquakes* in Spanish. As we said earlier, we have not included Using Students' Native Language in our lists of during-reading or postreading activities in order to avoid redundancy; it is important to remember, however, that employing students' native language is just as viable an option while they are reading a text or after they have read it as it is before they read. Thus, you might want to give Filipino students a study guide in Tagalog, or you might want to allow Hmong students to sometimes respond to what they read in Hmong.

Even teachers in multilingual classrooms, however, seldom speak Spanish, or Tagalog, or Hmong. That is where Engaging Students and Community People as Resources becomes valuable. In all probability, other students in your class, students in other classes in your school, and people in the community do speak the language or languages spoken by your English language learners. Bringing these children and adults into your classes as resource people has tremendous advantages. The most obvious of these is that they can communicate effectively with your students who are not yet proficient in English. Another advantage is the satisfaction, sense of belonging, and sense of pride that the resource people will get from assisting in your classroom. It is often difficult to convey to parents who are unfamiliar with U.S. schools and may not be that secure in their own English that they are welcome at school, that you really want to work with them to help their children succeed. By bringing such parents into the school as resource people, you convey to them that they are not only welcome, but needed. And again, as is the case with using students' native language, engaging people as resources is just as viable an option while students are reading a text or after they have read it as it is before they read.

With respect to the final prereading activity, Suggesting Strategies, the key word is *suggesting*. SREs are not designed to teach strategies—for example, to teach students how to make inferences or how to summarize a selection. As part of an SRE, however, you may want to alert students when a particular strategy they have already been taught is likely to be useful, perhaps by saying something like, "Because this chapter has a lot of new information, it would be a good idea to write a four- or five-sentence summary of it soon after you've read it."

For information on why you might want to teach strategies even though doing so is not part of the SRE framework, we suggest Michael Pressley's

"What Should Comprehension Instruction Be the Instruction Of?" (Pressley, 2000). For specific information on how to teach strategies, we suggest Graves, Juel, and Graves (2001).

During-Reading Activities

During-reading activities include both things that students themselves do as they are reading and things that *you* do to assist them as they are reading. Like prereading activities, during-reading activities are frequently recommended (see, for example, Aebersold & Field, 1997; Bean, Valerio, & Stevens, 1999; Beck, McKeown, Hamilton, & Kucan, 1997; Ciborowski, 1992; Fountas & Pinnell, 1996; Richardson, 2000; Schoenbach et al., 1999; Wood, Lapp, & Flood, 1992; Yopp & Yopp, 1992). In proposing possible during-reading activities for SREs, we have again attempted to list a relatively small set of categories that suggest a large number of useful activities that will help your students gain more from what they read.

We list Silent Reading first because we believe strongly that this should be the most frequently resorted-to during-reading activity, both for English language learners and for other students. The central long-term goal of reading instruction is to prepare students to become accomplished lifelong readers, and most of the reading students do in life—in the upper elementary grades, in the middle grades, in secondary school, in college, and in the world outside of school—will be silent reading. Although more than practice is required to develop proficient readers, it is both a basic rule of learning and everyday common sense that one needs to practice repeatedly the skill he or she is attempting to master. If teachers choose appropriate selections for students to read and have adequately prepared them to read these selections, then students will often be able to read them silently on their own (see Freeman & Freeman, chapter 2, and Krashen, chapter 3, in this volume).

For English language learners, choice of material—including, whenever possible, ensuring that the reading level of the material matches the reading level of the learner—and your support, including adequate preparation, are especially important keys to a successful silent reading experience. It is also important for teachers to keep in mind that some English learners are more proficient at reading than at listening.

Reading to Students can serve a number of functions. Hearing a story or expository material read aloud is, to begin with, a very pleasurable experience for many children and also serves as a model of good oral reading. Reading the first few paragraphs of a piece to students can help ease them into the material and can serve as an enticement to read the rest of the selection on their own. Reading to students can make texts that might otherwise be inaccessible to them quite accessible. And finally, some texts really come alive when they are read aloud. In these instances, reading aloud, or playing an audiotape for the same purpose, may be particularly appropriate. The power of Martin Luther King, Jr.'s "I Have a Dream" speech, for example, is certainly better grasped when listening to an actual recording of the speech than when reading the material silently. Many English language learners at more advanced levels also find audiotapes useful because they can replay sections to better hear and understand what is being said. Of course, reading some or all of the text to your English learners in their native language or having more advanced students or other resource people do so is another option.

Guided Reading refers to a broad range of activities that you use to focus students' attention on particular aspects of a text as they read. Guided Reading can be used to assist students in such thought-demanding activities as selecting main ideas, focusing on specific themes, and forming generalizations. Guided Reading often begins as a prereading activity, perhaps with your setting directions for reading, and is then carried out as students are actually reading. For example, in order to help students understand ethnic stereotypes, you may have them jot down some of the adjectives used to describe individuals of different ethnicities as they read and compare two articles on the same current event written in *Ebony* and *Newsweek*. Such activities can help students really learn from their reading.

To be sure, one long-term goal of schooling is to enable and motivate students to read without your assistance. Thus, with less challenging selections or as students become increasingly competent over time, your support can be less specific and less directive and perhaps consist only of a suggestion: "After reading this chapter, I have a suggestion for you. Try reading it with a partner and stopping after each section to take notes. This should help you understand and remember the material better."

Oral Reading by Students is a relatively frequent activity in some classrooms but a much less frequent one in others. As we previously mentioned, most of the reading students will do throughout their lives is silent reading. Nonetheless, oral reading has its place. Oral reading is needed in the early stages of play production, when children can select their parts and practice them by reading orally in pairs. Poignant or particularly well-written passages of prose are often particularly appropriate for oral reading. Reading orally can also be helpful when the class or a group of students is studying a passage and trying to decide on alternative interpretations or on just what is and is not explicitly stated in the passage. Students often like to read their own writing orally. And finally, oral reading offers you some direct insights into students' reading proficiency. Thus, while oral reading need not be a frequent activity, it can be a useful one and something to include among the many alternatives you offer students.

At the same time, we strongly recommend that oral reading in front of classmates be reserved for those English language learners whose English reading fluency is well developed. For English learners who do not yet read English fluently, oral reading in front of peers can be a difficult and even painful experience. Many second-language speakers, especially adolescents, are very self-conscious about pronunciation. Consequently, reading orally in front of peers can be a risky situation for many English learners.

When English learners do read orally, it is usually best to deemphasize pronunciation. Instead, as students are learning to read English, support their movement toward understanding what they read. Many English learners also move through a "silent period," a phase during which they can understand somewhat but choose not to make an effort to speak (Terrell, 1981). Teachers should expect students in such a silent period to continue to learn and grow, but they should also respect that many students need to have time to gain more confidence and realize that others in the classroom will support and encourage their oral language growth.

Finally, Modifying the Text is sometimes necessary to make the reading material more accessible to students. This can be especially true for English language learners in the early stages of their English development. For example, if a chapter in a social studies or science textbook is particularly lengthy and contains many concepts that will be new to students, you might want to select parts of the chapter to be read. For some English learners, you might even rewrite the text to simplify it, perhaps creating an outline-like version for them to read—although this is not something most teachers have the time to do very often.

Another way to modify the text is to draw a pictorial or graphic representation of the main ideas and ask students to examine these representations. Or you, or a resource person, might modify a text by substituting a version in a student's native language for the English version. Still another means of modifying a text is to find an alternative text that better matches your students' proficiency. Suppose, for example, some of your eighth-grade English learners have difficulty reading the history text your class is using; you may want to have them read a parallel chapter from a fifth-grade history text instead. There may be other times when you feel that your textbook's treatment of a topic is inadequate, and you need to find supplemental readings to help develop your students' understanding. Each of these cases represents an example of modifying a text to increase the possibility that your students will have a successful reading experience.

Postreading Activities

As is the case with prereading and during-reading activities, postreading activities serve a variety of purposes. They provide opportunities for students to synthesize and organize information gleaned from reading a text and to understand and recall important points and details. They provide opportunities for students to evaluate information and ideas, the author's stance, their own stances, and the quality of the text itself. They provide opportunities for students to respond to a text in a variety of ways: to reflect on the meaning of the text, to compare differing texts and ideas, to imagine themselves as one of the characters in the text, to engage in a variety of creative activities, and to apply what they have learned within the classroom walls and in the world beyond the classroom. You can also use postreading activities to evaluate your students' understanding and responses.

Not surprisingly given their many functions, postreading activities are recommended widely (see, for example, Aebersold & Field, 1997; Alvermann, 2000; Bean et al., 1999; Ciborowski, 1992; Fountas & Pinnell, 1996; Gambrell & Almasi, 1996; Schoenbach et al., 1999; Wood et al., 1992; Yopp & Yopp, 1992), and in most classrooms they are used very frequently. In proposing possible postreading activities for SREs, we have again attempted to list a relatively small set of categories that suggest a large number of useful activities.

Questioning, either orally or in writing, is a frequently used and frequently warranted activity. Some teachers use questions almost exclusively as a means of assessing students' understanding. Although this is one valid use of questions, it is important to realize that questioning can serve many other instructional functions as well. Questions can encourage and promote students' higher order thinking, and they can nudge students' interpretations, analysis, and evaluation of the ideas created and gleaned from reading. Questions also can elicit creative and personal responses—when you ask, for example, "How did you feel when…?" or "What do you think would have happened in the experiment if…?" Of course, teachers are not the only ones who should be asking questions after reading. Students can ask questions of each other, they can ask you questions, and they can ask questions they plan to answer through further reading or by searching the Internet.

Discussion, whether it is in pairs or small groups or involves the entire class, is also very frequent and often very appropriate. Discussions can be powerful learning experiences for English language learners, but only if such learners feel comfortable and safe in the group and are able to take risks with their developing language. When a discussion activity is well structured, it reinforces the main points of the material, thereby helping students who may have had difficulty understanding some of the basics of the material. Discussion gives the teacher an opportunity to extend and raise the level of all students' thinking about the material; equally importantly, it gives students opportunities to offer their personal interpretations and responses to a text and to hear those of others. Discussion is also a vehicle for assessing whether or not reading goals have been achieved: to evaluate what went right about the reading experience, what went wrong, and what might be done differently in the future.

Building Connections is a tremendously important part of making reading meaningful for students. Only by helping students build connections between the ideas they encounter in reading and other parts of their lives can we ensure that they come to really value reading; read enough so that they get to be really proficient readers; and create, remember, and apply important understandings from reading. In multilingual classrooms, connections that would be automatically made by native speakers may have to be explicitly pointed out.

Several sorts of connections are important: relating the material to students' lives, relating it to current issues, and relating it to previously learned material. For example, after a group of Somali youngsters living in New York City read a description of the daily life of children in a small town in the Midwest, they might compare these children's daily lives to their lives in New York and their lives in Somalia.

Writing is a postreading task that probably should be used more frequently than it is. In recent years, there has been a good deal of well-warranted emphasis on the fact that reading and writing are complementary activities and ought often to be dealt with together. Writing can be used to help students discover and learn ideas, understandings, and their own responses; to reinforce concepts gleaned and created during reading; and to assist later recall of those ideas, understandings, and concepts.

Writing can be particularly useful for assisting English language learners, especially those in the earlier phases of English development. When teachers consistently use writing as a means of instruction, students are often more comfortable responding in writing than they are responding aloud. Also, for those in the early phases of English learning who have some native-language writing facility, allowing and encouraging writing in the native language is extremely beneficial. Of course, if the teacher cannot read or speak the students' native language, she or he must rely on the students' own incentives and accuracy. Even though this situation is less than optimal, writing without feedback is more beneficial than not writing at all. To make writing more feasible for students with minimal English skills, you may sometimes have to ask students to simply copy words or short parts of the text that the class is reading until they gain more proficiency.

Drama offers a range of opportunities for students to get actively involved in responding to what they have read. By drama, we refer to any sort of production involving action and movement: Short plays, skits, and pantomimes are among the many possibilities. Drama often affords English language learners special possibilities for learning and participating in class, because ideas and concepts in reading materials become more evident through facial expressions, gestures, and other movements. Additionally, practicing the lines of a play is likely to be a nonthreatening and fruitful way of building fluency.

Artistic, Graphic, and Nonverbal Activities constitute additional possibilities for postreading endeavors. In this broad category, we include visual art, graphics, music, dance, and media productions such as videos, slide shows, and audiotapes, along with constructive activities that you might not typically think of as artistic—often graphics of some sort, such as maps, charts, timelines, family trees, symbols, diagrams, and the like. Other possibilities include constructing models or bringing in artifacts that are somehow responses to the selected reading.

Artistic and Nonverbal Activities are particularly useful because they are fun, they may be a little different from typical school tasks, and they provide opportunities for students to express themselves in a variety of ways, thus creating situations in which students with various levels of English proficiency can excel. This is not to say that such activities are frills, something to be done just to provide variety. In many situations and for many students, including English learners, artistic and nonverbal activities offer great potential for learning information and for responding to what they have read.

Under Application and Outreach Activities we include both concrete and direct applications, such as conducting a survey after reading about simple survey methods, and less direct ones, such as having students work together to change some aspect of student interaction in your classroom after reading about summits and councils on racial tensions in the United States. We also include activities that extend beyond the campus. For instance, English language learners might interview their older relatives to see if things in their native country were actually the way they are described in the text they read in class. Obviously, there is a great range of application and outreach options.

We include Reteaching as the final postreading activity as a reminder that it is often needed. No matter how well you plan, or how sturdy a scaffold you construct for students, some students may not succeed as fully with a reading selection as they need to. When it becomes apparent that students have not achieved their reading goals or the level of understanding you deem necessary, reteaching is often in order, and the best time for reteaching is usually as soon as possible after students first encounter the material. In some cases, reteaching may consist simply of asking students to reread parts of a selection. In other cases, you may want to present a minilesson on some part of the text that has caused students problems. And in still other cases, students who have understood a particular aspect of the text or resource persons who speak the various languages spoken in your multilingual classroom may assist English language learners in achieving full understanding.

Sample SREs for Multilingual Classrooms

In this section, we will consider three SREs. The first is for the simplest situation a teacher in a multilingual classroom faces, one in which the reading task is readily manageable for both the native English speakers and the English language learners in the class. This situation requires a simple SRE and only one version of it. The second SRE we describe here is for a more challenging situation, one in which the reading task is fairly demanding for both the native English speakers and the English learners. This requires a more complex SRE, but still only one version of it. The third SRE we describe is for a still more challenging situation, one in which the reading task is somewhat demanding for native speakers and very demanding for English learners. This requires a still more complex SRE—a differentiated one in which some students engage in activities that others do not.

A Simple SRE for an Easy Narrative

Suppose that you are working in a class of 30 fifth graders that includes six English language learners, four of whom speak Spanish as their native language and two of whom speak Vietnamese. Suppose further that these six students have been in your school since kindergarten, that their conversational

English is quite good, and that the class is somewhat unusual in that all 24 native speakers are strong readers. The class is reading a straightforward and engaging narrative, Andrew Clements's award-winning *Frindle* (1998), and your primary purpose in having them read the story is simply that they enjoy this thought-provoking yet fast-paced, humorous tale. As a matter of fact, you deliberately picked this story because you thought that both your English learners and your native English speakers could handle it quite well. In this case, none of your students needs an elaborate SRE. Prereading instruction might consist of only a brief motivational activity; the during-reading portion of the SRE might consist entirely of students' reading the novel silently; and the postreading portion might simply involve their voluntarily discussing the parts of the story they found most humorous or interesting. So the SRE for *Frindle* would look like this:

Prereading:	Motivating
During-reading:	Silent Reading
Postreading:	Optional Small-Group Discussion

The SRE for *Frindle* is brief—because neither your students, the story itself, nor their purpose for reading the story requires a longer or more supportive SRE.

A More Substantial SRE for a Social Studies Text

Suppose that you are again working with this same class of fifth graders—a class that includes six English language learners whose conversational English is quite good—but this time you are working on social studies. The class is reading the first chapter of Michael L. Cooper's *Indian School: Teaching the White Man's Way* (1999), and their goal is to learn the most important information presented in this chapter. In this situation, you might provide prereading instruction that includes a motivational activity, the preteaching of some difficult vocabulary (e.g., *interpreter* and *proposition*), and a prequestioning activity in which students pose who, when, where, what, how, and why questions that they expect to be answered in the chapter. For the during-reading portion of the lesson, you might read part of the chapter orally and then have students read the rest of it silently, looking for answers to their questions. Finally, after students have finished the chapter, they might break into discussion groups of three or four and answer the questions they posed during prereading. After this, the groups might come together as a class and share their answers. So the SRE for this group of fifth graders reading the first chapter of *Indian School* looks like this:

Prereading:	Motivating
	Preteaching Vocabulary
	Prequestioning
During-reading:	Reading to Students
	Guided Reading
Postreading:	Small-Group Discussion
	Answering Questions
	Large-Group Discussion

Several characteristics of this SRE are particularly worth noting. For one thing, it is considerably more substantial than the SRE for *Frindle*. This is a sturdy structure, intended to support students successfully reading and learning from a more challenging text. For another, you selected the activities you did based on your assessment of your fifth-grade students, the selection they were reading, and the purpose of their reading it. And even though this combination of prereading, during-reading, and postreading activities was specifically designed for this particular combination of students, text, and purpose, it is only one of a number of combinations you could have selected. There is no unique combination of pre-, during-, and postreading activities that constitutes the ultimate or only choice. There are usually a number of choices that will be appropriate in a particular situation—along with an even larger number that will *not* be appropriate.

A Differentiated SRE for a Challenging Science Text

Now consider the planning you might do and the SRE you might construct for a chapter on waves in a fifth-grade science text (Hackett & Moyer, 1991). This is the same class as before—a class that includes six English language learners (four of whom speak Spanish as their native language and two of whom speak Vietnamese) whose conversational English is quite good. Nevertheless, they still need plenty of assistance in working with technical and academic language. Somewhat similarly, your native English speakers also need some assistance, though not as much as your English learners.

After reading the chapter, you decide that the important reading purposes are for students to understand the concept of waves, note some of the properties of waves, describe several different types of waves, and come away with the understanding that waves are important physical phenomena, a scientific topic they will meet again and learn more about in later grades. Thinking again about your students, you decide that they can handle the chapter, with your help. You also realize that your English learners will need more help than your native speakers, and that you therefore need to construct a differentiated SRE.

Again considering the chapter, you identify the specific concepts you want to stress, and you note that the chapter contains some material students do not need to deal with at the present time. You also note that the chapter is 10 pages and about 3,000 words long, and you estimate that it will take most of your native speakers 20 to 30 minutes to read through it once and most of your English learners perhaps 45 minutes to do so. You also realize, however, that reading it through once is not going to result in the sort of learning you want students to achieve, regardless of how proficient their English is.

All this thinking—these considerations about your students, the chapter, and the purposes of reading it—is in your mind as you plan the SRE. With these considerations in mind, you come up with a basic set of pre-, during-, and postreading activities that all students will participate in. But you also come up with additional activities intended for only your English learners. Figure 5.3 shows an outline of this SRE, with the additional activities for English learners in italics.

For the prereading that all students will do, you decide to include a motivational activity that will relate the topic of waves to something they are familiar with and can readily see and feel. You include a motivating activity because you believe that some sort of motivation is almost always a good idea and because students will not automatically be interested in waves. For the activity, you have students demonstrate a wave by arranging themselves in a line across the front of the room and then successively standing up and sitting down—much as fans do at a football game. Following this demonstration (students will probably have to practice the wave several times before it becomes rhythmic and looks very much like a wave), you point out that all waves have certain characteristics, among which are *amplitude* and *frequency*, two characteristics of waves that they will learn about. You then briefly explain these concepts and have students demonstrate several different wave forms, changing the amplitude of their wave by raising both hands rather than standing up and changing its frequency by standing up and sitting down or raising and lowering their hands at different rates. Finally, you draw several wave forms on the board to illustrate the different amplitudes and frequencies waves can have.

**FIGURE 5.3 Differentiated scaffolded reading experience for a chapter
on waves**

Planning		
Students	*Selection*	*Purpose*
Thirty fifth graders, including six English language learners	Chapter on waves in a fifth-grade science text	To understand and recall the concepts of waves, wave particles, and typical waves

Implementation		
Prereading Activities	*During-Reading Activities*	*Postreading Activities*
Motivating: Acting out the motion of a wave.	Reading to Students: Read the first section of the chapter aloud to students.	Discussion: Small groups discuss the chapter and add information to the discussion guide you gave them. *English learners may have dual-language discussion guides.*
Preteaching of Concepts: Teaching the concepts of amplitude and frequency.	Modifying the Text: Make an audiotape of the chapter available to English learners.	
Building Text-Specific Knowledge: Use the headings in the chapter to show its organization and have students predict some of its content.	Guided Reading: Students read the chapter silently, referring to the chapter headings on the board *or their dual-language outline* as they do so.	Reteaching: Reteach and extend major concepts as necessary. *English learners may need more reteaching.*
Using Students' Native Language: *Give English learners an outline of the chapter with headings in both English and Spanish or Vietnamese.*		Writing: Have students write an imaginative tale, perhaps one in which a wave goes berserk, and share their writing with the class. *English learners may or may not share orally.*

Motivating students also might include stressing that waves are an important scientific concept; reminding them that they are already familiar with some sorts of waves, such as those in oceans or lakes; and asking them what other sorts of waves play parts in their daily lives. Microwaves and television waves are likely responses.

Next you move to directly teaching the concepts of amplitude and frequency as they apply to waves. You begin by writing *amplitude* and *frequency* on the board; then you define each concept. As you give each definition, you try to act out the meaning with gestures and sketch a visual representation on the board. Because the amplitude of a wave is the height of the wave from its origin to its crest, your drawing of a wave includes a line from the base of the wave to its highest point. This, you explain, is the wave's amplitude. Because the frequency of a wave—the number of cycles of the wave that pass through a given point in a certain amount of time—is a dynamic concept, it is challenging to illustrate. But a memory from your childhood suggests an approach. You show the students an extended "slinky." Then, you draw a line on the board and, with a student's help, gradually pull the slinky through it, counting each circle on the slinky as it crosses the line. When you finish counting, you explain that you have just demonstrated a wave's frequency. You then remind students that their own wave had amplitude and frequency; its amplitude was perhaps a foot or two, and its frequency might have been 10 cycles a minute. Finally, you might ask students if they know of other words or phrases that express concepts similar to amplitude and frequency. ("Height," "size," and "how often something happens" are possible responses.) Of course, these brief activities have not fully taught these complex concepts, but having had this instruction, students will be better prepared to more fully understand them when they come up in the chapter.

To further prepare students to deal with both the content and the organization of the chapter, you next write the headings and subheadings from the chapter on the board, being sure to preserve the features of the text used to show subordination: For example, the superordinate topics might be printed all in capital letters and left justified, while the subordinate topics might have just the first letter of each word in capitals and be indented. Then you ask students to identify the superordinate and subordinate topics by noting their placement and the type of letters used. Finally, you ask students to brainstorm what they can learn just from reading the headings. For example, the first heading, "How Do Waves Transfer Energy?" clearly indicates that one thing waves do is transfer energy. You write this on the board and continue through the rest of the outline with the class, jotting down information students glean from the outline.

As an additional prereading activity for your English learners, you (or a student or community resource person) might create an outline that shows the chapter headings in both English and Spanish and another that shows the headings in both English and Vietnamese; you would then briefly go through each of these with your English learners. Note that you will need some other activity for your native English speakers at this time—perhaps gathering illustrations of waves and making a bulletin board display; perhaps some independent reading or journaling.

For during-reading activities that all students will undertake, you might plan to read the first section of the chapter aloud to ease them into it. After the first section, your native English speakers will finish the chapter by reading silently to themselves, referring to the list of headings on the board to be sure they understand the structure of the chapter. Before students begin their listening or reading, however, you remind them that they should not try to learn everything in the chapter, but should focus their attention on the topics discussed in the outline—the properties of waves and the different sorts of waves described.

Next you consider during-reading activities for your English learners. Because you have discovered that the six English learners in your class do particularly well when they can both read and listen to a challenging text, the major additional during-reading activity you plan is having students listen to a tape and follow along in the book. You carefully prepare the tape, reading slowly and enunciating clearly, and listen to the finished tape to be sure it is sharp and clear. Even so, you remind your English learners that they can stop and replay the tape whenever they need to, and that they will probably need to read or listen to much of the chapter more than once. You also encourage them to use the dual-language outlines of the chapter to track their progress and further their understanding. Because your English learners will require more time to read the chapter, you will again need to have an additional activity ready for your native speakers.

In deciding on postreading activities for all students, you take into account the fact that the chapter is challenging, and that you definitely want students to remember the major concepts dealt with in it. Therefore, you prepare and hand out a discussion guide that parallels the chapter outline you wrote on the board, and give students 20 minutes to discuss the concepts in it in small groups. You might or might not provide a dual-language version of the discussion guide. Each group is asked to focus on a particular concept and to select one or two important facts about that concept that they will teach to the rest of the class. You are careful to place the English learners in groups in which there are students who will be supportive of their participation. Afterward the class comes back together, and each group reports one piece of information they discovered about waves. Because it is likely that some students will need extra work with some concepts in the chapter, you might offer to join any group in which students expressed such a need.

Next, because many of your students have a creative side and because you believe that waves and related concepts might prompt interesting creative writing or other creative activities, you suggest that students work independently or in small groups to create stories, poems, drawings, and perhaps even dramas in which waves play central roles. One idea you might suggest, in case some students need a prompt to get started, is that they create something in which a wave goes berserk. (Note that you may need to teach the word *berserk* to most students.) Finally, once students have completed their creations, they either present them orally or post them around the room.

There are no totally separate postreading activities for your English learners. However, you realize that English learners are particularly likely to need extra work on some of the concepts covered, and you are prepared to spend extra time with them if need be. Similarly, you understand that some English learners may not want to do oral presentations; at the same time, you know that if they do oral presentations and are successful at them it will be a very positive experience. You therefore monitor your English learners carefully as they are working on their creative writing endeavors and offer guidance about making oral presentations on an individual basis.

All in all, most students in the class might spend three or four days with this SRE, and some English language learners as well as some other students (not all of your native English speakers are likely to be equally strong readers) might spend an additional day. Your purpose in designing these activities, and the purpose in planning and carrying out any SRE, is a straightforward one: You want to do everything possible to ensure that *all* students have a successful reading experience. As we suggested before, we believe that a successful reading experience is one in which students glean and construct meaning from the selection, learn from it, respond to it, and enjoy it. Importantly, our goal includes students' realizing that they have been successful and recognizing that they have dealt competently with the selection. Of course, not all students will be totally successful with every selection they read, but as much as possible, students need to conclude their reading of a selection feeling that they worked on it, that the effort they put into it paid off in at least partial success, and that similar effort in the future will result in similar payoffs. If students are to become lifelong readers who not only *can* read but voluntarily *choose to* read, they must believe in themselves as readers.

Concluding Remarks

An SRE is a particular kind of lesson plan that relies heavily on the concept of scaffolding and on a number of other instructional concepts developed and validated over the past three decades (Fitzgerald & Graves, in press; Graves

& Graves, 2003). More specifically, an SRE is a set of prereading, during-reading, and postreading activities designed to assist a particular group of students in successfully reading, understanding, learning from, and enjoying a particular reading selection. In our judgment, SREs can be an extremely important part—albeit only one part—of a comprehensive and balanced reading and language program for both English language learners and native English speakers.

We believe that SREs should be used frequently in multilingual classrooms. They should be used whenever the class as a whole or a sizable group of students within the class is reading a text that they will be more successful with if they get some assistance from you. SREs markedly increase the likelihood that students' reading experiences will be successful and rewarding, and repeatedly engaging in successful and rewarding reading experiences will produce students who are better readers, are more knowledgeable, more fully understand the topics they read about, and are more likely to become independent and lifelong readers. Success breeds success.

Finally, there is the matter of how much scaffolding to provide. From a conceptual standpoint, we believe that the question has a straightforward answer: You provide enough scaffolding that students will succeed with the reading they are asked to do, but not so much that they do not have to work to achieve that success. From a practical standpoint, however, we believe that the answer is anything but straightforward; in fact, it is in answering this question that much of the art of teaching comes into play. As a professional, you must first become as informed as possible about your students, the subjects you teach, the texts you use, and the goals you have for your students. Then, you need to both ask and answer the question of how much scaffolding it will take to lead those students to successful reading experiences while at the same time challenging them enough to keep them actively involved, in ways that will produce real learning.

REFERENCES

Aebersold, J.A., & Field, M.L. (1997). *From reader to reading teacher: Issues and strategies for second language classrooms.* Cambridge, UK: Cambridge University Press.

Alvermann, D.E. (2000). Classroom talk about texts: Is it dear, cheap, or a bargain at any price? In B.M. Taylor, M.F. Graves, & P. van den Broek (Eds.), *Reading for meaning: Fostering comprehension in the middle grades* (pp. 136–151). New York: Teachers College Press; Newark, DE: International Reading Association.

Anderson, L.M. (1989). Classroom instruction. In M.C. Reynolds (Ed.), *Knowledge base for the beginning teacher* (pp. 101–115). New York: Pergamon.

Anderson, R.C., & Armbruster, B.B. (1990). Some maxims for learning and instruction. *Teachers College Record, 91,* 396–408.

Applebee, A.N., & Langer, J.L. (1983). Reading and writing as natural language activities. *Language Arts, 60*(2), 68–175.

Bean, T.W., Valerio, P.C., & Stevens, L. (1999). Content area literacy instruction. In L.B. Gambrell, L.M. Morrow, S.B. Neuman, & M. Pressley (Eds.), *Best practices in literacy instruction* (pp. 175–192). New York: Guilford.

Beck, I.L., McKeown, M.G., Hamilton, R., & Kucan, L. (1997). *Questioning the author: An approach for enhancing student engagement with text.* Newark, DE: International Reading Association.

Beed, P.L., Hawkins, E.M., & Roller, C.M. (1991). Moving learners toward independence: The power of scaffolded instruction. *The Reading Teacher, 44,* 648–655.

Betts, E. (1946). *Foundations of reading.* New York: American Book.

Brown, A.N., & Palincsar, A.M. (1989). Guided cooperative learning and individual knowledge acquisition. In L.B. Resnick (Ed.), *Knowing, learning, and instruction: Essays in honor of Robert Glaser* (pp. 393–451). Hillsdale, NJ: Erlbaum.

Cazden, C.B. (1992). *Whole language plus: Essays in literacy in the United States and New Zealand.* New York: Teachers College Press.

Ciborowski, J. (1992). *Textbooks and the students who can't read them: A guide to teaching content.* Cambridge, MA: Brookline Books.

Cooke, C.L. (2002). *The effects of scaffolding multicultural short stories on students' comprehension, response, and attitudes.* Unpublished doctoral dissertation, University of Minnesota, Minneapolis.

Fitzgerald, J., & Graves, M.F. (in press). *Scaffolding reading experiences for English-language learners.* Norwood, MA: Christopher-Gordon.

Fountas, I.C., & Pinnell, G.S. (1996). *Guided reading: Good first teaching for all students.* Portsmouth, NH: Heinemann.

Fournier, D.N.E., & Graves, M.F. (in press). Scaffolding adolescents' comprehension of short stories. *Journal of Adolescent & Adult Literacy.*

Gambrell, L.B., & Almasi, J.E. (Eds.). (1996). *Lively discussions! Fostering engaged reading.* Newark, DE: International Reading Association.

Graves, M.F., & Graves, B.B. (2003). *Scaffolding reading experiences: Designs for student success* (2nd ed.). Norwood, MA: Christopher-Gordon.

Graves, M.F., Juel, C., & Graves, B.B. (2001). *Teaching reading in the 21st century* (2nd ed.). Boston: Allyn & Bacon.

Graves, M.F., & Liang, L.A. (in press). On-line resources for fostering understanding and higher-level thinking in senior high school students. *National Reading Conference Yearbook.*

Jenkins, J.J. (1976). Four points to remember: A tetrahedral model of memory experiments. In L.S. Cermak & F.I.M. Craik (Eds.), *Levels of processing in human memory* (pp. 429–446). Hillsdale, NJ: Erlbaum.

King, M.L., Jr. (1963, August 28). *I have a dream* [Speech delivered on the steps at the Lincoln Memorial in Washington, DC]. New York: Scholastic.

Palincsar, A.S. (1986). The role of dialogue in providing scaffolded instruction. *Educational Psychologist, 21,* 73–93.

Pearson, P.D. (1996). Reclaiming the center. In M.F. Graves, P. van den Broek, & B.M. Taylor (Eds.), *The first R: A right of all children* (pp. 259–274). New York: Teachers College Press; Newark, DE: International Reading Association.

Pearson, P.D., & Gallagher, M. (1983). The instruction of reading comprehension. *Contemporary Educational Psychology, 8,* 317–344.

Pressley, M. (1998). *Reading instruction that works: The case for balanced teaching.* New York: Guilford.

Pressley, M. (2000). What should comprehension instruction be the instruction of? In M.L. Kamil, P.B. Mosenthal, P.D. Pearson, & R. Barr (Eds.), *Handbook of reading research* (Vol. 3, pp. 545–562). Mahwah, NJ: Erlbaum.

RAND Reading Study Group. (2002). *Reading for understanding: Toward an R&D program in reading comprehension.* Santa Monica, CA: RAND Education.

Raphael, T.M. (2000). Balancing literature and instruction: Lessons from the Book Club project. In B.M. Taylor, M.F. Graves, & P. van den Broek (Eds.), *Reading for meaning: Fostering comprehension in the middle grades* (pp. 70–94). New York: Teachers College Press; Newark, DE: International Reading Association.

Readence, J.E., Moore, D.W., & Rickelman, R.J. (2000). *Prereading activities for content area reading and learning* (3rd ed.). Newark, DE: International Reading Association.

Richardson, J.S. (2000). *Read it aloud: Using literature in the secondary content classroom.* Newark, DE: International Reading Association.

Routman, R. (2000). *Conversations.* Portsmouth, NH: Heinemann.

Schoenbach, R., Greenleaf, C., Cziko, C., & Hurwitz, L. (1999). *Reading for understanding: A guide to improving reading in middle and high school classes.* San Francisco: Jossey-Bass.

Snow, C.E., Burns, M.S., & Griffin, P. (Eds.). (1998). *Preventing reading difficulties in young children.* Washington, DC: National Academy Press.

Stauffer, R.G. (1969). *Directing reading maturity as a cognitive process.* New York: Harper & Row.

Taylor, B.M., Pearson, P.D., Clark, K., & Walpole, S. (2000). Effective schools and accomplished teachers: Lessons about primary-grade reading instruction in low-income schools. *The Elementary School Journal, 101,* 121–165.

Terrell, T.D. (1981). The natural approach in bilingual education. In California State Department of Education (Ed.), *Schooling and language minority students: A theoretical framework* (pp. 117–146). Los Angeles: Evaluation, Dissemination and Assessment Center, California State University.

Tierney, R.J., & Readence, J.E. (2000). *Reading strategies and practices: A compendium* (5th ed.). Boston: Allyn & Bacon.

Vygotsky, L.S. (1978). *Mind in society: The development of higher psychological processes* (M. Cole, V. John-Steiner, S. Scribner, & E. Souberman, Eds. and Trans.). Cambridge, MA: Harvard University Press. (Original work published 1934)

Warton-McDonald, R., Pressley, M., & Hampston, J.M. (1998). Literacy instruction in nine first-grade classrooms: Teacher characteristics and student achievement. *The Elementary School Journal, 99,* 101–128.

Wood, D.J., Bruner, J.S., & Ross, G. (1976). The role of tutoring in problem-solving. *Journal of Child Psychology and Psychiatry, 17*(2), 89–100.

Wood, K.D., Lapp, D., & Flood, J. (1992). *Guiding readers through text: A review of study guides.* Newark, DE: International Reading Association.

Yopp, R.H., & Yopp, H.K. (1992). *Literature-based reading activities*. Boston: Allyn & Bacon.

CHILDREN'S LITERATURE CITED

Byers, B. (1987). Sam's storm. In M. Aulls & M.F. Graves (Eds.), *Going to the fair and other stories*. New York: Scholastic.

Clements, A. (1998). *Frindle*. New York: Aladdin.

Cooper, M.L. (1999). *Indian school: Teaching the white man's way*. New York: Clarion Books.

Hackett, J.K., & Moyer, R.H. (1991). Waves. In *Science in your world, Level 6*. New York: Macmillan/McGraw-Hill.

Jimenez, F. (1999). *The circuit: Stories from the life of a migrant child*. Boston: Houghton.

Simon, S. (2001). *Earthquakes*. New York: Scholastic.

CHAPTER 6

Making Content Instruction Accessible for English Language Learners

Ana Hernández

The everyday demands of classroom instruction increase in complexity from year to year—with respect to curricular demands, accountability, and the diversity of the student population. New state frameworks and instructional trends require grade-level curricular standards to continually change. The demands of accountability vis-à-vis state standards and student performance on standardized tests influence district policies regarding instructional practices and how to best address the needs of the burgeoning numbers of English language learners.

In addition, the linguistic diversity of English language learners has important implications for the design of programs intended to address the range of levels of English language learners' oral fluency, literacy skills, and cognitive growth. A variety of materials can be used to engage learners in English language content instruction; however, if these students are to attain grade-level standards in English language subject matter instruction, they must master communicative and cognitive skills as well as master strategies for reading and learning from expository text, the staple of content instruction and the dominant type of text included in materials employed to teach content. This formidable mix of demands requires an answer to these two questions: (1) How can teachers effectively manage the complexity of skill, content, and English language development instruction and also make this instruction accessible to English language learners? (2) What are the implications for determining appropriate instructional materials?

This chapter will present ideas and strategies to help teachers optimize the education of English language learners in subject matter instruction. The potential to teach language and to enable access to learning across content areas will be addressed through four key instructional dimensions: communication-based instruction, content-based instruction, cognitive development, and study skills. Implications for appropriate instructional materials will also be addressed.

Communication-Based Instruction for English Learners

Communication-based instruction can be an effective tool for providing English language learners access to content area learning. Communication-based instruction is designed to parallel the way children acquire their first language. Krashen's (1982) acquisition-learning hypothesis holds that infants acquire language subconsciously rather than cognitively learning the language (see Crawford, chapter 7 in this volume, for an expanded description). When learning content in a second language, students need instructional approaches that allow them to interact with and construct meaning from lessons presented in class. Language is the medium for learning and communicating important subject matter. For students learning *in* the language rather than *about* the language, effective communication is interactive, authentic, and meaningful, with ample opportunities to hear and respond in the target language and to get feedback from native speakers, the teacher, instructional assistants, volunteers, and other English language learners.

Direct and indirect modeling of English language structures and conventions with corrective feedback can and should be included in communication-based instruction through directed lessons according to Fillmore and Snow (2000). Gersten and Baker (2000) also believe that English learners need formal feedback if they are to learn the language; however, they point out that merging content instruction with English language development usually truncates the amount of time devoted to learning the second language. They believe that sheltered instruction (instruction designed for making sure English language learners understand content instruction) usually does not include adequate English language development in the context of writing. Like Snow and Fillmore (2000), they believe that this phenomenon has a deleterious effect on student writing.

The written conventions of the target language should be linked to oral communication and content through daily language lessons in writing, spelling, and grammar that are connected to the related readings of the content curriculum, not taught as isolated and unrelated skills. Connecting daily language lessons to related reading succeeds in linking written language conventions to oral communication and content by demonstrating for English language learners the ways in which writers use literary devices such as figures of speech, similes, idiomatic expressions, metaphors, imagery, analogies, and the prosodic features (rhythm, intonation, and phrasing) of the dialect. The readings help demonstrate the use of grammatical structures and spelling conventions across genres of literature and expose English language learners to new vocabulary development in context rather than in isolated word lists that have no meaning or connections to their world (see Dutro & Moran, chapter 10 in this volume).

In content instruction, it is important for students to learn the structures of the English language in order to interpret the work of related readings across subject matter instruction. The ability of English language learners to succeed in "content" learning has to do with how well they can infer meaning, draw conclusions, learn terminology, analyze problems, and synthesize information from various sources, which means they need to transfer and apply reading and language conventions across the curriculum. Students make gains in language acquisition by interacting with speakers of the English language in meaningful contexts, and their English language oral fluency increases as they begin to respond and sustain communication in the target language— just as accuracy in reading and writing develops with daily involvement in purposeful application. When language is regarded as a medium of learning, it offers a context for communicating the thinking process in the subject matter without the need to translate content.

The Benefits of Sheltered Language Strategies

Sheltered language strategies allow students to develop knowledge of subject matter areas through their English language. Through these strategies, teachers ensure that lessons are comprehensible to learners of different English language proficiency levels and also provide English language development (see Graves & Fitzgerald, chapter 5; García & Beltrán, chapter 9; and Dutro & Moran, chapter 10, in this volume).

An effective sheltered instruction technique is to draw from the learners' background knowledge in the area of study. Relating the subject matter to the students can involve not only asking questions regarding what they have learned in school about the content but also eliciting what students know about the topic from their own life experiences and personal connections. If the teacher observes that students lack sufficient background or personal information or connections about the subject, then lesson planning needs to present basic foundations of the subject matter through the use of visuals, realia, hands-on experiences, guest speakers, field trips, or related readings. During content instruction, complex concepts and information can be clarified through demonstrations and experimentation. Lesson delivery should include simplification of explanations and vocabulary development by means of showing examples, demonstrating differences and similarities, and speaking with simpler syntax and added gestures. As the students acquire more oral fluency and comprehension, the complexity of content that they can handle can increase gradually as a result of their more frequent communication in context-reduced discourse (Mohan, 1986). It is important to maintain a comfortable participatory learning environment that allows students to practice their English language without fear of making errors, seeking clarification, or taking linguistic risks.

Giving students an amount of "wait time" to interpret information or to process questions related to content is encouraged before demanding a response. Students learning content via a new language may have difficulties with cognitively demanding tasks or with discussions presented in context-reduced situations with few external supports for meaning. Students may want to participate, but they may have difficulty formulating a response or incorporating appropriate content vocabulary learned in class. It is important for the teacher to frequently check learners' comprehension by collecting and evaluating student work samples in the subject area. Monitoring a student's degree of complexity in the use of the English language is another way of measuring progress in English language acquisition through communication-based instruction.

In addition to the sheltered strategies presented for communication and comprehension of content learning, there are other approaches to stimulate a communicative setting in the classroom. The next two sections present opportunities for positive peer and teacher-student interactions in a community of learners that allows for negotiation of meaning through conversations and discussions.

The Benefits of Student Interaction

English language learners benefit from language modeling and reinforcement of linguistic structures through peer interaction in the classroom. Students then have the opportunity to learn the target language in a natural communicative setting through the use of authentic and meaningful language. Providing an opportunity for daily peer interaction in the classroom allows for the academic and language success of the students. The interaction gives students a chance to develop an understanding of one another's culture. This enables positive cross-cultural attitudes to develop among the learners because the diverse languages and cultures represented in the classroom are assigned equal status (see George et al., chapter 13; Boyd-Batstone, chapter 14; and Gallego et al., chapter 16, in this volume).

There are programs that tend to group students in separate classrooms by language dominance; native speakers are grouped together for their daily program, while English language learners are assigned to other classrooms. If at all possible, native speakers and English language learners need the opportunity to participate jointly in content learning through team teaching situations in which student groups are integrated for instruction (see Coppola, chapter 8 in this volume). According to Cummins (1981), children best learn the English language when they are actively involved in the process of communicating with one another. Therefore, activities should include the integration and joint participation of speakers of the target language with English learners whenever possible (see also Crawford, chapter 7 in this volume).

Peer participation incorporates collaborative learning through mixed groupings comprised of various levels of language production and content expertise. A variety of groupings—pairs, triads, and small groups—can facilitate learning and meet the linguistic and instructional demands of all learners. Students in such settings have the opportunity to gain insights on how others access curricular knowledge and process information in their English language. Social learning theorists have shown that students learn and are motivated by observing others' actions and their consequences (Bandura, 1977)—for example, by observing someone persist in a task and achieve success. Student motivation can, therefore, be strongly influenced by the study behaviors modeled in class: They can observe how other learners manipulate the expository material contained in textbooks, handouts, computer-generated printouts, or library references. There is no better way to learn reading strategies for nonfiction material than to see other students infer meaning from a text. Interaction encourages students to become educational and social partners in the process of learning. Such partnerships lower the anxiety attached to seeking necessary assistance when presented with new concepts or difficult content materials in class. The resulting opportunities to verbalize content knowledge open doors for authentic peer dialogue.

The checklist in Figure 6.1 can be used with a partner to augment reading comprehension of nonfiction texts in the English language. It also can be used as a guide for teachers previewing text before reading or monitoring comprehension during the reading process.

FIGURE 6.1 Strategies for enhancing reading comprehension

DIRECTIONS: Use this checklist as a guide to help you understand the material when you read the selection alone or with a partner.

1. Preview the material: What text features do I need to find by scanning text?

___ Title and subtitles   ___ Labels

___ Illustrations and/or photographs   ___ Graphics, visual aids, maps

___ Boldface and/or italicized words

2. Predict content: What is the topic? What are the main ideas?

Write a prediction: _____

_____

3. Check for comprehension: Do I understand the material?

___ Quickly skim through the material to get an overview.

___ Divide the reading selection into smaller sections.

___ Read first and last paragraphs to understand what the material will cover.

___ Begin reading sections; stop to summarize and ask questions.

___ Reread if confusing, and stop more frequently to summarize.

___ Refer to graphics and visual aids to further clarify main ideas.

___ Clarify vocabulary by using context clues and checking glossary or dictionary.

___ Read summaries at the end of each section or chapter to identify important concepts.

___ Write down the main idea for each section or page you read.

If you are working with a partner:

___ Tell your partner what you have just read.

___ Your partner will ask you questions to clarify your understanding.

___ Have your partner tell you what he or she has read.

___ Ask your partner questions to clarify his or her understanding.

___ Together, write or make a graphic organizer to summarize the information.

___ Repeat this process as long as needed.

4. Key Words: Which words helped you understand the text?

List vocabulary related to the topic: _____

_____

5. Clarification. What information is unclear?

I/we need clarification in the following areas: _____

6. Reading Level: Was the reading level appropriate? ___ yes ___ no

Select one: Difficult   Just right   Simple

I was/We were unable to understand the text because _____

The Benefits of Teacher-Student Interaction

Equally important for English language learning is modeling by and interaction with the teacher. Teachers must provide students with modeling of the strategies needed to comprehend content material and content instruction. Teachers can, for example, model active listening skills by maintaining eye contact with a speaker and watching his or her gestures. Teachers can direct students how to use textbooks, reference materials, or environmental print in the classroom to enhance understanding of the subject matter. Learning to take notes, make an outline, pose a question, or otherwise seek help can also be demonstrated.

Effective teacher-student interaction involves interacting equally with all students during whole-class or small-group instruction. Providing students with equal access to the curriculum may require certain academic interventions, mediated structures, or other additional assistance. It may be necessary to prompt or give additional response time to newcomers or beginning-proficiency students who are in need of teacher guidance and reassurance.

A critical aspect of the development of language and content learning is providing a setting for English language learners to negotiate meaning in daily instructional interactions. *Negotiation of meaning*, a term coined by immersion experts (Cloud et al., 2000), is the process by which participants arrive at understanding one another. It is the collaboration needed in conversations or discussions to express needs, ideas, thoughts, and intentions; it also involves helping others extend and refine their communication skills. The strategies used in the negotiation of meaning are both verbal and nonverbal. A verbal strategy might involve expanding answers to refine the language with the use of semantics, settling on an appropriate rate of speech or providing simplified vocabulary, paraphrasing, or sentence structure to clarify meaning. A nonverbal strategy might incorporate facial expressions and gestures to match what students hear with what they see or do.

As students begin to acquire higher proficiencies in the English language, teacher-student interactions need to gradually model more complexities in language structure. According to the input hypothesis of Krashen (1985), input promotes progress when it is more advanced than the learner's level of proficiency. The learner acquires the ability to function in a new language by listening to input a little more sophisticated than his or her actual level of language production. Vygotsky's (1978) theory of the Zone of Proximal Development is another way to view this means of language learning. According to Vygotsky, children can learn within a range: tasks children can complete independently are at one end of the range, and tasks they cannot complete, even with assistance, are at the other end. The zone most productive for children is between these extremes, where there are tasks children can complete when assisted by a knowledgeable or more competent other.

Face-to-face interaction with the teacher tends to provide useful visual cues and nonverbal language to augment comprehension of subject material presented in the lesson. This provides the opportunity for English language learners to engage in content learning through the process of creative construction. The teacher has an opportunity in the classroom to model correct language use and to provide indirect and direct error correction. He or she can provide optimal language input and allow for maximum student output by utilizing higher-order thinking and questioning skills (see Dutro & Moran, chapter 10 in this volume).

Content-Based Instruction for English Learners

According to Cloud and colleagues (2000), there are three goals for content area instruction, which the authors term "goals of integrated instruction": content, language, and general skills goals. *Content goals* include conceptual learning of knowledge and skills required by the subject matter. *Language goals* address learning the precise vocabulary words and sentence patterns needed to communicate content. Achieving *general skills goals* means attaining study skills that promote both language and content learning. In content-based instruction, students are not only learning to communicate in the language of the subject; they are communicating *about* the subject by constructing meaning.

Subject matter is taught through communicating content and concepts in a meaningful construct, not through rote drills or practice of isolated skills at the end of a lesson. English language learners need to use language in purposeful contexts as a means to learn content. Instructional approaches should include progression from concrete to abstract thinking, including a rich use of oral and written language forms. Instructional units may be presented through thematic and interdisciplinary approaches so as to allow students to transfer concepts across curricular areas. Learning to create and compile sets of data for a math project, for example, can result in students understanding how to interpret charts, tables, and graphs in science or social studies textbooks (see Crawford, chapter 7 in this volume).

Lessons may need to be sequenced with careful planning so that students can be exposed to information needed as a prerequisite for another subject matter, particularly in the areas of math and science. For example, students may need to have a math lesson on liquid measurement before they can perform a particular science experiment. English language learning should not be a barrier to learning scientific thinking requiring analysis, inference, synthesis, formulation of conclusions, or evaluation; these higher-order thinking skills appear in content standards across the curriculum and are necessary for students' success in subject instruction (see Laturnau, chapter 12 in this volume). Students should be guided to see that these thinking processes are common in everyday life situations; lessons can then be adapted to demonstrate how the critical thinking used in their personal lives can be transferred to academic thought.

Classroom lessons incorporate the use of the English language to communicate content standards and follow-up activities. The underlying premise of content-based instruction is based on student-centered activities, the performance of which ensures comprehension and mastery of lessons. According to Mohan (1986), the term *activity* refers not just to something we get English language learners to do but rather to a combination of performed action and acquired theoretical understanding. In Mohan's understanding, an activity is a basis for a knowledge framework. Activities need to include the daily practice of newly learned skills through experiential approaches and an understanding of how what is learned is linked to the activity; Mohan refers to this as an *expository* approach, in that it is verbal and explicit. It is the combination of an action situation and a theoretical knowledge structure that creates the framework for an activity.

English language learners need to be exposed to both sides of the knowledge framework. One side is addressed by involving students in general theoretical concepts through communicative approaches and support from visual aids. The purpose of this component of the framework is to explain background information of concepts and classification of the topic; present the principles through methods, techniques, and strategies; or evaluate goals and appropriateness through the use of visual displays found in graphs, tables, charts, symbols, and other representations of the rules and norms (Mohan, 1986). The other side engages practical knowledge as presented through a discourse of pictures, film, drama, or experiential events. These specific, practical aspects of knowledge demonstrate concrete examples within the topic material by describing, sequencing, and making decisions in action situations (Mohan, 1986). Pictures or photostories in manuals or guides provide the "who/what, where, and when" of the real world. Films or videos demonstrate processes, procedures, or routines for science and math. Acting out a situation can present the conflicts, alternatives, or decisions involved when addressing school safety, first aid administration, or substance abuse. Incorporating experiential activities that relate to the English language learners' background knowledge connects the framework to what they already know or have experienced in life (see Graves & Fitzgerald, chapter 5, and García & Beltrán, chapter 9, in this volume).

Graphic organizers can help the visual representation of knowledge in content-based instruction. Their purpose is to organize information by using labels to arrange important aspects of concepts or topics into patterns. Organizers are used in a variety of ways to facilitate prereading, postreading, prewriting, revising, summarizing, comparing, and other arrays of symbolic information (configurations and organizational patterns that display information graphically prior to developing an essay, responding to a reading, summarizing information, researching a report, etc.). The implications are dramatic for the instruction of English language learners because the process of preparing arrays of symbolic information helps them build a framework for learning key ideas and vocabulary. Bromley, Irwin-DeVitis, and Modlo (1995) argue that graphic organizers help simplify the learning process and produce understanding. Organizers help construct knowledge into categories, which assists the brain in sorting through thought and language. The organizers provide mental tools for the English language learner to remember key ideas through a combination of visual and verbal language. Bromley et al. describe four basic organizers through which knowledge is constructed: *hierarchical*, *conceptual*, *sequential*, and *cyclical*. Hierarchical graphics are main concepts ranked by levels and sublevels, such as a flow chart of linear classifications. A conceptual organizer is a central idea supported by facts, such as a mind web or Venn diagram. A sequential category provides a chronological order of events, as in a timeline. Cyclical patterns depict circular successions or cycles (e.g., precipitation, evaporation, and condensation in the rain/water cycle). English language learners can augment their comprehension in subject matter instruction by learning to select and apply graphic organizers to construct meaning in content learning.

Accessing Comprehension Skills in Content Learning

Comprehension is the outcome of a reader interacting with a text and constructing meaning. Because the ability to process information resides in the reader, the cognitive processes that lead to more advanced comprehension skills can be taught to English language learners. Texts can be used as references when students discuss points of view or main ideas and support them with examples. The teacher can check for accuracy when students summarize information, sequence events, infer conclusions, or compare and contrast points of view. Students who are unable to access a text due to the readability level may have high cognitive ability but lack proficient literacy in the second language. These students can still benefit from class discussions by adding their own personal experiences or observations related to the topic, while the teacher attempts to bridge the gap between what students already know and what they are about to learn. The text can be read to the students, or recorded text can be played. As the students acquire content literacy in the English language, they will be able to increase their participation in reading and writing appropriately for their age and level of proficiency (see Coppola, chapter 8, and George et al., chapter 13, in this volume).

Students can become more efficient in locating and processing written information when they establish a purpose for reading and learn strategies for inferring meaning from content materials. Many times, English language learners are confronted with reading material in a subject matter that is beyond their reading level. Comprehension strategies for content areas can be taught in lessons to address their literacy needs. Before reading a text, the instructor can provide a brief overview of the content material being presented to formulate a purpose for the reading. A stimulating class discussion can access students' backgrounds and cultural knowledge of the subject prior to the lesson; students can discover and better understand ideas through sharing concrete experiences and examples before reading the text.

When students *are* reading the material, they may need teacher guidance in order to access information. The teacher may provide guided questioning; model dividing the text into sections; direct students on how to use study guides, outlines, or notes; or even teach how to set a pace for their reading. In setting a pace for reading, students need to know how to determine what parts to read intensively and what parts to ignore; it is imperative to show English language learners how to determine when passages can be skimmed or scanned. Chapters or books do not need to be read from cover to cover or in a linear way; students can skip sections, flip pages, find key headings, browse, tab pages, or attach sticky notes. Knowing how to use the parts of a book—indexes, tables of contents, glossaries, maps, tables, or charts—also can help English language learners access information quickly. English language learners need to understand the difference in format between fiction and nonfiction materials because ultimately students will need to use nonfiction materials to research information when furthering their studies in a particular area. It is important to point out to students how expository information is organized in textbooks because the textbooks can serve as models for students as they write outlines, notes, or reports and can facilitate comprehension.

The list of steps in Figure 6.2 can assist English language learners in accessing information from textbooks, particularly when the material presented is beyond the reading level of their English language. The teacher can use this guide with his or her students when textbooks in various subject areas are introduced in class.

By embedding language objectives in content instruction, one can explain how mechanics and conventions in one subject matter parallel written formats in other curricular areas. Students need to be aware that making an outline, writing a summary, adding supportive details, and comparing and contrasting two topics are interdisciplinary skills applicable across the curriculum. Once students learn the value of these academic cognitive skills in one subject area, they can learn how to transfer strategies learned from one domain to

FIGURE 6.2 Guide to enhancing comprehension of features in content area textbooks

1. Provide an overview and allow students to preview the material.
2. Assess students' backgrounds and experiences related to the subject matter before beginning a unit.
3. Demonstrate layout and features of the textbook by identifying the purpose of the following elements: title page, table of contents, unit sections, glossary, index, appendixes, and other references.
4. Examine format of text pages by identifying chapter headings, subtitles, boldface/italicized words, columns, margins, guide words/vocabulary.
5. Point out the use of visual elements designed to assist with comprehension of text: illustrations, photographs, charts, graphs, symbols, maps, diagrams, tables, chronologies.
6. Guide students regarding how to find introductions, directions for procedures, definitions of terms, steps for experiments, enrichment activities, study guides, review questions, and summaries.
7. Explain how to cut through text density and technical vocabulary to find important passages and key concepts using skimming or scanning.
8. Describe importance of concise language in explaining certain terms, symbols, and expressions, as in mathematics.
9. Demonstrate differences between primary and secondary sources cited in textbooks, such as diaries, journals, autobiographies, other literature, links to arts/technology.
10. Monitor reading comprehension as students work with textbooks to read and locate information.

another. English language learners have to know how to recognize high-frequency words that appear in texts in order to facilitate the reading process and increase fluency. Many high-frequency word lists are available from publishers and can be included in reading/writing folders for students or enlarged for use as classroom charts.

It is important to provide English language learners with independent reading time when they can research information with a reading buddy who can help interpret important information from texts or demonstrate the use of technology for research in the classroom. Students should be encouraged to consult with peers and engage in small-group discussions about their topics of study, taking advantage of materials used in class. By demonstrating how ideas and text are bound together in nonfiction materials, teachers can enable English language learners to succeed at the tasks of reading, writing, and comprehending subject matter.

Accessing Content Vocabulary

Proper language development depends on the explicit and implicit language of the curriculum (Genesse, 1994). We employ explicit language when we teach language arts through standards, the language skills learned progressively at each grade level. Implicit language is engaged when language is the medium and not the objective of the lesson. Language is embedded in the curriculum, allowing for authentic continuous language development and exposure to the target language during content learning.

It is essential to familiarize English language learners with clear content vocabulary related to the unit of study. Excessive vocabulary, however, impedes students' ability to understand lessons or materials presented in class by obscuring the message and overloading students with sentence complexity and difficult vocabulary unrelated to the content standard. Content-obligatory language is related to mastery of content standards (Cloud et al., 2000); it is the vocabulary required to understand and communicate about the content. Content-obligatory language can be entered in student journals as it is introduced in lessons; students can then be asked to explain and illustrate obligatory language through examples. Vocabulary charts also can be hung in the classroom as environmental print for English language learners to reference as needed. More abstract vocabulary can be introduced by providing concrete experiences (e.g., observing *metamorphosis* in a lab setting or walking along a stream to learn about *erosion*)—supplemented by visual aids such as pictures, photographs, diagrams, videotapes, pictionaries, and transparencies—and by having students create their own graphic organizers. Teacher manuals and support materials can provide numerous other suggestions for teaching vocabulary development. The organizer in Figure 6.3 can help students define content-obligatory language in subject-area instruction.

Content-*compatible* language stretches, refines, and expands language growth beyond the students' present levels of attainment. Compatible language is not required for the mastery of content; its acquisition is driven by students' expected growth in English language development and subject-area learning. Rich experiences in vocabulary development—such as learning multiple word meanings, doing word studies, using word banks, or making semantic maps—can yield rich word usage and an understanding of the contexts in which words appear. Students can also enter content-compatible vocabulary in journals, learning logs, and study guides. In daily writings, students can demonstrate understanding of key elements of language by comparing and contrasting definitions, providing synonyms or antonyms, writing their own definitions, or summarizing information using the new vocabulary.

When reading in content areas, students can attempt to read entire paragraphs even if they encounter unfamiliar words, so as to determine whether certain words are essential to the comprehension of a passage. Is the meaning clear, or is it uncertain because of unknown vocabulary?

FIGURE 6.3 Organizer for teaching content vocabulary

DIRECTIONS: Complete the vocabulary map. Use context clues, a glossary, or a dictionary to complete sections.

Topic: _____ Word: _____	Picture
Meaning	Word Analysis ____ ____ ____ prefix root suffix
Synonym	Sentence

English Learners and Cognitive Development

According to Piaget's theory of universal developmental stages for cognitive reasoning (1959), young children construct understanding in the context of their own activity. They progress from concrete to more abstract thinking, from figurative to operative aspects of cognition. Therefore, students learn more easily when they can manipulate objects rather than use abstract thought. The implications of this theory are that English language learning should follow instructional approaches that progress from concrete to abstract and employ rich learning experiences that develop cognitive thinking.

When the environment supports the learner, meaning is constructed in accordance with the learner's background knowledge or his or her use of the primary language to explain complex thought. This allows for already existing structures, referred to by Piaget as schemata, to adjust to new information being presented in the English language. Schemata are defined as previously acquired knowledge structures that help students process and organize new information and translate it into cognitive and linguistic growth. This information on how students construct knowledge parallels the common underlying proficiency model introduced by Cummins (1979, 1987), which posits that knowledge learned in one language transfers to a second language once students have acquired the linguistic skills to express that knowledge.

According to Cummins (1981), it takes an average of five to seven years to acquire cognitive academic language proficiency (CALP), a level at which English language learners can use higher-order thinking skills—analysis, synthesis, evaluation, generalization, conclusion formulation, etc.—in language and thought. Lack of linguistic development in either the primary or the English language can have negative effects on cognitive development.

The trend within content areas is to create learning environments that promote purposeful activity via sustained exploration of themes that are interdisciplinary. Some classrooms re-create time periods in history through the use of student plays, art projects, journal writing, guest speakers, field trips, artifacts from museums, exploratory materials, music of the times, literature and poetry, mathematical activities, and scientific experiments. For English language learners, extending beyond the textbook offers new ways to access and actively construct knowledge about a given subject or theme.

English language teachers should present content area instruction by a concrete approach that creates an exploratory and discovery-type learning environment in which students learn by doing—conducting experiments, observing and collecting data, etc. This approach empowers students to do their

FIGURE 6.4 Lesson planning for content instruction

Subject	Date	Content Standard
Language Objective		___New Concept ___Review ___Reteach
Instructional Materials		Experiential Activities (concrete to abstract)
Content-Obligatory Language Mastery of Concepts: Words and Phrases		Content-Compatible Language Refinement and Growth: Integrated Vocabulary
Teacher Modeling Strategy		Opportunities for Peer Interaction
Lesson Procedures		

Monitoring Comprehension	Study Skill Taught?	Assessment	Homework

own thinking, value their contributions, and participate as active learners in the classroom. It can also augment textbook-oriented lessons, which tend to present information accumulated through fact-finding and driven by extensive use of language and concept load. Figure 6.4 provides a sample teacher lesson plan for content learning.

Accessing Cognitive Development in Mathematics

Consider cognitive development in mathematics: Teaching literacy in the context of mathematics has led to an emphasis on the relation between the ability to read and the ability to solve mathematical problems. First, teachers need to find out if a learner's inability to solve problems is caused by the readability level of the materials or by the reader's lack of literacy proficiency in the first or second language. Appropriate modifications might involve simplifying the language of the material or mediating reading strategies for content learning with the student. Teachers should also determine whether errors leading to mathematical miscalculations are caused by a lack of basic computational skills or by failures in reading comprehension.

Students should be asked to explain the meaning of mathematical terms and phrases such as "greater than," "round to the nearest," "least common denominator," and "find the product of." Another indication of whether mathematical language has been internalized is students' understanding of synonyms related to mathematical terminology. For example, students can name all the different ways to say "add" in problem-solving situations, or can create a list of related terms, such as *sum, increase, combine, addition, include, total, in all,* and *all together.* English language learners need to internalize mathematical terms and phrases connected to their grade-level standards in order to attain a level of skill mastery in the continuum of cognitively demanding and undemanding tasks (Cummins, 1987). Whenever new linguistic skills must be used to communicate, active cognitive involvement occurs. Cummins (1987) defines cognitive involvement as the amount of information that must be processed simultaneously or in close succession by the individual to carry out the activity or task. Thus, if students lack development in mathematical language, the task of problem solving becomes cognitively demanding. However, as students acquire the content vocabulary and relate the terms to the mathematical procedures, the cognitively demanding tasks move up the continuum to become cognitively undemanding until finally they are mastered and become processed automatically. Students need to be aware of the steps in effective mathematical problem solving, including using context clues, finding key words, interpreting questions, eliminating unrelated facts, knowing which operation to use, drawing pictures, and writing equations or numerical sentences. English language learners need to know how problems are structured and what strategies are needed to solve different types of problems. English language learners must fundamentally know that the processes employed to solve problems involve both reading strategies *and* mathematical thinking.

The thinking can be either cognitively demanding or undemanding depending on how well the students have been prepared to learn and apply the mathematical language to the cognitive process. The checklist in Figure 6.5 provides strategies to assist students in solving mathematical problems.

FIGURE 6.5 Strategies for problem solving in mathematics

DIRECTIONS: Use this checklist of strategies to help you find the best method for solving mathematical word problems.

_____ Read and think aloud the problem.

_____ Decide what the problem is asking.

_____ Identify and list the important facts. Eliminate unnecessary data.

_____ Simplify the language or numbers in the problem.

_____ Sort material and analyze the parts.

_____ Find and underline key words or terms.

_____ Redefine the problem in a familiar context.

_____ Act out the problem in your head or with a partner.

_____ Draw pictures to help visualize the problem. Label the pictures with the numbers in the problem.

_____ Estimate or round off the numbers in the problem.

_____ Work the problem backward.

_____ Find a logical solution to the problem.

_____ Determine whether the problem has multiple steps.

_____ Choose the operation(s) you need to solve the problem; write a formula for applying it.

_____ Find a pattern or rule appropriate to the problem.

_____ Organize and label relevant information.

_____ Determine whether you need to use tools such as rulers, compasses, protractors, calculators, scales, balances, measuring cups, thermometers, or clocks. Do you need multiplication charts? Determine whether metric or standard measurements apply.

_____ Determine whether you need to compile data: Add graphs, tables, charts, diagrams, or maps, as needed.

_____ Check results; discuss process with partner; ask for clarification.

Study Skills as Learning Tools for English Learners

In content instruction, English language learners not only must learn specialized subject matter and language skills associated with the content area but also must develop basic study skills to enhance learning across the curriculum. It is important to teach English language learners study skills and the learning tasks for which they are appropriate because many of those students come to school after fragmented years of instruction. Some are trying to cope with overwhelming linguistic and academic demands; some are trying to adjust to changes in a new country of residence; and still others may have parents with limited schooling who can provide little in the way of academic learning. Many have not been properly taught how to set or achieve general skills goals. As researchers have observed, successful and unsuccessful students differ greatly in their use of study skills (Gall, Gall, Jacobsen, & Bullock, 1990).

Study skills can help English language learners identify general learning goals associated with academic success (Pérez & Torres-Gúzman, 1996). For example, parents should encourage students to set aside a routine time and quiet place to study at home where supplies are readily accessible. Parents need to learn how they can provide motivational support and promote good study habits for their children with the help of educators and the school system.

Much of children's success in school depends directly on their ability to *listen*, because listening is the primary medium of classroom learning. Listening skills, like many other study skills, are learned behaviors that affect academic performance.

According to Pérez and Torres-Gúzman (1996), students need to prepare themselves for a *thinking* curriculum. This includes not only knowing how to select and organize materials but also how to collect, integrate, and process information. Pérez and Torres-Gúzman recommend that students learn to set a purpose for reading and commit themselves to develop critical reading skills by reading daily. English language learners need to apply multiple strategies for reading comprehension and literary analysis. Understanding ways to use semantic maps and word analysis, outline passages, and write and report information supports the growth of cognitive processes that will nurture and facilitate learning.

*Meta*cognitive processes, which Jones (1986) defines as "thinking about what one knows and how to control one's learning process" (p. 9), involve (a) knowledge about one's own study skills and habits, including one's strengths and weaknesses as a learner; (b) the ability to direct the success of one's study behavior by selecting an appropriate learning strategy for a particular study task—for example, taking notes, reviewing for a test, or breaking down large tasks; and (c) the ability to monitor the effectiveness of a given learning strategy and know when to switch to an alternative study skill when a given learning strategy is unsuccessful. Students who have a limited repertoire of learning strategies may continue to use a given learning skill even when it is inappropriate. That is why it is so important to teach English language learners multiple study skills that they can use to self-monitor their learning. Researchers have found that students who perceive themselves as being in control of their own destiny and responsible for their own learning are more motivated to continue learning new skills (Schmeck, 1988).

The current interest in study skills instruction is part of the push for higher standards of performance for English language learners. As curricular standards become more rigorous, students will need more sophisticated strategies to succeed and compete in academic settings. Unless they receive study skills instruction along with language and content teaching, many English language learners are likely to become overwhelmed and achieve less. Figure 6.6 is a matrix of study skills that contribute to successful learning. Desirable learning strategies are listed first, followed by guided prompts and suggested actions. The second guide, in Figure 6.7, shows study skills that assist students in self-monitoring their progress.

The Implications for Instructional Materials

Today's instructional materials are not just a grade-level math, science, or social studies text full of information, skills, exercises, and questions. Classroom materials are more complex and elaborate than ever before and include related and extended readings of primary documents, novels, poetry, legends, biographies, research, plays, and other forms of text; however, the use of expository text, as opposed to narrative text, still dominates content instruction. To enable English language learners to meet state standards, expose them to the same historical and scientific perspectives afforded other children, and give them an opportunity to learn from the instructional materials used to teach content, classroom materials for communication-based instruction must be written in a way that facilitates and promotes comprehension, especially for the English language learner. As all students progress through the grades, higher and higher proportions of what they read are expository in nature.

How comprehensible is the text for any reader? One aspect of that comprehensibility is related to text structure, which can be very problematic for English language learners. Among the plethora of text structure features, text coherence has been found to promote or impede the comprehension of text depending on the absence or presence of certain text characteristics and depending on the degree of effectiveness of the specific characteristic when it *is* present. Seminal studies on this feature of text were conducted by Beck, McKeown, Omanson, and Pople (1984); Beck and McKeown (1988); Beck, McKeown, and Gromoll (1989); and Beck, McKeown, Sinatra, and Loxterman (1991). According to García (1994), text coherence is the quality of text that would assist the reader in connecting pieces of text information and combining this information with prior knowledge to develop a coherent representation of the text. It is comprised of five factors: (1) the explicitness of the text, (2) easily inferred causal relations, (3) relevancy, (4) consideration of prior

FIGURE 6.6 Student guide to study skills

Learning Strategy	Student Prompt	Action
Organizational Skills	Space Management	
	Can I find my work and books easily?	Find a safe place.
	Do I know where to find classroom materials?	Locate their proper place.
	Do I use charts and references when needed?	Use environmental print.
	Am I storing or filing materials correctly?	Find system procedures.
	Do I have a place to do homework?	Find a quiet place at home.
	Time Management	
	Am I using time wisely at school?	Stay on task.
	Do I balance school, fitness, and social activities?	Prioritize activities.
	Am I handing in assignments on time?	Write down due dates.
	Am I prioritizing assignments properly?	Determine relative importance and appropriate order.
	Self-Management	
	Do I get enough rest at night?	Set a sleep schedule.
	Am I allowing time to eat properly?	Eat healthily and regularly.
	Am I avoiding harmful substances?	Say no to drugs.
Work Habits	Assuring Access	
	Are my supplies and books readily available?	Have materials ready.
	Are my binders and folders organized and available?	Use tabs and label materials.
	Do I have the proper homework materials?	Obtain appropriate materials.
	Following Procedures	
	Do I exhibit regular attendance and punctuality?	Maintain daily schedule.
	Am I familiar with classroom and school rules?	Learn classroom and school rules and policies.
	Do I follow directions in class, in labs, and at the library?	Learn proper procedures.
	How do I retrieve materials at school?	Learn school regulations.
	When is my homework due?	Keep an assignment sheet.
	How do I fulfill class requirements?	Know the grading policies.
	Applying Oneself	
	Do I memorize material?	Dedicate time and apply learning strategies.
	Do I apply what I am learning in class?	Practice new study skills.
	Do I study for tests?	Prepare for exams.
	Do I complete assignments?	Finish work on time.
	Am I doing homework?	Complete and return assignments.
	Do I review returned assignments and tests?	Examine, and learn from, returned work.
	Am I breaking down big tasks into subtasks?	Chunk text into sections and set reading pace.

FIGURE 6.7 Student guide to study skills: Staying ahead

Learning Strategy	Student Prompt	Action
Monitoring Performance	Methods	
	How can I remember information?	Take notes, underline.
	How do I begin to write?	Brainstorm ideas, organizers.
	What is the process for writing?	Develop a plan with steps.
	How do I initiate a research project?	Narrow topic, locate info.
	How do I reference suitable sources?	Cite work, write bibliography.
	How can I comprehend while I read?	Ask questions, summarize.
	What do I do with unfamiliar vocabulary?	Use word analysis, look it up.
	How do I begin to read a chapter in a text?	Skim, scan and chunk text.
	How do I learn how to use a textbook?	Learn layouts and purposes.
	What do I do if the text is too difficult?	(1) Use visual aids in text.
		(2) Get the main ideas.
		(3) Partner up, seek help.
	Self-Evaluation	
	How do I check my work?	Revise/edit, self or peer.
	How do I overcome challenges?	Keep positive thinking.
	How can I improve the quality of work?	Use your best effort.
	Do I understand the content?	Clarify, ask questions.
	Am I paying attention in class?	Participate, collaborate.
	How can I avoid falling behind?	Complete and turn in all work.
	When do I seek help?	Try first, then ask to clarify.
	Staying Ahead	
	How can I be a better test taker?	(1) Know material covered.
		(2) Study for exams.
		(3) Use test taking tips.
	How can I find my strengths and weaknesses?	(1) Check quality of work.
		(2) Review tests, grades.
		(3) Conference with teacher.
	How can I improve my work?	Practice weak skills, tutoring.
	How can I do better in school?	(1) Set attainable goals.
		(2) One step at a time.
		(3) Celebrate success.
	How do I keep a positive self-image?	(1) Take pride in accomplishments.
		(2) Be determined, believe you can do it.
		(3) Know you're not alone.
		(4) Keep a positive attitude.

knowledge, and (5) reference cohesion (placement of pronouns and their antecedents). All texts vary in the quality of the writing, and if text structure features such as text coherence affect comprehension, it follows that consideration of these same text features should be important in the selection of materials that are used with English language learners. Students who comprehend more of what they read will have more to discuss.

Materials for content instruction need to reflect relevant grade-level content standards and provide opportunities for practice through diverse learning modalities. A variety of materials can be used for content learning, including state-adopted textbooks, trade books, realia, manipulatives, charts, posters, models, audiocassettes, videotapes, software, Laser disks, CD-ROMs, slides, maps, globes, laboratory kits, and overhead transparencies. It is necessary for books to support English language instruction with well-illustrated visuals and graphics. Content materials should have simple layouts that facilitate reading and attract the reader's eye to the main points. The typeface should be appropriate to the grade level—not too big, not too small depending on the age of the reader. Boldface captions and titles appeal to students, make the reading easier, and guide students through text. Materials should be free of cultural bias.

Classroom texts for English language learners should be of the same quality—with respect to both content and appropriate-level readability—as materials for the regular program. Unfortunately, classroom materials for content instruction are not always written for English language learners; some are standard textbooks adopted for the regular classroom. These textbooks, of course, present materials in a fashion suitable for mainstream instruction, without paying attention to the needs of diverse populations. Newer editions may have references on how to modify instruction for English language acquisition by providing strategies for enhancing comprehension. When subject matter is taught to English language learners, they must learn how to apply effective comprehension skills to the expository formats found in textbooks.

Publishers must give more attention to the creation of at least one teacher and one student component—among the myriad of ancillaries that usually accompany a content textbook—to address the needs of English language learners. There are simply too many teachers that need specific, explicit, and systematic instruction available to them for the varying levels of language acquisition that their students represent. Therefore, publishers should assume the responsibility for providing a supplemental student and teacher component that would incorporate many of the recommendations made in this chapter and in the other chapters in this volume for instruction of English language learners.

Concluding Remarks

Instructing English language learners in content areas continues to pose demands and challenges in classrooms across the United States. The increase of linguistic diversity and the wide range of literacy skills affect the manner in which content instruction is taught across the grade levels. It is extremely difficult to meet the academic needs of the English language learners by merely combining teacher lectures with textbook readings and activities. Therefore, planning and implementation of more effective strategies are needed to assist students in developing the language and academics of the content area. The degree of complexity of academic demands continues to escalate as linguistic and cognitive accountability are set for English language learners by state norms and standards. Curricular materials must align selections and lessons to state frameworks and continue to increase the rigor of academic complexity regardless of the students' level of English proficiency or knowledge of content background. For many English language learners, content instruction is now a moving target of opportunities for curricular access and success in school.

This chapter presented strategies and ideas to optimize the education of English language learners in subject-matter instruction through the discussion of four key instructional dimensions. Various elements woven through content learning can increase mastery of expository texts inclusive of subject vocabulary development, presentation of text features, strategies for comprehension, and cognitive thinking skills. Communicative-based instruction models that incorporate the teaching of English language structures and language conventions through purposeful application and comprehension of content lessons are appropriate and encouraged. The cognitive progression from practical to theoretical thinking provides meaningful constructs for concept learning. The research that supports effective instructional approaches for English language learners advocates learning from experiential activities to build a knowledge base for abstract thought. Researchers support helping students conceptualize new information through the use of concrete materials, embedding language objectives in content learning, and graphically organizing the thought processes. If English language learners can receive the tools for learning, then there should also be opportunities to succeed in school by learning adequate study skills along with language and content instruction. Finally, publishers must work to support teachers and students as they create textbooks that are the primary source of information used in content instruction.

REFERENCES

Bandura, A. (1977). *Social learning theory*. Englewoods Cliffs, NJ: Prentice-Hall.

Beck, I.L., & McKeown, M.G. (1988). Toward meaningful accounts in history texts for young learners. *Educational Researcher, 17*, 31–39.

Beck, I.L., McKeown, M.G., & Gromoll, E.W. (1989). Learning from social studies texts. *Cognition and Instruction, 6*, 99–158.

Beck, I.L., McKeown, M.G., Omanson, R.C., & Pople, M.T. (1984). Improving the comprehensibility of stories: The effects of revisions that improve coherence. *Reading Research Quarterly, 19*, 263–277.

Beck, I.L., McKeown, M.G., Sinatra, G.M., & Loxterman, J.A. (1991). Revising social studies text from a text-processing perspective: Evidence of improved comprehensibility. *Reading Research Quarterly, 26*, 251–276.

Bromley, K., Irwin-DeVitis, L., & Modlo, M. (1995). *Graphic organizers: Visual strategies for active learning*. New York: Scholastic.

Cloud, N., Genesse, F., & Hamayan, E. (2000). *Dual language instruction: A handbook for enriched education*. Boston: Heinle & Heinle.

Cummins, J. (1979). Cognitive/academic language proficiency, linguistic interdependence, the optimum age question and some other matters. *Working Papers on Bilingualism, 19*, 121–129.

Cummins, J. (1981). The role of primary language development in promoting educational success for language minority students. In California State Department of Education (Ed.), *Schooling and language minority students: A theoretical framework* (pp. 3–49). Los Angeles: Evaluation, Dissemination, and Assessment Center, California State University.

Cummins, J. (1987). Bilingualism, language proficiency, and metalinguistic development. In P. Homel, M. Palij, & D. Aaronson (Eds.), *Childhood: Aspects of linguistic, cognitive, and social development* (pp. 57–73). Hillsdale, NJ: Erlbaum.

Fillmore, L.W., & Snow, C. (2000). *What teachers need to know about language*. [Special report from ERIC Clearinghouse on Languages and Linguistics.] Available at http://www.cal.org/ericcll/teachers/teachers.pdf.

Gall, M.D., Gall, J., Jacobsen, D., & Bullock, T. (1990). *Tools for learning: A guide to teaching study skills*. Alexandria, VA: Association for Supervision and Curriculum Development.

García, G.G. (1994). *Effects of text coherence and English language proficiency on the comprehension of fifth grade students*. Unpublished doctoral dissertation, University of California at Los Angeles.

Genesse, F. (1994). *Integrating language and content: Lessons from immersion. Educational Practice Report No. 11*. Santa Cruz, CA: The National Center for Research and Cultural Diversity and English Language Learning.

Gersten, R., & Baker, S. (2000). What we know about effective instructional practices for English-language learners. *Exceptional Children, 4*, 454–470.

Jones, B.F. (1986). Quality and equality through cognitive instruction. *Educational Leadership, 43*(7), 4–11.

Krashen, S.D. (1982). Theory versus practice in language training. In R.W. Blair (Ed.), *Innovative approaches to language teaching* (pp. 15–30). Rowley, MA: Newbury House.

Krashen, S.D. (1985). *The input hypothesis: Issues and implications*. White Plains, NY: Longman.

Mohan, B. (1986). *Language and content*. Reading, MA: Addison-Wesley.

Pérez, B., & Torres-Gúzman, M. (1996). *Learning in two worlds*. White Plains, NY: Longman.

Piaget, J. (1959). *The language and thought of the child*. London: Routledge & Kegan Paul.

Schmeck, R.R. (1988). Individual differences and learning strategies. In C.E. Weinstein, E.T. Goetz, & P.A. Alexander (Eds.), *Learning and study strategies: Issues in assessment, instruction, and evaluation* (pp. 171–191). San Diego, CA: Academic Press.

Vygotsky, L.S. (1978). *Mind in society: The development of higher psychological processes* (M. Cole, V. John-Steiner, S. Scribner, & E. Souberman, Eds. and Trans.). Cambridge, MA: Harvard University Press. (Original work published 1934)

Teaching English Language Development: Rethinking and Redesigning Curriculum

Communicative Approaches to Second-Language Acquisition: The Bridge to Second-Language Literacy

Alan N. Crawford

nglish-as-a-second-language (ESL) instruction is the keystone of programs designed to meet the academic needs of English language learners. It is especially important in settings where only small numbers of students speak the same mother tongue or where a lack of trained personnel and appropriate instructional materials prevents the implementation of programs of bilingual education. It is also the major element of those full bilingual education programs in which we use the primary language for academic instruction while students develop sufficient English to benefit from academic instruction in their new second language.

Communicative approaches to second-language acquisition are based on concepts, theories, and hypotheses that converge around the constructivist paradigm. At this point, we should examine the dichotomy between the direct instruction and constructivist paradigms of instruction.

Direct instruction models focus on the disassembly or fragmentation of curricular elements, so that isolated skills and concepts can be mastered along a linear paradigm. They are teacher centered. Conversely, a constructivist view of instruction focuses on the construction of meaning, using what the learner already knows and combining it with new ideas to be integrated. It is learner centered, an important factor in working with students from diverse backgrounds who are often at risk in any case. In a constructivist framework, language acquisition is embedded in function within a meaningful context—not in an artificial or fragmented way (see Dutro & Moran, chapter 10 in this volume). The purpose of this chapter is to link the constructivist paradigm to communicative approaches to second-language acquisition.

One important element of the paradigm is Vygotsky's (1978) Zone of Proximal Development, "the distance between the actual developmental level as determined by independent problem solving and the level of potential development as determined through problem solving under adult guidance in collaboration with more capable peers" (pp. 86–87). This key concept emphasizes the social dimension of learning, which grows out of the support of parents, teachers, older siblings, and other caregivers. The collective wisdom of a cooperative learning group has an obvious role to play here as well.

A second element is scaffolding, which consists of the temporary support provided by teachers when students are engaged in a task within their Zone of Proximal Development. Bruner (1978) described scaffolding as a temporary launching platform designed to support and encourage children's language development to higher levels of complexity. Pearson (1985) explained the temporary nature of scaffolding as the gradual release of responsibility. Good teachers intuitively use such scaffolding strategies as questioning, prompts, rephrasing, illustrations and other visual resources, graphic organizers, demonstrations, dramatizations, gestures, and comprehension monitoring. These strategies enable students to sustain active participation in learning activities.

Approximation is a related process in which English language learners imitate language and test hypotheses about it. The process of approximation underlies oral and written language in that students are acquiring new skills and understandings within the context of authentic wholes. Students exhibit behaviors in which they approximate the language behavior of their models, growing closer and closer to their levels of proficiency. In his view of successive approximation, Holdaway (1979) describes the process as one in which Vygotsky's adults and more capable peers use the output from learner responses to construct, adjust, and finally eliminate the scaffolding that permits learning to progress.

A Historical Perspective

Until recent years, most students in the public schools have tried to learn a second language using such grammar-based approaches as the grammar-translation and audiolingual methods. The grammar-translation approach is most familiar to us as the one used in the foreign language courses we took in high school and college in the 1950s and even later (Chastain, 1975). We learned vocabulary in terms of our first language, from lists in which teachers paired words in the foreign language with their English counterparts. We studied the grammar of the new language again in terms of our own; our first language was the window through which we learned our new, second language. We rarely became capable of communicating in that language as a result of the classes we took; at best, we scored well on tests of grammar, read with halting comprehension, and translated with difficulty.

The audiolingual approach is rooted in structural linguistics and behavioral psychology. This combination results in a methodology based on a grammatical sequence combined with mimicry and the memorization of pattern drills, but without the heavy grammatical analysis of the grammar-translation approach (Chastain, 1975). The audiolingual approach is characterized by the following principles: (a) It is based on the unconscious mastery of sequenced grammatical forms; (b) learning is the result of teaching patterned oral drills; (c) the emphasis is on correct oral production of grammatical forms in response to oral stimuli; (d) language skills are acquired in the natural sequence of listening, speaking, reading, and writing; and (e) there is no reference to the primary language during instruction (Finocchiaro, 1974).

The typical audiolingual lesson consists of a dialogue followed by a series of related pattern drills. The purpose of the dialogue is to present the meaning of the vocabulary or grammatical element being taught within the context of a real situation. For example, a dialogue to introduce the grammatical concept of prepositions of position might appear as follows:

Patricia: Where is the book, Armando?

Armando: It's on the chair, Patricia.

Patricia: No, it fell under the chair.

Armando: Pick up the book, and put it in the box.

We would teach this dialogue using a repetition drill, illustrating it with pictures or dramatizing it with actual objects and students. We would then practice the new elements using pattern drills that develop a habitual response through repetition. The students respond based on a stimulus or cue from the teacher, making one incremental change in the pattern at a time. They usually begin by responding as a total group; as they gain confidence, smaller groups respond separately, until individual students are confident enough to respond alone. The result is usually an artificial and boring program based on a grammatical continuum that does not reflect the sequence in which elements are acquired naturally.

In recent years there have been major changes in educators' conceptions of how a second language is acquired and how this acquisition is best promoted in elementary and secondary classrooms. There has been a major paradigm shift away from grammar-based approaches to language acquisition and toward those we call *communicative*. This change has been particularly apparent in the second-language acquisition of English language learners (see Freeman & Freeman, chapter 2 in this volume).

Underlying Principles of Communicative Approaches

Krashen's Hypotheses

Krashen (1982) offers five important hypotheses that underlie current practice in most communicative approaches to second-language acquisition.

THE ACQUISITION-LEARNING HYPOTHESIS. In his acquisition-learning hypothesis, Krashen describes the difference between the infant's subconscious acquisition of the primary language and the high school French student's conscious learning of a second language. We *acquire* language subconsciously, along with a feel for correctness. *Learning* a language, on the other hand, is a conscious process that involves grammatical rules. Of course, infants are almost always successful in acquiring language, while high school foreign-language learners usually are not.

Gee (1992) expands Krashen's concept of acquisition to incorporate a social factor that encompasses Vygotsky's Zone of Proximal Development and also the concept of approximation:

> Acquisition is a process of acquiring something subconsciously by exposure to models, a process of trial and error, and practice within social groups, without formal teaching. It happens in natural settings that are meaningful and functional in the sense that acquirers know that they need to acquire the thing they are exposed to in order to function and that they in fact want to so function. (p. 113)

THE NATURAL ORDER HYPOTHESIS. According to Krashen's natural order hypothesis, grammatical structures are acquired in a predictable sequence, with certain elements usually acquired before others. He has concluded that the orders for first- and second-language acquisition are similar, but not identical. Krashen does not conclude, however, that sequencing the teaching of language according to this natural order is either necessary or desirable. The content of grammatical approaches to second-language acquisition is organized around sequences of grammatical structures. When infants acquire the primary language, by contrast, the content is whatever they need and are interested in at the time.

THE MONITOR HYPOTHESIS.   Krashen's related monitor hypothesis describes how the learner's conscious monitor or editor functions so as to make corrections as language is produced in speaking or writing. Several conditions are necessary for the application of the monitor: (a) sufficient time to apply it, rarely present in most ordinary oral discourse, especially in classroom settings; (b) a focus on the form or correctness of the message, rather than on its content; and (c) knowledge of the grammatical rule to be applied. These conditions serve to illustrate why so few students learn to understand and speak another language in a grammar-translation or audiolingual high school or university foreign-language course.

THE INPUT HYPOTHESIS.   Krashen's most important contribution is the input hypothesis, in which he concludes that progress in language development occurs when we receive comprehensible input, or input that contains structure at a slightly higher level than what we already understand (see also Hernández, chapter 6 in this volume). The input hypothesis corresponds to Vygotsky's Zone of Proximal Development. The context of the input provides clues that maintain the integrity of the message. According to the input hypothesis, a grammatical sequence is not needed: Grammatical structures are provided and practiced as a natural part of the comprehensible input that the learner receives, much as it occurs with infants acquiring their primary language. Krashen characterizes this comprehensible input as "caretaker speech" about the "here and now."

THE AFFECTIVE FILTER HYPOTHESIS.   In the affective filter hypothesis, Krashen concludes that several affective variables are associated with success in second-language acquisition. These include high motivation, self-confidence and a positive self-image, and low anxiety in the learning environment. Krashen (1981) relates the input hypothesis to the silent period—the interval before speech—in either the primary or second language, in which the learner listens to and develops an understanding of the language before beginning to produce language.

Other Underlying Principles

Results from recent research have led to other major changes in educators' conceptions of how a second language is acquired and how this acquisition is best facilitated in the elementary and secondary classroom.

SIMILARITIES BETWEEN PRIMARY- AND SECOND-LANGUAGE ACQUISITION. An important similarity between the acquisition of primary and second languages is the formation of an incomplete and incorrect *interlanguage* by both primary- and second-language learners (Selinker, Swain, & Dumas, 1975). Most children move through similar stages of development in this incomplete language. It is often called *telegraphic speech* because it resembles the incomplete patterns we used to use to convey meaning in telegrams (Terrell, 1982). Selinker et al. point out the danger that this interlanguage may become fossilized in the absence of native-language speakers, stopping short of its continued development into fluency.

In a related study, Ervin-Tripp (1974) conducted a meta-analysis of research comparing first- and second-language acquisition. She found that the development of syntax by second-language learners parallels the order of development in primary-language learners (see also Krashen, chapter 3 in this volume). Dulay and Burt (1974b) similarly found that learners from diverse language backgrounds tend to acquire English grammatical structures in approximately the same order. Chinese- and Spanish-speaking children, for example, acquired the copula at approximately the same stage of language development, even though the copula is present in Spanish but not in Chinese. Their conclusions give rise to questions about the actual effects of interference from the primary language. Dulay and Burt (1974a) subsequently found that fewer than 5% of children's errors in the second language could be attributed to interference from the primary language, which suggests additional reservations about the use of an ESL curriculum based on grammatical sequences.

Chamot (1981) pointed out another similarity: the lack of student interest in abstract language concepts. Instead, she infers that students should use language for functional purposes based on immediate needs and interests, just as infants do.

The effects of *correction* are also similar in both primary- and second-language acquisition. According to Terrell (1982) and Krashen and Terrell (1983), we should view correction as a negative reinforcer that raises the affective filter and the level of anxiety in a language classroom, whether composed of children or adults. When there is no interference with comprehension, we should recognize that the correction of errors is no more effective in a second-language acquisition program than it is when infants acquire their primary language. Some caregivers may expand incorrect or incomplete forms, such as "Daddy go bye-bye," and say "Yes, Daddy went to work." There is little evidence, however, that this expansion has any positive effect.

These similarities between primary- and second-language acquisition are not consistent with either the grammar-translation or the audiolingual approach to second-language learning. Infants acquiring their primary language do not rely on grammatical rules or on systematic acquisition of vocabulary. With its emphasis on early production instead of a silent period, on correct production instead of an interlanguage—acceptable even though it may be immature and incomplete—and on grammatical sequence instead of functional and communicative competence, the audiolingual approach bears little resemblance to how either primary or second languages are acquired successfully.

Other Factors Associated With Second-Language Acquisition

Many investigators have found strong associations between the successful acquisition of a second language and affective factors. Oller, Hudson, and Liu (1977) reported that positive self-esteem was associated with performance in second-language instruction. Gardner and Lambert (1972) found a strong relation between students' motivation to learn a second language and their attitude toward the group that the language represents. In a related vein, Saville-Troike (1976) found that negative stereotyping of English language learners' cultural group can have a negative effect on their efforts to learn a second language spoken by those who hold that negative stereotype.

The age of English language learners is another factor associated with second-language acquisition. Because students typically enter school when they first arrive in the United States, they enter beginning second-language acquisition programs at many different ages and grade levels. Although the age of entry into programs is therefore determined by age at arrival instead of the optimum age for second-language acquisition, it is useful to examine the effects of age on acquisition.

According to Lenneberg's (1967) critical period hypothesis, primary-language acquisition must occur before the onset of puberty. Snow and Hoefnagel-Höhle (1978) investigated the implications of the critical period hypothesis for second-language acquisition and found that subjects from 12 to 15 years of age and adults made the fastest progress in acquiring Dutch during the first months of learning. At the end of the first year, those from 8 to 10 years of age and from 12 to 15 years of age achieved the highest proficiency in Dutch and those from 3 to 5 years of age were lowest, indicating that Lenneberg's hypothesis was not supported for second-language acquisition.

In an analysis of similar studies, Krashen, Long, and Scarcella (1979) found that adults developed second-language proficiency faster than children, that older children developed faster than younger children, and that those who had natural exposure to second languages during childhood tended to be more proficient than those who began as adults. Cummins (1980) also concluded that older students acquired second-language cognitive academic language proficiency (CALP) more rapidly than younger students because of the greater development of CALP in the primary language and its interdependence with CALP in the developing second language.

Ervin-Tripp (1974) concluded that older language learners are more effective in learning a second language than younger learners because they take advantage of the generic similarities of languages in learning the second one. They learn new symbolic representations for concepts and ideas they already have words for in their primary language. They have better skills in managing memory heuristics, and they have greater capacity to solve problems and form generalizations.

Collier (1987) examined the relationship between the age of English language learners and their acquisition of English. She found that students who entered the ESL program at ages 8 to 11 were the fastest achievers and that they reached the 50th percentile in all subject areas within two to five years. The lowest achievers entered the program at ages 5 to 7; they were one to three years behind students from 8 to 11 years of age. In contrast to the findings of Krashen et al. (1979), and of Ervin-Tripp (1974), Collier found that students from 12 to 15 years of age had the most difficulty acquiring English. It was projected that they would need from six to eight years of instruction to reach grade-level norms in academic achievement. (See García & Beltrán, chapter 9 in this volume.)

Collier (1989) later analyzed other research on age and academic achievement in English and found that students who had primary-language academic instruction, whether in English or another native language, generally required from four to seven years to reach national norms on standardized tests in reading, social studies, and science but as little as two years in the areas of mathematics and language arts, including spelling, punctuation, and grammar. She also found that those students from ages 8 to 12 who had at least two years of schooling from their home country in their primary language needed from five to seven years to reach the same levels of achievement in English reading, social studies, and science, but only two years in mathematics and language arts. Young students with no schooling in the primary language from either the home country or the new host country needed seven to ten years of instruction in reading, social studies, and science. Adolescent students with no second-language instruction and no opportunity for continued academic work in the primary language—both those with a good academic background and those with interrupted schooling—were projected, in the main, to drop out of school before reaching national norms.

Communicative Approaches to Second-Language Acquisition

Krashen's hypotheses and related similarities between first- and second-language acquisition indicate that approaches to second-language acquisition should provide comprehensible input, focus on relevant and interesting topics instead of grammatical sequences, and provide for a silent period without forcing early production. There are approaches to second-language acquisition that meet these criteria. They are categorized as *communicative* approaches, and two that are very appropriate for elementary and secondary classrooms are the total physical response method and the natural approach.

Total Physical Response Method

Asher's (1969, 1979, 1982) total physical response or TPR method is an important communicative approach in the initial stages of second-language acquisition. The TPR method provides for comprehensible input, a silent period, and a focus on relevant content rather than on grammar or form. The emphasis of TPR is on physical responses to verbal commands, such as "Stand up" and "Put your book on the desk." Because little emphasis is given to production, the level of anxiety is low.

Teachers can give lessons to small groups or to an entire class. In the beginning, the teacher models one-word commands. This is done first with a few students, then with the entire group, then with a few students again, and finally with individual students. The teacher might say, for example, "Sit," and then model that command by sitting down. Later the teacher would issue the command without modeling. As the students' levels of language increase, the teacher begins to use two- and three-word commands, such as "Stand up" and "Close the door." The students demonstrate their comprehension by physically carrying out these commands.

The order of commands is varied so that the students cannot anticipate which is next. Old commands are combined with new ones in order to allow for review. Whenever the students do not appear to understand, the teacher returns to modeling. After a silent period of approximately 10 hours of listening to commands and physically responding to them, students then begin to give those same commands to other students. It is important for the teacher to maintain a playful mood during classroom activities.

Teachers can extend the total physical response approach to higher levels of proficiency by using the strategy of *nesting* commands. The teacher might say the following:

"Ivan, take the ball to Noriko, or close the door."

"Teresa, if Ivan took the ball to Noriko, stand up."

"If he closed the door, put your hand on your head."

A high level of understanding is necessary to carry out such commands, but no oral production is needed. Parents of young children will recognize that their infants can understand and carry out such commands long before they begin to speak themselves.

Natural Approach

Terrell's (1977) original concept of the natural approach was based on three major principles: (1) Classroom activities were focused on acquisition—that is, communication with a content focus leading to an unconscious absorption of language with a feel for correctness but not an explicit knowledge of grammar; (2) oral language errors were not directly corrected; and (3) learners could respond in the new second language, the primary language, or a mixture of the two.

Krashen and Terrell (1983) later presented four principles that underlie the natural approach to language acquisition. The first is that comprehension precedes production, which leads to several teacher behaviors: The teacher uses only the new second language, focuses on topics of interest to the students, and helps the students maintain comprehension.

The second principle is that production emerges in stages, ranging from nonverbal responses to complex discourse. Students can begin to speak when they are ready, and oral language errors are not corrected unless they interfere with communication.

The third principle is that the curriculum is made up of communicative goals. The syllabus consists of topics of interest, not a grammatical sequence. And finally, classroom activities must maintain low student anxiety, lowering the students' affective filters. The teacher accomplishes this by establishing and maintaining a good rapport and friendly relations with and among students.

Terrell's (1981) natural approach is based on three stages of language development: (1) preproduction (comprehension); (2) early production; and (3) emergence of speech.

PREPRODUCTION STAGE.   The teacher provides topical, interesting, and relevant comprehensible input in the first stage, which closely parallels Asher's TPR approach. The teacher speaks slowly, using gestures to enhance comprehension. Students may respond with physical behaviors—shaking or nodding their heads, pointing at pictures or objects, or saying "yes" and "no." It is important that input is dynamic, lively, fun, and comprehensible. Using a pet turtle, the teacher might say,

> This is a turtle. His name is Casper. Is he green? Who wants to hold him? [Hands turtle to student.] Who has the turtle? Does Niko have the turtle? Yes, he does. Does Graciela have the turtle? No, she doesn't.

This basic input can be repeated with other objects in the classroom. The teacher also can use large-format illustrations and posters. For example,

> Here is a picture of a farm. Are there animals in the picture? Yes. How many animals are there? [Elicits correct response.] Yes, four. Point to the horse. Where is the goat?

If each student in the group is given a different illustration, the teacher might provide such input as,

> Who has a picture of an airplane? Yes, Wolfgang, you do. Is the airplane large? Wolfgang, give your picture to Zipour. Who has a picture of a truck? Yes, María has a picture of a truck.

These examples include three primary preproduction techniques: using TPR, using TPR and also naming objects, and using illustrations. Appropriate student responses include movement, pointing, nodding or shaking the head, and using the names of other students in the group. We should remember that nodding the head for an affirmative response and shaking it for a negative one are not appropriate in all cultures; students also may have to acquire these non-verbal behaviors. Because the emphasis at this stage is on listening comprehension, verbal responses in the primary language are also acceptable. This may be a problem if the teacher is unable to understand the students' mother tongue, but they usually find a way to help the teacher understand.

Classroom props facilitate expansion of this and subsequent stages of the natural approach. Manipulable or concrete objects are helpful, including flannel boards and puppets. Large colorful illustrations, such as those in travel posters and Big Books, are also very useful. Other sources of free color illustrations include calendars (outdated or otherwise), large posters available from textbook and trade book publishers, food group posters available from the National Dairy Council, and colorful illustrations in the annual reports of many large corporations—usually available on request through announcements in major business magazines.

EARLY PRODUCTION STAGE.   In the stage of early production, the students begin to produce one-word responses, lists, and finally two-word answers, such as "little sister" and "in house." Some of these responses, such as "me like" and "no want," are grammatically incorrect or incomplete. But Krashen and Terrell (1983) remind us that error correction has a negative effect that raises anxiety level and is not helpful. According to Crawford (1986), we should view these errors as *immature* language, not incorrect language. In the presence of good models, most of these errors will disappear in time, just as they do among infants developing their primary language.

Several types of questions can be used to elicit one- and two-word responses from students as they transition into the early production stage:

Question Type	Question
Yes/no	Are you reading?
	Do you like movies?
Here/there	Where is the picture of the boat?
Either/or	Is this a watermelon or an orange?
One-word	How many apples are there?
Two-word	What toys are in the picture?

As in the preproduction stage, these strategies should be integrated into activities that permit a variety of responses, ranging from physical responses from those not ready for language production, to brief oral responses from those who are.

Does Bo-Gay have a picture of a tree? [Yes.] Is the tree blue? [No.] Who has a picture of a boat? [Jaime.] Does it go fast or slow? [Fast.] Where is the picture of the car? [There.] Look at Eladia's picture. How many children are there? [Four.] What are they doing? [Playing ball.]

As the students begin language production, conversations should increasingly require one-word responses. Within the same lesson, the teacher can address questions calling for longer responses to those children who are ready.

Sven, show us your picture. What is in Sven's picture? [A hamburger and French fries.] Yes, we see a hamburger and French fries. What is on the hamburger? [Ketchup.] Is there sugar on the hamburger? [No. Laughter.] What else is on the hamburger? [Tomato, mustard.] How does it taste? [Very good.] What do you like with a hamburger? [Nachos and a soda.] I like a milk shake with mine.

Terrell suggests other formats to elicit language from the students:

Activity	Example
Add-on sentence	I like cake.
	I like cake and pie.
	I like cake, pie, and...
Open-ended sentence	Playing baseball is...

He also recommends the use of oral lists; interviews; and the discussion of charts, tables, graphs, newspaper advertisements, and pictures.

EMERGENCE OF SPEECH STAGE.   During the stage of emergence of speech, students begin to produce structures that are longer, more complex, richer in vocabulary, and more correct. This production proceeds from three-word phrases to sentences, dialogue, extended discourse, and narrative. At this stage, Terrell recommends such activities as games, group discussions, preference ranking, skits, art and music, radio, television, filmstrips, pictures, readings, and filling out forms.

Terrell (1981) suggests three general techniques to focus students in this stage on using language instead of on its form: games, affective-humanistic activities, and problem-solving tasks. Games are helpful for providing comprehensible input in low-anxiety situations. Affective-humanistic activity might include dialogues about personal topics (such as weekend activities), interviews, preference ranking, and the preparation of personal charts, tables, and graphs. An example of a chart that incorporates preference ranking follows (Crawford, 1994):

Favorite Pizzas

Name	Cheese	Sausage	Pepperoni	Tomato	Anchovy	Mushroom
Rita		X		X		X
Nguyen		X				
Abdul						
Sofik	X		X	X		
Petra		X		X		X

> Does Nguyen like pizza? [Yes.] What kind of meat does Nguyen like? [Sausage.] How many like tomato on their pizza? [Three: Rita, Sofik, and Petra.] How does Abdul like pizza? [He doesn't like it.] Which students like the same kind of pizza? [Rita and Petra.] Is there a topping that no one likes? What is it? [Anchovy.] How do we know? [Anchovy column is blank.]

Not only is the completed chart a valuable source of comprehensible input, but the process of gathering the data for the chart is, as well.

Examples of critical-thinking activities would include responding to higher order questions during read-alouds and contributing to the development of a semantic map.

The Curriculum Context of a Communicative Approach Program

Teachers who would advocate teaching the third-person present progressive tense to a child in a second-grade classroom would be incredulous at the suggestion that a parent teach the same concept to a 3-year-old at home. Of course, both children can use the tense correctly, and neither as the result of instruction. This leads us to conclude, as do Krashen, Terrell, and others, that the content of second-language acquisition programs should be based primarily on content, not on grammatical sequence.

TOPICAL CURRICULA. Because needed language structures emerge and are acquired naturally within the context of thematic lessons, a communicative ESL curriculum is usually organized around a set of topics in order to ensure the introduction of new vocabulary and concepts of interest and utility to the students. Grammatical sequences occasionally appear as a subcategory of some communicative curricula, as we shall see in the next section.

Terrell (1981) suggests that, at the elementary and secondary levels, a grammatical continuum is not appropriate in the language acquisition process. He recommends the use of a topical curriculum that deemphasizes the form or correctness of the message and emphasizes instead its content—and he suggests that the content should be limited to the following until students demonstrate production of more than one-word responses: following commands for classroom management; names of articles in the classroom; color and description words for objects in the classroom; words for people and family relationships; descriptions of students; school activities; areas within the school; names of objects in the school that are not in the classroom; clothing; and foods, especially those eaten at school.

Later in the acquisition process, other topics of interest to students are added, including students' families, their homes and neighborhoods, their favorite activities, and pleasant experiences they have had. They may also enjoy discussing their preferences with respect to food, colors, television programs and films, and other aspects of their lives.

Like Terrell, Asher (1982) advocates the use of a topical curriculum. He suggests, however, that it should be organized into behaviors, represented by action verbs or verb phrases; objects that these behaviors act on; and qualifiers or modifiers, such as adverbials, prepositions, adjectivals, and possessives. For example, the teacher might select the behavior "pick up," the object "marker," and the qualifier "green" to produce the command "Pick up the green marker." According to Asher, these elements can be combined and presented in a variety of creative and interesting ways.

Chamot (1983) offers several recommendations that very effectively tie the ESL program to the core curriculum. She suggests that vocabulary and concepts from content areas of the curriculum be used in ESL activities and that reading and writing instruction in English be increased for older students, especially those with literacy skills in the primary language. Instead of focusing on the correct pronunciation of words in oral reading, teachers should emphasize silent reading comprehension, including extensive experiences with expository text in the content areas of the core curriculum (see also Hernández, chapter 6 in this volume).

GRAMMAR IN THE COMMUNICATIVE APPROACH CURRICULUM.   In his last work, Terrell (1991) reexamined the place of grammar in communicative approaches with respect to adults. He postulated that, instead of relying on input to produce language following the silent period, many adults rely on output, indicating that grammar may have more importance than previously thought in their language development. Indeed, most of us who work in fields related to language acquisition recognize our own desire for references to the grammar of any language we attempt to acquire.

Terrell concluded that we can consider using grammar instruction as an advance organizer to help adult language learners make sense of input. He also recommended using meaning-form focus in activities that contain many examples of a single grammatical relationship—that is, activities in which one grammatical concept, such as the use of the preposition *with*, is intentionally exemplified repeatedly, as described by Rutherford and Sharwood-Smith (1985). Terrell further suggested that, by using the monitor, in which learners are aware of their production, they might acquire their own output, instead of acquiring comprehensible input only from others. Although he addressed this discussion to adults, it has obvious implications for more capable secondary school English language learners. Teachers should give serious consideration to the expressed wishes of those of their students who request some type of referencing to grammar. This is not recommended, however, for elementary and intermediate level students.

Access to the Core Curriculum Through Sheltered English

A major issue in the acquisition of English as a second language is the extent of access to the core curriculum during that process. In a study of programs for limited–English-proficient students in California, Berman et al. (1992) concluded that most English language learners, especially those at the intermediate and senior high school levels, did not have access to aspects of the core curriculum that would permit them to receive a diploma. Instead, they were clustered in what was characterized as a steady diet of classes in ESL.

Many communicative strategies can be adapted to provide access to this core curriculum through a scaffolding process called *sheltered English instruction*. The topics treated in this highly contextualized instruction are the important content areas of the core curriculum.

Strategies for Providing Access to the Core Curriculum

Sheltered English instruction in the content areas of the curriculum adds substantially to the knowledge and vocabulary that students acquire and need as a base for comprehension as they read and think in any language (Krashen,

1985). These strategies are consistent with the philosophy of communicative approaches to second-language acquisition, and they additionally provide access to academic areas of the curriculum in such a way that communication is maintained.

Cummins (1981) provides a set of intersecting continua that are very useful for conceptualizing the issue of balancing the complexity of curriculum content with demands for language proficiency (see Figure 7.1). The vertical continuum extends from cognitively undemanding (e.g., a conversation about what students ate for lunch) to cognitively demanding (e.g., a third-grade mathematics lesson about the distributive principle for multiplication).

Cummins's intersecting horizontal continuum extends from context-embedded—for example, a science lesson on classification, taught with concrete manipulatives—to context-reduced: an abstract lecture/discussion, for example, about the principles of democracy. Sheltered English instruction will be most effective in subject areas of the curriculum that can be presented

FIGURE 7.1 Classifying cognitive level and contextual support of language and content activities

	Cognitively undemanding	Cognitively demanding
Context enhanced	Art lesson Playing kickball Conversation about lunch Playing a board game Singing a song	Mathematics lesson using manipulatives Conducting a science experiment about evaporation Making a map of the schoolyard Watching the news on television
Context reduced	Beginning reading skills Talking on the telephone Listening to the news on the radio Reading a set of instructions	Responding to higher order reading comprehension questions Participating in a debate on capital punishment Taking the SAT or the GRE

concretely, such as mathematics, science, art, music, and physical education. Although there are aspects of the social studies that can be taught concretely, such as geography and map skills, there are so many abstract concepts taught in this area that instruction might well be delayed until students acquire additional English proficiency.

The purpose of a sheltered English instruction approach to the core curriculum is to provide a focus on context-embedded activities, ensuring that comprehensible input is provided while treating increasingly cognitively demanding aspects of the core curriculum. The Los Angeles Unified School District (LAUSD) (1985) prepared a set of English-language teaching strategies that provide the necessary scaffolding in content areas for intermediate English language learners. They recommend that teachers simplify input by speaking slowly and enunciating clearly, using a controlled vocabulary within simple language structures. Where possible, teachers should use cognates and avoid extensive use of idiomatic expressions (see Cummins, chapter 1, and Freeman & Freeman, chapter 2, in this volume). They suggest that, to maintain comprehension, teachers make frequent use of nonverbal language, including gestures, facial expressions, and dramatization; they also recommend the use of manipulatives and concrete materials, such as props, graphs, visuals, overhead transparencies, bulletin boards, maps, and realia. Teachers should check frequently for understanding by asking for confirmation of comprehension; by asking students to clarify, repeat, and expand; and by using a variety of questioning formats. Schifini (1985) recommends a focus on student-centered activities—especially at the secondary level, where lecturing and textbook use predominate.

Richard-Amato and Snow (1992) provide valuable strategies for content area teachers of English language learners. For mainstream teachers, they recommend providing a warm learning environment, recording lectures and talks on tape for later review, rewriting some key parts of text material at lower levels, asking native–English-speaking students to share notes with English language learners, and avoiding competitive grading until students have achieved sufficient English proficiency to compete successfully with native speakers (see Graves & Fitzgerald, chapter 5 in this volume). In addition to the strategies suggested by LAUSD and Schifini earlier, they recommend that teachers reinforce key concepts frequently, establish consistent routines in the classroom, and provide sufficient wait time for students to respond to questions; that corrections be in the form of expansion and mirroring in correct form; and that teachers avoid forcing students to speak until they are ready. They also suggest that teachers frequently summarize and review, demonstrate that they acknowledge and value the language and culture that students bring to the classroom, and make effective use of teaching assistants or aides who speak their students' primary language.

There are several other strategies that provide scaffolding for English language learners in sheltered English instruction. The highly contextualized interactions that take place in cooperative learning can make the difference between what Krashen (1985, 1991) describes as submersion—or "sink or swim"—and immersion, the type of scaffolded subject matter instruction described earlier. Cooperative learning is most effective when, in the words of Vygotsky, more capable peers—that is, stronger speakers of English—are included in groups with English language learners at various levels.

Sheltered English instruction is an *intermediate* strategy. It is appropriate for students who have successfully emerged from the third stage of the natural approach.

Other Supportive Strategies

There are many other strategies that provide the scaffolding needed in sheltered English instruction. Thematic teaching units provide a broader context for students' understanding in the content/language integration fostered by such instruction in English. Elementary teachers will find that they can organize units around literature themes, such as *change*. They might begin with literature study in *The Very Hungry Caterpillar* (Carle, 1983), examining change in the metamorphosis of a butterfly. Through the integration of mathematics and science, they can study change by graphing the amount of rust on a piece of metal over time. In the area of social studies, they can analyze change in behavior as one grows older. The concept of change is revisited throughout the curriculum in all content areas, providing reinforcement of vocabulary and language structures that are used often.

At the secondary level, Short (1991) suggests close collaboration between ESL and content teachers, so that a theme such as deforestation might be the focus of a unit of study in both the language and science classes in which English language learners are enrolled. Chan and Chips (1989) recommend previewing lessons in the primary language, providing audiotapes for students to use after lessons, providing extra wait time for English language learners to think about their responses to questions, providing study guides, and conducting read-alouds of textbook materials before they are read by the students themselves.

Finally, students should learn academic content from the core curriculum in the primary language until they are ready for sheltered English instruction—

which should occur when they reach a level of intermediate fluency in English. Schifini (1985) describes these intermediate learners as those who can engage in extended discussion in English. Teachers will find that a student who has mastered a numeracy concept in the primary language, for example, will find the same concept much more comprehensible in the second language than one who is learning the concept for the first time. It is for the latter student, in fact, that primary-language instruction in that subject area is vital. Students who have developed language proficiency at an academic level in their primary language will show gains with respect to both their further understanding of the numeracy concept and the second-language development that will surely accompany it in sheltered English instruction.

Extending Communicative Approaches Into L2 Literacy

Until only a few years ago, it was commonly held that English language learners should not begin learning to read and write in English until they had reached an intermediate level of English fluency. We now recognize that the processes of reading and writing in English can begin early in the acquisition process, especially for those students who have developed literacy skills in the primary language. In addition, literacy can play a major role in support of the acquisition of English as a second language. Krashen and Terrell (1983) describe reading in the second language as an important source of comprehensible input. In the same way that we find parallels between communicative approaches to second-language acquisition and sheltered English instruction, we can identify many aspects of communicative approaches that parallel access to literacy in students' new second language—English (see also Krashen, chapter 3 in this volume).

Communicative Approaches and a Constructivist View of Reading

The convergence between communicative approaches to second-language acquisition and literacy is particularly prominent in the constructivist paradigm. Goodman (1986) views learning as proceeding from whole to part, without any basis in a sequence of skills. He places the major focus on authentic language use in the real world. Both principles are consistent with communicative approaches to second-language acquisition. Smith (1995) reinforces the importance of authenticity in stating that "literacy is a social phenomenon. Individuals become literate not from the formal instruction they receive, but from what they read and write about and who they read and write with" (p. 57). We can readily interchange listening and speaking for reading and writing in the Smith citation. Rigg (1991) has identified the major purposes of language within the constructivist paradigm, including the construction of knowledge and the creation and communication of purposeful and authentic meaning.

These mutually supporting concepts about the constructivist paradigm are entirely consistent with the underlying principles of communicative approaches to second-language acquisition. Let us now examine some approaches and strategies to reading and writing that promote second-language acquisition within that perspective.

Early Literacy Experiences That Emerge From Communicative Approaches

Most English language learners have had some emergent literacy experiences at home and in the community—recognizing cereal and soft drink labels, knowing brands of automobiles, being read to and watching a parent read, referring to a calendar, or writing a check. They have begun to understand the underlying concept of print as representing spoken ideas, often even in the second language they are only beginning to understand.

A print-rich environment in the classroom is an important step toward providing meaningful material to read. Students do not need to know letter names or sound-symbol correspondences to begin recognizing and discussing their own names, labels, and other forms of print to which they are exposed. Surrounding them with sources of print in the classroom will serve to supplant missing or inadequate experiences.

The Key-Vocabulary and Language Experience Approaches to Reading

If students have an extremely limited background in the language of initial instruction, and especially if that must be English as a second language, then the key-vocabulary approach of Veatch, Sawicki, Elliott, Flake, and Blakey (1979) provides a bridge to literacy from a strong, communicatively based second-language acquisition program. As a part of the natural approach, Terrell (1981) recommends that key words be written on the chalkboard in the second language for older students who are literate in their primary language. In the early production stage of Terrell's natural approach, students may express themselves quite appropriately in one- or two-word utterances as they begin to acquire a second language. It is altogether proper that they also begin to read the key vocabulary that they have expressed.

They may later produce lists of related ideas, such as foods to eat at a carnival or fair, words that describe a favorite friend, or things to do after school. These topics and this output reflect the oral language common in the early production phase of Terrell's natural approach to language acquisition.

During an individual meeting with the teacher, each student in the key-vocabulary approach selects a word of personal importance. The teacher writes it on a card. After the student traces the word with a finger, the teacher records it in a key-word book and also records a sentence or phrase about the word that is dictated by the student. The student then reads the dictation back to the teacher and illustrates it. Finally, the student copies the word and the sentence.

Most bilingual teachers who teach reading in the mother tongue recognize that student motivation to begin reading and writing in English early is strong. Although it is most beneficial for students to learn to read and write in the primary language (Cummins, 1986, 1989; Krashen & Biber, 1988), where possible and necessary, teachers can begin an early introduction to literacy in English in order to take advantage of that motivation.

Moving from the dictation of key vocabulary to predictable language patterns in the language experience approach (LEA) is a natural step, and one that quickly leads to more traditional LEA strategies (Heald-Taylor, 1986). A dictation about foods to eat at a football game might result in each of several students dictating an idea conforming to this predictable pattern:

We eat hot dogs at the football game.

We eat popcorn at the football game.

We eat peanuts at the football game.

Using the LEA in the second language is an excellent way to initiate students into print of interest and relevance to them (Moustafa & Penrose, 1985; Nessel & Jones, 1981). According to Crawford (1993), LEA also provides a means through which students can experience literature in their second language that is above their ability to read and comprehend. After a teacher or paraprofessional tells or reads a story aloud, the students can then dictate the story back—that is, retell it for the teacher or aide to record, although probably in a less complicated version than the original. Peck (1989) found that listening to stories in this way helps students develop a sense of story structure, which should be reflected in the dictated version and in enhanced abilities to predict, in this and other stories. Dictating a text allows students to think, talk, read, and write about a piece of literature and also to be exposed to its valuable cultural content. At the same time, they are actively interacting with it at a level of comprehension and of English-language proficiency appropriate for their stage of development. They will be able to activate background knowledge from this experience that will transfer positively into the second language when they later read the literature for themselves in their new language.

Beginning an LEA activity with a piece of literature or a story often will result in a better structured dictation than the random list of sentences that often results from an LEA dictation stimulated by an illustration, a manipulative, or some other prompt. Heller (1988) recommends adding several components to traditional LEA procedures, including activating background knowledge, setting a purpose and identifying a target audience for the dictation, discussing a model LEA dictation, modeling of metacognitive strategies by teachers who describe their thoughts about creating an interesting story, and asking the students to make notes about the story they will dictate. They can then discuss, edit, and rewrite the collaborative chart story in much the same way that the writing process would be applied in independent writing.

The key-vocabulary and language experience approaches should be implemented with caution to ensure that the second-language acquisition program does not evolve into an English literacy program presented before the student is ready. Being able to read and write in the mother tongue is always the most desirable base from which to establish literacy in English later, because of the positive transfer of literacy skills to English.

Shared Reading

Another valuable form of written text for English language learners early in the reading process is the Big Book, particularly those Big Books with predictable or repetitive language patterns. Teachers read to students, who then read *with* them and finally back *to* them, although this "reading" may consist, at the beginning, of telling the story while looking at the illustrations (Trachtenburg & Ferruggia, 1989). Using Big Books provides an opportunity for the teacher to model reading, so that students can observe what they will later do in their own independent reading. In addition, students begin to notice correspondences between letters in familiar texts and the sounds they represent (Holdaway, 1979).

According to Lynch (1986), the shared-reading process begins with talking about the book language that has probably already been acquired by students whose parents or siblings read to them at home. For those who lack this experience, shared reading is of particular importance. English language learners will tend more than other students to come from homes where printed material is scarce or where parents' own literacy skills may be limited. We cannot make assumptions about the conceptual knowledge about print that they bring to the classroom (Crawford, 1993).

Students look together at the cover and at illustrations inside a book, and then begin to understand that they can make predictions based on what they already know, their background knowledge, and what they think the author wants to say to them. As the teacher begins to read the story to them, they will note and discuss connections between their predictions and the story.

Many teachers are concerned about how students can begin to read a Big Book or a predictable book before they have learned to read—that is, to decode or call out the words. Smith (1988) describes the process as one of demonstration, in which a teacher or parent reads a Big Book to a student, who in turn reads it back to the teacher or parent. As students gain confidence through this early successful experience with reading and through a process of approximation, they begin to read with increasing accuracy and faithfulness with respect to the actual text. When students read to the teacher as a group, there is an even greater sense of success, because individual errors are not important. Students can either correct themselves or go right on, with a correspondingly low level of anxiety about reading. This process parallels the need for a low level of anxiety in the acquisition of a second language and the role of correction in that process.

Students in this activity begin to identify which parts of the text tell which parts of the story, and they soon begin to recognize certain words of interest to them. In terms of the frequency of their appearance in primary texts or the number of syllables they contain, these words are not necessarily easy words from an adult's point of view. But they are easy from a student's point of view, in terms of interest and utility. Such easy words as *elephant* and *yellow* are more likely to be readily remembered and identified on second or third reading than such difficult words, to a student, as *than* and *from*.

As Lynch (1986) points out, repetition of familiar stories leads to increased success, not to boredom on the part of the students. Students' ability to predict will grow, and they will increase the kind and variety of cues they use to predict, moving from illustrations and background knowledge of a story to familiar words and other visual cues. Graphophonic cues—the phonics and structural analysis skills of so much concern to some educational decision makers—emerge later as a *result* of this process, not as its cause (Smith, 1988).

Vocabulary Development

When English language learners read in their second language, their lack of vocabulary knowledge is often an obstacle to comprehension. This can be a problem in their primary language as well, because they may have insufficient academically related background knowledge and, as a result, less of the primary-language vocabulary development that would ordinarily accompany it. We can consider vocabulary as an aspect of background knowledge, but we will treat it separately here in order to examine several concepts that relate more specifically to vocabulary.

Let us consider two different aspects of vocabulary development for English language learners. One is the richness of language that surrounds them. We know that students learn the meanings of words when their experiences with them are highly contextualized, not when they are studied in isolation. It follows, then, that a richer language environment should result in increased exposure to contextualized vocabulary and, therefore, to increased understanding of the meanings of words (see Cummins, chapter 1, and Freeman & Freeman, chapter 2, in this volume).

We often postpone or even eliminate instruction for English language learners, however, in the very areas of the curriculum where new vocabulary words will be offered in the most highly contextualized ways: science, social studies, art, music, health. According to Crawford (1993), we must ensure that these areas of the curriculum are provided English language learners and that they are presented so that contextualized exposure to a rich vocabulary is promoted. Instruction in these areas should include the use of cooperative learning, problem solving, and other vocabulary-rich strategies.

Nagy, Anderson, and Herman (1987) found that, though the proportion of words read that were actually learned was low, a major factor in vocabulary development by third-, fifth-, and seventh-grade students was the sheer volume of reading that students did and the amount of vocabulary to which they were exposed. Stanovich (1986) elaborated this idea further in his examination of individualized differences and the so-called "Matthew effect": namely, that those who read more (the rich) read better (get richer). Similarly, Smith (1986) observed that good readers read, while poor readers take tests and do drill sheets.

In the case of some literature or content selections, there is the occasional need for direct instruction of a few vocabulary words that must be grasped clearly if the text is to be understood. There will be other words not known to the students that need not be addressed through direct instruction because they are not critical to understanding the selection or because their meaning can be grasped quickly through the context in which they appear.

Many of the strategies recommended for the activation or development of background knowledge constitute direct approaches to vocabulary instruction. Semantic mapping is one of these strategies, but its application should be limited to those key and conceptually difficult vocabulary terms that are more in the realm of background knowledge. Otherwise, there will be little time left for reading after prereading activities are completed.

A partial or complete read-aloud of a literature selection as a prereading activity can be equally productive. The teacher may analyze some words through brief discussion following that activity. They will have been presented in context, and someone in the group will likely have some knowledge of any given new vocabulary word. Others may be analyzed by reviewing the illustrations in a story or an appropriate illustration, manipulative, or visual aid provided by the teacher. Because illustrations provide important visual information, paging through a selection and discussing them provides a contextualized opportunity for presenting new vocabulary and also for making predictions about the text (see Graves & Fitzgerald, chapter 5 in this volume).

The Writing Process

A major principle of the constructivist view of language is the interdependence of listening, speaking, reading, and writing. Hudelson (1984) observed that English language learners address these four language processes as a totality, not as separate entities. According to Fitzgerald (1993), writing begins when children can draw, and there is no need to wait for reading. We can certainly extend these ideas to English language learners, who should be encouraged to write in English early, especially if they have writing skills in their primary language. The errors they make should be viewed in the same way that we view errors in oral production, as a part of the natural process of acquisition.

Conclusions

English language learners need a communicative approach to learning English as a second language because of its focus on meaning, rather than on form. When English language learners have intermediate English proficiency, they should have access to the full core curriculum through the careful application of communicative approach strategies in sheltered English instruction, with the focus of this instruction on maintaining comprehension.

At an appropriate time, English language learners should receive instruction in English reading and writing through strategies that ensure continued comprehension and communication. A constructivist view of reading instruction is very consistent with communicative approaches to second language acquisition with its focus on the construction of meaning.

REFERENCES

Asher, J.J. (1969). The total physical response approach to second language learning. *Modern Language Journal, 53*, 3–17.

Asher, J.J. (1979). Motivating children and adults to acquire a second language. *SPEAQ Journal, 3*, 87–99.

Asher, J.J. (1982). The total physical response approach. In R.W. Blair (Ed.), *Innovative approaches to language teaching* (pp. 54–66). Rowley, MA: Newbury House.

Berman, P., Chambers, J., Gandara, P., McLaughlin, B., Minicucci, C., Nelson, B., et al. (1992). *Meeting the challenge of language diversity*. Berkeley, CA: BW Associates.

Bruner, J. (1978). The role of dialogue in language acquisition. In A. Sinclair, R.J. Jarvella, & W.M. Levelt (Eds.), *The child's conception of language* (pp. 241–256). New York: Springer-Verlag.

Chamot, A.U. (1981). Applications of second language acquisition research to the bilingual classroom. *Focus: National Clearinghouse for Bilingual Education*, 1–8.

Chamot, A.U. (1983). Toward a functional ESL curriculum in the elementary school. *TESOL Quarterly, 17*, 459–471.

Chan, J., & Chips, B. (1989, April). Helping LEP students survive in the content-area classroom. *Thrust*, pp. 49–51.

Chastain, K. (1975). *Developing second-language skills: From theory to practice*. Chicago: Rand McNally.

Collier, V.P. (1987). Age and rate of acquisition of second language for academic purposes. *TESOL Quarterly, 21*, 617–641.

Collier, V.P. (1989). How long? A synthesis of research on academic achievement in a second language. *TESOL Quarterly, 23*, 509–539.

Crawford, A.N. (1986). Communicative approaches to ESL: A bridge to reading comprehension. In M.P. Douglass (Ed.), *Claremont Reading Conference Yearbook* (pp. 292–305). Claremont, CA: Claremont Reading Conference.

Crawford, A.N. (1993). Literature, integrated language arts, and the language minority child: A focus on meaning. In A. Carrasquillo & C. Hedley (Eds.), *Whole language and the bilingual learner* (pp. 61–75). Norwood, NJ: Ablex.

Crawford, A.N. (1994). Communicative approaches to second language acquisition: From oral language development into the core curriculum and L2 literacy. In C.F. Leyba (Ed.), *Schooling and language minority students: A theoretical framework* (2nd ed., pp. 79–131). Los Angeles: Evaluation, Dissemination and Assessment Center, California State University.

Cummins, J. (1980). The cross-lingual dimensions of language proficiency: Implications for bilingual education and the optimal age issue. *TESOL Quarterly, 14*, 175–187.

Cummins, J. (1981). The role of primary language development in promoting educational success for language minority students. In California State Department of Education (Ed.),

Schooling and language minority students: A theoretical framework (pp. 3–49). Los Angeles: Evaluation, Dissemination and Assessment Center, California State University.

Cummins, J. (1986). Empowering minority students: A framework for intervention. *Harvard Educational Review, 56,* 18–36.

Cummins, J. (1989). *Empowering minority students.* Sacramento, CA: California Association for Bilingual Education.

Dixon, C.N., & Nessel, D. (1983). *Language experience approach to reading and writing: LEA for ESL.* Hayward, CA: Alemany Press.

Dulay, H.C., & Burt, M.K. (1974a). Errors and strategies in child second language acquisition. *TESOL Quarterly, 8,* 129–143.

Dulay, H.C., & Burt, M.K. (1974b). Natural sequences in child second language acquisition. *Language Learning, 24,* 37–53.

Ervin-Tripp, S.M. (1974). Is second language learning like the first? *TESOL Quarterly, 8,* 111–127.

Finocchiaro, M. (1974). *English as a second language: From theory to practice.* New York: Regents.

Fitzgerald, J. (1993). Literacy and students who are learning English as a second language. *The Reading Teacher, 46,* 638–647.

Gardner, R., & Lambert, W. (1972). *Attitudes and motivation in second-language learning.* Rowley, MA: Newbury House.

Gee, J.P. (1992). *The social mind: Ideology and social practice.* New York: Bergin & Garvey.

Goodman, K. (1986). *What's whole in whole language?* Portsmouth, NH: Heinemann.

Heald-Taylor, G. (1986). *Whole language strategies for ESL students.* San Diego: Dormac.

Heller, M.F. (1988). Comprehending and composing through language experience. *The Reading Teacher, 42,* 130–135.

Holdaway, D. (1979). *The foundations of literacy.* Sydney: Ashton Scholastic.

Hudelson, S. (1984). Kan yu ret an rayt en Ingles: Children become literate in English as a second language. *TESOL Quarterly, 18,* 221–238.

Krashen, S.D. (1981). Bilingual education and second language acquisition theory. In California State Department of Education (Ed.), *Schooling and language minority students: A theoretical framework* (pp. 51–79). Los Angeles: Evaluation, Dissemination and Assessment Center, California State University.

Krashen, S.D. (1982). Theory versus practice in language training. In R.W. Blair (Ed.), *Innovative approaches to language teaching* (pp. 15–30). Rowley, MA: Newbury House.

Krashen, S.D. (1985). *Inquiries and insights: Second language teaching, immersion, and bilingual education.* Hayward, CA: Alemany Press.

Krashen, S.D. (1991). *Bilingual education: A focus on current research.* Washington, DC: National Clearinghouse for Bilingual Education.

Krashen, S.D., & Biber, D. (1988). *On course: Bilingual education's success in California.* Sacramento, CA: California Association for Bilingual Education.

Krashen, S.D., Long, M.A., & Scarcella, R.C. (1979). Age, rate and eventual attainment in second language acquisition. *TESOL Quarterly, 13,* 573–582.

Krashen, S.D., & Terrell, T.D. (1983). *The natural approach: Language acquisition in the classroom.* New York: Pergamon/Alemany.

Lenneberg, E. (1967). *Biological foundations of language.* New York: Wiley.

Los Angeles Unified School District. (1985). *Strategies for sheltered English instruction*. Los Angeles: Author.

Lynch, P. (1986). *Using Big Books and predictable books*. New York: Scholastic.

Moustafa, M., & Penrose, J. (1985). Comprehensible input PLUS the language experience approach: Reading instruction for limited English speaking students. *The Reading Teacher, 38*, 640–647.

Nagy, W., Anderson, R.C., & Herman, P. (1987). Learning word meanings from context during normal reading. *American Educational Research Journal, 24*, 237–270.

Nessel, D.D., & Jones, M.B. (1981). *The language-experience approach to reading*. New York: Teachers College Columbia University.

Oller, J., Jr., Hudson, A., & Liu, P. (1977). Attitudes and attained proficiency in ESL: A sociolinguistic study of native speakers of Chinese in the United States. *Language Learning, 27*, 1–27.

Pearson, P.D. (1985). Changing the face of reading comprehension instruction. *The Reading Teacher, 38*, 724–738.

Peck, J. (1989). Using storytelling to promote language and literacy development. *The Reading Teacher, 43*, 138–141.

Richard-Amato, P.A., & Snow, M.A. (1992). Strategies for content-area teachers. In P.A. Richard-Amato & M.A. Snow (Eds.), *The multicultural classroom: Readings for content-area teachers* (pp. 145–163). White Plains, NY: Longman.

Rigg, P. (1991). Whole language in TESOL. *TESOL Quarterly, 25*, 521–542.

Rutherford, W., & Sharwood-Smith, M. (1985). Consciousness raising and universal grammar. *Applied Linguistics, 6*, 274–282.

Saville-Troike, M. (1976). *Foundations for teaching ESL*. Englewood Cliffs, NJ: Prentice-Hall.

Schifini, A. (1985). *Sheltered English: Content area instruction for limited English proficient students*. Los Angeles: Los Angeles County Office of Education.

Selinker, L., Swain, M., & Dumas, G. (1975). The interlanguage hypothesis extended to children. *Language Learning, 25*, 139–152.

Short, D.J. (1991). *Integrating language and content instruction: Strategies and techniques*. Washington, DC: National Clearinghouse for Bilingual Education.

Smith, F. (1986). *How education backed the wrong house*. [Keynote address]. California Reading Association, Fresno, California.

Smith, F. (1988). *Understanding reading*. Hillsdale, NJ: Erlbaum.

Smith, F. (1995). *Between hope and havoc*. Portsmouth, NH: Heinemann.

Snow, C.E., & Hoefnagel-Höhle, M. (1978). The critical period for language acquisition: Evidence from second language learning. *Child Development, 49*, 1114–1128.

Stanovich, K.E. (1986). Matthew effects in reading: Some consequences of individual differences in the acquisition of literacy. *Reading Research Quarterly, 21*, 360–406.

Terrell, T.D. (1977). A natural approach to second language acquisition and learning. *Modern Language Journal, 6*, 325–337.

Terrell, T.D. (1981). The natural approach in bilingual education. In California State Department of Education (Ed.), *Schooling and language minority students: A theoretical framework* (pp. 117–146). Los Angeles: Evaluation, Dissemination and Assessment Center, California State University.

Terrell, T.D. (1982). The natural approach to language teaching: An update. *Modern Language Journal, 66*, 121–132.

Terrell, T.D. (1991). The role of grammar instruction in a communicative approach. *Modern Language Journal, 75,* 52–63.

Trachtenburg, P., & Ferruggia, A. (1989). Big books from little voices: Reaching high risk beginning readers. *The Reading Teacher, 42,* 284–289.

Veatch, J., Sawicki, F., Elliott, G., Flake, E., & Blakey, J. (1979). *Key words to reading: The language experience approach begins.* Columbus, OH: Merrill.

Vygotsky, L.S. (1978). *Mind in society: The development of higher psychological processes* (M. Cole, V. John-Steiner, S. Scribner, & E. Souberman, Eds. and Trans.). Cambridge, MA: Harvard University Press. (Original work published 1934)

CHILDREN'S LITERATURE CITED

Carle, E. (1983). *The very hungry caterpillar.* New York: Putnam.

CHAPTER 8

Meeting the Needs of English Learners in All-English Classrooms: Sharing the Responsibility

Julie M. Coppola

Immediately upon entering the old brick building that houses the North School, one encounters evidence that this is a school community that celebrates the linguistic and cultural diversity of its students. A graph of native languages spoken by each grade level covers one wall. Large photographs of students from a variety of ethnic backgrounds cover another. Handwritten greetings in many languages welcome visitors and signal the entrance to the Learning Center, which houses the English as a Second Language (ESL) program. The noise level in the Learning Center is high. Leah, the ESL teacher, smiles and shakes her head:

> You know, sometimes my students come into the Learning Center, and they talk and talk and talk, and I try to calm them down, and they say, "But you don't understand. I don't talk all day."

Leah teaches ESL to 34 kindergarten through fifth-grade English learners, who together represent 16 countries and 10 languages. The Learning Center is a hub of activity for Leah, a certified ESL and elementary teacher with eight years of teaching experience, and for her students, who share this space with the special education staff. Throughout the school day Leah closely monitors her daily master schedule, which must be attended to regularly as Leah pulls out students from their general education classrooms to work in the Learning Center. Depending on the hour and the day, students are scheduled to work on English literacy development, English oral language development, or general education classroom assignments.

Down the hall from the Learning Center is Dan's fifth-grade classroom. Dan, with more than 20 years of experience at the North School, has seen his classroom become increasingly diverse over the years. This year, six of Dan's 22 students receive ESL instruction in the Learning Center with Leah—five days a week, 45 minutes per day. Among this group are four Spanish-speakers, one Korean-speaker, and one child from Israel who speaks Hebrew and French and who is learning English as his *third* language. Leah also is responsible for helping these students with the language and literacy demands of the fifth-grade language arts/social studies curriculum. In previous school years, Leah addressed this need with additional pull-out sessions in the Learning Center. But as Leah and Dan's school system is encouraging collaboration among specialists and classroom teachers, Leah and Dan decided to coteach in Dan's classroom during this daily one-hour block and eliminate the need to pull out students. From Leah's perspective, this is a long-overdue change.

> I'm trying very hard to work with teachers on how to make modifications in the classroom for these kids. If a teacher is doing a particular unit, I don't feel they should always come to me and say, "This is the unit I am doing. Can you help these kids?"

Dan too, was ready for a change. Over the years, he reports, there have been increasing numbers of students in his classroom who receive ESL support services; however, he remarks, he has had little training or experience in teaching English learners.

> Probably the only formal [training] I've had has been staff development—mainly within this building. Most of my teaching has been language arts, so frequently when the students are assigned to language arts, they are pulled out to go to the ESL room for their reading instruction and language development instruction. They've been in some of the classes but often not very consistently in the past because of their pull-out schedule for ESL.

Dan believes that coteaching with Leah will allow him to better know the English learners in his class—and will enable them to participate more fully in his fifth-grade classroom curriculum.

> This [coteaching] seems to have a chance of working, whereas previously when the students were in the classroom for one thing, they weren't in the classroom consistently, so they might have missed something. They might have been here on Monday, but then missed Tuesday and be here Wednesday and Thursday, but then miss Friday. It's hard enough for them to keep up with the curriculum, much less when they are pulled out of the class.

There was a strong literature component to the fifth-grade social studies curriculum, according to Dan. Each year he chose several historical novels related to the fifth-grade topic of U.S. History. He explains,

> The format is similar to that in language arts. These units focus on our understanding of the people and time, as well as on reading appreciation and skill development.

Current events was also an important piece of the fifth-grade social studies curriculum, according to Dan. Each week, students were required to read and summarize two newspaper articles that were then presented for in-class discussion. A social studies text also was used frequently. Dan did not report any modifications in his instructional practices, however, when English learners were in the classroom.

> I am always aware that I'm probably not very successful in reaching some of the kids. Whenever they are in the classroom, I try to help them be involved in whatever group they're in. Depending on their proficiency in [English], some of them get involved, and some of them are very peripheral in their small groups.

Dan and Leah, like many teaching professionals, are faced with meeting the complex language and literacy needs of the increasing number of English learners in all-English classrooms. In this chapter I illustrate the journey of Dan, a fifth-grade classroom teacher, and Leah, an ESL specialist, as they collaborate to plan instruction that will meet the language and literacy needs of their English learners.

Changing Classrooms, Changing Needs

The growing number of children who are learning English as a new language in school has dramatically increased the demands on classroom teachers. In a U.S. national survey of classroom teachers, however, only 20% of respondents reported that they were prepared to teach students from diverse language and cultural backgrounds (National Center for Education Statistics, 1999). In the absence of special programs designed to meet their language and literacy needs, most English learners are in general education classrooms with teachers who have received little or no training in effective instructional practices that allow English learners to become active, contributing members of their classrooms (Carrasquillo & Rodriguez, 2002). There is often little information readily available to general education teachers about how to meet their English learners' special language and literacy needs in all-English classrooms (Gersten, 1999). The result is diminished opportunities for English learners to receive meaningful language and literacy instruction in general education classrooms.

Furthermore, participation in special educational programs for English learners, such as pull-out ESL classes, does not guarantee academic success. In pull-out programs, students must contend with fragmented literacy instruction, limited access to the grade-level curriculum, and isolation from native–English-speaking peers (Ernst, 1994). Pull-out schedules frequently leave little time for classroom teachers and ESL specialists, like Dan and Leah, to communicate with each other about their students, creating tensions and uncertainties with regard to accountability for students' academic success. Questions also remain about the quality of language and literacy instruction in ESL classrooms. Arreaga-Mayer and Perdomo-Rivera (1996) found that the ESL classrooms they studied provided English learners with few opportunities to read and write extended text and even fewer opportunities to develop oral language skills. Valdés (2001) reported that instruction in the ESL classrooms she studied was characterized by traditional grammar-based exercises and infrequent opportunities for students to use oral and written language for communicative purposes (see Crawford, Chapter 7 in this volume).

The steadily rising numbers of immigrant children in U.S. schools require that all teachers be prepared to respond to the divergent abilities, needs, and experiences of this fastest growing segment of the school-age population (National Council for Accreditation of Teacher Education, 2000). Research on pull-out models of remedial reading instruction demonstrates the need for collaboration among all those involved in the education of a school's neediest learners (Allington & Walmsley, 1995). Yet there has been little emphasis on the need for collaboration among those responsible for the education of English learners. By examining a collaborative effort between a general education classroom teacher and an ESL specialist, this chapter will demonstrate one way in which literacy instruction for English learners can be improved. First I examine the literacy instruction of six English learners in two settings: their fifth-grade classroom and their ESL classroom. Next I examine the children's opportunities to learn when their classroom teacher and their ESL teacher collaborate to implement a literature unit in the children's fifth-grade classroom. I conclude with insights gained from their collaboration that I believe can inform and guide classroom teachers and ESL specialists in their efforts to meet the needs of their English learners.

The collaborative project described here was an outgrowth of two workshops on effective instructional practices for English learners conducted by a

Boston University faculty member for a suburban school district with a growing population of English learners. The focus of these workshops was strategies for learning about students' home and background experiences and ways to build on this knowledge with respect to English learners in literacy instruction. Prior to the start of the workshops, I contacted all teachers who had enrolled and asked them to participate in a study to examine the effectiveness of a particular teaching strategy presented in the workshops: the critical autobiography (Brisk & Harrington, 2000). In the larger study, six teachers implemented the critical autobiography in their classrooms. This chapter focuses on two of the teachers in the larger study, Dan and Leah, who decided to collaboratively implement the critical autobiography as one component of a literature unit in Dan's fifth-grade classroom.

Critical Autobiography

Effective instruction of English learners is dependent on a teacher's knowledge about a host of factors—linguistic, cultural, economic, political, and sociological—that shape students' lives and their opportunities for academic development (Bartolome, 1994; Durgunoglu & Verhoeven, 1998). Linguistic factors include the nature of various languages and the ways in which native languages and English are used in the home, community, and school. Cultural factors encompass cultural values, communication and discipline practices, and parental participation in schooling. Economic and political factors include opportunities for social and economic mobility for members of language-minority groups in language-majority settings, along with their society's language and immigration policies. And sociological factors comprise attitudes toward minority languages and ethnic groups in addition to immigrants' reasons for immigration and their ties to their native countries. According to Zeichner (1993), "It is each student's individual life experiences influenced in unique ways by factors such as…ethnicity, language, [and] culture that affect the academic development of students" (p. 10).

In a critical autobiography, English learners and their teachers, working together, first investigate how these factors influence students' daily lives. For example, to explore the role of linguistic factors, a student's individual and/or family use of the native language and of English throughout the day may be documented in a language diary. Classroom activities—such as graphing family and individual language use patterns, surveying school and local libraries for availability of books and newspapers in English and the native language, or charting hours of television viewing in each language—help students see that linguistic factors affect their opportunities to use and learn English and their native language. Students and teachers can investigate students' ties to their native countries by examining family, classroom, or schoolwide travel patterns and discussing the influence of these ties on the home, the community, and academic achievement. Students can see that the ease or difficulty in travel to native countries plays an important role in family or community decisions to maintain native languages. Students can learn about the many different reasons for their families' immigration by interviewing their parents and reading first-person accounts of immigration. After class discussion and analysis of these factors, each student writes a critical autobiography—a personal narrative in which the student explores the effects of these factors on his or her life.

The larger study investigated what teachers learned about the English learners in their classrooms through their critical autobiographies and the influence of this knowledge on their teaching practice. The data presented here demonstrate the ways in which Dan and Leah's collaboration on the critical autobiography project influenced literacy instruction for their English learners in both their general education and ESL classrooms.

Methods and Sources of Data

Throughout the six-month study, my role was that of participant/observer. I first observed the teachers in their classrooms at the beginning of the study, prior to their taking part in the workshops. I observed literacy instructional periods and focused on literacy instructional practices. Next, I observed the teachers as they participated in the two workshops. The first workshop focused on the factors that affect English learners; the second, on guiding students through their investigation of the factors and their writing of a critical autobiography. I observed the teachers in their classrooms one to two times a week as they explored the factors with their students, and as their students wrote and shared their critical autobiographies. In Dan and Leah's classrooms this took place over a six-week period. As the students were writing and revising their critical autobiographies, I occasionally helped the English learners with English grammar and vocabulary. Finally, I observed the teachers in their classrooms at the end of the study. I conducted in-depth interviews with the teachers prior to the workshops; at the middle of the study, after their students had written their critical autobiographies; and at the end of the study.

All the teachers participated in a group reflection session at the end of the study.

As in most ethnographic studies, data collection and analysis were ongoing throughout the study. Each data source was analyzed for emerging themes, regularities, patterns, and topics as suggested by Strauss and Corbin (1999). Data analysis related to teachers' knowledge about English learners was based on the theoretical framework we discussed, comprising the factors that affect English learners. The coding framework for teaching practice included literacy instructional practices, literacy materials, and instructional episodes and was informed by recommended practices in language and literacy instruction for English learners. These included, but were not limited to, instances when the teachers (a) used visuals to make content comprehensible; (b) planned opportunities for English learners to speak, listen, read, and write for meaningful purposes; and (c) provided opportunities for students to write about or share background experiences (see Graves & Fitzgerald, chapter 5; Crawford, chapter 7; García & Beltrán, chapter 9; and Dutro & Moran, chapter 10, in this volume). A research assistant trained in coding procedures independently reviewed the data, and we conferred to compare responses and resolve any coding differences.

In the larger study, I organized the data from each of the six teachers into individual case studies (Yin, 1994), and I then conducted a cross-case analysis of all six cases (Miles & Huberman, 1994). The effects of the implementation of the critical autobiography on teacher knowledge of their English learners were reported in Coppola (2001). In this next section, I present Dan and Leah's efforts at collaboration.

Early Efforts: Struggling to Meet the Needs of English Learners

I interviewed Dan and Leah at the start of the school year prior to the workshops on teaching English learners; in their interviews, they were positive about their coteaching arrangement. Dan was hopeful, in particular, that coteaching would help him include the English learners in his classroom in more class activities; as we have seen, this had not happened in the past as often as he would have liked. Dan also was concerned because when his class was engaged in small-group activities, he often allowed his students to form their own groups. The English learners were usually not asked to join a group, so most often they were left to form a group of their own. Dan hoped that teaching with Leah would help him plan instruction that would involve the English learners together with their fifth-grade peers. Leah was also enthusiastic about the coteaching, which she thought would provide her with an opportunity to model teaching strategies in Dan's classroom that would benefit the English learners.

In early October, prior to the workshops, I observed Dan and Leah's classrooms during literacy instructional periods. Although in their interviews Dan and Leah had been positive about their coteaching plans at the start of the school year, these classroom observations demonstrated that, over a five-day period, the English learners did not attend their language arts/social studies class. Dan and Leah did not coteach. Instead, Leah continued to pull out the students for special instruction in the Learning Center where students had few opportunities to learn or use the English language or literacy necessary for participation in their fifth-grade classroom.

Throughout the observation period, Leah began each planned coteaching session by speaking with Dan at his desk, as the following field notes demonstrate:

> After Leah and Dan finished talking, Leah spoke to each of her students, who were seated at their desks with their notebooks open. The students packed up their notebooks and followed Leah out of the classroom. Leah explained the change in the plan to me.
>
> Leah: This is current events day. We decided that the children who do not get the newspaper at home, or the ones who would not benefit from the current events discussion, will go to the Learning Center with me.

Field notes taken during another observation period in Dan's classroom revealed a similar chain of events:

> Today the plan is for the students to remain in Dan's classroom, and Leah will help the students as they work in cooperative groups to complete a reading/writing activity about the federal government. After conferring with Dan at his desk, Leah decided that her students would be better off with her in the Learning Center. The children will not be able to stay in the classroom the entire language arts/social studies block, however, because Leah had scheduled a pull-out session with another group of children. We pack up again and leave Dan's classroom.

After a shortened period in the Learning Center, Leah sent her students back to Dan's classroom for the remainder of the language arts/social studies class.

The students' week in their language arts/social studies class also was interrupted by an apple-picking field trip planned by Leah for all kindergarten through fifth-grade students who received ESL support services. As a result, the fifth graders did not participate in a scheduled social studies class review for a unit test, held in Dan's classroom.

On the second day of the test review Leah's students were prepared to remain in Dan's classroom, and they sat with their textbooks open on their desks. After another conference at Dan's desk in which Leah looked over the test, she again asked the students to pack their belongings and follow her to the Learning Center. Once in the Learning Center, Leah explained the change to the students:

> You are going to have a test in social studies, and I am going to change the test for you. I am going to make it a little simpler, with not so many different words. I'm going to make a new test for you.

Dan concurred with Leah's decisions to pull out the students during the language arts/social studies block: "Leah thought she would do better to take them out of the classroom today," he explained.

At the first workshop, Leah was discouraged: Coteaching was not going as smoothly as she and Dan had hoped. There were few opportunities during their busy days to coplan or to share information about their students. Leah continued to pull out the students from Dan's classroom for both their ESL and their language arts/social studies class times. The students were spending a significant portion of their school day away from Dan's classroom and their fifth-grade peers. And once in the Learning Center, the students most often worked on phonics or spelling. The English learners continued to have limited access to the fifth-grade curriculum.

During the second workshop on the critical autobiography, however, all the participants were provided opportunities to work together and share ideas about how to implement this strategy in their classrooms. Dan and Leah took advantage of this time.

Dan decided that a unit his class was beginning on the discovery and settlement of the New World would provide a good opportunity to explore the factors that affect English learners. He was concerned, however, that he would not be able to find a way to explore them with all the students in his class; he could not teach a unit solely to his English learners. Leah suggested the class read the book *Guests* (Dorris, 1994), the story of a Native American boy and his first encounter with white Europeans. Leah believed that the book's theme—being a stranger in a new place—not only provided many opportunities to explore the factors, but also provided ways to include all the students in the class. Dan agreed that the experience of being a guest would be a universal theme, and that other students —not only the English learners—would be able to relate parents' or grandparents' immigration stories. Dan added that there were several students in his class who were former ESL students who might also benefit from having an opportunity to share their immigration experiences. Dan and Leah also decided to try three days of coteaching the unit on the New World in Dan's classroom rather than five days, as previously planned. As they left the second workshop, Leah expressed the hope that this collaboration would "help integrate the students in Dan's classroom" and eliminate the need to pull out students.

Creating Opportunities to Learn: Collaborating for English Learners

Leah and Dan decided to concentrate on exploring cultural, linguistic, and sociological factors with their fifth-grade class. Leah volunteered to plan all the reading response activities. She wanted to plan activities—including classroom discussions, readings, and writing about rites of passage, gender roles and expectations, holidays, foods, and customs across cultures—in which English learners would have opportunities to share their background knowledge and experiences with their classmates. Dan planned all reading comprehension, vocabulary, and skill development activities.

Dan and Leah began each coteaching session by reading a chapter of *Guests* aloud to the class. Dan reported that the response activities provided many opportunities for the English learners in his classroom to talk and write about their immigration experiences—which, he explained, "came very naturally from reading the book *Guests*." Other students were asked to research and share parents' or grandparents' immigration stories. All the children in the classroom shared, compared, and contrasted cultural traditions and the use of languages other than English in their homes and communities. Finally, all the children talked and wrote about a time when they were a stranger in a new place. As the class read and responded to the story, Leah and the English learners remained in Dan's classroom, and the English learners participated in all classroom activities.

After reading *Guests* and investigating the factors, Dan and Leah gave all the students in the class a choice of writing assignments. One choice was to write a critical autobiography; four of the six English learners chose this assignment. Dan explained,

> It flowed naturally. It came out of reading the book *Guests,* and the result of
> reading the book was a critical autobiography. It was an autobiography with
> a real focus—being a stranger in a new place.

In a small group, the English learners first brainstormed a list of topics to be included in their critical autobiographies. Dan and Leah reminded the students to revisit their class discussions on the factors as they were selecting topics. The children decided, with Leah's help, to write about languages spoken at home, cultural traditions, reasons for their family's immigration, adapting to a new environment, and the experience of being a guest.

Leah and the English learners remained in Dan's classroom for the writing sessions. Dan described the classroom scene:

> Four days we worked on writing in class, where all the students were working,
> so it was a very busy kind of classroom. It was mainly a busy writing and talk-
> ing kind of atmosphere during the whole class.

The final day of in-class writing was devoted to peer editing. Rather than allowing the students to select their own partners, Dan and Leah made sure that each English learner was paired with a native-English speaker.

The English learners continued to work on revising and editing their critical autobiographies in the Learning Center during their pull-out ESL class. They also practiced their oral presentations with Leah. When their critical autobiographies were completed, the students shared them orally with Dan and Leah and with their classmates in Dan's classroom (see Graves & Fitzgerald, chapter 5, for similar activities before, during, and after reading).

Dan and Leah were pleased with the outcomes of their collaboration. When I first met Dan, he had experienced, as we know, limited success in involving English learners in classroom activities. Dan learned that when English learners were provided opportunities to talk about their background experiences, they actively participated in class discussions:

> Definitely they said more than they would normally say. I think they were
> delighted to talk about some of their traditions—specifically we were talking
> about different celebrations, rites of passage. They were very pleased to tell
> about these different kinds of things that they do. I couldn't stop watching
> Luis while the others were presenting their critical autobiographies—I have
> never seen such involvement on his face. I have never seen such interaction

with a lesson. Certainly [the English learners] don't tend to respond a lot. Definitely they said more than they would normally say.

Dan noted that these students' increased classroom participation did not end with their critical autobiographies:

> One of the students about two weeks later brought in a current events article about *quinceañeras*, with big pictures and everything, and shared that with the class. So we all remembered that that was what she had mentioned in [her critical autobiography].

Leah also noted the value of providing English learners with opportunities to build on their background knowledge in their fifth-grade classroom:

> I found a great deal of enthusiasm for doing this project and for doing all this writing. They are not crazy about writing. It is hard work for them. But when they were writing about their own experiences, when it was their own life, there was a lot of enthusiasm.

Leah added that writing about familiar experiences also provided a meaningful context for skill development:

> It was a very good format to teach them how to organize, to talk about grammar, to talk about punctuation. Their own writing about their own experiences and their own countries—I thought that was very motivating.

Dan observed that when his English learners were given opportunities to talk about their background experiences, he in turn learned about *their* abilities. According to Dan, "It was a revelation how well they could do. They came up with some very nice pieces of work." Leah, too, reported that the students achieved more than she had expected.

Dan also spoke about interactions between the English learners in his classroom and their fifth-grade classmates:

> Something else that I learned, and I think it is a really profound thing, is what the other students learned [about their classmates]. Sometimes there is not that much interaction between the two groups, and maybe the [English learners] have never had a platform to stand up and talk about some meaningful things. So I thought that was very, very neat.

Leah reported that her teaching in Dan's classroom changed during their collaboration:

What was happening [before] was that the teacher was teaching, and I was just helping those kids try to understand what the teacher was doing. This has really given me the opportunity to get more involved. With this project I've been really able to work with the kids and really guide them and direct them. It's really been more of a coteaching situation with them with this particular project than it has been. There was only pull-out during their ESL time, and I used that time to help them with their project.

Leah attributed this change to the critical autobiography's being a collaborative project that provided opportunities for her students to share their background knowledge and experiences with their classmates and teacher:

There hasn't been an attitude of "These kids have a whole lot to bring to the class, and let's create opportunities for that to happen." As we've been doing this unit, I've seen more drawing on the kids' own experiences, more opportunities for them to talk to the class about their experiences.

Dan was pleased and relieved to discover that he could successfully include all students *and* cover his required curriculum:

Thank goodness it was a project that could work with all fifth-graders. I would have done a literature unit anyway, so this did not take any more time than another literature unit. When we first spoke, that was certainly on my mind—could I possibly give up the time—and the other part was I couldn't have done [this activity] with just the [English learners].

Dan reported that he planned to continue to provide opportunities for the English learners in his classroom to share and build on their background experiences: "To try and bring out their experiences—that's something I am more likely to do now." Leah reported that she planned to work with Dan to identify ways in which English learners' background experiences could be connected to the curriculum. Dan added that he planned to collaborate with Leah to ensure that English learners' needs were considered as he planned whole-class and small-group activities. Leah, too, was optimistic about the remainder of the school year:

I am really looking forward to the rest of the school year, because I will be interested in seeing how for the rest of the curriculum we're able to draw on the students' culture and their personal experiences and integrate them and pull them in. It's been fun. I have really enjoyed being in Dan's classroom and figuring out ways to make that happen.

Dan agreed:

I hope this is something we can do throughout the year and not just for this project, although this project has been super. But to keep working in this way, because it has been good for the kids and for me.

Conclusions

Throughout the collaboration, the English learners had more opportunities to learn about reading and writing in both their fifth-grade and ESL classrooms. In Dan's classroom, English learners had more opportunities to read, write, and talk about extended text; they participated in and completed more grade-level literacy instructional tasks and had opportunities to work on these tasks with native-English-speaking fifth-grade peers. The English learners shared their background experiences orally and in writing, and they participated in instructional activities that allowed them to build on their background knowledge. Throughout the collaboration, English learners continued to attend pull-out ESL classes; instruction in the ESL classroom, however, was devoted to extra practice on, and reinforcement of, grade-level literacy instructional tasks or preparation for a forthcoming lesson in their fifth-grade classroom.

Dan and Leah's efforts add to our understanding with respect to planning effective literacy instruction for English learners in all-English classrooms. The English learners in Dan's classroom benefited when their classroom teacher and their ESL teacher collaborated on an instructional unit that considered the language and literacy learning needs of all the students.

Dan and Leah benefited as well. Working together, they made changes in the kinds of learning opportunities they provided their English learners. Dan learned that he could make modifications in his instructional planning and classroom practices so as to include English learners and provide more opportunities for their language and literacy development to take place together with their grade-level peers. Leah was able to plan instruction in the ESL classroom that better prepared the students for grade-level literacy experiences. Providing classroom and ESL teachers with opportunities to collaborate and share their expertise may be a first step in establishing a literacy learning environment in which all teachers are prepared to assume responsibility for meeting the needs of English learners.

REFERENCES

Allington, R.L., & Walmsley, S.A. (1995). *No quick fix: Rethinking literacy programs in America's elementary schools.* New York: Teachers College Press; Newark, DE: International Reading Association.

Arreaga-Mayer, C., & Perdomo-Rivera, C. (1996). Ecobehavioral analysis of instruction for at-risk language minority students. *The Elementary School Journal, 96*(3), 245–258.

Bartolome, L. (1994). Beyond the methods fetish: Toward a humanizing pedagogy. *Harvard Educational Review, 64*(2), 173–194.

Brisk, M., & Harrington, M. (2000). *Literacy and bilingualism: A handbook for all teachers.* Mahwah, NJ: Erlbaum.

Carrasquillo, A., & Rodriguez, V. (2002). *Language minority students in the mainstream classroom* (2nd ed.). Philadelphia: Multilingual Matters.

Coppola, J. (2001, April). *Teachers learning about diversity: Effects on instruction.* Paper presented at the annual meeting of the American Educational Research Association, Seattle, WA.

Durgunoglu, A., & Verhoeven, L. (1998). *Literacy development in a multilingual context.* Mahwah, NJ: Erlbaum.

Ernst, G. (1994). Beyond language: The many dimensions of an ESL program. *Anthropology and Education Quarterly, 25,* 317–335.

Gersten, R. (1999). Lost opportunities: Challenges confronting four teachers of English-language learners. *The Elementary School Journal, 100*(1), 37–56.

Miles, M., & Huberman, A.M. (1994). *Qualitative data analysis* (2nd ed.). Thousand Oaks, CA: Sage.

National Center for Education Statistics. (1999). *Teacher quality: A report on the preparation and qualifications of public school teachers.* Washington, DC: U.S. Department of Education.

National Council for Accreditation of Teacher Education. (2000). *NCATE Standards.* Washington, DC: Author.

Strauss, A., & Corbin, J. (1990). *Basics of qualitative research: Grounded theory procedure and techniques.* Thousand Oaks, CA: Sage.

Valdes, G. (2001). *Learning and not learning English: Latino students in American schools.* New York: Teachers College Press.

Yin, R. (1994). *Case study research: Design and methods* (2nd ed.). Thousand Oaks, CA: Sage.

Zeichner, K. (1993). *Educating teachers for diversity: NCRTL special report.* East Lansing, MI: National Center for Research on Teacher Learning.

CHILDREN'S LITERATURE CITED

Dorris, M. (1994). *Guests.* New York: Hyperion.

CHAPTER 9

Revisioning the Blueprint: Building for the Academic Success of English Learners

Gilbert G. García and Dolores Beltrán

Today's Blueprint for English Learners

Most successful projects are successful because they are planned. Success cannot be left to chance. Learning works the same way. It is most successful in a classroom when it is carefully planned and executed in explicit lessons that are responsive to the needs of the student. Even though we know that a second language is best acquired naturally over time when students are meaningfully engaged in academically rigorous tasks in low-anxiety language-learning contexts, creating such contexts within the formal context of school is often extremely difficult. Planning such a curriculum and implementing it within the time constraints allotted for reaching fluency in English for English learners is also very difficult. It can be done, however—but it takes careful planning. It requires a blueprint for success that must be designed with the same rigor that is inherent in the blueprints for any building (see Dutro & Moran, chapter 10, in this volume).

Consider the roof above your own head for a moment. Look around you and consider the essence of the building you are in. The building did not come to be without careful planning. You can be sure that several professionals collaborated to create a blueprint. Engineers surveyed the land and tested the soil. Architects analyzed the surrounding environment and revised their plans according to building codes and recommendations made by structural engineers. Once finalized, the blueprint was taken to a contractor to plan and execute the construction. The blueprint became a building, but only as a result of the careful planning and inspections that preceded it. This same process applies to the creation of instructional blueprints for the academic success of English learners.

Many educators expect that all students will master the designated language arts curriculum with equal success within the same amount of instructional time allocated to teach English speakers literacy. English learners are expected to simultaneously learn English literacy and acquire English as a second language in an English immersion setting. In these settings, the challenge facing both teachers and English learners is that most skills found in the regular language arts program must also be taught to and learned by English learners in the same developmental sequence and under the same time constraints as for English speakers, even though these learners do not begin with the same language base. These are inordinately high expectations; they are equivalent to providing a contractor with a set of blueprints designed to be built on an inadequate foundation. Bilingual programs use the primary language as the foundation for literacy. Foundations must be built on solid ground; they must be deep enough, and sufficiently reinforced for the building to withstand the most violent forces of nature. All blueprints must be designed with such a foundation. The same set of blueprints is certainly not appropriate for all buildings, because of varied mitigating circumstances; yet we presently face a growing movement in education to apply the same set of blueprints to ensure the literacy success of all learners, including English learners.

This "New Literacy," as Gutiérrez (2001) calls it, is a mandated pedagogy of one-size-fits-all language and literacy learning curriculum that ignores the linguistic differences between English learners and English speakers. Forbidding the use of the primary language is the most important characteristic of this literacy movement. As Gutiérrez observes,

> consider this typical scenario in a California classroom. One child is English language dominant, a second is Spanish language dominant with little understanding of Academic English. Both are emergent literates in their primary language. Yet, academic reform in California assumes these two students participate on a level playing field and ostensibly treats them, in pedagogical terms, identically. However, this mandated pedagogy simultaneously limits the Spanish-speaking child from using her complete linguistic and sociocultural repertoire to learn and, once again, privileges the English dominant student in the learning environment. (p. 567)

Alarmingly, this pedagogy is increasingly being embraced as the blueprint for success for English learners across the United States. Owing to a prevailing desire among legislators and the majority of their constituents for a "quick fix" that will create a nation of readers at any cost, English literacy learning curricula for English learners have been constructed on a linguistic foundation of quicksand that imperils their academic development.

Many educational researchers (August & Hakuta, 1997; Cummins, 2000; Fillmore & Snow, 2000; Fitzgerald, Garcia, Jimenez, & Barrera, 2000; Gersten & Baker, 2000; Goldenberg, 2001; Tharp, 1997) agree that the primary language should play a role in the literacy development of English learners (see also Section I of this volume). In spite of this supportive basis for primary language instruction, however, Gutiérrez (2001) points out that advocates of the New Literacy espouse a pedagogy that defies logic and ignores the most precious capacity children bring with them to school—their language: "Language, the most powerful tool for mediating learning, in this case the children's primary language, is excluded from the students' learning toolkit" (p. 565).

An alternative to this existing practice for beginning-kindergarten English learners would be to double the time devoted to beginning literacy. This could be accomplished by increasing the number of preschool programs and targeting English language development (ELD) as the focus of this preschool curriculum. For English learners whose first school experience is kindergarten, we need to find ways of moving to a full-day kindergarten with at least half the day devoted to English language development. An alternative is to offer kindergarten English learners a K^x year, a second year of kindergarten, and to devote the first kindergarten year exclusively to English language development instead of the academic literacy curriculum currently in place. One hour of literacy instruction devoted to simultaneous literacy instruction and language acquisition is simply not adequate.

This instructional accommodation would serve to ameliorate the huge language gap that impedes the literacy success of many English learners. This same model could be applied to newcomers in subsequent grade levels. In such cases, chosen content would provide the basis of a yearlong English-immersion instructional ELD curriculum intended to prepare students to more fully participate in a mainstream literacy curriculum that is intended to fit the needs of all learners, and that is also based on a set of blueprints originally designed for English speakers, not English learners.

The blueprints for instructing English learners must be examined and refined to ensure that the language arts curriculum for English learners is constructed on comprehensive and sound research-based classroom practice designed to be flexible and adaptable enough to meet the complex needs of all second-language learners in all programs of choice in U.S. schools. Whether schools or parents opt for bilingual or immersion programs, the need for research-based classroom practice applies. The New Literacy is, we believe, a blueprint for a "house of cards" that will result in modest gains in the primary grades in literacy achievement on standardized tests, but will doom the English learner to a school career of declining literacy achievement, as measured by the same standardized tests. For far too many English learners the decline is exacerbated with each successive year, until frustration and failure lead to dropping out. For the majority of those students who remain in school, the ability to pass the high school exit exam will be diminished greatly. All too few, therefore, will make it out of high school—let alone graduate from a university.

More than a decade ago, Figueroa, Fradd, and Correa (1989) found that there was no "substantive body of empirical data on actual, well-controlled interventions...that improve the academic abilities of students who are English-language learners" (p. 17). Recently, Gersten and Baker (2000) cited the paucity of controlled empirical investigations; they found only nine studies with sufficient controls that support appropriate practice. They resorted to conducting a qualitative multivocal research synthesis (Ogawa & Malen, 1991), wherein promising practices were identified from a series of professional work groups that included academics and practitioners.

It is no surprise that our operative blueprints for the academic success of English learners have been created by many who are less than skilled architects. Researchers and practitioners who have experience with English learners are often ignored when it comes to the formulation of policy that dictates practice. Instead, laymen increasingly create the blueprints and set the policies that directly affect English learners: Legislators, state and local school board members, superintendents, and even the public at large have, as it were, proclaimed themselves architects. Experienced and knowledgeable educators have been relegated to the role of contractors and been given the mandate to take these blueprints and build the house, disregarding what they know about best instructional practices for English learners.

The Pillars of Effective Instructional Practice

Our understanding of English learners is evolving. There is still a dearth of empirical studies in the research literature that involve English learners and their literacy development. By contrast, there is a proliferation of studies that allow claims to be made about beginning reading pedagogy that are based on reliable empirical research. Some educational architects who create blueprints for the literacy success of English speakers use this same research base to justify the design of their instructional programs for English learners. We believe these claims are frequently misleading and most often unjustified if taken only at face value. We contend that applying the same teaching practice for literacy learning to both English speakers and English learners is not always supported by the research. We need more empirical studies of English learner populations to inform the architects of instructional pedagogy for English learners.

Despite the paucity of research, some noted researchers have reconceived the pillars of English learner pedagogy, based on new understandings of the needs of English learners. We have carefully considered the existing literature and have adopted the Five Standards for Effective Pedagogy advocated by the Center for Research on Education, Diversity & Excellence (CREDE) (2002), based at the University of California, Santa Cruz, as a basis for this discussion; we believe that they are necessary elements in any successful blueprint for English learners. These principles are described by Dalton (1998) in a research report:

> The Standards for Effective Pedagogy and Learning were established through CREDE research, and through an extensive analysis of the research and development literature in education and diversity. The Standards represent recommendations on which the literature is in agreement, across all cultural, racial, and linguistic groups in the United States, all age levels, and all subject matters. Thus, they express the principles of effective pedagogy for all students. Even for mainstream students, the Standards describe the ideal conditions for instruction; but for students at-risk of educational failure, effective classroom implementation of the Standards is vital.

The research consensus summarized by Dalton (1998) and advocated by CREDE (2002) can be expressed as five standards; to this compendium, we have added only one standard, placing it first before the five that we also adopt. It represents our strong belief that primary language use is essential and must be included in the instructional blueprints for all English learners.

The first pillar—native language, or primary language use—is both the main beam and the central pillar that supports literacy development in all sound instructional blueprints for English learners. Professional organizations, researchers, and practitioners generally agree that primary language use is an essential component for literacy success. The International Reading Association (2001), for example, has a position statement on second-language literacy instruction that recommends that educators recognize the value of initial instruction in the mother tongue and acknowledge that schooling in the official language and the home language are not mutually exclusive. Cummins

(1981) has long advocated recognizing the contribution that primary language makes to the acquisition of a second language in his explanation of what he calls the Common Underlying Proficiency (CUP) model. This model describes the cornerstone axiom of bilingual programs: Begin literacy instruction for English learners in L1 (primary language) instead of in L2 (second language). Cummins writes,

> What this principle means is that in, for example, a Spanish-English bilingual program, Spanish instruction that develops Spanish reading and writing skills (for either L1 or L2 speakers) is not just developing Spanish skills, it is also developing a deeper conceptual and linguistic proficiency that is strongly related to the development of literacy in the majority language (English). In other words, although the surface aspects (e.g., pronunciation, fluency) of different languages are clearly separate, there is an underlying cognitive/academic proficiency which is common across languages. This "common underlying proficiency" makes possible the transfer of cognitive/academic or literacy-related skills across languages. (p. 19)

(See also Cummins, chapter 1; Krashen, chapter 3; Graves & Fitzgerald, chapter 5, in this volume.)

Even if primary-language literacy is not the goal of instruction, primary language is still a valuable asset for second-language acquisition. Some noted researchers and practitioners advocate extensive use of the primary language throughout the elementary grades because it will increase students' English reading test performance (Ramirez, Pasta, Yuen, Billings, & Ramey, 1991). Dutro (2001) believes that the more comprehensive the use of primary language, the greater the potential for academic success:

> In order for students to continue to develop their natural language and foster their intellectual growth, it is necessary that they continue to use and expand their primary language while they learn English.... The primary language should be used for study requiring formal language use, during time dedicated to learning in that language, rather than simply for informal purposes. Since cognitive development is not language dependent, learning in the mother tongue supports language, literacy and content learning in English. (pp. 12–13)

Similarly, Goldenberg (2001) states,

> Learning to read and write in one's primary language is helpful for acquiring literacy in a second language.... The fact is that most scientific studies—as opposed to opportunistic uses of data—show that instruction in students' first language can help them develop literacy and academic skills in a second language. (p. B1)

Gersten and Baker (2000) advocate using native language "strategically." For example, they suggest using the native language to teach higher order thinking skills or to introduce complex concepts and afford students opportunities to read more challenging texts. Moreover, they also believe teachers must explicitly point out differences between Spanish and English.

The remaining five pillars are the Five Standards for Effective Pedagogy advocated by CREDE (2002). A detailed explanation of each standard can be found at the CREDE website (http://www.crede.ucsc.edu/tools/research/standards/stand_indic.shtml). These standards are

1. Teacher and Students Producing Together (Joint Productive Activity)
2. Developing Language Across the Curriculum (Language Development)
3. Making Meaning: Connecting School to Students' Lives (Contextualization)
4. Teaching Complex Thinking (Challenging Activities)
5. Teaching Through Conversation (Instructional Conversation)

There is much for architects of instructional blueprints for successful literacy learning and second-language acquisition by English learners to consider in these standards. We value the home language as an essential classroom resource and agree with the conclusions represented by the CREDE standards, recognizing them as pedagogical principles that consistently emerge in research-based practice (see Dutro & Moran's international principles in chapter 10 of this volume).

Building the Foundations for Second-Language Literacy

The revisioning of a blueprint for success requires careful attention to particular foundational requirements. In the case of the academic success of English learners, the basic foundations that are provided by curriculum resources, knowledgeable teachers, and family and community networks of support must be examined and questioned.

Is the Academic Success of English Learners Supported by a Solid Curriculum Framework?

The building of any structure calls for a thorough, detailed blueprint for its foundation and structural supports. The blueprint plan must address the personal specifications and requirements of the client. It is expected that blueprints will vary according to the purposes of each client and the intended use of the resulting structure. If curriculum frameworks are viewed as structural supports for teaching and learning, then they should provide pathways for teachers and students in the construction of academic proficiency. The question to pose is whether or not state curriculum frameworks have adequately provided for the specialized instructional support needed for the second-language development of English learners.

Most states' frameworks in language arts display gaps in the instructional scaffolding required for students to develop literacy in a second language. They seem to provide sketchy conceptual support and lack clarity and practical utility from the point of view of classroom teachers in the field who work with English learners—especially when those teachers are new and inexperienced. According to Kenji Hakuta, in his testimony on the education of language-minority students before the United Commission on Civil Rights on April 13, 2001,

> the focus should be on what ultimately matters most—[English language learners'] long-term performance and success. It is unreasonable to expect ELLs to perform comparably to their native English-speaking peers in their initial years of schooling (hence the need for standards specific to ELLs) and holding them to this expectation too early in their educational careers can be detrimental to their academic progress, not to mention their self-esteem. (p. 3)

In response to the urgent need to ensure comprehensive rigor and provide viable opportunities for students to achieve grade-level competency, standards must be established for the English language development of English learners. These standards must ensure equity and help close gaps in the structural design of curriculum frameworks (see Laturnau, chapter 12 in this volume).

The standards movement will have little meaning if it cannot respond to the needs of all students. In June 1997, Teachers of English to Speakers of Other Languages (TESOL) took the lead in the United States in establishing academic standards to mark the second-language development of English learners in grades pre-K through 12. The TESOL standards for ESL instruction were developed to acknowledge the central role of language in the achievement of content and to provide teachers with a resource to focus on the unique instructional needs of learners who are still developing proficiency in English. At the same time, California Assembly Bill AB 748 mandated the development of a standards-based assessment for ELD instruction to be based on statewide

ELD standards for English learners. Both efforts represent promising steps, with far-reaching implications for national reform.

The establishment of these ELD standards was intended not to replace standards being developed in other content areas, but rather to serve as indicators of linguistic scaffolds to be used by teachers in building the foundations for academic conceptual development in the second language. Valdés (1998) echoes the sentiments of English learner advocates as to the significance of these ELD standards when she states that they "directly address the confusion surrounding the goals of English-language study by delineating progress indicators" that English learners need in order to have "unrestricted access to grade-appropriate instruction in challenging academic subjects" (p. 14).

Is Instructional Opportunity Designed and Executed by Knowledgeable Professionals?

Within the metaphor of construction and design developed in this chapter, the role of the teacher can be depicted as that of a contractor who must translate the blueprint and vision of the architect and client into actual practice. Despite the fixed dimensions and scale of architectural design, actual construction is an organic process of adjustment and modification that requires flexibility and accommodation to the context of the building site—for our purposes, the classroom. Making adjustments and modifications defines the work as the contractor takes into consideration the availability of resources, possible flaws in the plan, and potential changes in need.

With the dramatic and amazing demographic shifts occurring all over the United States, there have been greater demands placed on new and experienced teachers to expand their understanding and skills to meet the needs of English language learners. It has been reported that 42% of U.S. teachers have at least one ELL in their classrooms (Moss & Puma, 1995). Moreover, education reforms targeting all students in the United States have raised the educational bar that must be cleared in order to finish school and participate in the economic and social world of the 21st century. Teachers need a wealth of content and pedagogical knowledge to respond creatively and skillfully to the complex needs of English learners.

There are increasing calls among experts for teaching expertise necessary to build from and on the structural frameworks provided by curriculum designers and theoreticians in their instructional blueprints for English learners. Hakuta (2001) alerts us to the considerable variability within the population of English learners that necessitates "additional teaching skills and theoretical knowledge beyond that which is taught mainstream teachers in order to effectively instruct this population" (p. 11). Fillmore and Snow (2000) maintain that today's teachers specifically must know how language figures in education to help them teach literacy to English learners. They argue for a foundation in educational linguistics as a necessary teacher competency that would support teachers' practice in assessing and meeting individual language needs, and respecting linguistic and cultural diversity. Walqui (2001) adds to the discussion of the need for a specific type of teacher expertise in her comprehensive framework for professional development rooted in a deep understanding of the complex interrelationships between teachers and students and the schooling of language-minority students. In Walqui's view, the realities of teaching English learners are embedded in the complexity of teachers' attitudes and expectations for their performance and ability. Teachers' perceptions have all too often relegated English learners to patterns of poor achievement and unrealized potential in unchallenging curricula focused on lower level skills. She states,

> Teacher preparation programs and opportunities for on-going professional growth need to build visions that run counter to these realities, visions that set the goal high and achieve it. They then need to deconstruct the processes that led to success so that teachers have multiple examples of what is possible with English learners, and can initially emulate some of these practices to eventually recreate and construct their own. (p. 53)

Although limited and quite startling, in comparison to the tremendous need for training at the national and local level, there have been efforts that can be recognized as exemplary models for those who seek to prepare teachers to educate English learners and for teachers who seek to improve their practice. These models provide comprehensive frameworks of methodological and affective accommodations for use in teacher education and professional development efforts. For example, the U.S. National Board for Professional Teaching Standards, through its highly acclaimed National Board Teacher Certification process, has established English as a New Language certification standards for teaching professionals to use as a basis for the rigorous, reflective process of documenting expertise in teaching English learners. These professional standards provide for benchmark proficiencies of professional knowledge and insight in the areas of language and language development, culture and diversity, teaching and learning, assessment, reflective practice, and linkages with families.

Additionally, recommendations to establish explicit links between the California Standards for the Teaching Profession and the teaching of English language learners were outlined in a policy paper prepared by the Joint Policy Committee of the California Council on the Education of Teachers, the California Association of Colleges of Teacher Education, the State of California Association of Teacher Educators, and the Independent California Colleges and Universities Council on the Education of Teachers (2001). This document serves as a model of essential policies and practices for teacher preparation and licensing to ensure that the needs of all California students, including English learners, are provided for by means of explicit and appropriate pedagogy.

How Do the School, Family, and Community Reinforce Effective Practices?

Structural support, whether referring to the construction of buildings or the development of academic proficiency, is situated within a network of social, economic, and political forces that exist within our communities at large.

The network of support closest to the site of construction is the child's family. The child brings into the classroom his or her personal inventory of intellectual, cultural, and linguistic resources, developed within the structures of his family, home, and community—and these resources are replenished on a continual basis throughout his academic career. Parental support influences children's academic performance in varied and significant ways, reaching beyond merely assisting students with homework to shaping attitudes toward study and learning that have lifelong implications for their educational development. For English learners, however, the connection between classroom and family is diminished when linguistic and cultural barriers to full involvement exist. Opportunities for parents to use their primary language for academic support must be promoted on a wide scale so as to maintain the valuable link between home and school. Public opinion must be transformed to embrace community support for maximizing the positive effects of home language and cultural resources so that they can be seen not as detriments to academic performance, but as essential scaffolds for enhancing academic performance in English.

The current reality of misinformation and misguided political agendas at the larger community level has eroded the support necessary to ensure the educational success of English learners. Educational policymakers, politicians, and public opinion have been at work erecting insurmountable fences that virtually eliminate access to the plentiful and enriching resources that exist in the communities in which they are working to build achievement. The findings of Valdés (1998), in her study of English learners in secondary schools, add an additional dimension to the issue of community support at the policymaking level. She writes,

> Part of the difficulty is that most policymakers and members of the public have little information about what actually happens in schools. In spite of that fact, however, far-reaching decisions are often made about immigrant children, about how they should be educated and about which language should be used in their education. (p. 14)

Valdés also highlights the problem of lack of consensus among the research community relative to the issue of educating language-minority students. If this is the case, can we question the quality and appropriateness of the blueprints for the instruction of English learners established at the national, state, and local levels? Do these "architects" have to go back to their drawing boards?

In addition to setting out a clear and unambiguous set of learning objectives for English learners via national and state ELD standards and professional standards for the teachers of English learners as described earlier, instructional initiatives that create and sustain connections between students and families, schools and the home, and learning and community activism can provide vital and essential links between the efforts of schools and communities. These initiatives can lead to an expansion of the resources necessary to ensure that the pillars of pedagogy for English learners are built on solid and enduring foundations. The goal is to make school-based literacy practices and skills more accessible to linguistically and culturally diverse parents and to establish networks of individuals to help children learn. Effective schools contain many such networks (Taylor, Pressley, & Pearson, 2000), but these networks are often difficult to form, especially where there is a disconnection between the school and the community. The work of Luis Moll (1992) in tapping community knowledge for the classroom enabled parents and others in the community to play a significant role in helping their children academically. It represents a viable means of establishing partnerships that work to fundamentally change the relationship between schools and the community. California Tomorrow's Bilingual and Bicultural Youth, Families, Communities, and Schools Project provides access to an inspiring compendium of community activist projects throughout the United States in *And Still We Speak...Stories of Communities Sustaining and Reclaiming Language and Culture* (Dowell, 2001). Projects in Louisiana, Arizona, Massachusetts, Texas, New York, and California have emerged amidst the local tensions and struggles in ethnic immigrant communities. These initiatives focus on the education and support of their young people so that they develop the knowledge and skills that reach across linguistic and cultural barriers. Their common goal is survival and success without the loss of heritage and community networks of support—parents, families, and churches. In living rooms, church basements, university campuses, and private and public schools, community activist networks representing diverse language and ethnic groups have labored to make it possible for their youth to optimize their linguistic and cultural abilities for social and academic achievement in English and their native language.

Advocacy for English learners requires the complex network of participants from the broader school community—parents, teachers, and academics—to successfully build the foundations and framework necessary for their academic success. As has been outlined here, work to create a new blueprint for quality instructional opportunity in their respective spheres of influence has already taken place. This collective work challenges the inadequate and inappropriate design underlying present policy. Our examination of research, policy, and practice calls for renewed efforts toward the development of a plan for instruction that begins and ends with the child and that is responsive and purposeful. A new vision for English learners requires a new set of lenses enabling us to see through the blur resulting from "quick fixes" and "short tracks" and bring their unique requirements for instruction and assessment into sharper focus.

English Language Development: The Fifth Reading Block

Cunningham (1995) has advanced the idea that good reading instruction consists of four reading blocks: guided reading, independent reading, word work, and writing. Armed with the knowledge that good literacy instruction must comprise at least these four elements, there are many teachers who do indeed provide excellent instruction in these four reading blocks to their English learners. Although implementation of the four reading blocks is a necessary part of the blueprint for achieving simultaneous English literacy learning and second-language acquisition, it alone is not sufficient to accomplish this task. Instructional time must be allocated to a fifth block of instruction for English learners if they are to have an opportunity to develop English literacy while clearly and precisely acquiring the English language. Specifically, dedicated instructional time for daily focused English language development for all English learners is imperative.

The second CREDE standard, referenced earlier, highlights the importance of language development. Educational research identifies explicit language teaching as essential, but it does not always happen. Delpit (1995) argues that language must be taught explicitly, because it is not automatically acquired. Walqui (2000) believes that all subject matter classes must have a language focus. Studies conducted by Ramirez (1992) and Arreaga-Mayer and Perdomo-Rivera (1996) found that teachers were not effectively promoting language development in English language development settings. Gersten and Baker (2000) concluded in their examination of English learner practices that there is hardly adequate time devoted to language learning, because teachers often emphasize content at the expense of developing English language abilities: "The major problem highlighted in discussion of sheltered content instruction," they note, "was how time for language learning often is truncated or omitted altogether" (p. 459). Citing inadequate time for English language development as a major problem in current practice, they urge that we

> encourage researchers and educators to consider language learning and content-area learning as distinct educational goals, rather than assuming that increased use of oral language in school will automatically lead to increased academic learning and the development of higher-order thinking skills.... Providing time each day for English-language learners to work on all aspects of ELD and providing academically challenging content instruction (whether in their first language or in English) are more likely to occur when teachers take time to make goals clear and precise. (p. 460)

English language development has been increasingly recognized as the essential ingredient of literacy instruction for English learners, especially in states where English immersion is the dominant pedagogy for literacy instruction. For example, the criteria for the development of curriculum materials for reading in the state of California (California Department of Education, 1999) required publishers to submit ELD lessons that teachers must teach in a separate 30- to 45-minute daily teaching block sometime during the regular school day; this ELD instruction is in addition to the basic literacy instruction that all children should receive. California's requirement that state-adopted basal English language arts programs be comprehensive enough to include an additional component—a fifth reading block of English language development—helps assure that ELD is taught explicitly and daily, and that core literacy instruction is accessible to English learners. This California mandate acknowledges that English language development is a necessary component of literacy instruction for English learners.

Teachers must provide ELD instruction that is grounded in sound research and sound pedagogical principles in order to help English learners deal with the formidable challenge of learning the same developmental sequence of English reading skills under the same time constraints as an English speaker. Without the fifth ELD block, literacy instruction would take place in English without an appropriate language development foundation with implications for sustaining performance into the upper grades. Adding a fifth ELD reading block puts language development back into the language arts curriculum for English learners and makes it possible for them to be successful.

Basic Components of the Fifth Reading Block

Although primary language is the bedrock of language development, English language development instruction is a necessary foundation as well for academic success in literacy. ELD instruction must be built on specific pedagogical pillars and fused with the bedrock of primary language that English learners bring to each learning task. This fusion of L1 and L2 constitutes the essence of the language foundation that is such a critical component of the blueprint for academic success of all English learners that we call the fifth reading block.

There are many instructional elements and strategies that may be part of the ELD instructional repertoire that could be included in this fifth reading block; we will list some and give reasons for considering their inclusion. With the aforementioned pillars of pedagogy upon which strategies should be based, we offer the following suggestions as to how ELD lessons should be designed.

Ideally, English language development lessons should be literature based. There are many reasons for employing quality literature resources. Literature is a real and authentic source for quality models of language, and it provides students with an engaging and meaningful purpose for listening to and using language. Literature is an excellent conduit for developing an appreciation for the English language in meaningful contexts that provide children with models of the rhythms and intonation of the language. Students can easily become very familiar with the syntactical structures of the English language through repeated exposures to and discussions of the same piece of literature.

Literature can easily be matched to curricular themes, and the selection of relevant, appropriate texts provides English learners with child-centered motivational content that can be related to interests and learning goals. A student's culture can, as well, be represented and validated. Literature selections that provide maximum support for language development possess one or more of the following characteristics: a good story; plots with plenty of action; characters who engage in lively dialogue that can be dramatized easily; richly textured descriptions, in words and pictures presented in a predictable sequence with repetitive language; and sensitivity to multicultural issues. And, ideally, the selection will exist in several different versions. These desirable characteristics are especially relevant for students in the beginning stages of language acquisition—who must master the mainstream English curriculum, develop English literacy, and acquire English as a second language simultaneously. Careful selection of appropriate literature will pay handsome instructional dividends.

In many instructional contexts throughout the United States, teachers do not always have the liberty to select literature for English language development that possesses these characteristics. New Literacy policies apply pressure to conform and perform to mainstream expectations, without attention to the complex needs of English learners. Teachers complain that they have barely enough time to teach the mandated curriculum in preparation for the mandated state assessment. If these desired characteristics are not present in the literature that is part of the mandated literacy curriculum, how do teachers make the necessary accommodations to promote the success of their English learners? Regardless of the available resources, the activities that are found in English language development instruction should support the content objectives of the core literacy program. The intent of this support is to provide English learners with an opportunity to access the literature that is the mandated literature curriculum for their grade level, along with the content concepts and the content objectives. What is of crucial importance is that teachers employ essential core strategies during ELD to support their students' acquisition of the language in which they are simultaneously learning to read.

Strategies employed during the time designated for ELD must be just as explicit and systematic as the instruction for the major tasks of reading instruction. Certainly, we would not leave phonics instruction and comprehension instruction to chance. The implicit instruction in ELD that occurs when teachers teach in English is not sufficient for English learners' acquisition of the language; explicit instruction in ELD is essential. Strategies that honor children's primary language and employ their language as a resource for helping them acquire the English language are important to include in every instructional repertoire where English learners are involved. Strategies are cognitive in nature and should be consciously selected by teachers of English learners using the filter of the standards of effective pedagogy as specific strategies are selected and employed in daily ELD instruction.

Careful consideration of the standards will guide teachers' selection of appropriate learning strategies. For example, students could be involved in meaningful activities that allow them to interact with each other as they develop background knowledge before reading a selection. Making predictions and developing questions about a selection they are about to read can be undertaken as a joint productive activity. This is an example of incorporating one of these essential standards into an explicit instructional strategy designed to promote students' English-language acquisition. We recommend an evaluation of how effectively these standards are being applied to chosen strategies for English learners by applying the rubric established by CREDE to assess the implementation of the standards (http://www.crede.ucsc.edu/tools/research/standards/spac.shtml).

Teachers must model these strategies; beginning-level English learners cannot be expected to employ strategies of prediction or questioning without appropriate modeling. Indeed, we should not expect this from any learner. Explicit lessons and think-alouds must be employed, with the teacher demonstrating, over several days, how to make predictions and how to ask questions when preparing to read—until students are asked to do it with the teacher. Redundancy in the teaching model demonstrations is very important, and just as important is redundancy in the practice and application opportunities made available to English learners. The strategy can then be employed in joint productive activities wherein students are asked to do it with the teacher or in joint activities with other students in collaborative settings. Once the teacher models this strategy several times, and students are asked to do it with the teacher and with more capable peers, students should eventually be expected to predict and question on their own. This scaffolding is absolutely necessary for all skills and strategies—and it is also necessary for ELD instruction.

Each day's lesson must scaffold the next day's lesson in advance of the pacing of the regular curriculum. The goal must be observable growth and development in language acquisition and in relevant content objectives over the course of each series of lessons that are presented in addition to the core literacy instruction. Repetition and redundancy must be built into the ELD lesson plans: English learners need repetition beyond what struggling readers and native English speakers need. The key to success is that students must be required to produce oral language in each phase of the day's lesson appropriate to their level of language acquisition. Interaction is an essential ingredient of each phase: Cooperative activities that promote collaboration between and among students are staples of this instruction. English language development standards should be the focus of instruction, along with providing access to the content objectives and the skill work of each weekly literacy lesson plan.

Another critical characteristic of literature-based lesson plans for English language development are strategies for tapping schema. One way this may be accomplished is through a variety of multimedia options. For example, when students use a piece of literature, the content of the literature is previewed easily in a variety of media. The literature may exist in a movie version; or alternative videos, DVDs, or downloadable files from the Internet that are related to the themes or concepts of the selection will surely be available, and accessible. Only portions of the multimedia versions may be appropriate or necessary. Watching a two-hour movie is not suggested; a five-to-ten-minute clip from a movie or a video is sufficient to stimulate schema and provide an impetus for activating background knowledge. Videos and related media carry a wealth of information, and teachers and students need to understand that this activity is not a privilege, but rather a necessary instructional strategy for English learners.

The alternative to a multimedia springboard is a print springboard for developing schema for a richer understanding of the literature. For example, teachers may use visuals from the text or have students participate in a theme-related print experience that is also related to the content of the literature selection. This additional selection-related print experience becomes the catalyst for background building, vocabulary introduction, and language modeling. Working with such print alternatives should always be done before students actually encounter the literature selection used for instruction that is part of the mandated curriculum.

These experiences should be brief and authentic; they might include poems, songs, chants, jokes, riddles, informational text, or a short selection from the anthology. This same print experience could be repeated throughout the week, providing opportunities for language modeling, shared reading, and repeated exposures to targeted language structures. Both multimedia and print experiences prior to reading a literature selection can play a significant role in the development of children's schema and their English language development. Beginning with these print experiences, of course, children's English language development should include all the language processes of reading, writing, listening, and speaking.

Directly related to the use of print options for background building is the use of primary-language resources, such as translations of English selections. Many literature selections exist in a primary-language version; if they do not exist in a trade book version, some publishers have translated them for inclusion in a primary-language literacy program. Consider the power of building background by having students read a selection in their primary language first and then having a subsequent ELD lesson using the same selection in English, now that comprehension has been facilitated through reading, writing, listening, and speaking about the same text in the language the student completely understands.

If the literature is not available in translation, printed summaries of the selection are a possible alternative. Many publishers offer at least a summary of major literature selections from their English anthologies in various languages, in a print form and also in a recorded form. This provides teachers with an opportunity to do a preview/review of the selection that will validate children's primary language, enhance their comprehension of the English text, and facilitate their acquisition of English.

The primary language is the most frequently cited positive resource in the literature on English learners. Conceptual understanding is greatly enhanced when supported by the child's primary language; this language link to the home provides a comfort zone in the classroom that facilitates conceptual understanding and emotional stability in the classroom environment. Use of the primary language permits children to use their full language repertoire to help them acquire a second language and fully participate amid the conceptual onslaught of meaningless labels that English immersion entails. Understanding concepts with the help of the mother tongue leads to the acquisition of the English that these concepts, with very different labels, represent. These labels, however, are often the same labels, or nearly the same, in both the mother tongue and in English. In Spanish, for example, there are many opportunities to move from the known to the unknown by focusing on cognates. These cross-linguistic comparisons are an extremely effective way of quickly establishing meaning while using a new label (Fillmore & Snow, 2000; Rodriguez, 2001). Explicit comparisons between English-language structures and primary-language structures are an additional means of facilitating English-language acquisition by employing judicious use of the home language.

The most obvious means of tapping background knowledge and developing concepts in English are concrete physical activities. Many concepts that are key to understanding a selection can be developed through activities that physically involve students in the learning. For example, if a selection is about a big race, get students involved by having them race each other on the playground, being careful to use the key vocabulary that is necessary to understand all the academic language that a race involves: the starting line, the finish line, the distance (100 yards, a mile), the duration of the race (in time), and the order of finish (first, second, third, etc.). There is a wealth of vocabulary that students will come to know if they are involved meaningfully; physical activities around which students use the language are much more powerful than any of the previously mentioned strategies. These activities represent natural cooperative opportunities for English learners to build background, learn concepts, and master vocabulary—and they provide an excellent basis for language discussion and practice that will occur later in class.

Vocabulary development is an essential instructional activity in all ELD lessons. Literature inherently provides many opportunities to develop vocabulary and academic language. Idioms and multiple-meaning words can certainly be problematic when employing literature, but they are specific targets of vocabulary instruction that are important to English learners and plentiful in children's literature. "Picture walks" that take full advantage of the illustrations are one of the "must-do's" of instructional practices when reading any literature with illustrations. Creating English learner "word walls" is a systematic way of dealing with new vocabulary; students should be responsible for adding a few words a day to the word walls. These same word walls also may be used in the traditional ways that word walls are generally employed, such that these words reflect phonics and spelling patterns.

Students should also be the ones who collect objects to enhance vocabulary building; teachers cannot be the sole gatherers of realia. Students should also create visuals that represent the vocabulary they are learning, because until they can verbalize their understanding by telling, they must at least *draw* what they understand or they will never have sufficient practice to *own* the vocabulary essential for using the English language. Another useful strategy is to have students create their own dictionaries. They should have opportunities to discuss their definitions and their illustrations of chosen words with their peers.

Academic language must be identified, and opportunities must be given for students to know and employ these words in a meaningful context. For example, students should be given frequent opportunities to participate in problem-solving activities that place them in small cooperative groups wherein they naturally employ the vocabulary and academic language that are the focus of the lesson. In spite of the fact that classrooms in the United States tend to maintain an individualistic, competitive environment, cooperative settings are the way of the business world and are the most conducive learning environments for English learners, and they also function as purveyors of culture and acculturation, of translation, of the mediation of the meaning of the text (better known as entering the transactional zone [Smagorinsky, 2001]), of friendship, and of many positive influences too numerous to list.

Standards one and three clearly address this issue. English learners must be given ample opportunities to employ the English language, and cooperative activities are particularly conducive to promoting the use of the language structures targeted for instruction, practice, and application. These opportunities are designed to promote instructional conversations (Goldenberg, 1992/1993) and to promote the use of the language in a meaningful context. Students should be paired as often as possible with a "buddy" who becomes responsible for his or her buddy's English-language acquisition progress. Graphic organizers should be employed frequently within the fifth instructional block and can yield many benefits. Graphic organizers provide English learners with a means of synthesizing content and summarizing it—with a way to think and talk about the content in a succinct and abbreviated way (see Hernández, chapter 6 in this volume). Care should be taken to scaffold the instruction while employing graphic organizers to eventually reach the goal of having *students* be able to choose appropriate graphic organizers to demonstrate the best way of visualizing their thinking. For example, if students are asked to compare and contrast characters, the ultimate goal of using a Venn diagram is to learn that it is one way to visualize comparisons and contrasts. It must be employed, however, as a way of demonstrating the thinking, not as an exercise that is just an exercise. Students should also be taught to identify the *language* that the graphic organizer represents. For example, all graphic organizers are inherently replete with academic language that is represented by the graphics, and students should know what that academic language is. They should be well aware that the academic words *same* and *different* are words that are part of a Venn diagram, even though they do not appear anywhere in the diagram itself. Graphic organizers are a means to think and talk about the content of literature. They may be employed at any time, and they also provide a basis for many cooperative learning opportunities and for meaningful writing activities. (See Dutro & Moran, chapter 10 in this volume, for a discussion of academic language.)

Many children's literature selections contain excellent examples of how the English language works and of the functions of language (Gibbons, 1991). For example, the character of the Big Bad Wolf is *warning* the three little pigs—and warning someone is a common language function. In the same story, the Big Bad Wolf describes what he might do if the three little pigs do not heed his warning; describing is another common language function. Literature is replete with wonderful examples of the functions of language. The way that language works is also evident in the example "I'll huff and I'll puff and I'll blow your house down." In this example, the combination of the words *I* and *will* results in the word *I'll*. What better model for demonstrating how contractions work than one found in the context of authentic and captivating literature!

Daily lessons for English language development should provide daily support for English language acquisition, and that requires modeling that comes from abundant teacher models scaffolded over time through teacher think-alouds. This is a show-and-tell model, but it cannot stop there. Teacher modeling is essential, but it is not sufficient; students must be able to do it themselves. This eventually means that students must demonstrate their understanding by using the language themselves. There should be ample opportunities for teachers to employ think-alouds while reading the text, along with strategies like Questioning the Author (Beck, McKeown, Hamilton, & Kucan, 1997). These types of strategies are important for enabling students to develop comprehension while reading the text.

Daily lessons should also focus on skills that are developed in the core program and specific English usage issues that transcend grammar. English learners must learn to use the language and use it correctly. Therefore it is critical that English learners, at some point beyond the beginning level of language acquisition, have sufficient opportunities to develop correct English usage habits (Fillmore & Snow, 2000). It is also critical, certainly, for teachers to understand the various language acquisition levels and maintain appropriate expectations for language production commensurate with these stages; at some point, however, English learners need appropriate feedback. Corrective feedback will help assure that they also master the appropriate use of the language not only in form, but also in various contexts and with appropriate shades of meaning. These nuances of language acquisition are often overlooked, resulting in broken English that is reflected both in speech and in written expression (Fillmore & Snow, 2000; Gersten & Baker, 2000).

Literature is also a perfect vehicle for adaptation to a Readers Theatre script. Readers Theatre is a wonderful means of involving students in repeated readings of a text, with built-in rehearsals that promote reading fluency. Drama is one of the very best means of authentic assessment of a variety of literacy skills, including comprehension. The English learner classroom should have multiple opportunities to practice literacy skills, assess them, and demonstrate them through drama.

There should be a listening center in every classroom. Students need multiple opportunities to encounter the literature they are reading in a variety of modes, and listening to the text being read is another form of fluency practice that should occur frequently. This would apply, obviously, to audiotaped books or texts, but it also means providing students with the opportunity to enjoy an alternative instructional activity, available to students as an individual activity during class time. Students should also have an opportunity to listen to a variety of music in English and in their primary language—and these opportunities should not be confined to purely didactic purposes.

Written expression is also a necessary focus of this instructional block. Writing in English requires an extension of the oral skills that language-acquisition practices often ignore. Students will certainly acquire language when they are involved in meaningful activities, as we have described earlier, but writing skills must be taught explicitly. This requires constant exposure to sentence patterning, so that English learners eventually become familiar with the conventions of how sentences are put together in the language. Once students are familiar with most of the conventions, time can be devoted to the development of writing skills using the writing process. Eventually, just as with oral communication, teachers must be willing to move beyond what is said and concentrate on *how* it is said if English learners are to be able to write well. Corrective feedback is a necessary step in reaching this elusive literacy goal.

English learners must have multiple daily opportunities to acquire the English language. These opportunities must be provided during the school day, and with sufficient time to help ensure successful English literacy learning. These opportunities will be most effective if they are related to the core literature used for general literacy instruction, particularly in English-immersion settings where simultaneous English-language acquisition and English literacy learning is expected. The fifth reading block of learning activities, designed to promote English-language acquisition, must be an integral part of literacy instruction for English learners and one that augments the instruction in the other four blocks that English learners also must receive. In combination, these five reading blocks will produce a greater number of English learners that become English-literate.

Is the Structure Sound? Accountability and Assessment

It can be argued that present policies for assessing the literacy development of English learners fall short of providing a comprehensive, robust accountability system that builds and sustains instructional effectiveness. An initial question that must be asked is whether or not educators are receiving a complete picture of exactly what English learners know at any given point in their academic development. Most state-level standardized tests, local district benchmark assignments, and school-level tests assess English learners with respect to content expectations in English according to the same standards as their native English-speaking peers. The results are, surely, predictable: English learners are below grade level on tests that require mastery of complex levels of English academic language and content understanding. Fundamental questions about assessment remain to be answered, however. What are the tests in place telling us? And, more important, what are they *not* telling us about English learners?

Even though a few states have established measures that separately assess English language development so as to mark the progress of English learners, the problem of having timely and meaningful results to inform instructional practice still persists. Incomplete and inappropriate performance data for English learners have created a well-documented "assessment muddle" (Cummins, 1991; De Avila, 1990; Gersten & Woodward, 1994; Hakuta, 2001) that continues to imperil the academic success of English learners, chiefly because of what is left out. On account of an assessment blueprint that excludes pertinent factors related to language and the learning environment, English learners' lack of English proficiency may easily be confused with a learning disability and lead to their inappropriate placement in special education or remedial content classes (De Avila, 1990). The unfortunate result can be the referral of "too many or too few" English learners to special education (Gersten & Woodward, 1994). A proper "fit"—an appropriate choice of instruction that meets student needs—can be ensured only through consistent monitoring. "Because of the serious inadequacy of ELL assessments" in enabling suitable instructional fits for English learners' needs, however, existing assessments have the "potential to erroneously impact—and subsequently render inequitable—state-provided educational experiences" (Hakuta, 2001, p. 12).

Compounding the problem of meaningful and appropriate assessment is a lack of clarity with regard to the role of the primary language and to definitions of language proficiency in assessment. Studies show that it takes English learners from three to five years to develop oral proficiency in the second language, and from four to seven years to develop academic English proficiency (Hakuta, Butler, & Witt, 2000). Yet, in a national climate leaning toward English immersion, school districts are not waiting for English learners to establish English proficiency before they are instructed and assessed solely in English. Without the benefit of a policy that ensures primary-language support, it is difficult for teachers to verify if students understand or learn the objectives of a lesson. English learners need alternative forms of assessment that allow for all the ways they come to know and understand. Teachers of English learners need to know how their primary and second languages intersect with literacy development and how to measure their progress at appropriate intervals for purposes of instructional planning.

But to measure progress in language development, what constitutes proficiency must be clearly articulated and understood. Unfortunately, it is at this point in the assessment of language proficiency that a lack of consensus begins. Although most researchers and professionals in the field of second-language acquisition define second-language proficiency for K–12 students in ways that acknowledge the multiple dimensions of language competence and use that are needed in school settings (Bachmann & Cohen, 1998), varying points of view among researchers have created a dilemma in the educational field. The result is a plethora of definitions, theories, and proficiency tests (Del Vecchio & Guerrero, 1995), ranging from the view that language proficiency consists of 64 separate language components to a sociotheoretical perspective that language "develops within a culture for the purpose of conveying the beliefs and customs of that culture" (p. 4). While the debate continues, the educational community is pressured to rely on incomplete or inappropriate resources in making assessment decisions that have a direct impact on classroom instruction and on the academic progress of English learners.

"In order to get an accurate picture of ELLs' English language proficiency level for classroom placement purposes," recommends Hakuta (2001), "states should support the supplemental use of more authentic assessments of students' academic language that more closely mirror classroom demands" (p. 13). To accomplish this, the classroom must be given prominence as the cornerstone of achievement and the teacher as its architect, so that attention stays focused on education's most basic level—the classroom interaction between student and teacher. This view recognizes that the teacher works in partnership with the child, the school, and the community and that they must move toward explicit and specific achievement goals, with authentic measures in place to assess progress. Each partner works to enable the child to say, "I know what I need to learn, how I'm going to learn it, and how I'll know if I've 'made it' or how far I have to go to get there."

National, state, and local ELD standards provide specific and explicit goals with respect to English language development assessment and instruction that outline a viable linguistic pathway for achieving mainstream standards. Standards-based instruction based on ELD standards ensures academically rigorous and developmentally appropriate targets for ELD instruction, aligned with instructional practices designed to scaffold and maximize English learners' access to the core curriculum as they gain English proficiency (see Laturnau, chapter 12 in this volume, for a full description). In a standards-based instructional model, embedded assessment practices provide meaningful data on progress toward standards through authentic classroom tasks. These assessments must provide clear indications of all competencies (in L1 or L2) that students bring to the classroom, looking beyond social and communicative competence to academic competence and multiple literacies (listening, speaking, reading, and writing) with respect to each level of English proficiency. Moreover, language development assessment must reflect the evolving linguistic and academic needs of language-minority students. English learners represent great variety in their second-language development and their grade-level academic performance at any given point in their academic careers. Reliance on a single assessment can fail to measure all the dimensions of language proficiency and may reduce the possibilities for responsive and meaningful instruction.

The limitations of norm-referenced, discrete-skill language proficiency testing that are typically advocated by educational policymakers at the national and local levels gave rise to the development of integrative and pragmatic approaches to language testing (Oller & Damico, 1991). This alternative type of testing calls for language proficiency to be assessed "in a fairly rich context of discourse" so as to counteract the serious gap created by measures that reduce language to a single skill or a single domain, absent of any social context or link to human experience (Del Vecchio & Guerrero, 1995, p. 83). According to Lavadenz (1996), in order to ensure "equitable evaluative practices for students who have historically received negative and differential school treatment" (p. 33) viable tools for the assessment of English learners must reflect a broader, more realistic depiction of classroom performance.

To meet the complexity and scope of the need, then, assessment of language development must

- be flexible enough to respond to the learning rhythms and needs of individual students;
- be adaptable enough to be administered at any given point in instruction;
- provide multiple views of language and literacy performance;
- provide data that can be collected on an ongoing basis for continuous monitoring; and

- be accessible to students and parents in order to be understood, discussed, and utilized by all members of the school community.

The most viable and suitable tool for meeting these demands is authentic assessment. O'Malley and Valdez-Pierce (1996) define authentic assessment as the "multiple forms of assessment that reflect student learning, achievement, motivation, and attitudes on instructionally-relevant activities" (p. 4). Inventories or checklists, rating scales, cloze tests, portfolios, oral and written retells, and journals are examples of authentic assessment forms that reveal a wide range of abilities and knowledge acquired by English learners. These forms of integrative, pragmatic assessment, based on the authentic performance of literacy and language tasks, provide insight that can be understood by the network of academic supporters who collaborate at the classroom instructional level to monitor the linguistic, conceptual, and academic progress of English learners: teachers, students, and their parents. The result is a "loop of inclusion" through which many labor to build from what students already know and do toward new cognitive and linguistic understandings. An instructional blueprint designed and crafted to meet particular and explicit needs within an authentic system of accountability guides their work.

Conclusions

As advocates for English learners, we are claiming our rightful place at the design table as architect-practitioners to challenge the blueprint for English learners that has been proposed by the New Literacy policymakers. We recognize that in order to accomplish our task, we must build on the legacy of research and practice available to us to examine and reexamine what has worked before and what can work better.

In his critique of research on culturally and linguistically diverse populations, Obiakor (2001) remarks that "research, policy, and practice ought to go hand-in-hand," arguing that the education arena can no longer "ignore the presence of persons from culturally and linguistically diverse backgrounds" (p. 5). Obiakor calls for research that assists practitioners to understand the children they serve, in order to foster functional, goal-oriented decisions in our complex society. In order to achieve this requisite understanding, teachers, researchers, parents, community, and policymakers must work with rigor and high standards as partners in the study of practices that best support the academic success of English learners. Our work must be a continuous process of "revisioning the blueprint" in order to meet codes of excellence in educational workmanship and instructional artistry.

REFERENCES

Arreaga-Mayer, C., & Perdomo-Rivera, C. (1996). Ecobehavioral analysis of instruction for at-risk language-minority students. *The Elementary School Journal, 96*(3), 245–258.

August, D., & Hakuta, K. (Eds.). (1997). *Improving schooling for language-minority children: A research agenda.* Washington, DC: National Academy Press.

Bachman, L.F., & Cohen, A.D. (Eds.). (1998). *Interfaces between second language acquisition and language testing research.* New York: Cambridge University Press.

Beck, I.L., McKeown, M.G., Hamilton, R.L., & Kucan, L. (1997). *Questioning the Author: An approach for enhancing student engagement with text.* Newark, DE: International Reading Association.

California Council on the Education of Teachers, California Association of Colleges of Teacher Education, State of California Association of Teacher Educators, & Independent California Colleges and Universities Council on the Education of Teachers. (2001). Success for English language learners: Teacher preparation policies and practices. A position paper published in *Teacher Education Quarterly, 28*(1), 199–208.

California Department of Education. (1999). *2002 K–8 reading/language arts/English language development adoption criteria.* Available at http://www.cde.ca.gov/cfir/rla/2002criteria.pdf

Center for Research on Education, Diversity & Excellence (CREDE). (2002). *The five standards for effective pedagogy* [Online]. Available: http://www.crede.ucsc.edu/tools/research/standards/standards.html

Cummins, J. (1981). The role of primary language development in promoting educational success for language minority students. In California State Department of Education (Ed.), *Schooling and language minority students: A theoretical framework* (pp. 3–49). Los Angeles: Evaluation, Dissemination and Assessment Center, California State University.

Cummins, J. (1991). *Empowering culturally and linguistically diverse students with learning problems* (Report No. EDO-EC-91-5). Reston, VA: Council for Exceptional Children. (ERIC Document Reproduction Service No. ED333622)

Cummins, J. (2000). *Language, power and pedagogy: Bilingual children in the crossfire (Bilingual education and bilingualism, 23).* Clevedon, UK: Multilingual Matters.

Cunningham, P. (1995). *The Four-Blocks Literacy Model: How and why it really works* [Videotape]. (Available from Carson-Dellosa Publishing Co., PO Box 35665, 4321 Piedmont Parkway, Greensboro, NC 27425-5665)

Dalton, S. (1998). *Pedagogy matters: Standards for effective teaching practice* (Research Rep. No. 4). Washington, DC and Santa Cruz, CA: Center for Research on Education, Diversity & Excellence [Online]. Available: http://www.cal.org/crede/pubs/research/RR4.pdf

De Avila, E. (1990). *Assessment of language minority students: Political, technical, practical and moral imperatives.* Paper presented at the First Research Symposium on Limited English Proficient Student Issues, OBEMLA, Washington, DC.

Delpit, L. (1995). *Other people's children.* New York: Basic Books. (ERIC Document Reproduction Service ED 387274)

Del Vecchio, A., & Guerrero, M. (1995). *Handbook of English language proficiency tests.* Albuquerque, NM: EAC West, New Mexico Highlands University.

Dowell, C. (Ed.). (2001). *And still we speak...Stories of communities sustaining and reclaiming language and culture*. Oakland, CA: California Tomorrow.

Dutro, S. (2001). *Reading instruction for English language learners: Ten pedagogical considerations*. November 13, 2001, Noyce Foundation ELL study meeting [Online]. Available: http://www.noycefdn.org/literacy_programs/ecrwfiles/Ten_Considerations.pdf

Figueroa, R.A., Fradd, S.H., & Correa, V.I. (1989). Bilingual special education and this special issue. *Exceptional Children, 56*, 174–178.

Fillmore, L.W., & Snow, C.E. (2000). *What teachers need to know about language*. Special report from ERIC Clearinghouse on Languages and Linguistics [Online]. Available: http://www.cal.org/ericcll/teachers/teachers.pdf

Fitzgerald, J., Garcia, G.E., Jimenez, R.T., & Barrera, R. (2000). How will bilingual/ESL programs in literacy change in the next millennium? *Reading Research Quarterly, 35*, 520–523.

Gersten, R., & Baker, S. (2000). What we know about effective instructional practices for English-language learners. *Exceptional Children, 66*(4), 454–470.

Gersten, R., & Woodward, J. (1994). The language minority students and special education: Issues, trends, and paradoxes. *Exceptional Children, 60*(4), 310–322.

Gibbons, P. (1991). *Learning to learn in a second language*. Portsmouth, NH: Heinemann.

Goldenberg, C. (1992/1993). Instructional conversations: Promoting comprehension through discussion. *The Reading Teacher, 46*, 316–326.

Goldenberg, C. (2001, January 25). Commentary: These steps can help us teach Johnny to read. *The Los Angeles Times*, p. B11.

Gutiérrez, K.D. (2001). What's new in the English language arts: Challenging policies and practices, ¿ y qué? *Language Arts, 78*, 6.

Hakuta, K. (2001). The education of language minority students [Testimony to the United States Commission on Civil Rights, April 13, 2001]. *Multilingual News, 24*(6), 1, 10–14.

Hakuta, K., Butler, G.Y., & Witt, D. (2000). *How long does it take English learners to attain proficiency?* University of California, Linguistic Minority Research Institute, Policy Report 2000-1.

International Reading Association. (2001). *Second-language literacy instruction: A position statement of the International Reading Association* [Online]. Available: http://www.reading.org/pdf/1046.pdf

Lavadenz, M. (1996). Authentic assessment: Toward equitable assessment of language minority students. *New Schools, New Communities, 12*(2), 31–35.

Moll, L.C. (1992). Bilingual classroom studies and community analysis: Some recent trends. *Educational Researcher, 21*(2), 20–24.

Moss, M., & Puma, M. (1995). *Prospects: The congressionally mandated study of educational opportunity and growth: Language minority and limited English proficient students*. Washington, DC: U.S. Department of Education.

Obiakor, F.E. (2001). Research on culturally and linguistically diverse populations. *Multicultural Perspectives, 3*(4), 5–10.

Ogawa, R.T., & Malen, B. (1991). A response to commentaries on "Towards Rigor in Reviews of Multivocal Literatures: Applying the Exploratory Case Study Method." *Review of Educational Research, 61*(3), 307–313.

Oller, J.W., Jr., & Damico, J.S. (1991). Theoretical considerations in the assessment of LEP students. In E. Hamayan & J.S. Damico (Eds.), *Limiting bias in the assessment of bilingual students* (pp. 77–110). Austin, TX: Pro-Ed Publications.

O'Malley, J.M., & Valdez-Pierce, L. (1996). *Authentic assessment for English language learners: Practical approaches for teachers*. Reading, MA: Addison-Wesley.

Ramirez, J.D. (1992). Executive summary: Longitudinal study of structured English immersion strategy, early-exit and late-exit transitional bilingual education programs for language-minority children. *Bilingual Research Journal, 16*(1), 1–62.

Ramirez, J.D., Pasta, D.J., Yuen, S., Billings, D.K., & Ramey, D.R. (1991). *Final report: Longitudinal study of structural immersion strategy, early-exit, and late-exit transitional bilingual education programs for language minority children* [Report to the U.S. Department of Education]. San Mateo, CA: Aguirre International.

Rodriguez, T.A. (2001). From the known to the unknown: Using cognates to teach English to Spanish-speaking literates. *The Reading Teacher, 54*, 744–746.

Smagorinsky, P. (2001). If meaning is constructed, what's it made from? Toward a cultural theory of reading. *Review of Educational Research, 71*(1), 133–169.

Taylor, B.M., Pressley, M.P., & Pearson, P.D. (2000). *Research-supported characteristics of teachers and schools that promote reading achievement*. Washington, DC: National Education Association.

Tharp, R.G. (1997). *From at-risk to excellence: Research, theory, and principles for practice* (Research Report 1) [Online]. Available: http://www.cal.org/crede/pubs/research/rr1.htm

Valdés, G. (1998). The world outside and inside schools: Language and immigrant children. *Educational Researcher, 27*(6), 4–18.

Walqui, A. (2000). *Strategies for success: Engaging immigrant students in secondary schools*. Washington, DC: ERIC Clearinghouse on Languages and Linguistics. (ERIC Document Reproduction Service ED 442300)

Walqui, A. (2001). Accomplished teaching with English learners: A conceptualization of teacher expertise. *The Multilingual Educator, 2*(2), 51–56.

CHAPTER 10

Rethinking English Language Instruction: An Architectural Approach

Susana Dutro and Carrol Moran

I n this chapter we will present an approach for rethinking English language instruction using an architectural metaphor. We will lay out a blueprint for infusing English language development (ELD) throughout the instructional program, and describe the design features and general instructional principles that underpin high-quality, rigorous second-language teaching. In other words, we will outline how to conceptualize an ELD program, how to design instruction, and how to teach English for academic purposes.

We join Fillmore and Snow (2000) in their call for including linguistic knowledge in the wide range of competencies required of teachers. We further suggest that all teachers need not only linguistic knowledge, but also knowledge of how to design a comprehensive approach to ELD. We will present an approach for academic language instruction that helps resolve the acquisition versus direct teaching tension in the second-language literature and provides a workable model for incorporating language teaching throughout the instructional day.

Given the increasingly multilingual populations in our schools, to effectively prepare students for success in academic subjects teachers need a focused approach to teaching language in every classroom, in every subject area, every day. It is clear that the need for second-language instruction is growing steadily. In 1980 over half the teachers in the United States either had English language learners or had taught them previously, whereas only one in seventeen had had any coursework in teaching English as a second language (Hamayan & Damico, 1990). The number of English language learners in the United States has increased dramatically in the past decade. The most recent statistics indicate that there were nearly 3.5 million limited–English-proficient students in K–12 schools across the country in 1997–1998 (National Clearinghouse for Bilingual Education, 2000). These estimates are considered conservative. Clearly, the demand for teacher expertise in English language development is immediate and widespread. It is time for us to embrace this need and define the skill base needed by teachers if they are to successfully develop academic-language competence in all students.

The theoretical basis for our approach stems from the major issues in the second-language literature (Beebe, 1988; Bourhis, 1990). The research reveals a number of controversies related to language instruction (Hakuta & McLaughlin, 1996); the most influential of these lies in the debate regarding language acquisition versus language learning. (See also Freeman & Freeman, chapter 2, and Crawford, chapter 7, in this volume.)

The two theories—that second language is acquired in the same way as first language (Krashen & Terrel, 1983) or that it ought to be taught systematically and explicitly (McLaughlin, 1985)—have been discussed at length in the literature. Krashen's views on second-language acquisition in the classroom have greatly influenced practices in California over the past 20 years. Under the guise of "natural language acquisition," many teachers resisted direct teaching of language and instead provided cooperative learning environments in which students would learn from one another. There is significant evidence that, though more interaction occurred as a result, learning language in this way did not develop sufficient language skills for academic success (Schmida, 1996). We also have evidence that aspects of language can be developed in different sequences and can be learned more quickly through explicit formal teaching (McLaughlin, 1985). A comprehensive theory of classroom instruction should incorporate both informal and formal-language learning opportunities.

Another issue in language instruction is whether students should study language processes by looking at language as an object of study and analyzing the patterns and rules of the language, or *intuit* patterns and rules by engaging in purposeful language activity.

The blueprint we propose embraces these tensions and focuses on the development of academic language—the language of school, literacy, content, and higher learning. We advocate a rethinking of some common practices in ELD instruction and take the position that language instruction requires teaching English, not just teaching *in* English or simply providing opportunities for students to interact with each other in English. We believe ELD requires purposeful daily instruction both in a developmental program and as explicit preparation for content courses, with ample opportunities for both formal and informal learning across the curriculum and throughout the instructional day. This includes everything from interactive practice—building scaffolds from contextualized experiences wherein meaning is carried through visual cues, props, and gestures—to decontextualized input, which requires students to function with minimal supports. In the application or practice of skills to develop fluency, this instruction also consciously provides for output of language as an important part of the language-learning process, not just as an outcome of language development or a means of assessment (Swain, 1986).

The blueprint includes three components of ELD taught throughout the day (see Figure 10.1). The first component is a vertical slice of the curriculum. This is systematic ELD: English instruction as its own discipline, which follows a developmental scope and sequence of language skills that builds from simple to complex structures within the context of a range of everyday and academic-language functions (see García & Beltrán, chapter 9 in this volume).

FIGURE 10.1 Blueprint for teaching English throughout the day

Systematic ELD *Purpose* *Develop a solid language foundation* *Content* *Follows scope and sequence of language skills in diverse functional contexts* *Organized by level of English proficiency*	Reading/ Language Arts	Mathematics	History/ Social Studies	Science/ Health	Physical Education	Art
	Front-loading language teaching *Purpose*: *Ensure access to content instruction taught in English by preteaching for upcoming language demands.* *Content*: *Determined by demands of upcoming subject matter. Teaches sentence structures and vocabulary needed to engage with content skills or concepts.*					
	Maximizing the teachable moment *Purpose*: *(1) Help ensure access to English language expression throughout the day and (2) Utilize odd moments for expanding and deepening language.* *Content*: *(1) Unanticipated language needs as they arise and (2) Developing language skills as appropriate.*					

We term the second component of ELD "front-loading language." This instruction occurs throughout the day as a horizontal slice of the curriculum, across all content areas. The term *front-loading* comes from the investment world: Front-loading of ELD refers to focusing on language prior to a content lesson. The linguistic demands of a content task are analyzed and taught in an up-front investment of time devoted to rendering the content understandable to the student—which takes in not only vocabulary, but also the forms or structures of language needed to discuss the content. The content instruction itself switches back and forth from a focus on language to a focus on content and back to language.

The third component of English-language instruction maximizes the "teachable moment" by utilizing opportunities as they present themselves to use precise language to fill a specific, unanticipated need for a word or a way to express a thought or idea. Fully utilizing the teachable moment means providing the next language skill needed to carry out a task or respond to an impromptu stimulus—like using a thunderstorm to stimulate a discussion about weather. Maximizing the teachable moment means exploiting unique situational contexts for spontaneous learning and taking advantage of odd moments throughout the day to expand and deepen language skills.

This blueprint helps resolve the tensions in the literature by promoting an approach that provides opportunities for gaining competence in academic language in both formal and informal settings.

We suggest that each of these three components of ELD is essential to student success. (These three components are discussed in greater detail later in the chapter.) Such a comprehensive approach is not required to develop everyday language—but it *is* necessary if students are to acquire academic-language proficiency at the level required for college admissions or job interviews. To continue the architectural metaphor, we must first have a clear vision of what we are building—in this case academic language competence—before we elaborate the design features and instructional principles necessary to support our blueprint.

Academic Language Versus Everyday Speech

Academic language is different from everyday speech and conversation: It is the language of texts, of academic discussion, and of formal writing. Academic-language proficiency requires students to use linguistic skills to interpret and infer meaning from oral and written language, discern precise meaning and information from text, relate ideas and information, recognize the conventions of various genres, and enlist a variety of linguistic strategies on behalf of a wide range of communicative purposes. For both native English speakers and second-language learners, learning academic uses of language is a lifelong endeavor (see Cummins, chapter 1 in this volume).

Though much vocabulary and syntax may be acquired through informal interaction, the range of academic-language skills—which includes the linguistic structures used to summarize, analyze, evaluate, and combine sentences; compose and write text; interpret graphs, charts, and word problems; and extract information from texts (Fillmore & Snow, 2000; Scarcella, 1996)—must not be left to chance encounters; it must be developed continuously and taught explicitly across all subject areas. Achieving full proficiency in English includes far more than merely exhibiting fluency in conversation; it means English learners know English well enough to be academically competitive with their native English-speaking peers (Hakuta, Butler, & Witt, 2000).

Academic-language proficiency helps students achieve long-term success in school. Yet many students at intermediate and advanced levels of English proficiency receive no formal language instruction (California Department of Education, 2000), leaving them fluent in everyday language (or in what Cummins [1989] refers to as Basic Interpersonal Communication Skills or BICS), but with critical gaps in academic-language knowledge and vocabulary. Although immigrant students often gain oral fluency in English in about two years (Collier, 1987; Cummins, 1984), it takes them far longer to achieve the academic-language proficiency required for success in school. Furthermore, length of time in second-language environments does not by itself guarantee the development of academic competence: Despite years of meaningful input and opportunities for interaction in English, serious gaps in linguistic competence can remain (Scarcella, 1996). Even though there are many opportunities for language learning during the course of a day in a language-rich classroom environment, merely being exposed to, and even being engaged in, activity in English is not sufficient to assure the development of full academic proficiency (Doughty & Williams, 1998).

Developing Academic English: Functions, Forms, and Fluency

Teachers, like architects, must understand the design features necessary to construct successful blueprints—including the blueprint that we envision for

English language instruction throughout the day. Our formula for designing such instruction is "Functions, Forms, and Fluency." It consists of analyzing the concept and skill requirements of lessons in

- the language task (function);
- the necessary tools (forms of language) for carrying out that task; and
- ways of providing opportunities for practice and application (developing fluency).

This approach builds on Halliday's perspective, which treats meaning and use as the central features of language and approaches grammar from that stance (Bloor & Bloor, 1995; Halliday, 1973).

Here we attempt to draw parallels with Cummins's (1989) approach to academic language and the three design features essential to our approach. Figure 10.2 is helpful in operationalizing Cummins's definition of Cognitive Academic Language Proficiency (CALP) in a planning design of functions, forms, and fluency (see Cummins, chapter 1, and Crawford, chapter 7, in this volume).

Communicative competence depends on the integration of acquired language knowledge with proficient use of *forms* appropriate to *functions*:

> The acquisition of vocabulary, grammar rules, discourse rules, and other organizational competencies results in nothing if the learner cannot use those forms for the functional purpose of transmitting and receiving thoughts, ideas, and feelings between speaker and hearer or reader and writer. While forms are the outward manifestation of language, functions are the realization of those forms. (Brown, 1994, p. 231)

If teachers are to design effective ELD instruction in their classrooms, they must learn to analyze academic language in terms of its functions, forms, and fluency features and address these in their planning process. Like a master carpenter guiding an apprentice, teachers must anticipate the task to be learned, determine which tools are needed for the task, and provide opportunities for practice. Practice will increase students' competence and develop their skills—skills that can then be applied to other tasks.

Let us consider each of these three design features in greater depth.

Functions (Tasks)

Functions are the tasks or purposes and uses of language (Brown, 1994; Halliday, 1973). That is, we use language to accomplish something in formal

FIGURE 10.2 Conceptual model from CALP to functions, forms, and fluency

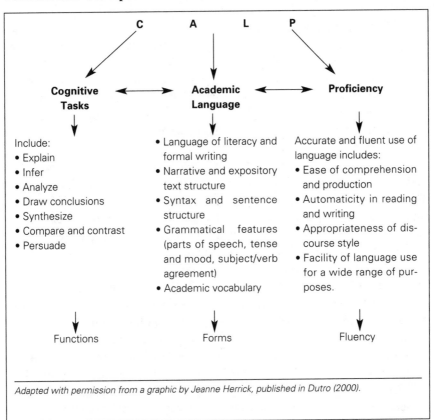

Adapted with permission from a graphic by Jeanne Herrick, published in Dutro (2000).

or informal settings, for social or academic purposes. Social purposes include expressing needs and wants, making jokes, exchanging greetings, indicating agreement or disagreement, and participating in personal conversations. Academic purposes include navigating written text, asking and answering informational and clarifying questions, relating information, comparing and contrasting, explaining cause and effect, drawing conclusions, summarizing, evaluating, justifying, persuading, and conducting research. Many language functions have both everyday and academic applications; some, such as writing a lab report, are specific to academics.

Functions are the cognitive tasks that drive us to connect thought and language. Taking Halliday's view that language is a "system of meanings" (Bloor & Bloor, 1995), we assert that teaching English language learners how to use language for a variety of academic and nonacademic purposes is both efficient and rigorous.

We argue that well-planned instruction and early use of academic language accelerate the acquisition of academic language proficiency. Through instruction that makes explicit the tools needed for different academic language functions, students learn the vocabulary and sentence structures needed for a range of cognitive tasks and uses of language. The utterances students learn, practice, and generate move from simple to complex depending on their level of English proficiency, always building toward the goal of fully proficient use.

Below we explore several language functions with examples across five levels of proficiency, based on commonly agreed-on stages of ELD (California Department of Education, 1999). Let us first consider the specific function of *describing* people, places, or things. It requires the speaker or writer to know how to use parts of speech—particularly verbs, nouns, and adjectives. Figure 10.3 illustrates possible utterances used to describe brown bears.

At the beginning level of proficiency, students may describe by using single words and phrases and basic nouns and adjectives ("brown bear"). By the early intermediate level they have progressed to basic subject-verb-object sentences using simple vocabulary: "The bear is brown. It has claws." At the intermediate level of proficiency the sentence is expanded and adjective use is more sophisticated ("thick," "sharp"), and at advanced levels descriptive sentences feature more complex sentence structures and ideas and more precise vocabulary. The language *function* is the same across the levels of proficiency, but the use of language is more complex and the content information is expanded.

FIGURE 10.3 Function chart for describing people, places, and things

Beginning	Early Intermediate	Intermediate	Early Advanced	Advanced
Brown; *brown* bear	The bear is *brown*. It *has* claws.	The brown bear *has thick fur* and *sharp claws*.	The brown bear *isn't a predator* even though it *has sharp claws and teeth*.	During their winter *hibernation*, brown bears *give birth to cubs*.

From Dutro & Prestridge (2001)

Another specific language function that falls under the umbrella of relating information is *locating objects in space*. For examples by level of proficiency, see Figure 10.4. The function of describing location calls for different vocabulary and grammar, particularly prepositional words and phrases (*on*, *behind*, *in front of*, *beneath*, *around*, *above*). A third example is the function of *relating past events*—describing action—which requires verbs, adverbs, and words that sequence (see Figure 10.5).

FIGURE 10.4 Function chart for locating objects in space

Beginning	Early Intermediate	Intermediate	Early Advanced	Advanced
Respond to direction: Put your plants *on* the table.	The corn *is behind* the beans.	*In* the garden, we planted corn *behind* the beans. We planted squash *in front of* the beans.	We buried a fish *beneath* the corn, squash, and beans to fertilize them.	The plants in our garden benefit from their *location*. The beans *grow around* the squash, providing nitrogen. The corn *grows above* the squash, providing shade.

From Dutro & Prestridge (2001)

FIGURE 10.5 Function chart for describing action

Beginning	Early Intermediate	Intermediate	Early Advanced	Advanced
Volcano, smoke, lava	The volcano *was smoking*.	*Last week*, the volcano *started smoking*. *This week*, it *erupted*.	*Previously*, the volcano *began to smoke*, and *this week*, it *erupted* violently.	It *has been two years since* the volcano *erupted* violently.

From Dutro & Prestridge (2001)

As illustrated in these figures, there are specific language functions (describing actions, locations, or things) embedded within larger functions (relating information) that make distinct linguistic demands on the language user. Competence in different language functions requires competence in comprehending and generating different parts of speech within different sentence structures. Increasing competence in any language function, however, impels the speaker or writer to use increasingly complex sentence structures. Consider these examples in relation to the language function of *expressing and supporting opinions*:

- It's better to be a farmer because it is safe. Hunting is dangerous.
- In my opinion, it would be better to be a farmer because farming is safer than hunting.
- I would have preferred to be a farmer, because hunters face many dangers.

Teaching English language skills from the perspective of language functions focuses attention on the language demands of a specific academic task (describing location, relating past events) in the context of specific content (strategic planting of crops, the eruption of volcanoes). But the benefits of learning to use a language function such as comparing, for example, extend beyond a given task, because once English language learners know how to compare, they can apply that skill to a range of contexts across many content areas. Consider Figure 10.6, which presents examples of comparison statements across diverse content areas.

Reading the chart from left to right demonstrates a progression of increased proficiency. Reading it vertically demonstrates a variety of comparative statements at a given level of proficiency. With this approach, then, learning interesting content—and how to talk and write about it—is not delayed until more advanced levels of proficiency are achieved. Instead, academic language is developed from the beginning stages of second-language learning. Competence in a range of language functions equips students to participate in content instruction and supports the acquisition of academic-language proficiency. Language thus becomes a vehicle, rather than a barrier, to learning.

Forms (Tools)

Once the functions of language are delineated, the second feature of our design plan for language learning is *forms*—grammatical features and word usage.

FIGURE 10.6 Function chart for comparing/contrasting

Beginning	Early Intermediate	Intermediate	Early Advanced	Advanced
triangle square three four	Triangles have three sides. Squares have four sides.	A triangle has three sides, *but* a square has four sides. They *both* have straight lines.	Triangles and squares *are alike because* they both have straight lines. They *are different because* a triangle has three sides and a square has four sides.	*Though* squares and triangles are similar because *both have* straight lines, a triangle is three-sided and a square is four-sided.
big ocean small lake	An ocean is *big* A lake is *small.*	An ocean is *larger than* a lake.	An ocean is enormous *compared with* a lake.	An ocean is vast; Even the largest lake is small by *comparison.*
Eagles fly, Seagulls fly, Penguins swim.	Eagles *can* fly. Seagulls *can* fly. Penguins *can* swim.	Eagles and seagulls *can* fly, *however* penguins *cannot.*	Eagles fly *high* Seagulls tend to fly *lower.* Penguins *can't* fly *at all.*	*Both* eagles *and* seagulls *have* the ability to fly. *However,* penguins *do not; instead,* they *are* able to swim.
pig spider	Wilbur *is a big* pig. Charlotte is a *small* spider.	Wilbur *is a young* pig, *but* Charlotte *is a grown* spider.	Wilbur *acts* immaturely and panics a lot, *but* Charlotte *remains* calm and reassuring.	Wilbur *appears* immature and excitable, *whereas* Charlotte *is always a* voice of reason.

From Dutro & Prestridge (2001)

These are the tools necessary for discourse, for reading and writing, for using complex language, and for engaging in cognitive processes. Forms include parts of speech, verb tenses and subject/verb agreement, the use of pronouns and conjunctions, and sentence structure or syntax (complex and compound sentences and word order).

As students progress through the grades the demand for complex language use in speaking, reading, and writing increases dramatically, leaving many English language learners unable to grasp more than the gist of what they read or hear. Limitations in students' knowledge of English—including lack of vocabulary and difficulty comprehending complex sentence structures—preclude their inferring subtleties, discerning irony, and comprehending relationships between and among ideas, characters, or events. A solid knowledge of language forms supports students as they deconstruct long sentences to make sense of them. The accurate and fluent use of grammatical forms helps ensure perception of the student as a proficient speaker, enabling full participation in academics and a respected voice to advocate for his or her positions and interests (Delpit, 1995).

Just as an architect understands the electrical system of a well-functioning building, so a teacher must understand the way English works. This requires more advanced linguistic knowledge than is currently possessed by most teachers. For example, teachers must recognize when and why to use perfect tenses ("He has been driving me crazy") rather than simple ones and how phonemes (sound units), morphemes (meaning units), and basic syllable patterns (consonant-vowel-consonant) work (Fillmore & Snow, 2000; Moats, 2000). They must understand the Anglo-Saxon, Latin, and Greek roots of English and how these affect orthography, morpheme patterns, and word usage. If teachers understand language well, they can explicitly teach these forms. So knowledge of the scope of English grammar, morphology, and phonology supports the teaching of reading and academic language to all students. This is basic teacher knowledge that our current student population demands.

Teachers of English learners must also understand the general sequence of how language forms are learned in a second language. For instance, a possible continuum of verb forms, from simple to complex, follows:

- present and past progressive tense ("is walking," "was not walking")
- future tense ("going to walk")
- present perfect tense (*have*/*has* + past participle: "She has been walking a mile each day for the past year.")
- phrasal verbs ("Walk down the street." "Walk up the path.")
- past perfect tense (*had* + past participle: "We hadn't been walking long when…")
- conditional form ("*If* we walk to the store, we *will* not be able to carry many bags.")

- future and conditional perfect tenses ("has been walking," "will have been walking"; "*If* she *had* walked, she *would have* gotten some exercise.")

- passive voice ("This novel *was written* by Ernest Hemingway." "This picture *was taken* by my grandfather.")

Clearly, this continuum is not fixed. Through innumerable interactions in classroom, playground, home, and community settings, students are exposed to a range of language forms and may recognize and use an advanced form while lacking competence in more basic ones.

VOCABULARY. We define *forms* to include not only grammatical forms but vocabulary. Knowledge of word usage along with a rich and varied vocabulary are critically important aspects of language proficiency and essential to academic success (Beimiller, 1999; Kame'enui & Simmons, 1998; Moats, 2000; Stahl, 1999). An intervention study showed that the vocabulary knowledge and reading comprehension gap between English language learners and native English speakers can be significantly reduced through enriched vocabulary instruction (McLaughlin et al., 2000).

One way to think of vocabulary is as comprising "general-utility" and "content-specific" words. Continuing our architectural metaphor, we refer to these, respectively, as "brick" and "mortar" words. "Brick" words are the vocabulary specific to the content and concepts being taught in a given lesson and might include words (to pick a random sample) such as *government*, *revolt*, *revolution*, *polarized*, *habitat*, *climate*, *arid*, *predator*, *adaptations*, *germinate*, and *mitosis*. Traditionally, this is the vocabulary teachers preteach at the beginning of a content area lesson or unit. In the earlier grades, many of these words are nouns—*giraffe*, *hoof*, *stem*, *leaf*—and can be illustrated or labeled. In later grades these words tend to be conceptual.

"Mortar" words and phrases are the general-utility vocabulary required for constructing sentences—the words that determine the relation between and among words. They are the words that hold our language together, and understanding them is essential to comprehension. Some examples of mortar words are

- connecting words required to construct complex sentences: *because, then, but, sometimes, before, therefore, however, whereas*

- prepositions and prepositional phrases: *on, in, under, behind, next to, in front of, between*

- basic regular and irregular verbs: *leave, live, eat, use, saw, go*

- pronouns and pronominal phrases: *she, his, their, it, us, each other, themselves*

- general academic vocabulary: *notice, think, analyze, direct, plan, compare, proof, survive, characteristics*

Many mortar words and phrases are basic vocabulary that may be unfamiliar to students who are learning English. Such vocabulary is best taught explicitly in the context of language use, as these words do not generally stand alone, but function within the context of a sentence or phrase along with brick, or content, words. Without deliberate instruction in the use of these words, students may not discern the time/place relationships among the rest of the words in a sentence or passage.

Linking functions and forms.   To illustrate the importance of addressing both brick and mortar vocabulary in language teaching that links function and form, let us consider again the language function of *comparison*. Students are called on to compare across content areas. Teachers might expect students, for example, to describe the similarities and differences among geometric shapes or between the values of numbers (*larger/smaller, less/more*), the relative nutritional value of different foods, the characteristics of bats and owls, or the personality traits of two characters in a novel.

Some possible brick vocabulary useful in discussing the similarities and differences between marine mammals and ocean fish, for example, is shown on the Venn diagram in Figure 10.7. This vocabulary is essential to expressing the idea that there are physical and behavioral similarities and differences between these two types of animals. However, the brick (content-specific) words of the Venn diagram do not by themselves equip students to demonstrate their comprehension of that idea. They also need mortar words and phrases in order to generate the sentences that make it possible to make the comparison.

By removing the brick words that are specific to content, the mortar words and phrases used in sentences are revealed. For example,

Marine mammals are warm-blooded, but fish are cold-blooded.

_____ are _____, but _____are _____.

The basic subject/verb/predicate adjective structure of this comparison sentence can be adapted by varying the verbs (e.g., *have, are, can, do, use*) or conjunctions (*however, whereas*). The ability to manipulate these basic sentence structures using a variety of content is necessary for demonstrating conceptual understanding in a lesson calling for comparison.

FIGURE 10.7 Venn diagram of brick words for marine mammals and fish

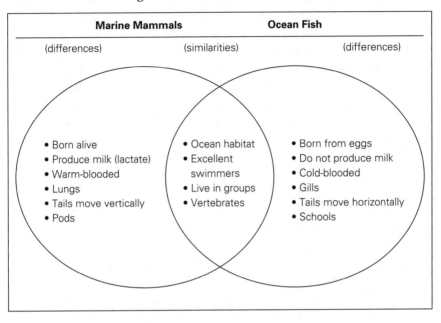

As illustrated previously (see Figure 10.6), comparative sentences range from simple to complex. Thus, the level of difficulty in a comparison task can be modulated by teaching the mortar vocabulary and sentence structure at levels of complexity appropriate to students' language skills, allowing students to engage in the work regardless of their level of English proficiency.

Another essential point is that these sentence frames can be used for comparing *any* two things. Explicitly teaching mortar vocabulary and how to construct various sentence frames helps students learn not only to compare marine mammals and ocean fish, but how to use language *to compare*, generally. Students will then be more apt to transfer those skills to making comparisons of triangles in mathematics, or of cultures in social studies. Wall charts labeled "Words and Phrases for Comparing" and "Sentence Frames for Comparing" serve as ongoing, practical references and become resources for student writing—and in conjunction with the instruction we have described, they enable students to develop metalinguistic awareness.

Functions (such as comparison) and forms (the vocabulary, grammar, and syntax necessary to express that) are two of the three design features of our instructional blueprint for teaching English. The third is *fluency*.

Fluency

Accurate facility in a wide range of language functions and grammatical forms, along with a rich vocabulary, is required for academic success: Consider standardized testing, classroom participation, reading literature and informational text, writing essays, and presenting oral reports. *Fluency* refers to the ease of both oral and written comprehension and of the production of speech and writing. It is the facility with which a speaker, reader, and writer uses language. *Accuracy* is the precision and correctness with which students speak, write, and comprehend written and oral language. Students develop fluency through focused and deliberate engagement with a range of uses of language—both oral and written—together with many opportunities to practice newly learned structures in different contexts.

In cases in which students have studied a language but had few everyday interactions in it, they may not understand speech in that language as well as they can read and write it (Canale & Swain, 1980). Most English language learners, however, are exposed to English through the media and in everyday interactions; for these students, receptive language generally precedes (and often exceeds) expressive language. Teachers of such children must consciously model language forms and vocabulary above the students' current expressive level while maintaining comprehensibility.

Now that we have established our conceptual framework and presented its components and design features, the next section of this chapter will take a more practical approach.

General Principles for English Language Instruction

English language instruction should provide not only ample opportunities for meaningful and engaging uses of language for a wide range of social and academic purposes, but necessary instruction in how English works. It should be deliberate, strategic, and purposeful. This section will present six guiding principles of English language instruction, drawn from the literature in cognitive psychology, language acquisition, and instructional practice. To develop high levels of language proficiency, we contend that teachers must

1. build on students' prior knowledge of both language and content;
2. create meaningful contexts for functional use of language;
3. provide comprehensible input and model forms of language in a variety of ways connected to meaning;

4. provide a range of opportunities for practice and application so as to develop fluency;

5. establish a positive and supportive environment for practice, with clear goals and immediate corrective feedback; and

6. reflect on the forms of language and the process of learning.

Let us look more carefully at each of these principles.

Prior Knowledge

Building on students' prior knowledge is essential. The value of tapping into the prior schema that we use to organize information and ideas has been apparent for a number of years, owing to the work of cognitive psychologists (Palinscar & Brown, 1984; Rumelhart & McClelland, 1986) as well as socioculturalists (Au, 1980; Heath, 1983). This body of work recommends using such strategies as semantic mapping, graphic organizers, and story walking. It is essential that every lesson take into account what students bring to the lesson and build on that existing knowledge and on prior language skills. Native language used strategically can solve some specific problems in connecting new learning to prior concepts or language forms (Gersten & Baker, 2000).

Meaningful Contexts

We know that creating context is vital if students are to map new knowledge onto prior knowledge or new forms and labels onto existing concepts. That is why a functional approach that creates purposeful settings for language use is so important. Moving from the concrete to the abstract is another basic principle. The use of visuals, gestures, graphic organizers, and word banks to reinforce concepts and vocabulary is effective in this regard (Gersten & Baker, 2000). Using simulations, gestures, realia, and theater is valuable in the early levels of English proficiency; comparisons, metaphors, and analogies (Marzano, 1998) are more suitable at higher levels of language functioning.

Comprehensible Input Connected to Meaning

Language, whether it is one's first or second language, is learned through modeling within a communicative context (Long, 1991). This holds true with respect to tasks ranging from engaging in simple speech to writing a complex essay. Learning occurs when modeling is clear; information is presented in small, comprehensible chunks; and frequent feedback is provided. Input, modeling, and output occur within clearly defined pedagogical tasks facing the learner, such as applying for a job, buying a house, planning a trip, or applying for college (Doughty & Williams, 1998).

Practice and Application

The goal for language learners is to move from the stage during which capacity is limited and language skills are new to automatic processing (Brown, 1994). Creating situations for focused interaction through debates, theater, interactive writing, and the like gives students opportunities to try their new language learning.

Cooperative group work around a situational task offers students the chance to use language purposefully. Cooperative learning is most beneficial when tasks are highly structured (Gersten & Baker, 2000); language output and practice are likewise maximized when tasks are structured—and when groups are small (preferably dyads or triads) and there are group incentives for appropriate language use (Moran, 1996). There is evidence that well-designed cooperative learning tasks afford students far more practice in speaking and listening than teacher-centered activities (Gersten & Baker, 2000). Though English language learners at similar levels of proficiency do not make more errors with one another than when speaking to fluent speakers, they cannot help one another discern how to correct these errors (Lightbrown & Spada, 1999) and do not provide one another the needed corrective feedback.

Safe Environment, Clear Goals, Corrective Feedback

For English learning to occur, students need a safe learning environment, clear output goals, and opportunities for practice and feedback. Krashen's (1985) "affective filter" described the importance of creating a safe, comfortable environment in which students can acquire a second language through engagement in natural situations. Scarcella (1996) concludes from her review of the literature of the 1980s that policies like those of the California Department of Education discouraged direct teaching of language and corrective feedback. She suggests a need to revisit these policies.

Scarcella found two main areas of weakness in her college students' English skills. The first is that limited knowledge of vocabulary and word usage results in misuse of words or word forms, mishandling of diction (using conversational words in academic writing), and use of acoustic approximations (e.g., the novel *Catch Her in the Right*). The second linguistic weakness is a limited understanding of English morphology and sentence structure, resulting in misuse of articles, pronouns, and nouns, misuse of verb tenses, and the inability to handle causative and conditional structures (Scarcella, 1996).

Marzano observes that "the simple act of setting instructional goals produces significant gains in student learning"; coupled with feedback regarding progress toward these goals, this is "one of the most straightforward and powerful techniques a teacher can employ" (Marzano, 1998, p. 128).

Feedback must be perceived as such, that is, not simply conversational or even written "recasts" of student speech or writing. Reyes relates end-of-the-year interviews with sixth graders who were surprised when apprised of their continuing spelling and grammatical errors. "Why didn't she tell me?" they wondered, expressing the expectation that the teacher's role included providing explicit feedback (Reyes, 1992).

Particularly in settings with few native English speaking models, teachers must create many opportunities for English learners to learn, use, and receive corrective feedback on academic language for the purpose of building the linguistic competencies required to achieve grade-level content standards.

Though we agree it is important to create an environment in which mistakes are seen in a positive light, clear goals and corrective feedback must be a part of the equation to develop academic language skills to an advanced level. Teachers have the responsibility to provide feedback so students can improve their performance and internalize correct usage (Lightbrown & Spada, 1999; Marzano, 1998).

Reflection on Forms and Process

Modulating cognitive and language demands by lowering cognitive demands when the language demand is high and vice versa allow students to move back and forth from a focus on concept to a focus on language form. Sharing this process with students will help them learn how to move back and forth effectively when learning new language forms, thus avoiding cognitive overload. Preteaching critical vocabulary prior to student reading (Rousseau, Tam, & Ramnarain, 1993) allows students to focus on form before focusing on content.

Metalinguistic reflection is particularly effective with English language learners, who can reflect on their native language to give them insight into the new language forms they are learning (Moran & Calfee, 1993). Encouraging students to reflect on the process by which they are learning language will help them to manage their own future learning situations.

Operationalizing the Blueprint: Three Components of English Language Development

Systematic English Language Development

Systematic ELD is designed to build a solid foundation in English language using an organized method that does not leave the development of forms or fluency to random experiences or chance encounters. It is the vertical slice of the blueprint; it is its own discipline. It is distinct from other disciplines in that the focus of instruction is on explicitly teaching English—functions, forms (including brick and mortar vocabulary), and fluency—for the purpose of increasing communicative competence in listening, speaking, reading, writing, and thinking, for both social and academic purposes.

Current ELD practices vary widely, and many English language learners receive limited or inconsistent assistance in learning English. The California Department of Education identified a number of problematic themes in the 1999 Language Census: (1) English learners of varying English proficiency levels are grouped together and are receiving the same ELD instruction regardless of ability; (2) ongoing assessment of students to determine progress in English proficiency is not conducted; (3) many English learners at advanced levels or in mainstream programs are not receiving ELD; and (4) ELD instruction is not tied to specific standards or expected outcomes.

Although it is beneficial to modify speech so as to assure comprehension, it is not necessary to limit utterances or restrict exposure (Lightbrown & Spada, 1999). Explicit instruction in language structures at and just above the level of proficiency accelerates learning and ensures that students learn less common usage and specifically academic forms. It makes sense, then, to anticipate the next level of language learning by means of focused instruction. Effective ELD instruction is targeted to the limits of what students can already do with English and teaches the skills needed to move ahead.

A well-planned, systematic ELD component lays out a scope and sequence of language forms as expected outcomes. Students are grouped by level of proficiency for this part of the instructional day. Ongoing assessment with respect to mastery of forms and the ability to apply them in different contexts drives instructional planning in order to ensure that learning is on track.

The systematic ELD component, which draws from Long's "focus on forms" (1988), does not practice isolated grammatical features, as in traditional grammar translation programs, but rather focuses on form within a meaning-based context (Doughty & Williams, 1998), and on communicative functions (e.g., using the past tense to describe what happened in a movie) relevant to the life experiences of learners.

The "focus on forms" framework operationalizes forms to include grammatical structures, syntax, and vocabulary. Instruction includes comprehensible input of forms, starting with extensive modeling; practice, with opportunities for relevant output—and with variation, so that students can define when the form is appropriate to the context; and application to develop proficiency. Lessons can be based on literature, content, or activities but must focus on the forms of the language.

TEACHING TOOLS: LEVELS OF PROFICIENCY. Training for a novice construction worker includes a careful introduction to each of the tools of the trade, starting with a simple hammer and saw and proceeding later to power tools. By the same logic, a novice learner of a second language should be introduced to the forms or structures—the tools—of the language in a developmental sequence: from simple, commonly used forms to more complex and abstract ones. As with the construction worker, this should not occur in an isolated laboratory, but rather in a functional context that enables immediate practical applications. Let us now look at how this systematic approach works at different levels of development.

At a beginning level, the focus of ELD instruction is often on understanding commands, or giving simple one-word responses in survival situations like getting what you need or following directions. As understanding develops, students learn basic common everyday vocabulary and simple grammatical present, past, and future tenses. They practice extensively, receiving instructional feedback from more experienced speakers and the teacher. Reading and writing are introduced at the beginning levels through labeling; modeling of sentence frames and practice in completing them with words from banks, webs, and other resources; and the use of predictable, patterned texts featuring basic vocabulary and sentence structures. Lesson plans may revolve around a particular grammatical form and provide for extended practice with that form, or may address a content theme that encourages opportunities for connecting new learning to prior schema and applies that learning to situations relevant to the life of the student.

Intermediate-level students are engaged in more reading and writing, and in using a variety of verb tenses and grammatical structures. There is tremendous vocabulary growth as students learn synonyms (e.g., *large/giant/huge*), antonyms (e.g., *fast/slow, strong/weak, addition/subtraction*) and basic idioms ("cut it out," "raining cats and dogs"). Writing might focus on forms and conventions, such as pronoun usage or past-tense verb endings; oral language experiences might include reporting, dialogues, skits, or games.

Systematic ELD instruction is currently rare at advanced levels, depriving students of the opportunity to master the academic language necessary to compete in higher education academic contexts. Extending vocabulary, particularly general-utility academic words, and practicing complex verb tenses are essential for reading more complex narrative and expository text and for thinking about the abstract concepts students will encounter as they proceed through school. Advanced-level ELD should focus on addressing persistent problem areas in grammar, working to develop fluency and automaticity in reading comprehension; teaching idioms, along with metaphors and other figurative language; and deconstructing expository text (Kinsella, 1997; see also Hernández, chapter 6 in this volume).

Intense attention to vocabulary development, modeling and clear instruction in reading comprehension strategies and written composition, the use of graphic organizers, and providing many opportunities to practice new skills are essential for older learners. Emphasis on metalinguistic understanding and intentional focus on how language works also can accelerate learning.

At each level of proficiency, ELD instruction can occur in large-group instruction or in smaller groups within the class or pulled across classes into appropriate levels of proficiency. Systematic ELD that is thoughtful and thorough lays a solid foundation for English language learners as they develop proficiency at each level—but it is not sufficient. Rather, English language development instruction must be incorporated into all content areas.

Front-Loading Language Teaching

The second component of a comprehensive ELD program is the horizontal slice of the blueprint, crossing all content disciplines. Front-loading involves strategically preteaching the vocabulary and language forms needed to comprehend and generate the language appropriate to an upcoming lesson—making an investment of classroom time to help ensure that content lessons are comprehensible to English language learners. Front-loading a content lesson anticipates the linguistic competence that the learning will require—as determined by the language requirements of the discipline in general and the lesson in particular—and intentionally teaches those skills.

A contractor needs specific tools for specific construction tasks, such as building a bookcase; if the task is to install a sink the tools are different, though they may overlap. So it is with respect to linguistic tasks. Students must have an array of linguistic skills in order to manage a range of language uses, purposes, and tasks; some of these, such as mastery of the regular and irregular forms of common verbs, overlap across disciplines and tasks, but using the conditional is particularly important to hypothesizing in science. So the teacher preparing students to hypothesize will consider how he or she wants students to make conditional statements and will teach students to use the appropriate language. Analysis of the linguistic demands of different cognitive tasks is at the heart of front-loading.

The ability to use many language tools is developed in a systematic ELD program, but this foundation alone will not provide English learners with the skills necessary to meet the range of language demands they will encounter across content areas. Front-loading in content area instruction is necessary to help students learn the specific language required to write a science lab report, frame an argument about the causes of a historical event, or summarize the plot of a novel—or to participate in a classroom discussion about current events or present an oral report on the need for recycling. Front-loading language teaches students the language of the content discipline.

CONTENT AREA INSTRUCTION. Content area instruction requires special attention directed at English language learners in every classroom that is not an ELD, ESL, or foreign language classroom. The primary approach to content area instruction for English language learners in U.S. schools is *sheltered instruction*. These classes are designed to simplify language demands and modify grade-level content instruction so as to make it accessible to students learning English; the adapted instruction is designed to provide an opportunity for English language learners to learn both content and academic language (Bunch, Abram, Lotan, & Váldes, 2001). Many mainstream content area teachers, however, receive little or no support regarding how to adapt their teaching methods to ensure that their English language learners have meaningful access to content.

The general principles of ELD hold true with respect to content area instruction (Moran, 1996). For one, content curriculum must be bridged to the knowledge and experience that students bring to the classroom (Díaz, Moll,

& Mehan, 1986; Heath, 1983). More generally, a positive and supportive environment for content instruction implies a sensitivity to the competing cognitive demands posed by challenging content and complex language. Organizational strategies—tools that fit a concept into a bigger picture as well as organize bits of information within a context or a topic (Calfee, 1981; Hernández, 1989)—are utilized at every level of the process. Meaningful contexts and practice through interaction with the language and concepts involved must be varied depending on the content and the function, but it is clear that interaction, whether in social studies, science, or mathematics, enhances learning (Hudelson, 1989; Reyes & Molner, 1991). Reporting or sharing is encouraged through a variety of modes of expression, both orally and in writing, and supported by the teacher's modeling and providing sentence frames and relevant vocabulary (Kinsella, 1997).

Research in the area of sheltered instruction has yielded some useful strategies. The Sheltered Instruction Observation Protocol (SIOP) model includes both content and language objectives, along with content concepts, in the preparation phase (Echevarria, Vogt, & Short, 2000). The Science-Language Integration rubric (Stoddart, Pinal, Latzke, & Canaday, 2002) defines five levels of teacher knowledge of content/language integration. The distinctions we define may help teachers progress through these levels in their understanding and in their ability to successfully integrate language and content.

SHELTERED INSTRUCTION VERSUS FRONT-LOADING FOR LANGUAGE. There are challenges involved in providing content instruction that is accessible and rigorous. As students progress through the grades, the linguistic and content demands made on them increase substantially, challenging even the best-intentioned and most knowledgeable teachers to bridge students' language proficiency in relation to the linguistic and content requirements of new subject matter. There is a risk of oversimplifying the content to accommodate the students' language level (Bunch et al., 2001); at the same time, because the primary goal of content instruction is to teach the knowledge and concepts of a discipline, the emphasis on content tends to dominate while language demands tend to be given short shrift. So sheltered content area instruction often leads to sacrifices in learning English, as teachers tend to emphasize content acquisition over building English language abilities and inadequate time is provided for English language learning (Gersten & Baker, 2000). Because of this lack of deliberate focus on the language required for accomplishing academic tasks, English language learners' linguistic skills cannot keep pace with the ever-increasing demands of the curriculum, and the gap between what they know and what they need to know continues to grow (Stanovich, 1986).

We suggest that front-loading the language required for content and content-related tasks begins to address this difficulty in the sheltered instruction model. By regarding language and content demands as distinct but related and complementary, we can help ensure that students receive adequate time and attention with respect to developing the linguistic competencies needed to support complex content learning.

When familiar content is used to explicitly teach and practice the essential language skills an upcoming content lesson requires, the content demand is lowered so that students can attend to the language learning. As a master carpenter would teach a novice the skills of measuring and sawing using basic cuts first, so it is with respect to front-loading language for content instruction: The math teacher explains the language of lines and angles with familiar geometric shapes before asking students to apply those terms to complex figures. Without this instruction, the student may miss the concept being taught, because he or she is preoccupied with attempting to understand what is meant, say, by the phrase *is parallel to*. But now that some of the key language has been taught, attention is more likely to be focused on the content instruction. The purpose of front-loading, then, is to anticipate and remove linguistic barriers to subject matter comprehension.

During the content lesson, the teacher does not forget about language skills; indeed, they will be thoughtfully practiced, reinforced, and revisited throughout the content lesson, as the emphasis shifts from language to content and back, as needed. It should be noted here that the emphasis in a front-loading lesson is on the language requirements of function-related tasks, requiring what we have termed "mortar" vocabulary. The content-specific vocabulary—or "bricks"—is generally taught in the content lesson itself.

THINKING THROUGH A FRONT-LOADING LANGUAGE LESSON.   Front-loading language instruction must be carefully thought through. A useful approach is to determine the language functions and identify the cognitive tasks that a given lesson targets. The teacher must first define those tasks by asking, What are the cognitive/linguistic demands of this assignment? Do I want the students to share information, tell a story, write an autobiographical essay, analyze a written math problem, or contrast animal behaviors? What is the linguistic load of the text? What are the demands of the readings in the discipline (textbooks, articles, websites), including chapter and section headings, charts, graphs, and maps?

Furthermore, what language forms will be needed to accomplish these tasks? What grammatical structures and vocabulary will be needed? Will the assignment require forming a question, or talking in the past tense? At this point it may be useful for the teacher to imagine the language he or she would like students to use, both orally and in writing. What kinds of sentences might students use to express the ideas being taught?

Next, what support is needed in order for students to learn to use these language structures? What are ways to engage students' interactions so as to further both the linguistic and conceptual goals of the lesson? And how can opportunities be structured for students to use these new forms appropriately and develop automaticity and comfort level (fluency)?

The purpose of both systematic ELD and front-loading is to develop competence in English. But whereas systematic ELD is organized by proficiency level based on competence with forms, front-loading language teaching is planned according to the demands of the content lesson and with a range of proficiency levels in mind.

By itself front-loading is not a comprehensive ELD program and may leave gaps in language knowledge; it is a complementary component to systematic ELD instruction. But we suggest that front-loading language enhances not only current sheltered instructional practices, but mainstream content instruction as well.

Maximizing the Teachable Moment

Finally, just as any good architect will take advantage of the natural terrain in designing a blueprint, we recognize the importance of contextual, incidental circumstances that create special learning opportunities.

Good teaching involves not only creating a language-rich classroom, but taking advantage of spontaneous opportunities to maximize learning—and make possible a more natural process of language acquisition. We call this informal, nonsystematic, yet potentially powerful aspect of English language development, which can occur at any moment during the school day, the "teachable moment."

How do serendipitous moments turn into learning opportunities? Teachable moments are captured when teachers assess the context and provide on-the-spot immediate input by briefly modeling, clarifying, or explaining a language need and providing an opportunity for practice. For example: Two students are in a conflict. The teacher insists students use "I" statements and models, "When you (do _____), I feel _____." This gives the students a language frame—the mortar words to plug the bricks into. The teacher can also supply the bricks—by asking, "Do you feel sad, mad, hurt?" and then modeling these bricks within the mortar frame.

Or, Gabriela walks in and says, "Look, teacher, I got new red *choose*," in her best approximation of *shoes*. Appreciating the new shoes with correct modeling—"Look at Gabi's new shoes" (with an emphasis on the sound of *sh*)—provides Gabi with immediate comprehensible input. A brief minilesson on the *sh/ch* distinction provides the clear goal, safe context, and instructional feedback needed to call attention to the distinction between these phonemes. An explanation of how English has two different sounds whereas Spanish uses one sound for both graphemes provides the relevant metalinguistic understanding.

Another example: Kenji walks into class and announces, "I earn $10 yesterday and I earn $10 tomorrow too." A quick assessment by the teacher suggests the opportunity not only to present a mathematics minilesson but also to focus on language forms (past and future tense verb distinctions), by having Kenji and his classmates talk through several word problems revolving around his earnings.

Or, a student is writing an essay discussing the benefits of going to college and is stuck on how to get from one paragraph to the next. This difficulty allows the teacher to provide an on-the-spot lesson on the mortar words needed for *transitions* to help the student's paper *flow*. A quick brainstorming regarding college preparation requirements helps the student fill in the brick vocabulary in this essay as well.

Teachable moments occur every day—from a butterfly flying into the room to the latest news headline—and during almost every lesson. Whether corrective feedback turns into learning or not depends on how the teacher handles the moment, the safety of the environment, how comprehensible the input is for the student, and whether or not opportunities for output are supported. Even given the most artful teacher, however, these random moments do not make up, as some teachers suggest, an entire ELD program. They are, rather, a series of serendipitous opportunities to accelerate the learning of a new language form or expand vocabulary in a functional context. They do not take the place of systematic ELD instruction nor eliminate the need for frontloading language for content instruction.

It is important to set clear daily goals with respect to both language and content development, and it is also important to know when to seize an opportunity that presents itself to teach a language skill at a perfect moment of receptivity. There are no hard-and-fast rules, though, for when to stay focused on goals and when to seize the moment. This is where teaching becomes an art, not a science. Just as an architect must balance the structural and aesthetic demands of his or her work, so must a teacher balance the science and the art of teaching.

Conclusions

Having presented the role of teacher as architect in implementing a well-designed approach to English language instruction, let us consider the knowledge base these architects will need. We return to Fillmore and Snow's (2000) discussion of what linguistic knowledge teachers must possess in light of the demographic and linguistic diversity in our world today. We agree that all teachers need to understand the linguistic features of English and have some ability to compare and contrast the most common languages of the students they serve. Furthermore, we believe that teachers need a fundamental understanding of the central role that academic language plays in learning and of the components of a comprehensive approach to ELD, including how to structure all three components—systematic ELD, front-loading language for content instruction, and maximizing the "teachable moment"—into their instructional day. They also need to be skilled in using the design features of functions, forms, and fluency to help plan their lessons. Finally, they need to be proficient enough with the above knowledge and skills to be able to create a rich language-learning environment. Perhaps future teacher preparation examinations will include tests of linguistic knowledge and of the underlying principles of English language development.

Studies by Haycock (1998) and others suggest that low teacher expectations with respect to language-minority students, as exhibited by assigning low-level tasks and providing minimal instruction, are widespread (see Coppola, chapter 8, and Chang, chapter 11, in this volume). English language learners face tremendous challenges in gaining both the linguistic and academic proficiencies required for academic success, and each student deserves thoughtful, rigorous, and well-designed instruction that is targeted to his or her level of language proficiency and provides for application of increasingly high levels of speaking, listening, reading, writing, and thinking skills. Our hope is that an architectural approach will help teachers, administrators, and policymakers rethink the structure and design of academic language instruction in schools. Further study might usefully focus on how best to develop teacher ELD knowledge, and research is needed on the most effective use of the constellation of ELD components and design features presented here.

We believe that the architectural approach provides a powerful metaphor for English language instruction. For one thing, it gives proper prominence to the *design* aspect of language instruction. If teachers take seriously their role in planning for the teaching of language every day, English language learners will gain the tools to build durable foundations and strong academic language structures that will allow them to function comfortably in any academic or applied setting.

REFERENCES

Au, K. (1980). Participation structures in a reading lesson with Hawaiian children: Analysis of a culturally appropriate instructional event. *Anthropology and Education Quarterly, 11*(2), 91–115.

Beebe, L.M. (Ed.). (1988). *Issues in second language acquisition: Multiple perspectives*. New York: Newbury House.

Beimiller, A. (1999). *Language and reading success* (Vol. 5: *From reading research to practice*). Cambridge, MA: Brookline Books.

Bloor, T., & Bloor, M. (1995). *Functional analysis of English: A Hallidayan approach*. New York: St. Martin's Press.

Bourhis, R.Y. (1990). The development of second language proficiency. In P. Allen, B. Harley, J. Cummins, & M. Swain (Eds.), *The development of second language proficiency* (pp. 134–145). New York: Cambridge University Press.

Brown, D.H. (1994). *Principles of language learning and teaching* (3rd ed.). Englewood Cliffs, NJ: Prentice Hall.

Bunch, G.C., Abram, P.L., Lotan, R.A., & Valdes, G. (2001). Beyond sheltered instruction: Rethinking conditions for academic language development. *TESOL Journal, 10*(2/3), 28–33.

Calfee, R. (1981). *The book*. Unpublished Project READ training manual, Stanford University, Stanford, CA.

California Department of Education. (1999). *English language development standards* [Online]. Available: http://www.cde.ca.gov/standards/eld.pdf

California Department of Education. (2000). *Language proficiency and academic accountability unit* [Online]. Available: http://www.cde.ca.gov/el/index.html

Canale, M., & Swain, M. (1980). Theoretical bases of communicative approaches to second language teaching and testing. *Applied Linguistics, 1*, 1–47.

Collier, V.P. (1987). Age and rate of acquisition of second language for academic purposes. *TESOL Quarterly, 21*, 617–641.

Cummins, J. (1984). *Bilingualism and special education: Issues in assessment and pedagogy*. Clevedon, UK: Multilingual Matters.

Cummins, J. (1989). *Empowering minority students*. Sacramento, CA: California Association for Bilingual Education.

Delpit, L. (1995). *Other people's children: Cultural conflict in the classroom.* New York: New York Press.

Diaz, S., Moll, L.C., & Mehan, H. (1986). Sociocultural resources in instruction: A context-specific approach. In California State Department of Education (Ed.), *Beyond language: Social and cultural factors in schooling language minority children* (pp. 187–230). Los Angeles: Evaluation, Dissemination and Assessment Center, California State University.

Doughty, C., & Williams, J. (Eds.). (1998). *Focus on form in classroom second language acquisition* (Cambridge Applied Linguistics Series). Cambridge, UK: Cambridge University Press.

Dutro, S. (2000). *Building bridges: Grades 4–6 English language & literacy RESULTS institutes.* Training materials prepared for the California Reading & Literature Project, San Diego, CA, for the California Professional Development Institutes for Teachers of English Language Learners.

Dutro, S., & Prestridge, K. (2001). *A teacher's guide to a focused approach for English language development.* Training materials prepared for the California Reading & Literature Project, San Diego, CA.

Echevarria, J., Vogt, M.E., & Short, D.J. (2000). *Making content comprehensible for English language learners.* Boston: Allyn & Bacon.

Fillmore, L.W., & Snow, C.E. (2000). *What teachers need to know about language.* Special report from ERIC Clearinghouse on Languages and Linguistics [Online]. Available: http://www.cal.org/ericcll/teachers/teachers.pdf

Gersten, R., & Baker, S. (2000). *Effective instruction for English-language learners: What we know about effective instructional practices for English-language learners.* Eugene, OR: University of Oregon, Eugene Research Institute.

Hakuta, K., Butler, Y.G., & Witt, D. (2000). *How long does it take English learners to attain proficiency?* (Policy Report 2000-1). Santa Barbara, CA: University of California Linguistic Minority Research Institute.

Hakuta, K., & McLaughlin, B. (1996). Seven tensions that define research on bilingualism and second language acquisition. In D.C. Berliner & R.C. Calfee (Eds.), *The handbook of educational psychology* (pp. 603–621). Washington, DC: American Psychological Association.

Halliday, M.A.K. (1973). *Explorations in the functions of language.* London: Edward Arnold.

Hamayan, E.V., & Damico, J.S. (Eds.). (1990). *Limiting bias in the assessment of bilingual students.* Austin, TX: Pro-Ed.

Haycock, K. (1998, Summer). Good teaching matters: How well-qualified teachers can close the gap. *Thinking K–16, 3*(2), 2.

Heath, S.B. (1983). *Ways with words: Language, life and work in communities and classrooms.* Cambridge, UK: Cambridge University Press.

Hernandez, H. (1989). *Multicultural education: A teacher's guide to content and process.* Columbus, OH: Merrill.

Hudelson, S. (1989). Teaching English through content-area activities. In P. Riggs & V.G. Allen (Eds.), *When they don't all speak English* (pp. 139–150). Urbana, IL: National Council of Teachers of English.

Kame'enui, E.J., & Simmons, D.C. (1998). Beyond effective practice to schools as host environments: Building and sustaining a school-wide intervention model in beginning reading. *OSSC Bulletin, 41*(3), 3–24.

Kinsella, K. (1997). Moving from comprehensible input to "learning to learn" in content-based instruction. In M.A. Snow & D.B. Brinton (Eds.), *The content-based classroom: Perspectives on integrating language and content* (pp. 46–68). White Plains, NY: Longman.

Krashen, S.D. (1985). *The input hypothesis: Issues and implications.* New York: Longman.

Krashen, S.D., & Terrel, T. (1983). *The natural approach: Language acquisition in the classroom.* Oxford, UK: Pergamon.

Lightbrown, P.M., & Spada, N. (1999). *How languages are learned* (Rev. ed.). New York: Oxford University Press.

Long, M.H. (1988). Instructed interlanguage development. In L.M. Beebe (Ed.), *Issues in second language acquisition: Multiple perspectives* (pp. 115–141). Rowley, MA: Newbury House.

Long, M.H. (1991). Focus on form: A design feature in language teaching methodology. In K. de Bot, D. Coste, R. Ginsberg, & C. Kramsch (Eds.), *Foreign language research in cross-cultural perspective* (pp. 39–52). Amsterdam: John Benjamins.

Marzano, R.J. (1998). *A theory-based meta-analysis of research on instruction* (Contract No. RJ96006101). Aurora, CO: Office of Educational Research and Improvement, Department of Education, Mid-continent Regional Educational Laboratory.

McLaughlin, B. (1985). *Second-language acquisition in childhood* (Vol. 2: School-age children; 2nd ed.). Hillsdale, NJ: Erlbaum.

McLaughlin, B., August, D., Snow, C., Carlo, M., Dressler, C., White, C., et al. (2000, April). *Vocabulary improvement in English language learners: An intervention study.* A symposium conducted by the Office of Bilingual Education and Minority Languages Affairs, Washington, DC.

Moats, L.C. (2000). *Speech to print: Language essentials for teachers.* Baltimore: Paul H. Brookes.

Moran, C. (1996). *Content area instruction for students acquiring English, Power of two languages.* New York: MacMillan/McGraw Hill.

Moran, C., & Calfee, R. (1993). Comprehending orthography: Social construction of letter-sound systems in monolingual and bilingual programs. *Reading and Writing: An Interdisciplinary Journal, 5,* 205–225.

National Clearinghouse for Bilingual Education. (2000). *Summary report of the survey of the states' limited English proficient students and available educational programs and services, 1997–98.* Washington, DC: Author.

Palincsar, A.S., & Brown, A.L. (1984). Reciprocal teaching of comprehension-fostering and comprehension-monitoring activities. *Cognition and Instruction, 2,* 117–175.

Reyes, M.L. (1992). Challenging venerable assumptions: Literacy instruction for linguistically different students. *Harvard Educational Review, 62,* 427–446.

Reyes, M.L., & Molner, L.A. (1991). Instructional strategies for second-language learners in content areas. *Journal of Reading, 35*(2), 96–103.

Rousseau, M.K., Tam, B.K.Y., & Ramnarain, R. (1993). Increasing reading proficiency of language-minority students with speech and language impairments. *Education and Treatments of Children, 16,* 254–271.

Rumelhart, D., & McClelland, J. (1986). *Parallel distributed processing.* Cambridge, MA: MIT Press.

Scarcella, R.C. (1996). Secondary education and second language research: Instructing ESL students in the 1990's. *The CATESOL Journal, 9,* 129–152.

Schmida, M. (1996). *I don't understand what she be saying: Reconsidering the interlanguage and semilingual theories and explanations for first language loss and limited SLA*. Unpublished manuscript, University of California at Berkeley.

Stahl, S. (1999). *Vocabulary development* (Volume 2 in the series from reading research to practice). Cambridge, MA: Brookline Books.

Stanovich, K.E. (1986). Matthew effects in reading: Some consequences of individual differences in the acquisition of literacy. *Reading Research Quarterly, 21*, 360–406.

Stoddart, T., Pinal, A., Latzke, M., & Canaday, D. (2002). Integrating inquiry science and language development for English language learners. *Journal of Research in Science Teaching, 39*(8), 26–45.

Swain, M. (1986). Communicative competence: Some roles of comprehensible input and comprehensible output in its development. In J. Cummins & M. Swain (Eds.), *Bilingualism in education* (pp. 116–137). New York: Longman.

CHAPTER 11

Multilevel Collaboration for English Learners: An Asian American Perspective

Ji-Mei Chang

Two major educational realities in today's schools are that all students must have equal access to the core curriculum, and that students must be given appropriate support in meeting state or district standards while being held accountable to a statewide testing mandate. Teachers and administrators who are striving to provide equal access and adequate support face severe challenges in schools that have a high enrollment of a diverse group of English learners. Many English learners in these schools, even though fluent in oral language, lag behind their English-speaking peers in academic performance; and such learners' statewide test scores are consistently below the 40th percentile.

Helping all learners meet state and district standards and access core curriculum requires careful planning and establishment of a culture of multilevel collaboration among all the key players—specifically, teachers, administrators, family members, and workers or volunteers associated with related community agencies. I focus here on Asian American English learners who

- are not traditionally perceived as model minority students (Chang, 1995a)

- approach their district's accepted levels of English oral language fluency—as judged by, for example, basic interpersonal communicative skills

- repeatedly score below the 36th or 40th percentile on statewide tests

- are from families with low or middle socioeconomic status (SES)

- may or may not have any school-identified learning disabilities (LD)

Hereinafter, these learners will be referred to as "the specified group," "specified learners," or "specified students." The specified group comprises individuals who, in addition to sharing these characteristics, either were born in the United States or are recent immigrants from different parts of Asia, including the East, the Southeast, and the Indian subcontinent.

The specified group's literacy and language needs are not being addressed effectively in schools because society often has the misperception that all Asian American students perform well in school. Yet, when Asians and Asian Americans are *not* model students, their educational reality is less than desirable (Chang, 1995a, 2001a). If they are poor, limited in English proficiency, and identified as having LD in school, Asian and Asian American students' school days are typically filled with squandered learning opportunities (Chang, 1995a). Schools, in general, do not have effective intervention programs for those students who demonstrate oral fluency but not academic language proficiency, so such students are often placed in sink-or-swim situations in mainstream classrooms. In addition, schools generally do not have teachers or other personnel with the expertise to address the specified needs of learners from some Southeast Asian regions. Hence, intervention is less effective for those who fail in school because of their lack of academic language proficiency as well as their unique socioemotional needs.

To overcome such challenges and avoid leaving the specified group behind, schools need to build multilevel collaboration among key players who can serve as strong student advocates. In many schools, once these learners fall too far behind their peers, they will be referred for special education placement. Based on the findings of a recent study (Chang, 2001a), it is particularly important for the specified group to receive proper school intervention early in schooling. Should they fall too far behind, there are very few options for schools to provide intervention beyond elementary school.

The type of special education program available to the specified group typically occurs in a more restricted environment than that of studying with English-speaking peers in an inclusive classroom. For example, instead of being placed in an inclusive classroom and supported with a special education resource program, these students might be placed in a special, more restrictive full-day class covering all core subject areas, reducing much-needed interactions with successful English-speaking peers. Owing to the extreme shortage of well-qualified special education teachers, these students are unlikely to receive much-needed English language intervention. Hence, a special education program becomes a placement rather than a service for the specified group (see García & Beltrán, chapter 9 in this volume).

This chapter explores potential ways to empower key players to reverse the course of driving the specified group to unnecessary failure in schools. In particular, I highlight practices that might generate successful schooling for all students through multilevel collaborations. Teachers and students need more than just increased funding to adjust to new testing mandates; instead, the community as a whole needs to help teachers combat the trend toward fragmented teaching aimed merely at boosting statewide testing scores in each classroom.

In essence, the specified group needs an enriched, inclusive English language learning environment, managed by well-qualified and responsive English language development (ELD) teachers—either in sheltered programs or in inclusive classrooms where integrated content knowledge can be delivered, such as by integrating language arts with history (Chang, 2002). In sheltered programs, core academic subjects such as social studies, science, and mathematics are taught in English while learners' second language development needs are still addressed. Sheltered language intervention programs are most effective when accomplished through teacher collaborations, as I have observed in my studies (Chang, 2002; see also Coppola, chapter 8 in this volume).

The issues raised in this chapter are critical to those learners from low-to-middle-SES family backgrounds enrolled in schools with too few qualified teachers and insufficiently responsive administrative leadership. A U.S. government report (Bush, 2001) documents that in 1998, 68% of fourth graders were unable to read at the basic level in the nation's highest poverty schools, and that 15 million students have graduated from high school in the last 15 years unable to read at the basic level. Furthermore, the U.S. Census Bureau has suggested that difficult times are ahead for U.S. schools, given the high enrollment of students coming from poor or low-income families (Rosenblatt & Helfand, 2001). The anticipated high enrollment of learners from low-income families, coupled with insufficient school and home support, inadvertently places some students at risk of academic failure.

Based on my research findings and field observations (Chang 1993, 1995, 2002), this chapter discusses what is needed in order for key players to initiate, implement, and sustain the multilevel collaborations necessary to help the specified group of learners. Also, to advocate for the specified group, the call for multilevel collaborations is further supported by evidence provided in the following sections. I first set forth a theoretical framework for multilevel collaborations. Included in this framework is the research tool that enabled my research team to effectively examine the components of multilevel collaborations and the implications of such collaborations for the specified group. I then explore the possibilities of a reconceptualized partnership based both within and beyond school confines. Finally, I examine several contexts in which multilevel collaborations seem to me both necessary and especially promising.

The Theoretical Framework for Multilevel Collaborations: Reconceptualizing a Home-School-Community Partnership

"Multilevel collaborations" refers to an integrated support system among key players from school, home, and community that effectively advocates for the specified group to enrich the social, language, and literacy learning environment for this group. The call for multilevel collaboration is rooted in an earlier study I conducted that systematically explored a home-school-community–based conceptualization of low-income, inner-city Chinese American children with limited English proficiency (LEP) and school-identified LD (or LEP + LD) (Chang, 1993). As previously noted, these children's entire careers in school were filled with lost learning opportunities (Chang, 1995a).

The 1993 study showed that when Chinese American children were poor, had LEP, and were lagging behind other Chinese or Chinese American children, they were more likely to be referred for special education assessment and to be placed in a pull-out LD resource program in an elementary school. By the time they entered middle school, most of them were dismissed from special education placement to make room for other, more behaviorally disruptive students. The findings also suggested that the important social, language, and literacy support for these children most often occurred outside their home and in the community, such as in after-school homework supervision and reading opportunities sponsored by the public library, YMCA, church, or Chinese Benevolent Association (Chang, Fung, & Shimizu, 1996; Chang, Lai, & Shimizu, 1995). Multiple learning sites exist in many Asian American communities. The key players may tap such resources to help the families and learners in the specified groups (see Yaden et al., chapter 15, and Gallego et al., chapter 16 in this volume).

Because collaboration is largely a social act, to implement an effective multilevel collaboration among key players each school team might best be guided by the sociocultural theories of education (Tharp, 1997) and of development (Rogoff, 1995). These theories have their roots in Vygotsky's (1978, 1981) sociocultural theory of learning and cognitive development. All three theories suggest that the development of an individual is influenced by more capable others through engaging and participating in sociocultural activities within meaningful contexts. Moreover, generating meaningful contexts may be guided by a set of sociocultural principles (Dalton, 1998; Tharp, 1997). The implementation of such principles and standards and the formation of a multilevel collaborative team may also be closely examined using Rogoff's (1995) planes of analysis. Such an analysis will allow the team to detect problems more objectively from a broader context.

Sociocultural Principles and Standards

The importance of cultural and social influences and experiences for individuals' learning and development was reported in two major synthesis reports regarding the general principle of learning (Bransford, Brown, & Cocking, 1999; Donovan, Bransford, & Pellegrino, 1999). "Participation in social practice," write Bransford and colleagues, "is a fundamental form of learning. Learning involves becoming attuned to the constraints and resources, the limits and possibilities that are involved in the practices of the community" (p. xii).

The recognition of social and cultural factors in one's learning and development further supports the emerging sociocultural theory of education (Tharp, 1997). The gist of this theory can be presented as follows:

> The individual learner is viewed not as a "receptacle" into which knowledge is poured by teachers nor as an "acquirer" who seeks and seizes new knowledge through individual effort. Rather, the learner is an active participant in teaching and learning; the *learner and teacher are participants in sociocultural activity* (Rogoff, 1995).
>
> While we value and use the explanations offered by cognitive science as to the structures, processes, and mechanisms of thinking, education must be concentrated on cognitive development. Sociocultural theory explains the cognitive development of all individuals—of any age, culture, or level of sophistication—through the same basic principles. In fact, the applications of the theory in schools have been based on the natural socialization of children by their parents and caretakers. The key to development lies in participation in sociocultural activities, activities often seen as so mundane that their powerful role in development is not noticed. (Tharp, 1997, p. 11)

Such a theory has been the organizing conceptual structure for CREDE. There were 30 research projects conducted under six programmatic strands: language learning; professional development; family, peers, school, and community; instruction in context; integrated school reform; and assessment (Tharp, 1997). CREDE's mission is to address issues of risk, diversity, and excellence involving the education of linguistic and cultural minority students and students placed at risk by factors of race, poverty, and geographic location. The researchers will also bring such issues to the forefront of discussions concerning educational research, policy, and practice (Tharp, 1997). My recent studies conducted among the specified group were supported by CREDE and were a part of the research strand on professional development (Chang, 2001a, 2001b, 2002). Through synthesis, I was able to explain who was influential within and beyond the school environment to affect the academic success of learners in the specified group.

Vygotsky (1978, 1981) argued against the widespread use of IQ tests and unassisted instructional practices. He further proposed the concept of the Zone of Proximal Development (ZPD) (Moll, 1990; Vygotsky, 1978), which reflects the difference between what an individual can accomplish independently in the way of problem solving and what he or she can achieve in collaboration under adult assistance. Vygotsky's theory influenced many researchers and scholars in the United States (Bruner, 1986, 1987; Moll, 1990; Monzo & Rueda, 2000; Newman, Griffin, & Cole, 1989; Rogoff & Wertsch, 1984; Rueda & Garcia, in press; Tharp, Estrada, Dalton, & Yamauchi, 2000; Tharp & Gallimore, 1988), as well as many researchers conducting second language studies (Lantolf & Appel, 1994). Assisting each school in forming and delivering the multilevel collaboration within its ZPD may be guided by CREDE's Five Standards for Effective Pedagogy. By participating in a multilevel collaborative team, each key player will be empowered to solve a complex problem.

The CREDE Standards

A school-based multilevel collaborative team would benefit from the sociocultural theory of education and the practice of scaffolding within the learner's ZPD as guided by the set of five effective pedagogical standards proposed by CREDE (Dalton, 1998; Tharp et al., 2000). CREDE's standards were the result of in-depth reading of literature and extensive research, which sought consensus among researchers, teachers, parents, administrators, and policymakers (Tharp, 1999a). The five principles evolved into CREDE's Five Standards, meaning the ideals for best teaching practices for all learners—across all cultural, racial, and linguistic groups in the United States, all age levels, and all subject matters—for mainstream students and particularly for those at risk of school failure (see García & Beltrán, chapter 9 in this volume).

Briefly, CREDE's Standards for Effective Pedagogy and Learning (Dalton, 1998) are as follows:

- Standard 1: Joint Productive Activity (JPA). Within the classroom, it urges teachers to facilitate learning through teacher-student or student-student collaboration toward a common product or goal so as to motivate and sustain learning.

- Standard 2: Language Development (LLD). It urges teachers to facilitate students' ongoing development in the language of instruction across the curriculum. Language development is critical to help learners acquire the tools for learning.

- Standard 3: Contextualization (CTX). It urges teachers to help students establish a foundation for learning by connecting new learning to students' lives.

- Standard 4: Challenging Activities (CA). It urges teachers to promote students' higher order thinking skills through modeling and joint productive activities.

- Standard 5: Instructional Conversation (IC). It urges teachers to engage students in small-group instructional activities wherein teachers may incorporate daily events, content knowledge, and students' prior experiences.

The same set of five standards was systematically employed for professional development, in the studies supported by CREDE (e.g., Chang, 2002; Estrada, in press; Rueda, 1998; Rueda & Monzo, in press; Tharp, Hilberg, Epaloose, Feathers, & Bird, 1999), and for engaging partners beyond schools (e.g., Chang, 2001b; Tharp et al., 1999). An assessment rubric to monitor the enactment of CREDE's standards, Standards Performance Continuum (SPC) (Hilberg, Doherty, Tharp, & Epaloose, in press) is available from CREDE's website (http://www.crede.ucsc. edu). In addition, following CREDE's sociocultural principles, Azmitia and Cooper (2001) and Cooper and Gándara (2001) studied the brokers and gatekeepers across the worlds of family, peers, schools, and community among junior high, high school, and college students as they navigated the path to college and careers.

The multiple applications of CREDE pedagogical standards across classroom, professional development, and home practices contexts (see Figure 11.1) will provide a basis for schools to forge multilevel collaboration among key players. In essence, each school has its own ZPD. When a school establishes multilevel collaborations, guided by CREDE standards, it is more likely to expand the school's ZPD to its fullest extent in supporting all learners, particularly those in the specified group.

FIGURE 11.1 Multiple applications of CREDE's pedagogical standards across classroom, professional development, and home practices

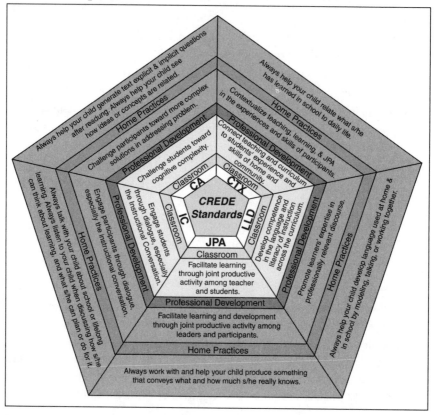

Planes of Analysis as a Research Tool

Planes of analysis (Rogoff, 1995), as a research tool, highlights the fact that whereas a phenomenon observed in any plane can be examined closely by foregrounding that particular plane, the phenomenon cannot be understood fully without reference to other planes in the background. Rogoff's planes of analysis helps address two research questions. First, what are the contexts that enhance the participating district and school's ability to institutionalize a research-based professional development and classroom intervention model with respect to the specified group? Second, what factors encourage or discourage willingness among key players to generate opportunities for multilevel collaboration with respect to the specified group?

The success or failure of multilevel collaborations among key players often is influenced by diverse factors within home, school, and community in the lives of specified learners. In examining what might affect the schooling of this group, the planes of analysis is an invaluable research tool. Rogoff's approach helps untangle the various factors that affect key players' ability to jointly support the specified group across the community, interpersonal, and personal planes. The development of true multilevel collaboration requires key players to participate fully in team planning and in implementing responsive intervention within and beyond the school. In the following sections, I provide brief descriptions of each plane and examples of how foregrounding each plane identifies issues relevant to the specified group.

THE COMMUNITY PLANE.   This plane signifies the school context, which embraces, at least, the shared rules, values, priorities, dominant teaching methods, and administrative priorities and practices in the school. The school is, of course, also subject to district and state mandates.

The current test-driven teaching practices and teacher and administrator shortages in many parts of the United States are two institutional factors rooted in wider cultural and economic realities. Statewide shortages of qualified teachers and administrators, particularly special education teachers and principals in many secondary schools, pose challenges to schools' day-to-day operations, classroom instruction, and teacher collaborations. Such shortages are particularly common in areas that have high enrollments of English learners from low-to-middle-SES family backgrounds. These schools may experience frequent changes in administrators and frequent shifting of administrative priorities—making it harder, for example, to sustain an effective sheltered program for English learners, as observed in my recent study (Chang, 2002), or to build collaborative teams that would effectively support all learners.

Over the past few years, states have increasingly used tests as a means to hold schools and districts accountable with respect to student performance. When a school becomes caught up in state-mandated testing and actively builds a testing culture, such action will, obviously, influence teachers' teaching practices. To raise test scores, these schools often emphasize drill-and-test approaches on bits and pieces of language and subject content. Such a teaching practice may not meet an objection in schools where students' families have vast financial and social resources to enrich their children's foundation for learning and development inside and outside of school. However, this heavy emphasis on the test-drill-test mode of teaching will further deprive the specified group of precious school-based language development opportunities, because many learners do not have optimal ELD opportunities beyond the classroom. Within such a school environment, teachers and school personnel are likely to define learning narrowly and to judge school achievement primarily by standardized test results, not by students' multiple abilities and learning potential. Such a testing culture has caused concerns on the part of educators and educational researchers (Paris, 1998; Popham, 2001).

THE INTERPERSONAL PLANE.   This plane embraces faculty support for ongoing collaboration, built-in scheduling for team preparation, an administrative structure that supports ongoing communication with parents and a home-school partnership, and a shared decision-making process about school-related issues. Collaborations occurring in this plane were observed in my recent studies (Chang, 2002) between teacher and teacher, teacher and instructional associates, teacher and administrators, teacher and family members, and teacher and community members. The community and personal planes (see below), of course, influence activities observed in this plane.

Observations made within the interpersonal plane underscore the importance of teacher collaboration. For example, numerous teachers in California hold emergency credentials but are not formally enrolled in an accredited credentialing program. Sustained district- or school-based professional development and multilevel collaboration are critical, not only for retaining these teachers but also for generating student achievement. If educational communities are serious about holding all teachers accountable for student learning, they must ensure that these developing teachers are teamed with effective teachers and are provided with built-in schedules for teamwork (see Coppola, chapter 8 in this volume).

THE PERSONAL PLANE.   This plane incorporates individuals' willingness and commitment to participate in, contribute to, change, and explore effective pedagogies for various groups of students. Individual commitment plays a critical role in initiating, implementing, and sustaining a multilevel collaboration. In each of my previous studies concerning the social, language, and literacy development of learners in the specified group, I was inspired by the personal commitment of an individual at school, at home, or in the community.

Furthermore, each key player's personal and professional development as it relates to the support of learners is inseparable from interpersonal and community factors. For example, as a school promotes its multilevel collaboration for the specified group, teachers' and administrators' personal commitments to such learners play a key role in reinforcing and sustaining a collaborative culture at the school site.

Rogoff's planes of analysis helped my research team analyze observational data in a coherent manner across three planes in a three-year participant observation study, conducted within a Title I middle school. (This study is discussed in greater detail later in the chapter.) These planes included school and district policies and support in the institutional or community plane; interactions between administrators and teachers as well as among collaborating teachers at the interpersonal plane; and individual teachers' commitment to the specified group at the personal plane. Together, the interactive effect among these factors across all three planes determined the educational reality of these learners in the specified group.

In a traditional home-school-community conceptualization, we assume that school is one coherent unit, with coherent goals and priorities. The data gathered from the planes-of-analysis model, however, indicate that there are conflicts within a school when it comes to delivering services to the specified group. Thus, the practices or actions of the teachers and administrators may need to be examined separately in order to see *how* an effective school intervention would or would not be delivered. My current view regarding the key players who influence learning in the specified group is grounded in what I consider a more realistic conception of the within-and-beyond-school partnership, rather than in a home-school-community partnership.

Multilevel Collaboration Within and Beyond School: A New Partnership

Schools' key players are teachers and administrators; their beliefs, commitment, and actions largely determine whether or not students have access to the district core curriculum and benefit from the implementation of standards. Key players outside of schools can be any family member, community agency, or network that serves as an advocate for these specified learners. Because many parents and guardians of the specified group, owing to language and acculturation issues, may not understand the U.S. school system and feel unprepared to intercede effectively, siblings or members of the extended family are also potential key players for the specified group beyond school. When my research team sponsored family literacy nights for the specified group, it was apparent that those who accompanied the participating students to these evening events ranged from parents to family friends (Chang, 2002).

Within-School Support From Teachers and Administrators

In recent studies, I further examined teachers' and administrators' impact on the specified learners' school performance because school administrators may trivialize the support that is critical to the specified group. From the perspective of a community plane, school administrators do not teach students directly. However, administrators' policies, mandates, and administrative priorities have a significant impact on the education of the specified group. The examples presented here are based on observations from the personal and interpersonal planes in my recent studies as well as ongoing fieldwork; these observations highlight the interrelationship between teacher and administrator support and the education of the specified group.

The first example comes from a study conducted with a Title I middle school (Chang, 2002). My research team observed and documented four teachers' commitment to multilevel collaboration to support the specified group. The observations were made in both the personal and interpersonal planes over the course of three years. On the personal level, the teachers were dedicated to, and capable of, providing a collaborative sheltered instruction program for incoming sixth-grade learners who matched the characteristics of the specified group. After observing a large number of the specified students fail in school, these teachers committed their summer hours to plan and initiate a sheltered instruction program for the incoming sixth graders, who traditionally were not included in the school's language and academic intervention programs. In this case, more than 60 students were identified in each of the two years that the program was supported by school administrators (the 1998–1999 school years). Almost all these students were members of the specified group.

In the interpersonal plane, these teachers met in and out of school regularly, often on their own time, to plan and implement a responsive program that integrated language arts and history, using themes selected from sixth-grade ancient history units. For example, in the unit on early men, students read and studied the trade book *Maroo of the Winter Caves* (Turnbull, 1984). One other important feature of the sheltered program was that not only was language arts integrated with history, but all core subject teachers also worked closely in math and science to form a truly collaborative team. Together, they provided a responsive instructional environment for English learners.

The participating teachers' commitments could not be sustained when administrators departed, and new administrators shifted the school's priorities. By the end of our two-year intervention study, my researcher team and I had observed a parade of three new school principals after the original principal left. Each new principal participated in planning or presenting the four project-sponsored family literacy nights (Chang, 2001b). The short tenure of each subsequent substitute principal at this middle school inadvertently led to several shifts in administrative priorities.

As we followed the Year I and Year II sixth-grade students to the seventh and eighth grades, none received any specified language intervention. In the meantime, the sheltered program for incoming sixth graders was dismantled by the new administrative team, although this program yielded consistent and positive gains, as observed in students' day-to-day performances as well as in students' statewide test scores over two consequent years. The joy and commitment of the participating teachers who were eager to continue the program, if administrative support was available, persisted over the term of the study; but the change in district and school administrative teams and their priorities terminated an effective program for the specified group. The dismantling was done without any consultation with the participating teachers or with the parents of the students within the specified group.

A second example, drawn from my ongoing fieldwork within schools serving Asian American students from low-to-upper-middle-SES homes, further illustrates the mutually inclusive roles of two key players within a school. Observations made across community, interpersonal, and personal planes suggest that many affluent schools openly promote Cantonese and/or Mandarin as foreign languages and teach them via a Chinese-English immersion program. The situation differs, however, in inner-city and urban schools serving children from low-income communities. Bilingual teachers from these schools report that when statewide testing was mandated in the late 1990s, they were not allowed by school administrators to speak in the primary languages of many children, even to help them to make sense of classroom instruction or to clarify concepts or directions. In a district that ostensibly supports bilingualism, their principals, hoping to improve students' statewide test scores, prohibited bilingual teachers from using a child's first language.

The administrators' justification for their stance was to get these children ready to take the statewide tests by second grade. In these cases, the school administrators and teachers not only inadvertently signaled to these young children that their home language was invalid for school learning, but they also stunted the normal progress that could have been made if these children used the language they brought to the instructional setting. Such an example shows that a top-down pressure to raise school's test scores is in many cases the end goal of formal schooling.

Such pressure forces teachers to abandon children's primary language and drill young children in early schooling solely on "state testing language." It is common to see that, even though many schools have adopted so-called research-based English reading programs, the administrative urgency to raise test scores quickly, along with the shortage of experienced teachers, means that drills on test-taking skills and reading test-like passages inadvertently fill many classrooms' instructional agendas and daily teaching time. Any effective pedagogies that promote teaching for understanding and demand multiple learning strategies and time to process are perceived in such schools as taking time away from efforts to meet state and district demands for high test scores. Essentially, fragmented test items presented in statewide tests define English language learning for these children with low SES.

An enriched learning environment is critical for diverse learners from nonmainstreamed and low-income communities. These children face a double jeopardy: They are challenged by poverty and/or LEP, and they are more likely to be taught by inexperienced teachers or a series of short- or long-term substitute teachers in their school. If we follow the top-down mandate to focus on test scores in order to help schools get more funding or be accountable to policymakers, then we knowingly fail a generation of children who learn test-taking skills but not the literacy skills necessary to function in a complex society.

In sum, securing both teachers' and administrators' coherent support within any school is critical if the specified group is to succeed in meaningful schooling. When teachers and administrators serve as advocates for learners and for future society, rather than for test scores, they are less likely to repeat the mistakes of the competency-based education of the 1970s, when test scores were raised, but functional literacy abilities declined.

Family and Community Support Beyond School

The persons who may serve as key players to support the specified group outside of a school vary among individual families and students. As previously noted, levels of acculturation, formal education, and English proficiency all contribute greatly to such a person's abilities and availability to monitor and support the specified group's school performance. I propose that the key player(s) outside of school from either family or community might be any person(s) who would fulfill the role of a parent in a middle-class family in supporting a learner from the specified group. To further illustrate this assumption, I present two examples in this section. Observational data were obtained from both my recent study (Chang, 2002) and previous studies (Chang, 1995b; Chang et al., 1996), guided by the planes of analysis.

In the first example, my research team observed that many parents with LEP were eager to help but unable to assist their child with completing homework beyond arithmetic computations (Chang, 1995b, 2002; Chang et al., 1995; Chang et al., 1996). Whether we worked with urban parents of elementary school children or suburban parents of middle school teens, the most common question raised by participating parents was "How can we help our child at home?" When these parents were not proficient in the school's instructional language, they sought support from people at community-based learning sites, such as various homework centers, or from friends. To the advantage of many such children, there were several community-based homework or learning centers available to sharpen these children's academic and language skills.

In addition, the shared culture of supporting children's schooling led many urban parents to make personal sacrifices and endure personal hardships, such as by working at two jobs in order to strive for the best possible education for their children. It was not unusual for these parents to arrange for their children to receive paid tutorial services to maintain school performance (Chang et al., 1996). Some even arranged for their children to take piano or violin lessons to help develop musical talent.

The integration of family and community as one strong support system is most important for the specified group of learners with special needs, particularly because many recent immigrants may not be familiar with the U.S. school system. For example, when a child is identified as "learning disabled," these parents may not understand that educational label because it may not exist in their home country. They rely on friends or community agents to guide them through the complex identification and special education placement process (Chang, 1995b, 1995c; Chang et al., 1995).

My colleagues and I consistently observed the same support system linking home and community for the specified group in the span from early 1990 to 2000, as well as across inner-city to suburban schools. Regardless of setting—whether in structured survey studies or in project-sponsored workshops for parents (Chang, 1995d) or family literacy nights (Chang, 2001b, 2002)—most of the participants reported that they must rely on their family or extended family, on friends, or on community agencies to fulfill their responsibility to support their child's schooling.

The second example I present illustrates the critical need for integrated home-and-community support for learners with special needs within the specified group, because of misconceptions about special education among some Asian American and Asian communities. The stigma associated with individuals with special needs touches the lives of every family member, particularly in Asian American and Asian communities. Misunderstandings and misconceptions about disabilities inherited in the community and the culture may alienate and hurt parents and family members who care for a member with such disabilities if support is not available from the community (Chang, 1995c). Hence, an integrated home-and-community support system plays a central role in generating much-needed support for everyone affected by such disabilities or special needs.

Beyond school, integration to support these families and individuals with special needs is well illustrated by Friends of Children with Special Needs (2002), a support group established by Chinese American families and communities in the Silicon Valley in Northern California. The most distinguishing feature of this support system is a purposeful integration among families and friends who have children, with or without special needs. Only through such genuine integration within an inclusive environment of families without special needs can families with special needs take full advantage of school and community resources and receive the support necessary to plan and care for their loved ones. Such integrated support also can ease tensions among the caretakers, who might otherwise be burdened by culturally inherited shame or discomfort over having a child with disabilities.

Challenges and Opportunities for Multilevel Collaborations

Owing to the existing and increasing diversity among the specified group, it would be difficult for any one teacher, administrator, or family or community member to generate responsive social, language, and literacy support for these learners. Multilevel collaboration, then, among key players from both within and beyond school promises to enhance education for the specified group greatly. The following sections present three areas that directly affect learners' academic performance.

Integrating Multiple Learning Sites and Diverse Prior Experiences

The specified group comes from diverse homes and communities; hence, these learners bring to the classroom an array of cultural resources beyond traditional school culture. To transform such diverse cultural resources into a valuable foundation, or funds of knowledge (Gonzalez et al., 1993), for their school learning, however, depends on multilevel collaboration among key players. When teachers and administrators are open and willing to collaborate with members of the specified group's home or community, classroom instruction can be better contextualized. For example, when abstract concepts are introduced, the metaphors, analogies, or multiple examples tapped as approaches for teaching for understanding (Gardner, 1999) more likely would be tied to these learners' real-life experiences.

As Figure 11.2 illustrates, there are multiple sites for such literacy learning activities within and beyond schools. An earlier descriptive study across school, home, and community in urban and inner-city communities identified multiple literacy-learning sites available to these children (Chang, 1993; Chang et al., 1996). The existence of such sites was consistent among both West and East Coast communities and suggests that multiple learning sites are common across many ethnic communities, constituting a valuable resource to support the specified group's school learning (see Yaden et al., chapter 15, and Gallego et al., chapter 16, in this volume).

FIGURE 11.2 Multilevel collaboration across multiple learning sites

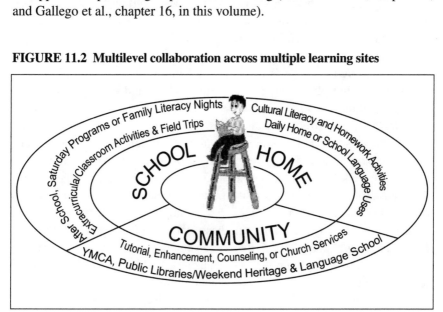

"Multiple sites of learning," as defined in a previous study (Chang et al., 1996), includes any site that engages learners in expanding their social and learning experiences through activities involving completing homework, borrowing books, reading newspapers and magazines, listening to stories, participating in field trips, discussing experiences and events, or acquiring a broad range of general information as a foundation for school learning—in addition to acquiring or learning English or learning their native language. The teams involved in multilevel collaboration to support the specified group may employ learning across multiple sites beyond the classroom.

Furthermore, inspired by First Lady Laura Bush (2001), pediatricians at the Boston City Hospital have successfully launched an early literacy program, Reach Out and Read (ROR), to provide community support to the families and parents of young children. This program is designed to further expand the multiple learning sites available for families, particularly those in the specified group. Tapping into the parents' trust in their child's physician, the doctors, nurses, and volunteers involved in ROR will, it is hoped, substantially enhance an awareness of the need for early reading and provide much-needed modeling to participating parents or guardians regarding effective ways to read to their child regularly. Community-based ROR is most critical for those families who are confined within poor and nonmainstreamed communities.

As children grow older, it is important for parents, guardians, and teachers to fully tap into children's prior experiences and their knowledge of the world in order to enhance their reading and literacy development. I am deeply impressed and influenced by Freire and Macedo's insight that "reading the world always precedes reading the word, and reading the word implies continually reading the world" (1987, p. 35). Linking these children's experiences across multiple learning sites within and beyond school, therefore, is likely to help the specified group comprehend reading passages, and it is best provided through instructional dialogues, modeling, and hands-on activities.

With the support of a multilevel collaborative team, teachers also are empowered to (a) actively bring in students' knowledge of their world in order to decrease the knowledge gaps of these unique learners as they struggle to understand what they read; (b) alter the trend, in some schools, to promote only the fragmented drill-and-test approach to raising test scores; and (c) become informed about the rich resources in these learners' homes and communities. Most learners within the specified group do not have homes or communities to provide them with opportunities for acquiring a body of general information relating to the dominant culture, and such a foundation is critical to absorbing the content knowledge offered in the core curriculum.

In my previous reading comprehension study involving teacher-parent collaboration at six inner-city and urban elementary schools (Chang, 1995d), the participating LD resource specialists were surprised by the urban students' limited knowledge of general information. Because these LD resource specialists were not familiar with these learners' backgrounds, the dialogues that were intended to help students clarify concepts and make sense from print often were disrupted or ineffectual.

Without the assumed prior knowledge, it was also challenging for urban learners to interact with one another and to carry out meaningful and extended instructional dialogues with one another in a cooperative learning group setting. The same phenomenon—having a limited world knowledge in the context of a dominant school culture and instructional language—also was observed in my study among the sixth-grade English learners enrolled in a Title I middle school (Chang, 2002). Ideally, a multilevel collaborative team will help both teachers and students bridge the worlds within and beyond the classroom. Essentially, multiple learning sites provide a pool of diverse Asian language and cultural informants who can help the specified group succeed in school.

Sustained Professional Development for Responsive Reading and Literacy Instruction

Reading instruction is a highly controversial issue, particularly when reading instruction is under pressure from sociopolitical forces and profit-making business agendas. In reality, children who are poor—English learners or not—have limited opportunities for learning to read, or developing literacy, so long as they are placed in a classroom taught by unqualified and inexperienced teachers. When the state or district shifts the focus on reading instruction, the amount of ongoing support and school- or district-based professional development must be made available to all inexperienced teachers.

Rueda and McIntyre (2002) differentiate further between reading and literacy. They note that balanced reading is not a comparison of whole language versus phonics, but of reading versus literacy. They shared two definitions of reading: reading is (1) individual psychological processes involved in decoding and comprehending text; or (2) as viewed by Snow, Burns, and Griffin (1998), reading is "the use of the products and principles of the writing system to get at the meaning of a written text" (p. 42). Literacy, on the other hand, includes reading as a necessary component, but also focuses more broadly not only on the act of reading but on the beliefs, attitudes, and social practices that literate individuals and social groups engage within a variety of settings and situations, including those involving technology (Pearson & Raphael, 1999).

The complexity of literacy is further enhanced when we address the multiple literacies brought in by diverse groups of learners (Gallego & Hollingsworth, 2000). Hence, when the public debates forge ahead on the do's and don'ts of reading and literacy instruction, ongoing professional development activities must help teachers and school administrators keep such debates in perspective. Educators must not narrowly define literacy as an act of reading taught either by phonics-based or literature-based instructional activities.

The need for sustained professional development can be supported even when we take a narrow view of reading instruction. For example, when the field of reading instruction embraced whole language and literature-oriented reading instruction, many inner-city and urban children performed poorly. Literature-based reading is culture specified, so unless we make a concerted effort to link literature to another cultural group's world experiences, we cannot expect children from diverse SES and cultural backgrounds to derive the full benefits of such instruction. To make the matter worse, fewer teachers learned or developed proficiency in responsive pedagogy suitable for young children from diverse cultural backgrounds. In other words, these children read literature that was far removed from their world experiences and typically, were taught by someone poorly prepared to deliver such important lessons.

In the late 1980s and early 1990s, when whole language instruction was prevalent in many schools, many experienced teachers continued to provide phonics lessons, even without their administrators' knowledge. They knew that they had always provided more balanced reading lessons by teaching students the code of English language as well as exposing students to a variety of children's books. Now that the pendulum has swung back to teaching phonics, given the current emphasis on statewide testing and ranking practices, many teachers are drilling students in phonics and returning to an outdated approach for the sake of raising test scores. Nowadays, it is common for teachers to claim that they have no time to emphasize reading for pleasure or reading for comprehension, particularly around the time when statewide testing is administered.

We might expect that many experienced teachers would employ a phonics approach but also enhance children's reading and literacy ability by exposing them to authentic text and children's literature. But what about the inexperienced teachers? If multilevel collaboration were the norm in all schools, then those inexperienced teachers would receive support and proper training in order to deliver responsive reading interventions in a manner that was theoretically sound and culturally responsive.

If professional development activities are offered in a top-down manner or in a one-shot training format, they will not yield positive and lasting effects insofar as classroom implementation is concerned (Joyce & Showers, 1983; Sprinthall, Reiman, & Thies-Sprinthall, 1996; Tharp et al., 2000; Tharp & Gallimore, 1988). It is rather common to observe such fragmented development activities for teachers, however, when a district adopts new reading programs. Although individual coaching and follow-up consultations that enable classroom teachers to provide responsive literacy instruction are costly, it is important that they be made available to teachers, particularly in high-poverty areas.

ELD and Special Education: Enrichment, Not Remediation

English language development is critical for the specified group. Given their characteristics, however, members of the specified group, particularly those identified as having LD, have limited opportunities to acquire English academic language proficiency and may depend largely on support from teachers and administrators (Chang, 1995a, 1995b, 2001a). Metaphorically speaking, both special education and ELD programs are poor stepchildren in the school system. They each have a separate parent for funding—with separate policies, restrictions, conflicts, and challenges. An English language learner, once placed within a special education program, generally is treated as an English speaker and receives little or no language support from the ELD program. At this point, collaboration between the special education teacher and the ELD teacher, supported by the multilevel collaborative team, is the most obvious and viable solution.

Currently, many special education teachers, as well as those with emergency special education credentials, subscribe to a deficit-oriented remediation emphasis. Many of them also are ill-equipped to promote and enhance the specified group's ELD language development. On the other hand, not all ELD teachers are fully prepared to address their students' special needs. Hence, once learners from the specified group are placed in special education, they are unlikely to receive a meaningful education without multilevel collaboration.

In current schools that face statewide testing and ranking demands, some learners in the specified group without any genuine LD have been referred mistakenly and placed in special education programs, seemingly to help raise a class or school's test scores. A multilevel collaborative team could help minimize any misidentification and misplacement of specified learners in special education programs by generating and pooling much-needed language expertise related to the specified group in the special education assessment process. This is one important step toward preventing a cycle of defeat among the specified group when these students are pulled out of their inclusive classroom environment.

Such teams also could play important roles in this area by, among other activities,

- exploring and implementing research-based intervention strategies for English learners with learning difficulties to enable their developing academic language, and accessing general curriculum (e.g., Gersten, Baker, & Marks, 1998; Morrison, 2001). Such a joint productive activity could be an important scaffold for a responsive collaboration between ELD and special education.

- providing ongoing and meaningful professional development to explore the possibilities of a true balanced reading and literacy instruction program (e.g., Rueda & McIntyre, in press)—one way to avoid producing word-callers who lack reading comprehension. Schools in high-poverty areas must have enriched early reading programs instead of just teaching children to "crack the code." These children need to be read to regularly, mimicking middle-class children's bedtime story reading.

- generating social capital for the specified group in order to develop the multiple literacies necessary for functioning successfully outside of school. Learners in the specified group are taught primarily by commercially prepared and drill-based basic reading programs on phonemic awareness, phonics, and decoding, with test-like short reading passages constituting their entire reading and literacy instruction in school. These learners do not have the same family support as their English-speaking peers from middle- and upper-middle-class environments. That support allows them to develop multiple literacies, including Internet literacy.

- providing relevant funds of knowledge that would be unique to the specified group and that are not readily observable by teachers in classrooms or available within teachers' own cultural experiences. This is one way for teachers to incorporate students' prior knowledge effectively through small-group instructional activities to help students gain more from reading and literacy activities. It also is critical for teachers to acknowledge that students' home language and culture are invaluable in school learning and in developing students' positive self-identity (see George et al., chapter 13; Boyd-Batstone, chapter 14; and Yaden et al., chapter 15, in this volume).

- generating substantial support for teachers and students, either in an inclusive or a special education classroom, by either (a) designing readily deliverable supplemental materials, such as audiotapes or videotapes, to allow teachers to provide individualized instructional packets or learning modules that learners in the specified group would learn at their own pace or repeat as needed, or (b) providing responsive instructional assistants, who would free the teacher to work regularly with the specified group.

- including and monitoring ELD goals in a learner's individualized education program (IEP) so as to fully realize the rights granted by the public law, Individuals with Disabilities Education Act (IDEA) Amendment 1997. This is one effective way to directly address the needs of these learners to be provided with enriched English language resources and support, beyond what a special education teacher could offer.

Conclusions

If we are serious about providing responsive and enriched language intervention for the specified group, collaboration with built-in support, time, and substance must be the norm. A multilevel collaborative team would empower administrators to actively foster a seamless collaboration between their ELD and special education programs; hence, the school would be able to establish the much-needed baseline and student-teacher performance record to adjust and validate such collaborations in the context of demands for accountability and the call to "leave no child behind."

Author Note

The current work was supported by the Education Research and Development Program, PR/Award No. R306A60001, the Center for Research on Education, Diversity & Excellence (CREDE), as administered by the Office of Educational Research and Improvement (OERI), National Institute on the Education of At-Risk Students (NIEARS), U.S. Department of Education (US-DOE). However, the author is responsible for the contents and discussion. I also extend thanks to Ward Shimizu, Research Associate, for ongoing discussion and the shaping of the chapter as well as to Dr. Robert Rueda and my San Jose State University colleagues Drs. June McCullough and Robert Cullan for extensive feedback.

REFERENCES

Azmitia, M., & Cooper, C.R. (2001). Good or bad? Peer influences on Latino and European American adolescents' pathways through school. *Journal for the Education of Students Placed at Risk, 6,* 45–71.

Bransford, J.D., Brown, A.L., & Cocking, R.R. (1999). *How people learn: Brain, mind, experience, and school.* Washington, DC: National Academy Press.

Bruner, J. (1986). *Actual minds, possible worlds.* Cambridge, MA: Harvard University Press.

Bruner, J. (1987). Prologue to the English edition. In L.S. Vygotsky, *Collected works* (Vol. 1., pp. 1–16). (R. Rieber & A. Carton, Eds.; N. Minick, Trans.). New York: Plenum.

Bush, L.W. (2001). *Ready to read, ready to learn: First Lady Laura Bush's education initiatives* [Online]. Available: http://www.ed.gov/inits/rrrl

Chang, J.M. (1993). A school-home-community-based conceptualization of LEP students with learning disabilities: Implications from a Chinese-American study. In J. Gomez & O. Shabak (Eds.), *The proceedings of the Third National Research Symposium on Limited English Proficient Students' Issues: Focus on middle and high school issues* (Vol. 2, pp. 713–736). Washington, DC: U.S. Department of Education, Office of Bilingual Education and Language Minority Affairs.

Chang, J.M. (1995a). When they are not all Asian model minority students... *Focus on Diversity, 5*(3), 5–7.

Chang, J.M. (1995b). LEP, LD, poor, and the missed learning opportunities: A case of inner city Chinese-American children. In L.L. Cheng (Ed.), *Integrating language and learning: An Asian-Pacific focus* (pp. 31–59). San Diego: Singular.

Chang, J.M. (1995c). Asian LEP children in special education: A need for multidimensional collaboration. In S. Walker, K.A. Turner, M. Haile-Michael, A. Vincent, & M.D. Miles (Eds.), *Disability and diversity: New leadership for a new era* (pp. 81–88). Washington, DC: The President's Committee on Employment of People With Disabilities in collaboration with the Howard University Research and Training Center.

Chang, J.M. (1995d). *Advancing and improving the knowledge base on content/scaffold reading comprehension strategies with parental involvement: An Asian LEP+LD student perspective* (Final Report). Washington, DC: U.S. Department of Education, Office of Special Education Programs.

Chang, J.M. (2001a, January/February). Monitoring effective teaching and creating a responsive learning environment for students in need of support: A checklist. *NABE News, 24*(3), 17–20.

Chang, J.M. (2001b). *Scaffold for school-home collaboration: Enhancing reading and language development* (Research Brief No. 9). Santa Cruz, CA: Center for Research on Education, Diversity & Excellence.

Chang, J.M. (2002). *Expanding knowledge base on teacher learning and collaboration: A focus on Asian Pacific American English learners* (Final Report). Santa Cruz, CA: Center for Research on Education, Diversity & Excellence.

Chang, J.M., Fung, G., & Shimizu, W. (1996, June). Literacy support across multiple sites: Experiences of Chinese-American LEP children in inner-cities. *NABE News, 19*(7), 11–13.

Chang, J.M., Lai, A., & Shimizu, W. (1995). LEP parents as resources: Generating opportunity-to-learn beyond schools through parental involvement. In L.L. Cheng (Ed.), *Integrating language and learning: An Asian-Pacific focus* (pp. 265–290). San Diego: Singular.

Cooper, C.R., & Gándara, P. (2001). When diversity works: Bridging families, peers, schools, and communities at CREDE. *Journal for the Education of Students Placed at Risk, 6*(1 & 2), 1–5.

Dalton, S.S. (1998). *Pedagogy matters: Standards for effective teaching practice* (Research Rep. No. 4). Santa Cruz, CA: Center for Research on Education, Diversity & Excellence.

Donovan, M.S., Bransford, J.D., & Pellegrino, J.W. (1999). *How people learn: Bridging research and practice*. Washington, DC: National Academy Press.

Estrada, P. (in press). Patterns of language arts instruction activity and excellence in first and fourth grade culturally and linguistically diverse classrooms. In H. Waxman, R.G. Tharp, & R.S. Hilberg (Eds.), *Observational research in culturally and linguistically diverse classrooms*. Cambridge, UK: Cambridge University Press.

Freire, P., & Macedo, D. (1987). *Literacy: Reading the word and the world*. Westport, CT: Bergin & Garvey.

Friends of Children with Special Needs. (2002). *About our organization* [Online]. Available: http://www.fcsn1997.org

Gallego, M.A., & Hollingsworth, S. (2000). *What counts as literacy: Challenging the school standards*. New York: Teachers College Press.

Gardner, H. (1999). *The disciplined mind: What all students should understand*. New York: Simon & Schuster.

Gersten, R., Baker, S.K., & Marks, S.U. (1998). *Teaching English-language learners with learning difficulties*. Washington, DC: ERIC Clearinghouse on Disabilities and Gifted Education.

Gonzalez, N., Moll, L.C., Floyd-Tenery, M., Rivera, A., Rendon, P., Gonzales, R., et al. (1993). *Teacher research on funds of knowledge: Learning from households* (Educational Practice Rep. No. 6). Santa Cruz, CA: National Center for Research on Cultural Diversity and Second Language Learning.

Hilberg, R.S., Doherty, R.W., Tharp, R.G., & Epaloose, G. (in press). Development and reliability of the Standard Performance Continuum. In H. Waxman, R.G. Tharp, & R.S. Hilberg (Eds.), *Observational research in U.S. classrooms: New approaches for understanding cultural and linguistic diversity*. Cambridge, UK: Cambridge University Press.

Joyce, B.R., & Showers, B. (1983). *Power in staff development through research on training*. Alexandria, VA: Association for Supervision and Curriculum Development.

Lantolf, J.P., & Appel, G. (Eds.). (1994). *Vygotskian approaches to second language research*. Norwood, NJ: Ablex.

Moll, L.C. (1990). *Vygotsky and education: Instructional implications and applications of sociohistorical psychology*. New York: Cambridge University Press.

Monzo, L., & Rueda, R. (2000). *Constructing achievement orientations toward literacy: An analysis of sociocultural activity in Latino home and community contexts* (49th yearbook of the National Reading Conference, pp. 405–420). Chicago: National Reading Conference.

Morrison, S. (2001). *English language learners with special needs*. Washington, DC: ERIC Clearinghouse on Language and Linguistics. Available: http://www.cal.org/ericcll/faqs/RGOs/special.html#journals

Newman, D., Griffin, P., & Cole, M. (1989). *The construction zone: Working for cognitive change in school*. New York: Cambridge University Press.

Paris, S.G. (1998). Why learner-centered assessment is better than high-stakes testing. In N.M. Lambert & B.L. McCombs (Eds.), *How students learn: Reforming schools through learner-centered education* (pp. 189–210). Washington, DC: American Psychological Association.

Pearson, P.D., & Raphael, T.E. (1999). Toward a more complex view of balance in the literacy curriculum. In W.D. Hammond & T.E. Raphael (Eds.), *Early literacy instruction for the new millennium* (pp. 1–21). Grand Rapids, MI: Michigan Reading Association.

Popham, W.J. (2001). *The truth about testing: An educator's call to action*. Alexandria, VA: Association for Supervision and Curriculum Development.

Rogoff, B. (1995). Observing sociocultural activity on three planes: Participatory appropriation, guided participation, and apprenticeship. In J.V. Wertsch, P. del Rio, & A. Alvarez (Eds.), *Sociocultural studies of mind* (pp. 139–164). Cambridge, UK: Cambridge University Press.

Rogoff, B., & Wertsch, J.V. (Eds.). (1984). *Children's learning in the "zone of proximal development."* San Francisco: Jossey-Bass.

Rosenblatt, R.A., & Helfand, D. (2001, March 23). A new boom in U.S. student population, census finds: Count enrollment of 49 million equals 1970 record. But immigration is a concern, especially in California. *Los Angeles Times*, p. A34.

Rueda, R. (1998). *Standards for professional development: A sociocultural perspective* (Research Brief No. 2). Santa Cruz, CA: Center for Research on Education, Diversity & Excellence.

Rueda, R., & Garcia, E. (in press). Assessing and assisting performance of diverse learners: A view of responsive teaching in action. In A.I. Willis, G. Garcia, V. Harris, & R. Barrera (Eds.), *Multicultural issues in literacy research and practice*. Hillsdale, NJ: Erlbaum.

Rueda, R., & McIntyre, E. (2002). Toward universal literacy. In S. Stringfield & D. Land (Eds.), *Educating at risk students* (pp. 189–209). Chicago: University of Chicago Press.

Rueda, R., & Monzo, L. (in press). Apprenticeship for teaching: Professional development issues surrounding the collaborative relationship between teachers and paraeducators. *Teaching & Teacher Education*.

Snow, C.E., Burns, M.S., & Griffin, P. (Eds.). (1998). *Preventing reading difficulties in young children*. Washington, DC: National Academy Press.

Sprinthall, N.A., Reiman, A.J., & Thies-Sprinthall, L. (1996). Teacher professional development. In J. Sikula (Ed.), *Handbook of research on teacher education* (2nd ed., pp. 666–703). New York: Macmillan.

Tharp, R.G. (1997). *From at-risk to excellence: Research, theory, and principles for practice* (Research Rep. No. 1). Santa Cruz, CA: Center for Research on Education, Diversity & Excellence.

Tharp, R.G. (1999a). *Effective teaching: How the standards came to be* (Effective Teaching Document Series No. 1). Santa Cruz, CA: Center for Research on Education, Diversity & Excellence. Available: http://www.crede.ucsc.edu/tools/research/standards/development.shtml

Tharp, R.G. (1999b). *Proofs and evidence: Effectiveness of the Five Standards for Effective Pedagogy* (Effective Teaching Document Series No. 2). Santa Cruz, CA: Center for Research on Education, Diversity & Excellence. Available: http://crede.ucsc.edu/tools/research/standards/effectiveness.shtml

Tharp, R.G., Estrada, P., Dalton, S.S., & Yamauchi, L.A. (2000). *Teaching transformed: Achieving excellence, fairness, inclusion, and harmony*. Boulder, CO: Westview Press.

Tharp, R.G., & Gallimore, R. (1988). *Rousing minds to life: Teaching, learning, and schooling in social context*. New York: Cambridge University Press.

Tharp, R.G., Hilberg, R.S., Epaloose, G., Feathers, M., & Bird, C. (1999). *School/community co-constructed school reform: Upscaling from research to practice in a Native American community*. Available: http://crede.ucsc.edu/research/sfc/intro5_6.shtml

Vygotsky, L.S. (1978). *Mind in society: The development of higher psychological processes* (M. Cole, V. John-Steiner, S. Scribner, & E. Souberman, Eds. and Trans.). Cambridge, MA: Harvard University Press. (Original work published 1934)

Vygotsky, L.S. (1981). The genesis of higher mental functions. In J.V. Wertsch (Ed.), *The concept of activity in Soviet psychology* (pp. 144–188). White Plains, NY: Sharpe.

CHILDREN'S LITERATURE CITED

Turnbull, A. (1984). *Maroo of the winter caves*. New York: Clarion.

CHAPTER 12

Standards-Based Instruction for English Language Learners

Joseph Laturnau

This chapter will examine the potential benefits of standards-based instruction for English Language Learners (ELLs), present a backward mapping process for designing standards-based instructional units, and review the design of two standards-based units for ELLs.

Standards-Based Instruction and ELLs

Standards-based instruction (SBI) is at the forefront of education reform because it presents a way to ensure that all students are exposed to challenging curricula and prepared to contribute positively to an increasingly complex world. SBI is characterized by *content standards*, which define what students should know and be able to do; *benchmarks*, which identify the expected understandings and skills for a content standard at different grade levels; and *performance standards* (or *indicators*), which describe how well students need to achieve in order to meet content standards.

By focusing on detailed descriptions of expected understandings—learning targets—SBI engages teachers in raising the expectations for all students, promotes the use of multiple assessment strategies that allow for students to reach proficient levels at different times and in a variety of ways, and requires teachers to differentiate instruction to meet the readiness levels, learning profiles, and interests of students.

ELLs need to be included in standards-based educational reform. According to Hakuta (2001), clear academic standards must be in place to confirm that ELLs should be held to the same expectations as mainstream students. Hakuta cautions, however,

> It is unreasonable to expect ELLs to perform comparably to their native English-speaking peers in their initial years of schooling (hence the need for standards specific to ELLs) and holding them to this expectation too early in their educational careers can be detrimental to their academic progress, not to mention their self-esteem. The problem enters when students are not pushed to go beyond this stage over time, are presumed to be at an elementary level, or are misdiagnosed as having educational disabilities by teachers unfamiliar with the needs of ELLs. (p. 3)

The gap between learning expectations as described in standards, particularly language arts standards, and the performance of ELLs as tempered by their initial and temporary limited English proficiency is in some cases widened by limited formal schooling. Two prominent efforts to bridge this gap have been undertaken by the California Department of Education (CDE) and the Teachers of English to Speakers of Other Languages (TESOL), a professional organization. CDE (1999) has produced English Language Development (ELD) Standards to assist teachers in moving ELLs to English fluency and to proficiency on the California English-Language Arts Content Standards. CDE has delineated five incremental levels of language proficiency—beginning, early-intermediate, intermediate, early-advanced, and advanced—and identified the linguistic competencies ELLs must develop to "catch up" with their monolingual English-speaking peers.

TESOL's English as a Second Language (ESL) Standards revolve around three goals for ELLs: (1) to use English to communicate in social settings, (2) to use English to achieve academically in all content areas, and (3) to use English in socially and culturally appropriate ways. Agor (2000), Irujo (2000), Samway (2000), and Smallwood (2000) provide sample pre-K–12 units that describe how teachers use standards as planning tools, observational aids, assessment guides, and ways of understanding language development. Snow (2000) discusses ways to help prospective and practicing teachers implement the ESL standards.

What promise does a shift to SBI hold for ELLs? Figure 12.1 highlights key SBI teacher practices (adapted from Latchat, 1998) and their implications for ELLs.

In summary, these practices point to significant changes in classroom practices and learning environments that have great potential for improving the educational outcomes of ELLs. Given the challenges they face in learning an

FIGURE 12.1 Key SBI teacher practices and their implications

In standards-based instruction, teachers...	The potential benefits for ELLs are that this shift...
Organize learning around what students need to know and need to be able to do to reach high levels of performance.	Has the potential to reverse the tendency to assign ELLs to unchallenging curricula and presents an opportunity for schools to engage in substantive communication with the parents of ELLs regarding achievement.
Broaden the focus of their teaching to include higher order thinking processes.	Sets high learning expectations for ELLs, who have traditionally been provided with instruction focusing on low-level skills.
Guide student inquiry by giving students work related to real-life tasks that require reasoning and problem solving.	Allows ELLs to build upon their prior knowledge and provides for diverse ways of solving problems.
Emphasize holistic concepts rather than fragmented units of information.	Focuses more on how ELLs think and what they understand rather than whether or not they have the one right answer.
Provide a variety of opportunities for students to explore and develop their understanding of concepts and situations over time.	Helps teachers understand how ELLs learn, places value on the linguistic and cultural backgrounds of ELLs, and allows ELLs to draft, reflect on, and revise their work.
Use multiple sources of information rather than a single text.	Allows for a variety of learning styles and offers multiple pathways and connections to academic success.
Work in interdisciplinary teams.	Improves communication between regular education and ELL staff and encourages an open dialogue about a school's expectations for ELLs.
Use multiple forms of assessment to gather concrete evidence of student proficiencies and achievement.	Complements diverse ways of knowing and learning and reveals productive "entry points" that build on students' strengths and lead to new areas of learning.

unfamiliar curriculum in a second language and in a different culture and school setting, many ELLs have difficulty negotiating the routines and expectations of the classroom. Tomlinson (2001) stresses the importance of the atmosphere of the classroom and school:

Atmosphere will signal without ambiguity whether the classroom is a place in which making a mistake is considered part of the natural learning process or a punishable event; varied ideas and perspectives are celebrated or rejected; diverse languages, cultures, and economic statuses are valued or problematic; and a student's current degree of skill and understanding is acceptable or inconvenient. (p. 45)

Designing Standards-Based Instructional Units

Latchat (1998) describes traditional approaches to schooling as often textbook driven, characterized by an emphasis on "covering" the curriculum, and highly activity based. Activity-based instruction typically includes three components. First is the selection of a topic from the curriculum, second is the design and presentation of instructional activities, and third is an assessment. Unfortunately, the demands and evaluative criteria of the final assessment are often kept secret from students, and once a grade or feedback is given, it is time to move on to a new topic, regardless of how much or how well students learned. Additionally, activities are often chosen primarily because they are fun and engaging for students (e.g., dinosaurs, rainforests) with little regard to what standards and benchmarks need to be taught and at what grade levels.

Current literature on planning for SBI (Mitchell, Willis, & Chicago Teachers' Union Quest Center, 1995; Wiggins & McTighe, 1998) advocates some form of *backward mapping* or *backward planning*, in which specific learning goals are identified and plans are made to ensure that those goals are achieved. Wiggins and McTighe delineate three stages in their backward-design process: (1) identify desired results, (2) determine acceptable evidence, and (3) plan learning experiences and instruction. This chapter suggests a similar backward mapping process to aid teachers in designing SBI for ELLs. Figure 12.2 is a graphic illustration of the process.

Identify Desired Results

The Standards oval in Figure 12.2 represents Wiggins and McTighe's "identify desired results" stage. The desired results are the standards being targeted. When designing a SBI unit, it is best to cluster standards, that is, to target a few standards that fit well together. For example, in a unit focusing on the U.S. Constitution, a teacher may choose some history and political science standards, as well as some language arts standards. A target of no more than three

FIGURE 12.2 The backward mapping process

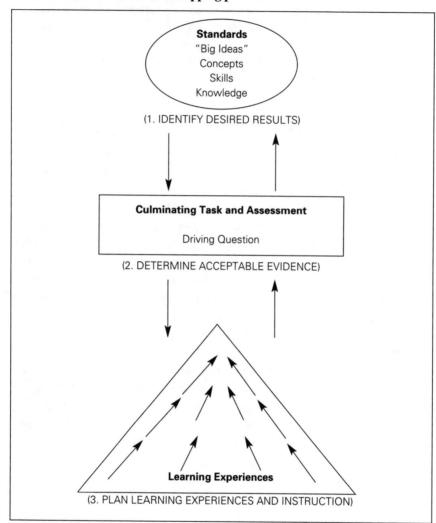

or four standards is suggested because the teacher needs to focus on standards that can be taught and assessed reasonably and effectively.

It is imperative that teachers understand what the standards and grade-appropriate benchmarks mean in regard to what student learning would look like. One strategy is to look closely at the verbs and the nouns in the standard. The verbs usually indicate the action the students need to take, and the nouns often represent the content or concepts. For example, a grades 6–8 history benchmark states, "Identify possible causal relationships in historical chronologies" (Hawaii Department of Education, 1999, p. 5). The important concepts are causal relationships and historical chronologies, and the students need to be able to identify them. But what does identify mean? If a student simply lists three causes of the U.S. Civil War, is that adequate? It is at this point in the planning process that teachers need to be able to articulate learning goals. Perhaps most teachers would agree that in this example, in addition to identifying the causes, students would also be asked to explain and justify their findings.

Another strategy teachers can use when seeking a better understanding of state standards is to refer to standards published by national professional organizations (e.g., the National Council of Teachers of Mathematics, the National Council of Teachers of English), which tend to be more descriptive and in depth. One valuable resource that covers all subject areas is *Content Knowledge: A Compendium of Standards and Benchmarks for K–12 Education* (Kendall & Marzano, 2000), which is also available online at http://www.mcrel.org.

Also represented in the oval in Figure 12.2 are the *concepts*, *skills*, and *knowledge* of the discipline and content. Attention to these overarching "big ideas" grounds teachers in thinking about what students need to know and be able to do. Reflective questions such as "What do social scientists do?" or a review of statements like "The primary purpose of social studies is to help young people develop the ability to make informed and reasoned decisions for the public good as citizens of a culturally diverse democratic society in an interdependent world" (Hawaii Department of Education, 1999, p. 1) help teachers to plan units that get to the heart of the discipline.

Determine Acceptable Evidence

The arrow in Figure 12.2 that points down from the Standards oval to the Culminating Task and Assessment rectangle represents the next step in the process in which acceptable evidence is determined. This step represents a fundamental difference from traditional activity-oriented instructional practices. According to Wiggins and McTighe (1998),

> The challenge is to postpone all thinking about what specific learning activities should frame a unit until the culminating performance tasks and other assessments are clear. *Educators need to know precisely what performances are required by the end of the unit before they can know what specific experiences and learnings need to occur.* (p. 41; italics added)

When designing the culminating task and assessment, it is important to consider the continuum of assessment methods (Wiggins & McTighe, 1998) to be used throughout the unit. For example, informal checks for understanding, observations, quizzes, academic prompts, and projects all vary in terms of complexity, time frame, setting, and structure.

For the purposes of this discussion, the culminating (or performance) task and assessment refers to a project-based activity. It is an engaging real-world activity that embodies all the selected standards and gives students a reason to achieve them. The task must directly match the standards identified, it must clearly describe expectations of students, and it must include specific criteria to evaluate quality. Culminating tasks are designed to build students' background knowledge, deepen their understanding, and result in applied learning. Additionally, culminating tasks typically seek to engage students in adult-like behavior, may include external audiences, and often require students to use technology to present what they have learned. Reference to state or district performance standards (or indicators) for the selected content standards can assist teachers in designing the culminating task and assessment.

Key to the second stage of the backward mapping process is one or more "driving" questions (sometimes referred to in various literature as "essential," "guiding," or "unit" questions), which are designed to stimulate student interest, energize instruction, and provide an unambiguous focus for the entire unit. Driving questions need to be open ended, have the potential for in-depth investigation, and connect to real-world issues. Driving questions typically start with "how" or "why." The culminating task in Mitchell et al. (1995) is stated as follows:

> Students will plan, organize, and carry out for the community a Pure Water Day. The day's activities will focus on issues of water purity in the community. These activities will be designed to answer the driving question: "[How] is the quality of our community's water affected by individual uses of land?" (p. 8)

The culminating task encourages student responsibility because the evaluative criteria are created (with student input if possible) before the unit is started and shared with students. Ideally, students are provided with exemplars to clarify learning expectations. Exemplars combine examples of student work at different levels of proficiency with teacher commentary on the quality of student work when compared to the desired outcomes. For example, if students were required to write a research paper about the causes of the U.S. Civil War, the teacher could provide them with examples of student papers about the causes of the American Revolutionary War that exceeded, met, or did not meet standards. From these samples, students can obtain a better understanding of how arguments can be presented, how a variety of informational sources can be incorporated, and how causal relationships can be explained. The task's performance assessment asks students to synthesize information and to show and justify what they know, emphasizes important learning/concepts, and is designed with complex and multiple steps to stretch student thinking. When appropriately constructed, performance assessments ensure real-world applications of student learning, meaningfully connect instruction with the discipline's big ideas and concepts, allow for a variety of student differences, and present opportunities for improving communication between schools and parents concerning student achievement.

Moon and Callahan (2001) present students with these instructions for the culminating task:

> Throughout history, progress (social, technological, artistic, etc.) has led people to believe that the time in which they are living is, in many ways, "the best of times." You have been employed by PBS to create a documentary from a particular historical era that will reflect on why that era was "the best of times".... From the perspective of your new role, write an essay or develop a monologue to be presented to the class that will convince others that, for you, these are "the best of times." (pp. 54–55)

Along with this scenario, students are provided with a three-point scoring rubric that describes performances that exceed, meet, or fall below expectations in the areas of historical accuracy, perspectives/point of view, persuasiveness, thoroughness, research skills, and referencing skills.

Plan Learning Experiences and Instruction

The arrow in Figure 12.2 that points down from the Culminating Task rectangle to the Learning Experiences triangle indicates that the selection and sequencing of instructional experiences and activities take place *after* the culminating task and assessment are determined. Again, this constitutes a significant difference between activity-based instruction, in which activities are the means and ends, and SBI, where activities are the means and standards are the ends (Harris & Carr, 1996).

The arrows inside the Learning Experiences triangle symbolize the different ways in which students need to be prepared in order to successfully complete the culminating task. For example, the authors of the "Pure Water

Day" task presented in Mitchell et al. (1995) identify six areas in which students need learning opportunities—creating, administering, analyzing, and reporting a water-use survey; understanding the water cycle; writing a persuasive editorial—to meet the expectations. If students struggle in any one of these areas, then the teacher needs to reteach or make other adjustments. Otherwise the students are inadequately prepared for the culminating task. In SBI, students may need more time and/or different avenues to achieve desired levels of achievement, that is, SBI focuses on student achievement, not simply the coverage of material.

When planning learning experiences, there are a number of reflective questions teachers can ask themselves. What materials/resources will be needed? How long will students need to complete each activity? What prior knowledge will students need in order to complete the activities? What exemplars can be shared with students? What informal and formal assessments can be used to measure student progress? How can instruction be modified or differentiated to ensure that all students have the potential to reach or exceed the expected learning outcomes of this unit?

The arrow in Figure 12.2 that points up from the triangle to the rectangle signifies that all the learning experiences were geared to preparing the students for the demands of the culminating task, while the arrow that points up between the rectangle and oval shows that the successful completion of the culminating task is an indication that significant progress toward the standards has been achieved.

Standards-Based Units for ELLs

When planning for the achievement of ELLs in the SBI approach, there are some unique considerations that teachers need to make in each of the three steps of the backward mapping process. As for Step 1 in Figure 12.2, Identify Desired Results, it is important that teachers understand the standards they are required to target and commit their efforts toward them. ELLs must have access to challenging curricula and the focus of instruction should be on their long-term success. ELLs may experience academic difficulties due to their limited English proficiency or lack of content understanding due to limited formal schooling; nevertheless, ways in which teachers can help ELLs make reasonable progress toward high standards must be explored and pursued. The previously described approaches taken by the California Department of

Education and TESOL are examples of how teachers, schools, and school districts make efforts to include ELLs in standards-based reform.

When considering Step 2 in Figure 12.2, Determine Acceptable Evidence, it is important to note that the assessment of ELLs is often problematic. Do the ELLs understand the directions for the task or prompt? Even if ELLs understand the directions, do they have the facility in English to show that they understand the knowledge, concepts, and skills that the unit has targeted? For example, if the performance task centers on the concept of photosynthesis, and the ELL understands the concept in his or her first language but cannot yet express it in English, what type of assessment that measures the ELL's true content understanding *and* yields useful information for planning future English language instruction can be administered? Using alternative or authentic assessments with ELLs, rather than relying solely on traditional forms of testing such as multiple-choice tests, allows for better assessment of the full range of student outcomes, and the information gained through the assessment can then be used to inform instructional planning. O'Malley and Valdez-Pierce (1996) describe and discuss the advantages of using eight types of authentic assessments with ELLs, including oral interviews, story retellings, projects, and demonstrations, and they provide a number of rubrics and checklists appropriate for classroom use.

Perhaps the most important question in Step 3, Plan Learning Experiences and Instruction, is, How can instruction be modified or differentiated to ensure that all students have the potential to reach or exceed the expected learning outcomes of this unit? This question is particularly important when planning for the achievement of ELLs. To answer this question the teacher must identify the cognitive and language demands of the unit, as well as its cultural relevancy to the students. The diversity among ELLs is great; they differ according to prior educational experiences, exposure to English, length of time in the U.S., learning styles, family literacy practices, socioeconomic status, sense of self, and other characteristics. These factors profoundly affect in idiosyncratic ways the learning readiness and rate of English acquisition of ELLs.

Examples of instructional accommodations or modifications that have proven effective with ELLs include providing instruction and materials in the students' native languages; demonstrating activities and strategies through teacher "think alouds" and modeling; setting language, content, and learning strategy objectives; tapping prior knowledge; using visuals/manipulatives; explicitly teaching key vocabulary; adjusting speech; utilizing cooperative learning methods; and teaching coping strategies. Figure 12.3 provides a brief rationale for these accommodations. (See also Graves & Fitzgerald, chapter 5; Hernández, chapter 6; García & Beltrán, chapter 9; and Dutro & Moran, chapter 10, in this volume.)

FIGURE 12.3 Accommodations that have proven effective for ELLs

Instructional accommodations for ELLs	Rationale
Provide native language instruction and materials.	The strategic use of the students' native language to focus on the development of higher order thinking skills and on the clarification and elaboration of key concepts and vocabulary has great potential for accelerating and enhancing ELLs' access to mainstream curricula. Additionally, when ELLs' native language is valued and utilized, they are more likely to have increased self-esteem and greater self-efficacy. Access to materials written in their native language supports ELLs' literacy and cognitive development (Hakuta, 2001).
Provide "think-alouds" and modeling.	ELLs benefit when teachers explain strategies and steps for tackling instructional tasks, check for student understanding before having students start the task independently, and present numerous examples of concepts being taught (Gersten, Baker, & Marks, 1998).
Set language, content, and learning strategy objectives.	Chamot and O'Malley (1994) contend that content should be the primary focus of instruction, academic language skills can be developed as the need for them arises from the content, and ELLs can learn and apply learning strategies to a variety of contexts if those strategies are explicitly taught.
Tap students' prior knowledge.	Instruction which values and continues to cultivate the educational and personal experiences ELLs bring to the classroom, rather than ignores or tries to replace these experiences, enables students to make meaningful connections with what is being taught (Cummins, 1994).

(continued)

FIGURE 12.3 Accommodations that have proven effective for ELLs (continued)

Instructional accommodations for ELLs	Rationale
Use visuals/manipulatives.	Concrete examples and experiences give ELLs a variety of ways of understanding the information being presented.
Teach key vocabulary.	Traditional instructional processes aimed at improving vocabulary acquisition in which students are given word lists to look up in the dictionary, followed by practice in a definition or synonym exercise, and then tested, do not work well with ELLs (O'Malley & Valdez-Pierce, 1996). Teachers need to utilize a variety of approaches and strategies (e.g., graphic organizers) to help ELLs gain a deep understanding of abstract concepts.
Adjust speech.	The Center for Applied Linguistics (1998) suggests 11 ways teachers can adjust their speech to increase comprehensibility: face the students; pause frequently; paraphrase often; clearly indicate the most important ideas and vocabulary through intonation or writing on the blackboard; avoid "asides"; avoid or clarify pronouns; use shorter sentences; use subject-verb-object word order; increase wait time for students to answer; focus on student's meaning, not grammar; and avoid interpreting on a regular basis.
Utilize cooperative learning methods.	Cooperative learning is a key instructional strategy for ELLs because it enhances interactions among students, promotes the development of positive academic and social support systems for ELLs, prepares students for increasingly interactive workplaces, and allows teachers to manage large classes of students with diverse needs (Holt, 1993).
Teach coping strategies.	ELLs may not have the confidence or facility in English to ask for help or clarification. They may also come from cultures where it is inappropriate to directly ask a teacher for help.

The two sample units featured in Figures 12.4 and 12.5 are appropriate for elementary ELLs. They are based on the *Hawai'i Content and Performance Standards II (HCPS II)*. The unit, "The Life Cycle of a Monarch Butterfly," adapted from a unit the author observed in a second-grade self-contained ESL classroom, focuses on science standards. The "My School Day in Hawai'i" unit, designed for newly arrived non-English proficient students in an ESL classroom, aims for progress toward achievement of language arts standards.

The inclusion of the two units in this chapter serves two purposes. First, the commentary provides insight as to the types of needs of ELLs and suggests ways in which teachers can make instructional accommodations in order for ELLs to reach high academic standards. Second, the units invite a professional dialogue regarding how teachers can plan for standards-based instruction. The following reflective questions are useful in determining the quality of the unit design and informing refinements to the unit plan. How complete is this unit? To what degree are the standards naturally integrated? How appropriate is the culminating task? How well do the assessments align with the standards? How well do the students learn the standards? How do the learning activities prepare students for the culminating task?

FIGURE 12.4 Sample unit plan: "The Life Cycle of a Monarch Butterfly"

ELL Unit Plan 1	Commentary
Title: "The Life Cycle of a Monarch Butterfly"	Historically, an unfortunate characteristic of many ESL self-contained classrooms has been an emphasis on discrete language skills at the expense of content area learning. In this case, however, the teacher has made a conscious, systematic effort to integrate language and content by providing age- and grade-appropriate curriculum.
Grade Level: Second	
Length of Time: Five to six weeks	
Unit Description: Students will observe and learn about the life cycle of monarch butterflies, complete a visual aid depicting the cycle, and orally present their understandings.	
Big Ideas: Science instruction engages students in describing objects and events, asking questions, constructing explanations, testing those explanations against current scientific knowledge, and communicating their ideas to others.	ELLs are vulnerable to educational discontinuities if academic instruction is delayed until they have mastered basic English skills. Programmatic and instructional accommodations need to be made to ensure that ELLs have access to rigorous and high-quality curricula.

(continued)

FIGURE 12.4 Sample unit plan: "The Life Cycle of a Monarch Butterfly"
(continued)

ELL Unit Plan 1	Commentary
Content Standards: Science **Domain I**: How Humans Think While Understanding the Natural World **Strand**: Science as Inquiry **Content Standard: 1**. Students demonstrate the skills necessary to engage in scientific inquiry. **Grade Cluster Benchmarks**: Generate ideas, questions, and/or predictions, about objects, organisms, events, places, and/or relationships in the environment; Collect and organize data using simple tools, equipment, and techniques; Appropriately communicate their investigations and explanations to an audience. (HCPS II, Science, p. 10, grades K–3).	This cluster of selected benchmarks asks students to make predictions, collect and organize data, and communicate their understandings. These skills are central to scientific inquiry. One or more language arts standards could be added, however, the three benchmarks adequately cover what will be assessed in this unit.
Driving Question: How do caterpillars turn into butterflies? **Culminating Task**: Students will complete a visual aid that depicts four stages of the life cycle of a monarch butterfly (i.e., egg, caterpillar, chrysalis, and emergence of butterfly) and use it to support their explanations.	The teacher needs to determine the circumstances under which the task will be completed by students. Will the students present in front of the whole class? A panel? One-on-one with the teacher? Some other arrangement?
Culminating Activity Assessment: The activity will be assessed according to the following criteria: _____ Student will complete a visual aid that is clearly labeled and appropriately depicts the four stages of the life cycle. _____ Student will use the visual aid as support to explain the life cycle. The explanation must include at least three facts or observations about each stage.	It is the teacher's responsibility to determine the answer to the question, "How good is good enough?" Based on the two criteria on the left, a rubric could be developed to determine the quality of the visual aid and the explanation. The explanation could be examined in terms of its science content as well as the student's facility with language.
Learning Activities: (1) The teacher starts the unit by utilizing the first two steps of the K-W-L approach (Ogle, 1986); that is asking students what they know about caterpillars and butterflies and then what they want to know about caterpillars and butterflies. The final step of the approach is reviewing what has been learned.	Instruction must start where the students are cognitively and linguistically. The teacher should note that it may be difficult to determine what ELLs really know, therefore a variety of instructional accommodations are needed (see Figure 12.3). (continued)

**FIGURE 12.4 Sample unit plan: "The Life Cycle of a Monarch Butterfly"
(continued)**

ELL Unit Plan 1

(2) The teacher gives students a number of questions to research for the duration of the unit. These questions are compiled from three sources: (1) student incomplete understandings and misconceptions taken from the know step; (2) student questions from the want step and; (3) other important questions the teacher feels students may have missed. To support student learning, the teacher may want to categorize (with student help if possible) the questions (e.g., on habitat, physical characteristics, etc.).

(3) The teacher provides students with opportunities to make daily observations of the caterpillar/butterfly terrarium, read a variety of literature to do research, and share their findings orally and visually.

Extension Activity: After reading and exploring the features of storybooks or poetry about caterpillars/butterflies, students can write and publish their own fiction or poetry that incorporates their understandings from the life cycle unit.

Commentary

The premise is that if students can answer these questions from their observations and research, then they will be adequately prepared for the culminating task.

These opportunities and activities must focus on what students will need to know and appropriate ways in which they can explain their understandings. A number of accommodations may be necessary for ELLs. For example, students can be provided with prediction and/or observation logs. These logs could have simple prompts like "This is what I saw" (and a space for the ELL to draw what was observed) and "This is what I noticed" (and a space for the ELL to write what was observed). Practice in taking and recording measurements may be needed. As the unit progresses, a "scientific vocabulary" glossary or pictionary can be developed individually or by the whole class. A variety of reading materials, in terms of cognitive and linguistic demands, as well as types of texts (e.g., expository, narrative) will be needed. Students may need to paired or grouped for some research activities and sharing out opportunities must be provided.

FIGURE 12.5 Sample unit plan: "My School Day in Hawaii"

ELL Unit Plan 2	Commentary
Title: "My School Day in Hawaii"	One of the first and most important tasks an ELL must undertake is to know school routines and expectations. Unless this understanding is reached, it will be difficult for the student to focus his or her energy on learning English, content, and skills. An important concept in the field of second language acquisition is "affective filter," which highlights the emotional component of second language learning and states that learning may be blocked when students are in a highly anxious environment. In addition to developing literacy skills and attitudes, this unit is intended to promote for the ELL a sense of belonging to the school. This unit could be adapted for ELLs at any elementary grade level.
Grade Level: Elementary non-English proficient students	
Length of Time: One to two weeks	
Unit Description: Students, with the teacher's assistance and guidance, will "research" daily routines at school and present their findings in a "published" book.	
Big Ideas: According to HCPS II, Language Arts (pp. 2–3), Hawaii's standards are organized around these key concepts: • Language is functional and purposeful. • Language processes are meaning-making processes. • Language allows for communication through symbolic forms. • Language is governed by conventions. • Language develops from a positive attitude about self as a reader, writer, speaker, and from engagement in meaningful literacy activities. • Language enables us to develop social and cultural understanding.	These are key concepts for both first- and second-language learning.
Content Standards: Language Arts **Component**: Reading **Content Strand**: Attitudes and Engagement	The two targeted benchmarks reflect the goals of language arts in Hawaii's schools, which are aimed at

(continued)

FIGURE 12.5 Sample unit plan: "My School Day in Hawaii" (continued)

ELL Unit Plan 2	Commentary
Content Standard: **5.** Demonstrate confidence as readers, and find value and satisfaction in reading and sharing reading experiences with others. **Grade Cluster Benchmark**: Share reading experiences with others (HCPS II, Language Arts, p. 10, grades K–1 & 2–3). **Content Standards**: Language Arts **Component**: Oral Communication **Content Strand**: Convention and Skills **Content Standard**: **3.** Apply knowledge of verbal and nonverbal language to communicate effectively. **Grade Cluster Benchmarks**: Speak clearly and expressively using nonverbal language to complement and enhance verbal messages; Use standard English pronunciation and grammar when speaking to be understood (HCPS II, Language Arts, p. 16, grades 2–3).	ensuring that all students develop knowledge about and appreciation of and facility in using the English language in ways that will serve them in all aspects of their lives. Progress toward these benchmarks jumpstarts non-English-proficient ELLs into the world of active English language use.
Driving Question: How can the story of a day at our school be told in a book?	Placing students at the center of the authoring, illustrating, and publishing processes is a powerful learning incentive.
Culminating Task: Students will read their illustrated book to their regular education teacher and to an adult at home.	The task requires students to complete their book, share it with others, and use English competently.
Culminating Activity Assessment: The activity will be assessed according to the following criteria: _____ Student will read the entire book with fluency, expression, and understanding. _____ Student will illustrate the book with pictures that support the text. _____ Student will illustrate the book with pictures that are colorful. _____ Student will read the book to his or her regular education teacher and return a signed form as proof. _____ Student will read the book to an adult at home and return a signed form as proof.	The assessment of this activity uses a simple checklist rather than a rubric because differentiating between levels of proficiency is not a priority. For example, if the student stumbles frequently while reading, it is more important to give him or her more practice opportunities rather than to determine his or her level of proficiency. Also, although the student will need to make illustrations, fine arts standards are not targeted in this unit.

(continued)

FIGURE 12.5 Sample unit plan: "My School Day in Hawaii" (continued)

ELL Unit Plan 2	Commentary

ELL Unit Plan 2

Learning Activities:

(1) Teacher explains to the student the criteria above for this activity (e.g., "By November 15 you will complete a book ... and ...").

(2) Teacher explains and reviews with student the school day.

(3) Teacher dictates and transcribes the story for student. Each bulleted item below may represent one page of the book, for example:

- My name is _____. I am in the _____ grade at _____ school.
- School starts at _____.
- From _____ until _____ we study _____. (or "The first class is _____.")
- Next we study _____.
- Recess is from _____ until _____. I like to _____.
- After recess, we _____ ,
- Lunch is from _____ until _____ . I like to eat _____.
- After lunch, we _____.
- School finishes at _____.
- (include "About the Author and Illustrator" page)

(4) Teacher explains to student that illustrations must support the story and be colorful.

(5) Student completes illustrations. Teacher gives suggestions as needed and checks for appropriateness.

Commentary

If students can internalize learning expectations, then chances are they will take more responsibility for their own success.

To tap into student's prior knowledge, the teacher, for example, may ask the student to share and compare his or her school day from his or her home country.

This is the point in the learning activities where the accommodations planned for ELLs are critical. The length of the book, the depth of details and descriptions, and the length and complexity of the sentences are the teacher's decision, based on the capability of the ELL. The flow of the book is an important consideration. For example, the consistent use of time or sequence words will support the reader. The student's prior knowledge is another important consideration. Obviously, to complete this task the student will need to know some things about print (e.g., English is read from left to right) and be able to tell time or understand sequence words like first, second, after, next, then, etc.

The main idea is that the illustrations must support the text. Fine arts standards are not a priority for this task and therefore there is no formal assessment link of the illustrations to fine arts standards.

An ESL teacher who has tried this unit commented, "Because the students illustrated each page, they could easily 'read' their writing by looking at their pictures."

(continued)

FIGURE 12.5 Sample unit plan: "My School Day in Hawaii" (continued)

ELL Unit Plan 2

(6) Teacher and student "publish" the book.

(7) Teacher gives student opportunities to practice reading (e.g., in front a small group of peers) to the point that the student can read with fluency and confidence.

(8) Student reads book to his or her teacher and to an adult at home and returns signed form to the ESL teacher. The form may include requests such as "Please comment on how well the child read the book" and "Please comment on the child's illustrations." The form may need to be translated into the family's home language and the family should be encouraged to respond in their home language if necessary.

(9) Teacher and student meet to determine if the criteria for the activity have been successfully completed. If not met, then teacher and student determine next steps to ensure completion.

Extension Activity: Student completes and shares similar book about his or her school day in his or her home country.

Commentary

The ELL experiences a sense of accomplishment and ownership, despite often being perceived as "limited or non-English proficient."

Teacher utilizes a variety of strategies to check comprehension (e.g., cloze, strip story).

An external audience reinforces a sense of purpose for the student. The form provides an opportunity to improve communication between the ESL teacher and the regular education teacher as well as between the school and the home. A regular education teacher, after seeing and listening to an ELL's book, commented that she "was impressed with the quality of work the ESL kids could do."

Opportunities for student self-assessment and timely, specific teacher feedback enhances learning.

This is a potentially valuable activity because it indicates that the life experiences of the ELLs are valued and that ELLs are viewed as informational assets to the classroom and the school. All students can benefit from learning about life and schooling in other countries.

The butterfly life cycle and the school day units have been presented here as vehicles to investigate the potential benefits of SBI for ELLs. Do the units incorporate effective elements of planning for SBI and effective instructional practices for ELLs? In what ways could these units be improved? How could these units be adapted to classroom situations in your school?

The achievement of high standards by all students presents a daunting challenge for schools, particularly those with student populations that reflect diverse cultural and linguistic backgrounds. The promise of SBI is that clear, high standards help to clarify that the purpose of schooling is to make the knowledge and skills essential to success in today's world accessible to all.

Author Note

This chapter was funded by the U.S. Department of Education under the Regional Educational Laboratory program, contract number ED01CO0014. The content does not necessarily reflect the views of the U.S. Department of Education or any other agency of the U.S. government.

REFERENCES

Agor, B. (Ed.). (2000). *Integrating the ESL standards into classroom practice: Grades 9–12.* Alexandria, VA: Teachers of English to Speakers of Other Languages.

California Department of Education. (1999). *English language development standards* [Online]. Available: http://www.cde.ca.gov/statetests/eld/eld.html

Center for Applied Linguistics. (1998). *Enriching content classes for secondary ESOL students: Study guide.* McHenry, IL: Delta Systems.

Chamot, A., & O'Malley, J. (1994). *The CALLA handbook: Implementing the cognitive academic language learning approach.* Reading, MA: Addison-Wesley.

Cummins, J. (1994). Knowledge, power, and identity in teaching English as a second language. In F. Genesee (Ed.), *Educating second language children.* New York: Cambridge University Press.

Gersten, R., Baker, S., & Marks, S. (1998). *Teaching English-language learners with learning difficulties.* Washington, DC: The Council for Exceptional Children.

Hakuta, K. (2001). *The education of language minority students.* Testimony to the U.S. Commission on Civil Rights, April 13, 2001 [Online]. Available: www.stanford.edu/~hakuta/Docs/Civil-RightsCommission.htm

Harris, D., & Carr, J. (1996). *How to use standards in the classroom.* Alexandria, VA: Association for Supervision and Curriculum Development.

Hawaii Department of Education. (1999). *Hawai'i content and performance standards II* [Online]. Available: http://doe.k12.hi.us

Holt, D. (Ed.). (1993). *Cooperative learning: A response to linguistic and cultural diversity.* McHenry, IL: Delta Systems.

Irujo, S. (Ed.). (2000). *Integrating the ESL standards into classroom practice: Grades 6–8.* Alexandria, VA: Teachers of English to Speakers of Other Languages.

Kendall, J., & Marzano, R. (2000). *Content knowledge: A compendium of standards and bench-marks for K–12 education* (3rd ed.). Alexandria, VA: Association for Supervision and Curriculum Development.

Latchat, M.A. (1998). Shifting to standards-based learning: What does it mean for schools, teachers, and students? In *Educating linguistically and culturally diverse students: An ASCD professional inquiry kit*. Alexandria, VA: Association for Supervision and Curriculum Development.

Mitchell, R., Willis, M., & Chicago Teachers' Union Quest Center. (1995). *Learning in overdrive*. Golden, CO: North American Press.

Moon, T., & Callahan, C. (2001). Classroom performance assessment: What should it look like in a standards-based classroom? *NASSP Bulletin, 85*(622), 48–58.

Ogle, D. (1986). K-W-L: A teaching model that develops active reading of expository text. *The Reading Teacher, 39*, 164–170.

O'Malley, J.M., & Valdez-Pierce, L. (1996). *Authentic assessment for English-language learners: Practical approaches for teachers*. Reading, MA: Addison-Wesley.

Samway, K. (Ed.). (2000). *Integrating the ESL standards into classroom practice: Grades 3–5.* Alexandria, VA: Teachers of English to Speakers of Other Languages.

Smallwood, B. (Ed.). (2000). *Integrating the ESL standards into classroom practice: Grades preK–2.* Alexandria, VA: Teachers of English to Speakers of Other Languages.

Snow, M. (Ed.). (2000). *Implementing the ESL standards for preK-12 students through teacher education*. Alexandria, VA: Teachers of English to Speakers of Other Languages.

Tomlinson, C. (2001). Standards and the art of teaching: Crafting high quality classrooms. *NASSP Bulletin, 85*(622), 38–47.

Wiggins, G., & McTighe, J. (1998). *Understanding by design*. Alexandria, VA: Association for Supervision and Curriculum Development.

Optimizing Culture as a Bridge to Literacy Learning

CHAPTER 13

Connecting Children, Culture, Curriculum, and Text

MariAnne George, Taffy E. Raphael, and Susan Florio-Ruane

Culture is man's medium; there is not one aspect of human life that is not touched and altered by culture. However, like the purloined letter, it is frequently the most obvious and taken-for-granted. —E.T. Hall

"I kent spiek so masch inliech I am from Gomenny ameriea is kool" (November)

"Des is a mannstar wat I dnng" (December)

 "I likt the part when ho motter went to school mif Molly and tray to tell the ticher thet the kits sott stop lauving to Molly. Not nice uf them." (April)

"Hi my name is Nels and we tackt about all the books like Pettrecha Polacko and the pescanco eggs. It was fun doing Book Club and now we will not see the same kids. Now we haf to stost of oveer and we red Famely stosis and The Sgrep Book and Rocksen Bocksen. So see you nekt teer Mrs. George." (June)

With the "shrinking" of our world and the multicultural nature of our population, schools in the United States have become a microcosm of society, serving a mosaic of children of diverse cultures, languages, and ethnic groups. If it has been commonplace for teachers to expect to teach pupils similar to them in language, cultural background, and economic standing, research predicts that in the next two decades more than half of all students in U.S. schools will be members of language and ethnic minority groups (see, for example, Nieto, 1999). This not only changes our image of teaching; it also changes the work of the teacher. How can we, as educators, affirm the diverse cultures and first languages of our students within the context of teaching the school curriculum? How can we help children like Nels connect learning English with home culture, so that school curriculum and text, as well as school learning, become relevant, effective, and affirming of Nels's emergent identity as a citizen of the United States?

This task would be difficult under the most generous of conditions. The task is taken up, however, in a contemporary climate of high standards, diminishing resources, and a press toward accountability with respect to both children and teachers. In this situation, the tendency may be to oversimplify, short-circuiting the powerful learning experiences our students need in order to acquire school literacy (Florio-Ruane, 2002b). Slimming down complexity, and working harder and faster at what we assume to be essentials of our task, risks ending up missing the forest for the trees. Nels's task is not just to learn a new language code—exclusively and out of context. It is to become part of a new community of discourse—and, as such, to grow more aware of his primary discourse, learned in the family and in German. This is a crucial part of learning in a multicultural society and a democratic form of government.

Literacy teaching and learning are crucial to sustaining a democratic society, and schools have the primary responsibility for this work. For decades, U.S. educators' assumptions have focused on literacy as a set of reading and writing skills, albeit with both aesthetic and functional purposes. Recently, however, educators and researchers have recognized literacy not only as a set of skills but also as cultural practice, which has led those of us in literacy education to reconsider the content of the literacy curriculum as well as instructional methods and assessment practices. Examples of this refocusing include examining the nature and potential of home-school-community relationships as resources for literacy education (e.g., Moll, 1992; see also García & Beltrán, chapter 9, and Chang, chapter 11, in this volume) and rethinking how to facilitate teachers' understandings of the relationships among culture, the literacy curriculum, and the texts used in teaching (e.g., Florio-Ruane, 2002a). In this chapter we focus on our collaborative research on literacy curriculum, instruction, and assessment in MariAnne George's third-grade classroom. We describe the work she and her students did to build meaningful connections among the literature they studied, their personal and critical responses to that literature, and their study of those texts as cultural artifacts.

Description of the Collaborative Inquiry

The authors of this chapter are members of the Teachers' Learning Collaborative (TLC), a network of teacher researchers from across southeast

Michigan, USA, who teach in settings from first through eighth grades and in preservice and inservice teacher education programs. A primary problem TLC members explored was reengaging low-achieving readers (see Florio-Ruane & Raphael, 2001; Raphael, Florio-Ruane, Kehus, et al., 2001). During the summer of 1998, members of TLC met together to begin to develop and study a pilot literacy curriculum framework called Book Club *Plus*. The overarching theme, Our Storied Lives, provided a context for linking students' reading, writing, and talking about texts—with students balancing their work between texts appropriate to their age level and those appropriate to their reading level (Raphael, Florio-Ruane, & George, 2001). The project combined curriculum design with research, both qualitative and quantitative, on teaching the curriculum as well as on teacher and student learning (see, for example, Berne, 2001; Raphael, Florio-Ruane, Kehus, et al., 2001). MariAnne George, the first author of this chapter, is one of the teachers participating in TLC, and it is her classroom that this chapter describes.

Setting the Scene

During the period of this project (1999–2001), MariAnne George taught in a suburban school that serves as a center for teaching English as a second language to students throughout the district. Thus, her classroom was both multicultural and multilingual. Two professors, Taffy E. Raphael and Susan Florio-Ruane, worked in teacher education programs at nearby universities. They shared a common understanding of literacy as a cultural practice, not simply as a set of skills and strategies. With support from the research center in which they worked (see Author Note on page 329), TLC was created to connect teachers who were seeking, by rethinking curriculum and instruction, to reengage struggling young readers. TLC found that the link between culture and literacy was a central one in the effort to help young readers see text as a meaningful part of their lives.

MariAnne's school has an unexpectedly diverse composition. A relatively prosperous suburb of Detroit, Michigan, USA, it is home to families from many parts of the world, many of whose members work in the automobile industry. In a way, this city is an exemplar of our time—a time in which the world is shrinking by means of rapid communication and transportation and the creation of international corporations from what were originally industries isolated by nation and even by region. As during World War II, a period that saw African Americans from the South migrate to "the motor city" in large numbers to help with the industrial work of the war effort (Sugrue, 1998), the Detroit metropolitan area is today a polyglot one, now with migrants from other nations. Today the auto industry draws immigrants from continents as diverse as Asia, Europe, and Latin America, giving rise to a new richness in the area's population. And despite deep educational and social divisions remaining between core city and suburbs, based on factors like racism and lack of economic opportunity (Farley, Danziger, & Holzer, 2000), the linguistic, cultural, ethnic, and social diversity of the area bears witness to a networked world economy and the criss-crossing of citizens within it.

Located historically, geographically, and socially within this setting, MariAnne's class of third graders was a richly multicultural and multilingual setting in 1999 (the year described in this chapter). But working in this setting posed dilemmas and problems that initially drew MariAnne to participate in TLC. That participation led to MariAnne's making local modifications to the emerging TLC curricular framework. The work she did in her class created a strategic research site in which to study the interweaving of literacy, culture, and text in the elementary school curriculum. This interweaving had implications for the learning of all students, but MariAnne's inquiry focused in particular on its role in the learning of students struggling to learn to read and write in English.

MariAnne, Susan, and Taffy were all interested in how the TLC curriculum work applied to the specific question of helping students construct their own knowledge of culture so that they could interact, share knowledge, and extend their appreciation and understanding of other cultures and experiences. We conjectured that in making culture "visible" to students, both teachers and students might better understand the critical role culture plays in literacy development. We hoped that our focus on culture would turn the diversity of backgrounds and first languages in MariAnne's room into *resources for* rather than *obstacles to* literacy learning. Students might find ways, we envisioned, to engage personally with the stories they read and told, thus making reading and response to literature more meaningful, engaging work.

We begin by describing the context in which this research occurred: the context of our diverse society and of a classroom using Book Club *Plus*—an innovative, integrated, and thematic approach to literacy instruction developed by members of TLC. Not by accident, the theme studied across the year within the Book Club *Plus* framework focused on culture, especially the rendering of lives in narrative. We called this overarching theme "Our Storied Lives," and we will describe it in this chapter. We then frame specific curricular activities in terms of the Our Storied Lives theme and the three units that make it up: Stories of Self, Family Stories, and Stories of Culture. In doing so, we describe our problems of practice, resources we found helpful in addressing them, and the results of our efforts. We also discuss what we have learned from this work, drawing on examples of classroom research including classroom charts, samples of individual students' work, and MariAnne's teacher research journal. We end with recommendations for helping teachers and students become engaged participants in exploring their own and others' storied lives.

Teaching About Language, Literacy, and Culture Through Book Club *Plus*

The structure and thematic content of Book Club *Plus* build from understanding self to understanding others, and promote engagement through compelling and personally meaningful texts and activities. Both organizational structure and thematic content help weave a meaningful fabric out of diverse activities, texts, and children—and help teachers make literacy learning more coherent for students across different instructional contexts and activities. Ultimately the study of self and family is aimed at understanding culture. Culture is one of the complex ideas explored as a theme in the yearlong curricular framework, "Our Storied Lives." The framework comprises three six-to-eight-week units: Stories of Self, Family Stories, and Stories of Culture. This progression of units allows us to begin with a focus on the self—something that accords with curricular materials across grade levels—and then contextualizes the self within the broader family, community, and society.

Each unit draws from a set of books that supports the particular focus that is fully developed with the Book Club book, the guided reading books or short stories, the teacher's read-aloud, shared reading books that are often the basis for minilessons during writers' workshop, and the classroom library, which supports students' Sustained Silent Reading (SSR). Each unit also includes a major culminating project that requires students to apply and integrate language arts skills and strategies along with ideas related to the overarching theme. Teachers alternated students' Book Club activities (two to three days per week) with Literacy Block (also two to three days per week). Literacy Block included guided reading, literacy center activities, and independent unit work activities.

To understand learning in this curricular context, we collected several types of information. Adopting a social constructivist stance with respect to learning (Gavelek & Raphael, 1996), we traced the children's understanding of culture in a variety of sociolinguistic activities that would yield a linguistic record of their thinking over the course of the school year. The first type of record involved whole-class charts, generated from discussions conducted at the beginning of the school year; in March, prior to the beginning of the Stories of Culture unit; and at the end of the school year. These classroom events involved MariAnne's framing the discussion in terms of two broad questions: What is autobiography? What is culture? We then analyzed these charts by reading and rereading them, looking for patterns among the responses. Three categories emerged: (1) features or traits characteristic of culture; (2) personal connections to the idea of culture, influencing students' experiences within their families and communities; and (3) examples of cultures, from students' backgrounds to the classroom as a culture.

The second type of record was based on individual students' written responses. These were captured by asking students to respond to the prompt "Tell me about yourself" on the first day of school, and again in early June. Interspersed with these responses were field notes and other artifacts of student learning across the three units, enabling us to track the process of cultural understanding—which looked very different as reflected in the first prompted writing than it did in the last one at year's end.

The third type of record was a set of texts created by children and generated through activities designed specifically to elicit students' individual writing about culture. In this context, the activity itself was as important as were the "texts" it involved: some oral, some written; some drawn; some represented in the work of eliciting family oral histories and artifacts. Across the board, however, these texts took a decidedly narrative form, involving such activities as writing family stories, drawing on interviews with or about members of their grandparents' generation; retelling stories in writing or orally; reading books related to the family stories; and creating a quilt square reflecting students' cultural heritage—an activity that stressed everyone's participation in culture and the diversity of cultural experiences among the students, as the squares were ultimately combined into a classroom quilt.

Stories of Self

We began the yearlong Our Storied Lives theme with the first unit, Stories of Self. In the belief that we must understand ourselves before we can understand others, instruction focused on activities, literature, and discussions that helped children look inward. We began the unit with two different activities designed to reveal students' conceptions about autobiography, genre, and the primacy of culture in their lives, along with students' initial writing abilities. The first activity involved a writing sample; the second, generating class charts in a whole-class setting.

During the first week of school, we asked students to write in response to the prompt "Tell me about yourself." Most of the responses read like laundry lists of statistical information: age, birthday, address, telephone number, number or name(s) of pets, and so forth. Few mentioned ethnicity or heritage. Erich wrote his response in German, "Mein papa heist Oliver. Mein mama heist Sophie…" while Arturo used a combination of Spanish and English, "I am from Mexico. Mi casa is Mexico City." After this writing activity, we turned our attention to teaching using the texts for Stories of Self and the curriculum framework of Book Club *Plus*.

The whole-class activity involved the children and the teacher constructing two class charts. First, MariAnne asked them to respond to the question "What is autobiography?" Then students responded to the question "What is culture?" Analysis of the charts revealed that the children's definitions of autobiography were relatively unformed. Typical responses included "writing a biography on an automatic machine" and "a special book about autos." Students had a vague idea about an autobiography's involving stories (like a biography), but little understanding of the content of those stories. Their responses to the question about culture—which included what kinds of foods you eat, where you are from, someplace other than the United States, and how you talk—were more closely linked to the construct. The responses indicated awareness, however, rather than deep or complex understandings. The two charts helped us ground children's developing understanding of culture and its history—and of how family histories and stories are grounded in cultural histories.

After these introductory activities, we began the Book Club *Plus* unit Stories of Self. In accordance with this theme, the texts we used for the teacher read-aloud, the Book Club discussion book, and the students' guided reading were autobiographical and featured high-quality, authentic multicultural literature. We hoped to help children make connections to their own personal experiences, expand their horizons, and expose them to ethnic groups, cultures, and experiences different from their own as they read texts written by authors describing their lives. Galda (1998) suggests that literature is both a mirror and a window. The stories told within books mirror who we are: our hopes, dreams, emotions, and cultural practices, and the ways we interact with each other and with our world. But literature is also a window, taking us to times and places and introducing us to people whom we may never otherwise encounter.

These texts were used within the Book Club *Plus* curriculum framework (see Raphael, Florio-Ruane, & George, 2001, and Raphael, Florio-Ruane, Kehus, et al., 2001, for a description of the framework and of teaching specific literacy concepts). Book Club *Plus* is based on the theory that language and literacy skills are learned in socially interactive settings that allow children to play with language and take risks. The framework provides an instructional format of discussion-based learning—some teacher led, some student led; some whole class, some small group. The ELL (English Language Learners) students had many opportunities to try out their new language in small-group situations such as book clubs, guided reading groups, and collaborative projects. For example, during one guided reading group, Luis became very excited when he initially opened the book *Family Pictures*, by Carmen Lomas Garza (1990): The text is written in both English and Spanish. "Would you like me to read it in Spanish?" he excitedly asked the small group. He then proceeded to read each page for us, trying to explain as best he could the relationship of the words to the illustrations. He then followed along as we read the English text, stopping us at key points to say the word in Spanish for us (from Teacher Research Journal, 1/6/00). This was the beginning of Luis's becoming an engaged reader: He seemed to value reading, and he clearly saw his home language as "cultural capital" (Bourdieu & Passeron, 1977, p. 30) that enabled him to make meaningful contributions to his teacher's and his peers' literacy learning and meaning making.

The Book Club *Plus* framework also provides extensive opportunity for students to engage in writing in support of their learning. Writing activities within the Stories of Self unit, like those in the entire framework, related to the theme and supported the inquiry of the unit. By ensuring that a variety of materials and methods adequately reflected the students' backgrounds and lives outside of school, we hoped to help our ELL students make the social, cultural, and linguistic transition to the English-speaking classroom. Narrative played a vital role in helping with this transition. The use of narrative as a means by which students come to understand their world has been written about extensively. Dewey (1902) asserted that the greatest asset in a student's possession—the greatest, moreover, that ever will be in his or her possession—is his or her own direct and personal experience. Stories, he writes, provide "life informing and life transforming" possibilities.

The sharing of narrative—life experiences or personal and family histories—can serve as a basic source for subsequent learning and sharing. Shared human experiences connect the past with the present and future. They help connect life experiences with ethnic heritage, and ultimately with the history of the world. Narrative can engender personal pride in family history—in a family's struggles and accomplishments. Stories endow experience with meaning, provide culturally shaped ways of organizing that experience, and reflect prevailing theories about the "possible lives" and "possible selves" in our culture (Rogers & Soter, 1997, p. 4). "Learning and thinking are always situated in a cultural setting and always dependent upon the utilization of cultural resources," writes Bruner (1996). Helping children transform these cultural products—stories—into cultural resources enables them to explore and express cultural differences in the classroom social network. And it is in experiencing differences that we discover ourselves as I's and you's (Freire, 1998).

We additionally emphasized narrative by asking students to create personal vignettes. These vignettes gave ELL students an opportunity to connect outside experiences with the formal curriculum. Some of the vignettes were prompted by artifacts, which were introduced in a shared reading of *The World of William Joyce Scrapbook* (Joyce, 1997). After the shared reading, children were asked to bring in an artifact that would reveal something important about them. Other writing involved creating a timeline of milestone events, one for each year of the child's life. Students worked with their parents to create the timeline, students then took turns presenting their life stories to their peers—adding to their sense of belonging to a community in which it is safe to tell their story. Many students attached photos, ribbons, awards, event tickets, and mementos (personal artifacts) to their timeline.

Home-school connection activities connected to students' writing became important vehicles for building meaningful bridges between home and school experiences. Furthermore, through some of their presentations, students began to make concrete the abstract concept of culture. And some have argued that the concept of culture is "the only means by which children can organize data about human behavior in contextual settings and develop an understanding of how and why groups of people differ from one another in their customs, habits, and traditions" (Soldier, 1989, p. 88). Such understandings help children make nonjudgmental, objective, cross-cultural comparisons.

The reading and, particularly, the writing activities pushed students' learning beyond school and unit boundaries. By legitimizing their voice and visibility through personal response, discussion, and writing, we empower all our students. By grounding these activities in stories of their own lives, we help students to see the importance of their own stories, and we set the stage for children to think about how each of their stories is grounded in those of their families (see Coppola, chapter 8, and Boyd-Batstone, chapter 14, in this volume).

Family Stories

From studying themselves as individuals, students moved on to considering their histories in terms of Family Stories. To make the concept of family stories visible, the unit featured books by and an author study of Patricia Polacco. Her books were chosen not only because she is a prolific author from our home state of Michigan, but also because all her stories are based on family events. Polacco draws from her rich, diverse family heritage—one branch of the family lived for generations as Michigan farmers, the other emigrated from Russia in the early 20th century—to create high-interest, engaging texts that include characters from diverse backgrounds. These family stories and histories are in turn grounded in cultural stories and histories. Thus, this strong, literature-based, literacy curriculum supports not only children's literacy learning, but their deepening understanding of culture.

The absence of stories of culture inside classrooms has limited what both teachers and educators can know, in Rogers and Soter's words, about "how children actually draw on the life-informing possibilities of narrative—or the nature of the personal and social understandings that children acquire as they transact with stories in the classroom" (Rogers & Soter, 1997, p. 4). Absent that element, calling for greater parent participation, community involvement, or curricular relevance is an empty gesture. We need to change both our texts and our contexts to encourage the use of the narrative and its role in learning about literacy and culture in our classrooms. Bruner states in this regard that "human learning is best when it is participatory, proactive, communal, collaborative, and given over to constructing meanings rather than receiving them" (Bruner, 1996, p. 84).

Polacco's books provided fertile ground for children to make personal connections between text and their own lives, and to involve their families in this discovery. We saw these connections in students' reading log entries as well as their discussions of text. For example, in her reading log response to *Picnic at Mudsock Meadow* (Polacco, 1992), Rita wrote, "If I was Waliam I wuld go away so I wont get in trouble and I will bring a luck coin and I wuld stay home but I was really him I would play something else" (2/21/00). Rita places herself in the context of the story, providing two alternatives to William's behavior. After listening to a teacher read-aloud of Polacco's (1994) autobiography, Cara connects two ideas—grandparents and storytelling—to her own family: "I called my grandma 'Grandy' not Babushka. She used to tell me stories but she called them Getting Warm Stories because they make you feel good inside."

Similar personal connections emerged as we listened to students' Book Club discussions. In a discussion of *Chicken Sunday* (Polacco, 1992), a student remarked, "My dad travels to lots of different places. He brings back eggs like that for us. But he just calls them 'P' eggs because he can't remember the word Pysansky" (2/22/00). In a subsequent whole-group discussion that day, students began to share other family events of which they were reminded by the book, with some students making explicit links to traditions in their native countries. For example, Angie described how "in the Philippines I liked Sundays because it was game day. We would walk to our neighbors' place and take out our sacrifices. My aunt would put money, candy, toys, and stuff like that...."

Throughout the study of Family Stories, students drew connections between the family activities in the stories and those in their own lives. It is interesting and perhaps noteworthy, however, that they tended to key in on events in the story and the memories they prompted of their own lives, rather than unpacking aspects of culture. Yet, from these connections, we can see the beginnings of their attention to similarities and differences in personal and family activities and settings.

The children's work in the Family Stories unit established a firm base for the explicit study of culture through exploring how their own and their family's stories grew out of their cultural heritage—and how literature represents many such stories of culture.

Stories of Culture

Because one of our research questions involved examining students' growing understandings of culture, we began the Stories of Culture unit by re-asking the question we had raised in September, "What is culture?" Using the context of a K-W-L lesson (Ogle, 1986), MariAnne pointed out a large sheet of yellow paper covering the front board. Students, familiar with the format, responded to her question by brainstorming ideas and categories of concepts that they believed related to culture. The first responses described their own backgrounds, perhaps because of their ongoing focus on self and family:

Mando: I'm of the Mexican culture because my mom and dad were born in Mexico.

Lana: I'm Philippine because my mom and dad were born in the Philippines.

For the next five minutes, students each described their heritage in terms of their ethnic histories (sometimes mentioning a single country, sometimes mentioning multiple ones). Students then identified many of the features of culture often described in social studies texts, including dress, hair, language, and foods. Starting with this relatively simple view, the children kept digging more deeply, trying to get a handle on this complex idea.

It is not surprising that these students faced challenges when trying to explain culture, because the term has a wide range of everyday and technical uses, conjures up all sorts of images, and has diverse connotations (Florio-Ruane with deTar, 2001; Lankshear, 1997). Culture can mean different things to different people in different contexts, and we cannot assume a common, unitary definition: It can be a *what* (content or product), a *how* (the process by which content or product is created and transformed), or a *who* (the agents responsible for creating and changing content or product) (Nieto, 1999). Culture can refer to artifacts, to ethnic or racial identity, to sophistication or class, or to otherness or difference. Culture can be associated with material objects, with visible displays (such as dress, or dances, festivals, and the like), or with other trappings, such as skin color or language or dialect—the objective or visible aspects of culture (Philips, 1983). Culture can be the components of the subjective or invisible aspects of a society: attitudes, values, norms of behavior, and social roles (Geertz, 1983). Culture can mean generating and circulating meaning, the process by which meaning is made and shared, the outcome of thought, the actions or creations of humans in a society, or the way people interact—essentially what ordinary people do every day (Bruner, 1996; Cole, 1996; Erickson, 1986).

We can see that many people have an interest in the technical meaning of culture. Moreover, the concept is also in the domain of folk wisdom (Bruner, 1996), as people make and use culture in their everyday lives, often with little conscious reflection. In schools and in classrooms, we see culture as both the everyday ways of being that come together inside one mandatory setting, and as the explicit and conscious study of these as part of formal education and the creation of a particular kind of cultural setting for learning—the classroom learning community (Rogoff, 1990; Schwab, 1976).

Over the course of generating what they knew about culture, the children in MariAnne's classroom began to raise questions that conveyed their grappling with more abstract ideas (for example, culture is both dynamic and complex; culture is built on traditions; culture reflects values; cultures come into contact with one another; there are cultures other than those based in ethnic traditions). In the next phase of the K-W-L lesson, MariAnne asked students to formulate questions to guide their upcoming study. Students generated questions that illustrated the depth of their thinking: How do cultures start? Do cultures end? Can you be in more than one culture? Can you join another culture? Where did the word *culture* come from? These questions and ideas stood in marked contrast to students' incoming understandings of culture as a set of physical features, differentiated only according to ethnic heritage.

The texts with which students engaged in this unit featured culture in prominent ways, with the emphasis on the cultural bases for family stories. Similarly, the texts they read involved family stories that conveyed important aspects of culture. Their Book Club book, *Molly's Pilgrim* (Cohen, 1983), conveys the immigrant experience through the eyes of the protagonist, who is adjusting to a new country, language, and set of customs. Teacher read-alouds included books such as Say's (1993) *Grandfather's Journey*, another tale of immigration and adjustment.

From videotapes of students' presentations, pictures of their artifacts, and MariAnne's teacher research journal, we can see how students proudly conveyed traditions associated with their ethnic backgrounds and also made meaningful connections across cultures. Miguel focused on the holiday Cinco de Mayo, celebrated by his family here and in Mexico; Nami, who is from Japan and would return there at the end of the school year, suggested it is a lot like Boy's Day in her native country. The following excerpt is from MariAnne's journal (3/30/00):

> Miguel started with the story of the French Army coming to Puebla, Mexico and the war on May 5th. Mexicans celebrate the 5th of May. He points out where Mexico is on a map of North America. We call it Cinco de Mayo since it's like a National Holiday. The teacher asks him to describe what they do on Cinco de Mayo. He describes carrying flags, mom dressing in costume, singing, dancing. "My family always has fun." Nami adds, "I think it is like Boy's Day in Japan."

Miguel conveyed a sense of place using the map in the room; detailed the importance of the holiday as a national event; and went beyond his planned presentation when MariAnne prompted him to do so.

Argen looked into his family's history to create a story that conveys the importance of honor within his culture and within his family. The following excerpt is from MariAnne's journal (4/13/00):

> Argen sets up his display before starting. He has a family picture depicting four generations. A large poster board is hung on which Argen has drawn his storyboard. A small chest is on the table. Argen begins his story pointing to

the pictures on the storyboard. "My great grandfather lived near New Delhi, India. He was digging in the back yard one day when he came upon a small chest of money...."

Argen then described how, in the time before his great grandfather lived, there were no banks, and people buried their family treasures. When his great grandfather dug up the treasure, he could have secretly kept it and used it for his family. Instead, he took the treasure to the village leader, because it was not his treasure to keep. Because he had been so honest, he became an honored and revered person in the community, and his family has held this honored status over time. Argen's decision to present this story conveyed a deep appreciation for how his cultural background is reflected in his current values and helps shape the way he thinks and acts.

Our third example conveys the importance of participation with respect to membership in the classroom as a community. Sasha had recently moved from Quebec and spoke very little English. Yet, having observed a few days of family stories, she wanted to be part of the presentations. The following excerpt is from MariAnne's journal (4/11/00):

> Sasha's mother could write some English, so she helped Sasha put together a display board and write out short sentences for each picture. Sasha's grandfather had played for the New York Yankees, so she knew she had an exciting and engaging story to share. When Sasha presented, I helped her with her English wording, and she was very proud to have been able to tell her story.

Sasha's story demonstrated how quickly she was able to determine what would make her visible and important to her classmates. Observing the other students share their stories, furthermore, gave her confidence to participate earlier than she might otherwise have participated as a new student, one who was not comfortable with the language. As a whole, the family stories helped children to know and praise their own and one another's cultural heritages. Not only did they seek out ways in which they were alike; they closely examined differences and celebrated these differences, rather than avoiding them or seeing difference as grounds for teasing.

These ideas arose in their book clubs as well. Because *Molly's Pilgrim* was written at grade level, students unable to read it independently had access to the text by reading with a buddy or with adult support. A prominent event in the story occurs when the title character is teased at school because she speaks "broken" English and does not dress like the other children. This particular story, with its account of a clash of cultural differences, had an impact on all the class. Students' reading logs from that particular day revealed how little patience they had for the behavior of the children who were teasing Molly, and their belief that the teacher should have been more protective (4/28/00):

- Molly's mom said that everybody who comes from a different country is a pilgrim. Molly's mom was right because everybody has a different culture from a different country.
- I likt the part when ho motter went to school mif Molly and tray to tell the ticher thet the kits sott stop lauving to Molly. Not nice.
- Molly is sade becasu pippols make funne have her.
- Molly is not god feeling. I like the book she is a got rater and she used other Language and other words. Her mom wand to go to school and take with the Teacher the asher girls are teasing. She rote a letter it says Jolly Molly, Your Eyes are awf'ly small. Jolly Molly, your nose is awf'ly tall.

In our ending discussion of the book, one student asked, "Why didn't the teacher stop the teasing?" Many others joined in, angry that the teacher had not stepped in to protect Molly and punish the other girls. After a few minutes more of discussion, one student summed it up best: "They just didn't understand; she was part of her old culture, caught in a new culture!"

Through their writing and discussion, students revealed a deepening concept of culture as it is reflected in their own lives and as it affects others' behavior. A culminating activity involved each child in designing a quilt square that conveyed his or her cultural heritage and that would become part of a classroom community quilt. The quilt would convey the multiple ways that cultures are represented along with the dynamic nature of culture: cultures intersect, and new cultures evolve from contact as well as conflict.

The children were encouraged to represent themselves pictorially. Laura had a drawing of herself in the center of her square, wearing a T-shirt with a large U.S. flag. Her arms were outstretched and in her hands were flags representing the countries of her heritage: Germany, Poland, Norway, and Ireland. Mia's square had her name in Chinese, pictures of native toys, a drawing of China, coins that were glued on, and a drawing of a bowl of rice, with a broken toothpick representing chopsticks. Erich chose to use actual artifacts on his square: coins from Germany, a small empty candy box, a label from a beer bottle, a small fabric flag, and a picture of the German coat of arms.

The quilt squares were assembled and the quilt was hung in the classroom in order to honor each child's own culture as well as the classroom community's diverse cultural heritage. The children had come to understand certain core principles about culture: Cultures borrow from one another;

cultures are learned; cultures are shared. We learn from one another through borrowing and sharing, and acquire ways of doing things from others that enhance our lives. When we add to our own culture, we do not take away from that culture but, rather, enrich it.

Principles for Teaching Literacy and Diversity

Principles about culture can be just mere words if taught mostly to be restated as evidence of tolerance of diversity or as themes in school celebrations of diversity (such as Black History Month or Women's History Month). It remains a great challenge to figure out how, in Dewey's (1938) terms, these principles can be experienced by students, be they young children or college students, in authentic school-based activities (see, for example, Chavez & O'Donnell, 1998). Though the importance of cultural knowledge to learning has been well documented, little has been studied and written about *how* children go about constructing their cultural knowledge, understanding their own cultural identity, and building cultural awareness. What we know, instead, is the extent to which ordinary classrooms privilege a "mainstream" culture reflective of so-called mainstream Caucasian, middle-class values. Little room is available inside the ordinary classroom for exploration of either that mainstream culture or the cultural identities screened out by it. By understanding how the teacher, the classroom context, and the curriculum support children in their construction of culture, a set of principles emerges that helps us guide our English learners toward reaching the highest possible level of English literacy—thus achieving education that enables all individuals to come into full possession of all their powers (Dewey, 1902). We have identified four principles that we believe are core with regard to teaching for literacy and diversity.

PRINCIPLE #1. CULTURE IS BOTH WEB AND WEAVING.   All children construct their knowledge through cultural lenses that reflect their cultural and economic backgrounds. However, according to Cushner, McClelland, and Safford (1992), "Culture is a secret" (p. 79). They state that learning about culture is made more difficult because most people generally know very little about themselves. Few people receive formal training about how to be a member of a culture; they learn through experience, through observing others, through trial and error, and through continuous reinforcement. For teachers then, the task of making the student's culture visible becomes a challenge.

The Our Storied Lives theme brought culture to the forefront. Focusing first on stories of self, students were able to draw upon the area in which they were experts—themselves. They saw culture as part of their own personal identities, a lived experience with the "everydayness" that members of a community take for granted. Yet, juxtaposing—in the literature and face to face—a variety of such "everydaynesses," they began to see that cultures differ, not according to individual idiosyncrasy, but systematically and by group. Stories of family, in particular the Patricia Polacco author study, showed families from within and without the U.S. mainstream. Students could see what holds a given family group together, how that may differ from what binds other family groups, and how family groups of all kinds share some fundamental characteristics.

This transition from family to *families*—from one's here and now to what has happened before, what might happen in the future, and how the cultural practices we take for granted are changing every day—gave culture its final due. The literature read and the types of activities carried out (e.g., Tell Me About Yourself prompts, timelines, personal artifacts, journal writing, home-school connection activities) made learning encounters more relevant and effective for MariAnne's ELL students. Drawing on children's cultural knowledge, prior experiences, and frames of reference helped create a classroom environment wherein teaching, learning, and culture became inseparable. The discussions, types of questions, and teacher scaffolding gave MariAnne the opportunity to build bridges between the cultural experiences of her ethnically diverse students, those of mainstream students, and the curriculum content. As students developed a personal connection with their teacher, they felt empowered by knowing that their voice and visibility were legitimized. They began to take risks to push their literacy development.

MariAnne also became aware of the importance of understanding her own culture and how it affected her classroom practices. She noted in her teacher research journal,

> This has become as much a learning experience and journey into self for me as for the children. It's strange how many times I've caught myself and asked, Why am I doing this? Is this a valid and useful practice for all children OR is this just an established classroom practice I've done over time? (1/31/00)

If we experience culture as webs of significance that we ourselves weave (paraphrased from Weber, cited in Geertz, 1983), then those webs can ensnare us, cutting us off from change in our own lives or from engagement with other webs being woven (Florio-Ruane, 2002b). Yet we also discover, as we study storied lives, that our webs are interconnected—linking one meaning system to another, facilitating contact rather than isolation (Anderson-Levitt, 2002). Viewed this way, culture is both the web and the weaving, and our capacity to undertake and understand multiple weavings attests to multiculturalism in our time is what Goodenough (1976) called "the human experience" (p. 4).

It is probably not surprising that this kind of complexity is the stuff of discussion and inquiry among contemporary cultural anthropologists. But more exciting—and perhaps more important—it is also the stuff of discussion and inquiry in MariAnne's third-grade classroom.

PRINCIPLE #2. STUDENTS AND TEACHERS—AND THEIR OWN STORIES—ARE PRIMARY RESOURCES. Curriculum that is responsive to the needs of all children in our schools and seeks the betterment of society has diversity or pluralism at its center. The emphasis is on basic understandings and generalizations about human beings rather than on goals and objectives related to desired changes in student behavior. The knowledge is accessible to students and connected to their lives and experiences outside of school. Learning is the process of integrating and connecting who we are with what we know. Instruction needs to connect culture, the curriculum, and learning, while bearing in mind that children come to us with differences in background knowledge, home and community experiences, and understandings about the functions of literacy.

The curricular framework based on the theme of Our Storied Lives offers both age-appropriate and ability-level texts as well as authentic writing and oral language activities (Raphael, Florio-Ruane, Kehus, et al., 2001). Opportunities for all students to actively engage and participate are seen in examples such as Nels's literature log entries, Mando's letter to Patricia Polacco, and Sasha's family story. In our efforts, narrative plays a significant role both as content (i.e., the stories we read, hear, and tell about culture) and as a way of thinking and representing knowledge to oneself and others (Bruner, 1996). This sharing of narrative (life experiences, personal and family histories) serves as a basic source for subsequent learning and sharing.

According to Bennett-Armistead,

> in addition to giving a teacher a look into the window of the child's self perception, narrative offers the child the opportunity to construct his own understandings of his culture and the world in general, as well as his place in it. (personal communication, 6/24/00)

Erickson (1997) has suggested that students and teachers be used as primary resources in the curriculum, critically examining their own autobiographies so they will approach culture not as a fixed or static state of being, but rather as socially constructed and changing. Critical examination is key here, lest storytelling merely reinforce extant knowledge and beliefs or reproduce "master cultural narratives" (Gee, 1992, p. 76) that both oversimplify and stereotype. Thus the construction and deconstruction of one's own stories help students and teachers develop a critical stance about their own and other people's culture and histories. "Skill in narrative construction and narrative understanding is crucial to constructing our lives and a 'place' for ourselves in the possible world we will encounter" (Bruner, 1996, p. 40).

Not all classrooms invite narrative (see, for example, Applebee, 1990; Rosen, 1987). In fact, in Egan's (1997) assessment,

> too often, literacy is taught without much regard for the richness of children's oral-culture background. With this in mind, the educational task becomes a matter of not ignoring or even suppressing those oral tools, but of stimulating and developing them in the first place, and then of introducing literacy and its associated intellectual tools in coordination with the oral. (p. 183)

In a sense, therefore, the Our Storied Lives approach to curriculum and instruction is itself countercultural. For better or worse, we know from research that the norms in a classroom are reflexively created in the relationships that occur among learners and teacher. To change one is to change the other.

PRINCIPLE #3. GOOD MULTICULTURAL LITERATURE ENABLES STUDENTS TO KNOW THEMSELVES AND OTHERS.   It is essential for children of all races and ethnicities to find books in which they see a wide variety of accurate portrayals of their own diverse cultures, histories, and everyday lives—books in which they can find and identify themselves. Angie, in her reading log entry about *Molly's Pilgrim*, demonstrated such connections as she drew from her knowledge of school, identified with her response to school (i.e., "doesn't cry"), and related personally to her pleasure at having teacher support:

> My prediction is that Molly's teacher is going to teach her and she is going to like school and she will make friends. My favorite part is that she doesn't cry at school. My favorite character is the teacher because she doesn not make fun of Molly. Sometimes a book makes me feel great to read it. (4/12/00)

Multicultural literature helps children explore universal topics and themes within the unique contexts of different cultures and peoples, while also presenting culture-specific perspectives and experiences. Children develop a heightened understanding of differences, yet also see common cultural connections in the form of underlying emotions, values, and needs.

The multicultural literature used throughout Our Storied Lives provided a rich base on which children could build their developing sense of culture. Personal and cultural knowledge was invited and engaged during ongoing classroom discourse about studied texts (through shared reading, guided reading, and book clubs). Children learned that making connections between the books used in school and the experiences of their personal and community lives was both valued by their teacher and essential to their learning. Classroom discussions on cultural issues helped not only in the development of the children's own cultural identity but also in the revising of their notions of cultural "others." The multicultural texts used in conjunction with discussion-based learning helped MariAnne's students move beyond just an understanding of the "4 F's of culture"—food, fashion, festivals, and folklore (Diamond & Moore, 1995, p. x); their understanding became more probing and complex, as evidenced by the questions they raised in their K-W-L chart (How do cultures start? Can you be in more than one culture? Can cultures change? Can you join another culture?). As Banks (1995) confirms, learning about different cultures and other aspects of diversity is an essential ingredient in learning to respect and value diversity.

PRINCIPLE #4. SCHOOLS AND CLASSROOMS SHOULD BE LABORATORIES OF MULTI-CULTURALISM. Learning occurs in the community of others (Dewey, 1902), and understanding the cultural dimensions of learning is essential for effective teaching (Hollins, 1996). In particular, understanding how children make sense of the abstract idea of culture and use this understanding to explore and construct their past, present, and future selves is especially important in today's educational settings. Children need opportunities to interact with others, to share their knowledge, and to extend their appreciation and understanding of others' cultures and experiences.

Above all, many opportunities must be provided for students to construct their own knowledge. There is evidence that when cultural literacy and social organization patterns are reflected in classroom practices, student participation and enthusiasm increases and school achievement improves (Au, 1980; Au & Jordan, 1981). In making culture visible to students and to themselves, literacy educators enable the school to be a place where culture is taken into account in ways that support the learning of all and where children can become culturally as well as academically competent.

All human beings have and make culture, and culture is reflected in people's communities—in everyday activities, relationships, and social processes. It is culture that provides the tools for organizing and understanding our world in meaningful and expressive ways. Culture both forms and makes possible the workings of a distinctly human mind (Bruner, 1996): "Mind creates culture, [and] culture also creates mind" (p. 166). Erickson (1997) probably states it most succinctly, "Culture can be thought of as a construction—it constructs us and we construct it" (p. 39).

Our schools are cultural institutions that can embrace or reject the diversity of cultures that surround them. Teachers are challenged to meet the traditional purposes of schooling: inculcating academic learning, passing on economic knowledge, and enabling the development of informed minds suitable for citizenship in a pluralistic democracy. In the process of meeting these purposes, we are compelled to look at our students closely and to be aware of their cultural knowledge, which influences how they view the world and ultimately how they respond to schooling; we are, after all, neither only what we inherit nor only what we acquire, but, instead, stem from the dynamic relationship between what we inherit and what we acquire (Freire, 1998). We must affirm and acknowledge students' cultural backgrounds, help them to develop positive self-images, and facilitate their ability to construct their own meanings from what they read and write (Delpit, 1995). In order for children in a pluralistic society to engage in and become part of the democratic process, they need to see themselves reflected within that process—to see themselves as part of the whole.

A good classroom climate is one in which all students feel they have the right to learn; are important and worthy; and have good ideas, significant experiences, valued insights, and talents to bring to their learning (Schwab, 1976). If a classroom functions this way, it can offer students opportunities to practice democratic learning.

Classrooms in which all voices are celebrated help children become more aware and appreciative of their individual culture and heritage, be open to the cultural ideas shared by others, and appreciate what other cultures have contributed to our country. Until we appreciate the wonders of the cultures represented before us, we cannot appreciate the potential of those who sit before us, nor can we begin to link students' histories and worlds to the subject matter we present in the classroom (Delpit, 1995). Examining ways in which classrooms can be inclusive so everyone belongs, everyone can be successful, and everyone is respected and valued will lead to the creation of an empowered student culture.

Conclusions

By means of conducting our own research and reviewing the research of others, we learned about the importance of teachers' awareness of their own thoughts about culture and of how they respond from their own cultural experiences to those who are from other cultural backgrounds (Florio-Ruane, 1997; Florio-Ruane, Raphael, Glazier, McVee, & Wallace, 1997; McVee, 1999). We know that teachers who are aware of their own thoughts and behaviors in cross-cultural interactions are better prepared to respond in ways that will improve teaching and learning (Au, 1980). This is important for several reasons. First, teachers are gatekeepers who are tremendously significant and powerful individuals in the lives of their students (Hollins & Spencer, 1990). Second, teachers serve as cultural accommodators and mediators—fundamental in promoting student learning (Diamond & Moore, 1995; Nieto, 1999). Third, teachers are important in identifying and creating meaningful ways to bridge the diverse backgrounds of their students in the construction of a classroom culture (Erickson, 1997). Fourth, for better or worse, teachers are agents of the educational meritocracy. As such, teachers need to build on what children do and do not bring to school with them as "cultural capital"—the resources that enable school success and its rewards.

In addition, teachers can be instrumental in recognizing as part of children's cultural capital those funds of knowledge (Moll, 1992) in their homes and communities which, though not ordinarily privileged in school, can be made valuable in school learning and inside the classroom community (Nieto, 1999). Finally, teachers are professionals and practitioners. As such they must be able to identify and evaluate the research perspectives used in the development of curriculum—instructional content, methods, and assessment—so that they reflect the multicultural perspectives of the diverse population they serve (Banks, 1995).

> Learning how to live and teach through diversity, including the inevitable struggles and contradictions, seems especially important. The sense of embracing diversity is developed through ongoing opportunities for personal interactions and transactions with people and contexts that are diverse in traditions, beliefs, language, and thought. Thus, becoming a literate teacher, in relation to diversity, means doing more than writing and reading *about* culture—it means learning to *be* diverse in perspectives, skills, and knowledge. It means understanding, influencing, and participating in the lives of diverse students, schools, and the wider society. —C.B. Dillard, 1997

Author Note

This project was supported, in part, under the Educational Research and Development Centers Program, PR/Award Number R305R70004 to the Center for the Improvement of Early Reading Achievement (CIERA), as administered by the Office of Educational Research and Improvement, U.S. Department of Education.

REFERENCES

Anderson-Levitt, K.M. (2002). *Teaching cultures: Knowledge of teaching first grade in France and the United States*. Cresskill, NJ: Hampton Press.

Applebee, A.N. (1990). *Literature instruction in American schools* (Report Series 1.4). Albany, NY: Center for the Learning and Teaching of Literature, State University of New York at Albany.

Au, K.H. (1980). Participation structures in a reading lesson with Hawaiian children: Analysis of a culturally appropriate and instructional event. *Anthropology and Education, 11*, 170–180.

Au, K.H., & Jordan, C. (1981). Teaching reading to Hawaiian children: Finding a culturally appropriate solution. In E.T. Trueba, G.P. Guthrie, & K.H. Au (Eds.), *Culture and the bilingual classroom: Studies in classroom ethnography* (pp. 139–152). Rowley, MA: Newbury House.

Banks, J. (1995). *Handbook of research on multicultural education*. New York: Simon & Schuster.

Berne, J.I. (2001). *Connected teacher learning: An examination of a teacher learning network*. Unpublished doctoral dissertation. Michigan State, East Lansing, MI.

Bourdieu, P., & Passeron, J.C. (1977). *Reproduction in education, society and culture* (R. Nice, Trans.). London: Sage.

Bruner, J. (1996). *The culture of education*. Cambridge, MA: Harvard University Press.

Chavez, R.C., & O'Donnell, J. (Eds.). (1998). *Speaking the unpleasant: The politics of (non)engagement in the multicultural education terrain*. Albany, NY: State University of New York Press.

Cole, M. (1996). *Cultural psychology: A once and future discipline*. Cambridge, MA: The Belnap Press of Harvard University Press.

Cushner K.H., McClelland, A., & Safford, P. (1992). *Human diversity in education: An integrative approach*. New York: McGraw Hill.

Delpit, L.D. (1995). *Other people's children: Cultural conflict in the classroom*. New York: New Press.

Dewey, J. (1902). *The child and the curriculum*. Chicago, IL: University of Chicago Press.

Dewey, J. (1938). *Experience and education*. New York: Collier.

Diamond, B., & Moore, M. (1995). *Multicultural literacy: Mirroring the reality of the classroom*. White Plains, NY: Longman.

Dillard, C.B. (1997). Placing student language, literacy, and culture at the center of teacher education reform. In J.E. King, E.R. Hollins, & W.C. Hayman (Eds.), *Preparing teachers for cultural diversity* (pp. 85–96). New York: Teachers College Press.

Egan, K. (1997). *The educated mind: How cognitive tools shape our understanding*. Chicago: University of Chicago Press.

Erickson, F. (1986). Voices, genres, writers, and audiences for the "Anthropology and Education Quarterly." *Anthropology and Education Quarterly, 17*(1), 3–5.

Erickson, F. (1997). Culture in society and in educational practices. In J. Banks & C. McGee-Banks (Eds.), *Multicultural education: Issues and perspectives* (3rd ed., pp. 32–60). Boston: Allyn & Bacon.

Farley, R., Danziger, S., & Holzer, H.J. (2000). *Detroit divided: A volume in the multi-city study of urban inequality*. New York: Russell Sage Foundation.

Florio-Ruane, S. (1997). Discovering culture in discussion of autobiographical literature: Transforming the education of literacy teachers. In C.K. Kinzer, K.A. Hinchman, & D.J. Leu

(Eds.), *Inquiries into literacy theory and practice* (46th yearbook of the National Reading Conference, pp. 452–464). Chicago: National Reading Conference.

Florio-Ruane, S. (2002a). How culture matters. Introduction to K.M. Anderson-Levitt, *Teaching cultures: Knowledge of teaching first grade in France and the United States*. Cresskill, NJ: Hampton Press.

Florio-Ruane, S. (2002b). More light: An argument for complexity in research on teaching and teacher education. *Journal of Teacher Education, 53*(3), 206–217.

Florio-Ruane, S., with deTar, J. (2001). *Teacher education and the cultural imagination: Autobiography, conversation, and narrative*. Mahwah, NJ: Erlbaum.

Florio-Ruane, S., & Raphael, T.E. (2001). Reading lives: Creating and sustaining learning about culture and literacy education in teacher study groups. In C.M. Clark (Ed.), *Talking shop: Authentic conversation and teacher learning* (pp. 64–81). New York: Teachers College Press.

Florio-Ruane, S., Raphael, T.E., Glazier, J., McVee, M.B., & Wallace, S. (1997). Discovering culture in discussions of autobiographical literature: Transforming the education of literacy teachers. In C.K. Kinzer, K.A. Hinchman, & D.J. Leu (Eds.), *Inquiries into literacy theory and practice* (46th yearbook of the National Reading Conference, pp. 452–464). Chicago: National Reading Conference.

Freire, P. (1998). *Teachers as cultural workers: Letters to those who dare teach* (D. Macedo, D. Koike, & A. Oliveira, Trans.). Boulder, CO: Westview.

Galda, L. (1998). Mirrors and windows: Reading as transformation. In T.E. Raphael & K.H. Au (Eds.), *Literature-based instruction: Reshaping the curriculum* (pp. 1–10). Norwood, MA: Christopher Gordon.

Gavelek, J., & Raphael, T.E. (1996). Changing talk about text: New roles for teachers and students. *Language Arts, 73*, 24–34.

Gee, J.P. (1992). *The social mind: Language, ideology, and social practice*. New York: Bergin & Garvey.

Geertz, C. (1983). *Local knowledge: Further essays in interpretive anthropology*. New York: Basic Books.

Goodenough, W.H. (1976). Multi-culturalism as the normal human experience. *Anthropology and Education Newsletter, 7*(4), 4–7.

Hollins, E.R. (1996). *Culture in school learning: Revealing the deep meaning*. Mahwah, NJ: Erlbaum.

Hollins, E.R., & Spencer, K. (1990). Restructuring schools for cultural inclusion: Changing the schooling process for African American youngsters. *Journal of Education, 172*(2), 89–100.

Lankshear, C. (1997). *Changing literacies*. Philadelphia: Open University Press.

McVee, M.B. (1999). Narrative and the exploration of culture, self, and other in teachers' book club discussion groups (Doctoral dissertation, Michigan State University, 1999). *Dissertation Abstracts International, 60*(10), 3634.

Moll, L.C. (1992). Bilingual classroom studies and community analysis: Some recent trends. *Educational Researcher, 21*(2), 20–24.

Nieto, S. (1999). *The light in their eyes: Creating multicultural learning communities*. New York: Teachers College Press.

Ogle, D. (1986). K-W-L: A teaching model that develops active reading of expository text. *The Reading Teacher, 39*, 564–570.

Philips, S.U. (1983). *The invisible culture: Communication in classroom and community on Warm Springs Indian Reservation*. New York: Longman.

Raphael, T.E., Florio-Ruane, S., & George, M. (2001). Book Club *Plus*: A conceptual framework to organize literacy instruction. *Language Arts*, *79*(2), 159–168.

Raphael, T.E., Florio-Ruane, S., Kehus, M., George, M., Hasty, N., & Highfield, K. (2001). Thinking for ourselves: Literacy learning in a diverse teacher inquiry network. *The Reading Teacher*, *54*, 596–607.

Rogers, T., & Soter, A.O. (1997). *Reading across cultures: Teaching literature in a diverse society*. New York: Teachers College Press.

Rogoff, B. (1990). *Apprenticeship in thinking: Cognitive development in social context*. New York: Oxford University Press.

Rosen, H. (1987). *Stories and meanings*. Sheffield, UK: National Association for the Teaching of English.

Schwab, J. (1976). Education and the state: Learning community. In *Great ideas today, 1995* (pp. 234–271). Chicago: Encyclopedia Britannica.

Soldier, L.M. (1989, winter). Children as cultural anthropologists. *Childhood Education*, pp. 88–92.

Sugrue, T.J. (1998). *The origins of the urban crisis: Race and inequality in postwar Detroit*. Princeton: Princeton University Press.

LITERATURE CITED

Cohen, B. (1983). *Molly's pilgrim*. New York: Morrow.

Garza, C.L. (1990). *Family pictures*. San Francisco: Children's Book Press.

Joyce, W. (1997). *The world of William Joyce scrapbook*. New York: HarperCollins.

Polacco, P. (1992). *Chicken Sunday*. New York: Philomel Books

Polacco, P. (1992). *Picnic at Mudsock Meadow*. New York: Putnam.

Polacco, P. (1994). *Firetalking*. Katonah, NY: Owen Publishing.

Say, A. (1993). *Grandfather's journey*. New York: Scholastic.

CHAPTER 14

Reading With a Hero: A Mediated and Literate Experience

Paul Boyd-Batstone

O n a springtime Saturday afternoon, I was sitting at the edge of a soccer field watching one of my fifth-grade students play goalie for a city league team. I was observing sandy-haired Josue, called "Güero" (blondie) by family and friends, in order to examine the contextual factors that influenced the ways he experienced reading literature. I wanted to see how cultural funds of knowledge appeared in my students' reader responses. This particular case study brought me to a soccer game—a significant part of Josue's life.

Josue stood in the goalie's box waiting, poised to defend his goal. His wiry, athletic build barely filled out his baggy goalie's uniform. His oversized gloves made his hands look like a cartoon character's as they rested on his knees. He leaned forward, peering intently at the action downfield. His team's attempts to score a goal had just been thwarted.

Suddenly the action changed direction and the two teams frantically pursued the ball toward midfield. Josue's teammates were being outrun, and the ball crossed into Josue's territory. The opposing team's forwards positioned themselves for an attack on Josue's goal—and none of his teammates was within reach of the ball to help defend against the attack. Just then, Josue daringly raced out of the goalie's box. Cries of "Güero! Güero!" sounded from the sidelines. He ran upfield to intercept the ball, risking leaving his goal exposed. Running at full speed, he booted the ball out of bounds—but then crashed into the opposing forward.

The forward was a much larger boy who sent Josue tumbling to the ground. Lying sprawled on the field, Josue grasped his right ankle and cried out in pain. The team's coach and Josue's father, on the sidelines, ran out on the field to attend to him. They checked his leg for broken bones, helped him

333

to his feet, exercised the bruised ankle, and inserted crushed ice into his knee sock. He tested his leg by raising it up and down. One of the parents called for a replacement player, but Josue declined and remained in the game. They finished playing, and his team won by a single goal. His heroic play at goalie had saved the game. I watched as he limped off the field and his teammates gave him congratulatory pats on the back. Josue was a hero.

Over an eight-month period, I observed Josue in and out of class because he was an exceptional reader—identified as a bilingual, Latino, gifted-and-talented student. So much attention is given to remediation of struggling readers, for obvious reasons; but I wanted to learn from this *skilled* reader in order to describe what Luis Moll (1992) terms a "mediated and literate relationship" (p. 453). As I discussed reading with Josue, and examined his writing in light of his family background and prior experiences, a persistent image of a hero emerged.

The purpose of this chapter is to examine how a successful Latino reader experienced literature. In doing so, I discuss a confluence of two theoretical perspectives: reader response theory, as set forth by Rosenblatt (1978, 1986) and Bakhtin (1981, 1983); and cultural funds of knowledge, as articulated by Moll and Greenberg (1990) and Moll and Gonzalez (1994).

The Theoretical Background

A composite theory of reader response and cultural funds of knowledge (Moll & Greenberg, 1990) provided the background for this study. The following section will examine the two theoretical strands and discuss how they intersect. Together, the two perspectives cast light on how Josue interpreted and used literary works to tell his own story.

Reader Response

According to Cox (1992), reader response theorists can be classified by the primary metaphor they employ to characterize their thinking. Bakhtin (1981) envisioned the reader and the text in a dialogue situated in a historical and cultural context. Benton (1983) imagined the reader transported into a secondary world that functioned as a magical space between reader and text. Harding (1937) and Britton (1982, 1984) conceived of the reader as a participant in the making of the story. Fish (1980, 1987) designed an interpretive community involving the writer, the text, and the reader. Iser (1978, 1980) devised the notion of a virtual text, existing between the text and the reader's representation of it. And Rosenblatt (1983), perceived as the fountainhead of U.S. reader response theorists, described reading literature as an experience of tapping a "live wire"; as one reads a work of literature, "a lived-through experience" takes place. For reader response theorists, reading a literary work is seen as a dynamic moment of making meaning.

More specifically, Rosenblatt's theory of reader response, drawn from James's (1890) stream of consciousness theory and Dewey's (1987) theory of aesthetics, describes an aesthetic reading experience. The experience, which remarkably parallels Bakhtin's concept of utterance, involves a "specific reader and a specific text at a specific time and place: change any of these, and there occurs a different circuit, a different event—a different poem" (Rosenblatt, 1978, p. 14). Words on paper do not, by themselves, constitute an experience. A lived-through experience occurs at the time of the response, when the *reader* makes the story come alive. Although reading for informational purposes (such as finding directions, or skimming a newspaper) is not an aesthetic experience; when reading a literary work, the reader takes on a qualitatively different stance—one that engages the mind experientially and creatively in reliving the story.

In Boyd-Batstone (1996) and Cox and Boyd-Batstone (1997), Rosenblatt's theory of reader response was applied to literature study in a bilingual classroom setting. It was found that students, given the invitation, freely described their responses to literature. In many cases, those responses reflected the students' cultural perspectives and their personal interpretations of their reading. Their expressions of response to literature became a profound resource for instruction.

The moment of a reader's expression, or utterance, captured for Bakhtin his understanding of reading as a dialogical relationship. Dialogue is a major theme of Bakhtin's (1981) thinking; the concept of *dialogics* originated in his critique of Dostoevsky's (1957) novel *The Brothers Karamazov*. Bakhtin saw the various characters as engaged in a struggle of ideologies that represented a variety of political and historical contexts. The counter position of the brothers with their opposing intentions and conflicting ideologies sparked his idea of the polyphonic novel. "These are different voices singing variously on a single theme," he exulted, citing Mikhail Glinka, one of Dostoevsky's favorite composers, as observing that "everything in life is counterpoint, that is, opposition" (p. 42).

Bakhtin expanded the notion of the polyphonic novel, along with the centrality of dialogue, to encompass ways of understanding a multilingual world. What Bakhtin (1983) perceived in the dialogical relationships found in a novel he expanded to larger spheres of language, culture, and life: "The single adequate form for verbally expressing authentic human life is the open-ended dialogue. Life by its very nature is dialogic" (p. 293).

Bakhtin (1981) conceived of a text as something malleable and under constant change, mediated by the forces of history, society, culture, and one's own intentions. In his concept, language in general and words in particular are not fixed units of thought; they have a much more pliable quality. One way to understand his thinking is to imagine words as forms shaped from elastic putty and handed from one speaker to another. Each conversant receives the putty in one form, reshapes it, and hands it off to someone else. The reservoir of available words is culturally arbitrated and historically situated, but each speaker retains the freedom to mold the words to fit his or her own intentions.

Dialogue is an exchange and a borrowing of utterances among multiple, and at times conflicting, voices. No single participant in a dialogue can claim sole ownership of the shape the words take. Words do not exist in a pure and untainted state; they are uttered or written by people who share spheres of influence and collections of ideas, or ideologies. Within a culture, words are handed down, preformed in social and historical contexts, but they are still malleable and yielding to individual appropriation:

> The word in language is half someone else's. It becomes "one's own" only when the speaker populates it with his own intention, his own accent, when he appropriates the word, adapting it to his own semantic and expressive intention. Prior to this moment of appropriation, the word does not exist in a neutral and impersonal language...but rather it exists in people's mouths, in other people's contexts, serving other people's intentions: it is from there that one must take the word, and make it one's own. (Bakhtin, 1981, pp. 293–294)

Dyson (1997) applied Bakhtin's concept of language to an elementary classroom setting. She characterized children as composers of language who "are not so much meaning makers as meaning negotiators, who adopt, resist or stretch available words" (p. 4). In linguistically diverse classrooms, negotiating meaning takes place as a polyphony of voices enter into dialogue. In dialogue, linguistically diverse students creatively employ one language to shape words into a meaningful form so as to communicate in another language.

Bakhtin (1981) recognized the creativity of a multicultural and multilingual consciousness. He envisioned an imaginative interdependence of cultures and languages coexisting with and elucidating each other:

The new cultural and creative consciousness lives in an actively polyglot world. The world becomes polyglot, once and for all and irreversibly. The period of national languages, coexisting but closed and deaf to each other, comes to an end. Languages throw light on each other: one language can, after all, see itself only in the light of another language.... All this set into motion a process of active, mutual cause-and-effect and interillumination. Words and language began to have a different feel to them; objectively they ceased to be what they had once been. (p.12)

According to Wertsch (1990), dialogue has profound implications for developing new sociocultural approaches to understanding ways of knowing. The polyphony of cultures and languages is not perceived by Wertsch as a barrier to learning but, rather, as multiple avenues to understanding. Therefore, the reading experience in a linguistically diverse classroom setting can be understood as a polyphony of voices discovering and negotiating meaning.

Rosenblatt and Bakhtin, then, together impart an aesthetic and sociocultural understanding of the reading experience. Rosenblatt's articulation of the aesthetic experience of reading literary works complements Bakhtin's dialogical understanding of the utterance of words, and of language use generally, in a social and cultural milieu. Whereas Rosenblatt affords insight into the moment of reading, Bakhtin provides a perspective within a sociocultural context. In other words, the reading experience is both dynamic and dialogical; it takes place in both the present moment and the present milieu. The two theorists laid a foundation for analyzing the personal and sociocultural ways in which linguistically diverse students experience reading literature.

Cultural Funds of Knowledge

Research in human development, conducted in Liberia by Cole (1971), applied a Vygotskian sociohistorical approach to pedagogical concerns. "Vygotskian" perspective posits that ways of knowing are embedded in a context that is mediated by historical, cultural, and social factors. It became apparent to Luis Moll, as a doctoral student working on Cole's project, that this work was relevant to issues regarding minority education in the United States.

Diaz, Moll, and Mehan (1986) initiated research into positive aspects of learning in Latino families; it was Moll and Greenberg (1990), however, who applied the term "funds of knowledge" to community analysis. Greenberg (1989) initially coined the term as he uncovered the social structure of Latino extended households. He found that a strong parallel existed between how household economic funds were held and dispersed and the way that *knowledge* unique to the culture was treasured and maintained. He began to identify the various "funds" that he encountered: for example, caloric funds, for furnishing daily sustenance; funds for maintaining land and shelter; and ceremonial funds, for carrying on familial traditions involving symbolic ritual. These funds, along with an abundance of other resources of knowledge, constituted "an operations manual of essential information and strategies households need to maintain their well being" (p. 2). Similar research was conducted by Warren, Rosebery, and Conant (1989) with Haitian Creole bilingual students in the Boston area and by McCarty, Wallace, Lynch, and Benally (1991) with a Navajo bilingual program in Rough Rock, Arizona.

Researching the positive aspects of learning in various cultural groups stood in direct contrast to more prevalent research conducted from a deficit model perspective. Moll (1992) contended that the research being conducted on bilingual education in the United States was asking questions that were flawed. The fault of the research, undertaken as it was from a deficit perspective, was, in Moll's view, its attention to the academic disadvantages of English language learners, or to what was lacking in their thinking. The research questions did not address the fact that most children attending bilingual classes came from working-class homes. Moll attempted to describe the resources of knowledge that students brought to the school setting. The underlying assumption was that a positive influx of culturally based knowledge would become a resource for the classroom rather than representing a deficit. As a result, teachers would develop instructional methods and curriculum built upon the students' prior knowledge, experience, and academic strengths. Thus, although uncovering funds of knowledge originated as an anthropological concept, it became a tool for informing instruction and opened a possibility for a shift in student-teacher relationships. Exploring funds of knowledge called on the teacher to step outside the classroom (see George et al., chapter 13 in this volume).

In relation to reading, Moll and Gonzalez (1994) formulated an instructional model in which teachers and students read and negotiated the meaning of written texts in light of the students' imagined worlds and funds of knowledge. The goal of the model was essentially for teachers and students to develop "mediated and literate relationships" (p. 453) as they explored knowledge funds through literacy. The composite term "mediated and literate relationships" emphasizes several key features of how literacy development is understood and conducted. "Mediated" refers to the historical, cultural, and social context in which knowledge is constructed. "Literate" refers to mastering the tools of using and interpreting words. "Relationships" acknowledges the dialogical nature of learning. In an instructional model that calls for mediated and literate relationships, the student and the teacher collaborate to uncover cultural knowledge funds. Dialog and negotiation of meaning is key to the process. The student and teacher work together to find conventional ways to express cultural insights and idiosyncratic ways of using words. The result is a creative product whether illustrated, oral, or written that bridges cultural and conventional learning.

Gonzalez (1995) and Moll and Greenberg (1990) advanced the idea of teachers and students collaborating to create culturally literate communities. Bringing the teacher back into the learners' community created new possibilities for educating all students, not simply English learners. Teaching students in such a way as to explore and understand their knowledge resources through literacy has powerful ramifications for reading instruction. The ramifications mean including students' perspectives of the reading experience, attending to reader responses as a source of instructional possibilities, modifying the curriculum to match the sociocultural resources students bring to the classroom, and extending personal ties with the families of linguistically diverse students to enrich the instructional process. In such a context, readers tell their own stories as they populate their reading with their own intentions, accents, and timbres—their reading shaped by the sociocultural contexts of home, school, and the larger community.

The Classroom Setting

Josue was in a fourth- and fifth-grade combination classroom that I taught in an urban Southern California school. It was part of a fledgling, bilingual gifted-and-talented education (GATE) program. The underlying impetus for developing a bilingual GATE program came from the school's teachers and parents. They realized that many of the Latino bilingual students displayed exceptional abilities in ways that were not readily apparent from objective measures of achievement such as standardized test scores. With the help of the school district's GATE office, students were identified as "gifted and talented" or "potentially gifted and talented" using a composite of criteria including Renzulli's (1977) model of considering levels of student engagement and teacher recommendations in addition to standardized test scores. (The category "potentially gifted and talented" was created by the school district to include students who demonstrated exceptional abilities—as reflected in teacher recommendations and an evaluation of academic work—that were not necessarily reflected in test scores.) The referral process involved teacher and parent requests to interview students for participation in the program. Enough students at each grade level were identified to initially establish four bilingual GATE cluster classrooms. Cluster classrooms were either single- or multigrade, and populated by essentially three types of students, who were identified as gifted and talented, potentially gifted and talented, and regular-education bilingual students.

The program began as a kindergarten-through-third-grade offering and later expanded to a late-exit transitional bilingual program with combination classrooms of grades 3–4 and 4–5. I had the opportunity to teach in the grade 4–5 combination classroom, and Josue was one of my students.

Because it created possibilities for creative engagement in all areas of the curriculum, language arts became a major focus of my classroom. The students were encouraged to be self-directed learners, using a writers' workshop format. They were asked to form their own reading groups around a book of their choice. They were required to produce four process-written pieces about the book, poetry, or a song based on their readings, and a creative project of their own design, and they were required to present their work to the rest of the class and to parents at the end of each writers' workshop session. I would meet with each group of students on a daily basis to discuss their readings, edit and evaluate their writing, and facilitate student-generated projects.

While working with the students, I became increasingly interested in their oral and written responses to reading. Informally, I noticed cultural aspects of the students' lives entering into their work. For example, students would include in their writing references to places near their homes, character names from pop culture, or even excerpts from stories told to them by their parents or grandparents. When it was warranted, I would ask students to interview their parents about family histories, stories, or experiences so they could make connections between their reading and their lives. And I encouraged the students to include those kinds of vignettes in their own writing.

When I began to talk with students about their lives outside the classroom, it proved to be enlightening. As I worked with these exceptional students, I began to realize that they had much to teach *me* about how successful Latino readers experienced literature. I wanted to identify what cultural resources they drew upon as they read and responded to literature—and that led me to conduct a more serious study of the intersection of the students' reader responses with their cultural backgrounds.

I then planned to examine individual case studies in depth. This would involve not only observing students in class and analyzing selected written responses to literature, but visiting participating students' homes, interviewing family members, and asking participants to create photo journals about their lives. I decided to ask students to apply to participate in a study—the application process, of course, included gaining their parents' approval and permission to make site visits for interviews. I also established as selection criteria that the students demonstrate fluency in reading in both Spanish and English and that they be identified as either gifted and talented or potentially gifted and talented. Josue was one of the selected case study participants.

Josue

Josue was selected to participate as a case study because his family agreed to invite me into their home as a teacher-researcher (at least three times during the course of the school year, for field-note taking) and because he met the following additional criteria: (a) a Spanish reading component score of at least 75.0 Normal Curve Equivalent (NCE) on the Individual Test of Academic Skills (ITAS, 1996)—whose reading component evaluates elements of vocabulary, comprehension, inference, and the ability to conceptualize the main ideas of selected reading material; (b) willingness to participate in the research, as demonstrated by completing an application form; and (c) designation as gifted and talented or potentially gifted and talented by means of the school district's assessment tools (Leiter International Performance Scale, 1927/1979, and/or Raven's Coloured Progressive Matrices, 1956/1986).

To ensure that the students were bilingual, scores were also collected from the Idea Oral Language Proficiency Test (IPT, 1988), which assesses fluency in English, and an English reading assessment based on Clay's (1985) running records—though neither of these measures was a requirement for participation in the research. For purposes of this study, running-record assessments scored a student's reading accuracy in terms of the percentage of words of selected paragraphs in English that were read correctly; the process also included a retelling of the story and a reflective response in written form to demonstrate comprehension.

As part of the application process, each student wrote why they wanted to be part of the study. (The application was written in Spanish for the benefit of the parents, so the students wrote their explanations in Spanish.) Josue wrote the following in his application:

> Yo quiero participar en esto por estudiar más y llegar a hacer alguién en la vida, para aprender otras cosas nuevas que yo no sé. [I want to participate in

this in order to study more and to make myself into someone in life, in order to learn other new things that I do not know.]

Family Background

Josue lived with his family in a four-unit apartment in a residential part of the downtown area of the city. Their apartment was on the second floor of the building; it was long and narrow, extending across the entire length of the building. The front room was the living/family room area, with an entertainment center including a television and a VCR. The room was split by a planter, creating a space for a dining area, which was filled with a large hardwood table that could seat eight people. Each time I visited, I sat at the table with Josue's parents to talk; as our conversation became more relaxed, I was invited to move to the living room. Although our discussions took place in Spanish, I have included only the English translations in this chapter.

Josue's family came from Chapala, Michoacán, in Mexico. His parents explained to me that this part of Mexico is famous for the fishing on Lake Chapala, and for its own brand of ranch life and rodeos. His mother's side of the family survived off the lake by fishing. She lamented the current condition of Lake Chapala, which over the years appeared to be drying up and receding. The impact was devastating to her parents' fishing business and forced them into retirement—and required other family members to find gainful employment elsewhere.

Josue's mother, who had not completed "primaria" (elementary school), lamented her experience in school, but she wanted her children to succeed academically:

> I hope that my son continues to study so that...well, school is good for you. When I went, I didn't reach more than fourth grade. I didn't study more than up to fourth grade and I missed out in studies.

Josue's father's family were butchers tied to Chapala's ranching industry. In school, his father completed "secundaria" (high school); he studied engineering, was very competent in math, and excelled in management. Moving to the United States, however, meant sacrificing his initial career dreams in engineering; he settled for a job working as a manager at a brick manufacturing company.

Each year in February, the family packed up their van and made a two-week trip to Chapala to participate in its festival days, full of dancing, fishing, rodeos, and bull riding. (Residents of Chapala shun bullfighting, which is traditional in other parts of Mexico, in favor of bareback bull riding.) Bull riding took place for six to eight hours a day during festival days, according to Josue's father. On one occasion, we sat together and watched an hour and a half of home videos of the festival days in Chapala. Josue's father talked with me while his mother prepared food for dinner. She served me sodas and we ate "Chapala style"—carne asada (roast beef) and caldo (soup)—as we discussed their lives.

One important aspect of the *ranchera* life was how one dressed. Josue's father took almost an entire hour to display the expensive Stetson hats he had given his son, as well as the leather vests and jackets, the belts and the boots, and the scarves that identify one's familial home. They would apparently spend any amount of money to be dressed well in "Chapala-style" ranch clothing. I inquired about the value of clothing in their family.

Teacher: It must be very valuable to you to spend so much money on these clothes.

Father: It is very expensive, yes, very valuable.

Mother: Well him [the father], he wants to buy everything for his son...whatever it is. When [Josue] was little, he bought him everything to dress like that. He liked to bring him those kinds of clothes. He would dress him with special scarves. He gave him vests. He also has a leather sport jacket and Josue does not like it, doesn't like it at all. And you know a sport jacket made of leather like this...you use it for all occasions. You know, these never go out of style.

His father made a comment under his breath about Josue and clothes: "Now he no longer uses boots; it's purely tennis shoes, nothing else." Josue's father's effort in showing me clothing, combined with his disapproving reference to Josue's current taste in sportswear, seemed to signal a shift in cultural priorities across generations from the ranching roots of Chapala to the sports influence in California.

Josue wore sports shoes because he loved playing goalie (*portero*, which literally means "gatekeeper"), on a city soccer league team that was coached by his paternal uncle. Their home was adorned with trophies that Josue had won and pictures of his soccer team. In spite of his relatively small stature, Josue had established himself as one of the best goalies in the league. One particular trophy was in a prominent spot, on the mantle over the fireplace. Josue took it down to show me that the previous year he had been selected most valuable player by his teammates.

Soccer was an important part of Josue's life, but there was another facet of his life that was important, too—the spiritual side. Josue told me about the various churches in Mexico where he had celebrated communion with his father. His father explained to me that he wanted Josue to know about all the representations of the Virgin Mary throughout his home state of Michoacán, so his family made it a custom to visit sites throughout Mexico in order to venerate the different Mexican manifestations of the Virgin Mary, such as La Virgin de Guadalupe and La Virgin de Talpa.

During the school year, like many other Catholic boys and girls his age, Josue celebrated his first communion. His parents had signed him up for catechism classes, and in short order he had demonstrated to the teacher that he was ready to receive communion. According to his mother, he diligently and quickly learned his catechism:

Mother: He is going to have his first communion and he has had just one class and he already knows the entire catechism. And there in the church school, the teacher, the one that gave the classes, says that he passed, because he learned it all. In other words, he likes to learn, he really likes to learn. And with just one class he is going to have his first communion on the 6th of December.

Teacher: Really? What church will it be?

Mother: It will be at La Placita Olvera [the oldest church in Los Angeles, on the city's first main street, dating back to the 1780s].... It is going to be beautiful. He already knows the catechism. He is...it is going to be wonderful...with one class he learned it. Oh, it's just that he is good...he reads something and in just a short while he says it from memory, if he is reading it. It's that he has a lot of imagination. You can tell, right?

Teacher: Yes, you *can* tell.

Mother: And it will be his first communion. And you know that with others it takes as much as two years of study and here this lady gives classes, but for La Placita Olvera. I don't know about other churches that are closer.

Teacher: I didn't know that it took up to two years.

Mother:	Yes, it took that long.... My daughter, the oldest one, took two years of study before her first communion. And this lady had done nothing more than given what they needed to learn, the catechism, on a sheet of paper, and he already learned it. In just one class. It's that he has a lot of capacity to learn.

I felt compelled to find out more about Josue's spiritual interests, so I asked to come to his first communion, and he and his parents readily invited me to attend. Although the event was first scheduled to be held at the historic La Placita de Olvera, the venue was changed because of the number of expected attendees and the limited space in the sanctuary. It was relocated to a small church about five miles away from the historic site.

The church was a taupe-colored stucco building in an industrial neighborhood of Los Angeles that seated about 200 to 250 people. As I entered, there was standing room only. Many of the families were tending to their children, who were freely moving about the sanctuary. The priest, in his forties, was a bearded European American who spoke a somewhat fluent Spanish, marred by numerous grammatical errors. The sermon was about each one of us being the hands of God. He expanded on the idea of God being powerless without the work of the people. He spoke in a church that was poor and in disrepair.

As I sat in the church observing the proceedings, an image of the heroic nature of being a teacher-researcher appeared to me. I was struck by the fact that the priest and I were the only ones in the congregation who could be classified as *gringos*, a slang Spanish term for English-speaking European Americans. We framed the congregation, as it were—the priest, standing by the altar at the front of the church, in front of a large cross, and I, the teacher-researcher, in the last pew at the back of the church, near the street—both *gringos* with the Hispanic congregants sitting and kneeling between us. In retrospect, the metaphor of reading with a hero began to take form at this point in the research process. Josue was taking a heroic step in his religious journey. I also realized that I shared a sense of the heroic with Josue.

In addition to observing Josue's home, his play on the soccer field, and his first communion, I gave Josue a disposable camera and asked him to compile a photo journal of what was important to him. Seeing the world through his eyes gave me additional insights into his funds of knowledge. Table 14.1 is a summary of the pictures he selected for his photo journal.

Josue placed the pictures in order of importance to himself; the themes explored in the photos included spirituality, family, sports, friends, and pets.

TABLE 14.1 The Photo Journal

#	Contents of photographs	Josue's Description	Theme
1	Wall in Josue's home showing photographs and a large print of the Virgin of Guadalupe	That's the Virgin. I trust her in everything.	Spirituality
2	Josue sitting on a desk with his younger sister standing on the desk behind him.	My little sister Guadalupe. I always play with her, wrestling. She is three years old.	Family
3	A family photograph displayed in a bouquet of flowers.	When we went to Chapala, my grandparents celebrated their 50th anniversary. We took a picture of the whole family.	Family
4	Display of a certificate with a trophy on either side. Flowers are behind the certificate.	My trophies from the [soccer] team I played in. We were in 1st place and they didn't score any goals on me. In ten games they scored only two goals.	Sports
5	Wrapped packages, flowers, and a certificate.	Mother's Day presents that we gave our mom. I gave her a Teddy bear and clothes.	Family
6	A boy in a soccer uniform squatting behind five trophies.	My cousin Gilberto. We're like brothers. We always play together.	Family/ Sports
7	A man with Josue, both squatting behind trophies and a soccer ball.	My coach: he'll be able to talk to me anytime. He's my uncle and my godfather.	Family/ Sports
8	Josue and a boy posing behind trophies and a soccer ball.	Another picture of my cousin and my trophies and the soccer ball. Because I like soccer.	Family/ Sports
9	Josue with a boy on the school playground.	My friend, Nicolás. He's one of my best friends.	Friends
10	Two boys on the school playground. One is looking at the camera.	And Richard. He played with us all the time in all the recesses. Soccer, basketball, everything.	Friends/ Sports

(continued)

TABLE 14.1 The Photo Journal (continued)

#	Contents of photographs	Josue's Description	Theme
11	Josue with a girl on the school playground.	I took a picture of Yubel, because we were all walking. I have my "Surge" sports drink.	Friends/ Sports
12	Josue with a boy and a girl.	More friends. Cindy and Nicolás. We're always together.	Friends
13	Josue with a girl on the school playground.	I took one picture alone with Cindy, just with her. We joke around together.	Friends
14	Josue with a black dog.	My dog, Spikey. I always play with him. When we finished playing a game, my uncle gave it to me. He got it from his friend.	Pets

Sports accounted for 42% of the pictures; family followed with 33%. Each one of the themes explored in his photo journal was evident in his writing in response to reading. And every time he wrote, the image of a hero emerged. Josue read with the intent of exploring the heroic.

Josue's Way With Books

Gaining an understanding into Josue's background and experiences gave me significant insights into his ways of experiencing literature. In our classroom, students formed literature study circles (Daniels, 1994; McMahon, 1992; Samway et al., 1991) around books that were of interest to them. Books were made available from an extensive classroom library of more than 600 titles in English and Spanish. The first book that Josue and his group selected to read was *You Shouldn't Have to Say Good Bye* by Patricia Hermes (1984). Although the book was not Josue's first choice, I had required that each reading group be gender balanced to the extent possible to avoid students forming exclusively boys or girls groups, so Josue acquiesced, saying in a note to me, "I choose [sic] this book because this is the only book that a girl got in our group. It is a great book for all four of us. I am going to enjoying [sic] it a lot for this year."

The book recounts a story of the loss experienced by a young girl, Sarah Morrow, as she sees her mother fight a losing battle with cancer. Responding to the story, Josue wrote two poems exploring issues of life, loss, and lasting connections. Interestingly enough, the first poem was written only as a first draft; it was filed in his writing folder as a kind of unfinished fragment. The poem is metaphorical, suffused with cosmic and personal images that convey loss and remembrance:

Stars Over Snow

And in the West,
a planet
swinging below a star.
Look for a lovely thing and you will find it.
It is not far.
It never will be far;
but in our heart you will always be around.

In the second poem, Josue is more prosaic. Each line reads like a statement about those who have died or those who remain alive, and the spiritual and cultural notion of a connection between the living and the dead is expressed:

You Shouldn't Have to Say Good Bye

This is my story. This is my life.
People that die can say good bye,
because when they die,
they miss people that are alive.
People alive pray for people alive,
so nothing could happen in their future.
People alive dream about people that die.
They miss the ones they have lost.

Josue's reflections on life and death were not limited to poetic musings. He wrote adventure stories that sometimes went unfinished, like television dramas that leave the viewer hanging in anticipation of the next installment. He incorporated a character named Robin into a story that had little relation to the book, except for the reference to imminent death:

Monday Night

One Sunday, Robin was telling her mom, "I want to be a movie star."
"Honey, you are too small to be a movie star," said her mom.

Days Later

"Mommy I want to go to the Mall to buy a beautiful dress," said Robin.

When they arrived at the Mall, they saw a lot of trailers going to the parking lot. A theater director was screaming and yelled, "We want a little girl with a great mind!" The director was telling the little girls, "No! Next. She's too big."

Then Robin walked in and she was perfect for the part. She practiced the script and she finished rehearsing the play.

Two Months Later

When the play was going to be previewed, she was nervous. A man changed the fake bullets and put real bullets in the gun.

(To be continued...)

The subsequent installment never appeared. Josue left the reader wondering if the real bullets were intended for Robin, her mother, or possibly the director. Nor does he reveal who the mysterious man is who switched the bullets, or his intentions in doing so. Several months later, while rereading the story, I asked Josue to fill in the missing details, but he said he could not remember how he intended to finish the story. What was evident, however, was the component elements of life and death revolving around a central figure, which reappeared in much of his writing.

The theme of life-and-death adventures grew to more heroic proportions as Josue selected to read the book *Jacob's Rescue* by Malka Drucker and Michael Halperin (1993). The book is an account of a Jewish boy in Poland during World War II who escapes the Warsaw Ghetto to live in the countryside with an adopted family. The boy loses his own family to the Nazi Holocaust, but lives to tell his own story.

Josue wrote several stories in response to *Jacob's Rescue*. The first two stories involved two powerful boys named Sergio and Oscar, who begin as enemies and later become friends. The dimensions of their relationship had worldwide significance in scope: They dared to attack the church and had the power to make world war or create world peace.

The Best Friends Attack I

Once upon a time a boy named Sergio and his best friend Oscar were troublemakers. Sergio was the bad boy of the city. Sergio told Oscar, "Let's break the windows of the church."

The next day the police caught them and took them to jail. They called Sergio and Oscar too. When they got out of jail, Sergio was a leader of a gang and Oscar was a leader of a gang too.

They always had wars with each other. They started World Wars III, IV, V, VI, VII, VIII, IX, until they reached to X. Then they found out that they were really best of friends.

(To be continued)

The sequel picks up with Sergio and Oscar recognizing their friendship. It brings the story to a conclusion as the friends unite against a common enemy. The twist to the story is that these powerful boys question their fighting and choose peace instead.

The Best Friends Attack II

Sergio and Oscar found out that they were best friends. Sergio asked, "How could this happen?"

Two months later, Sergio and Oscar were shopping, and Sergio's second leader of the gang [Alfredo] said, "Look at you. You are friends again."

Then that day, Alfredo tried to destroy them. Sergio and Oscar formed a gang. When Alfredo went to visit them, Oscar said, "Why do you want to fight us?"

Alfredo responded, "Let's be friends and have no more fighting."

Josue persistently dealt with issues of violence and evil on his own terms. In attempting to discuss the book *Jacob's Rescue* with the students in Josue's reading group, I realized that they were demonstrating little understanding of the historical context of the story—the Nazi occupation of Poland. I wrote the following entry in my teacher's journal about my own frustrations in dealing with the complex history underlying the story of *Jacob's Rescue*:

> The group doesn't seem to understand what the book is about. We don't have discussions about the story. I am spending the whole time untangling the confusion between the Nazis and the Polish soldiers, when the story actually took place, why the countries were at war, who were the Jews and why they were singled out by the Nazis. They don't seem to understand that people can be both Polish and Jewish...that one is a nationality and the other an ethnicity, that Nazis were a political party, not a gang...although many consider them gang members today....
>
> It is like they have been handed down a host of disjointed images of World War II through movies and film clips. When they get an actual story about the war, the story gets fragmented too.

My ineffective clarifying of the historical background of the book and my frustrated attempts to untangle the students' confusions gave me pause. I later realized that the students were exemplifying Bakhtin's theory of dialogics. Josue and his classmates lived in a world of fragmented images and fragmented notions of historical events such as the Holocaust. With help, Josue could have grasped more of the author's intent; but instead, he used his flawed understanding of the text for his own intentions—namely, to express an image of a hero in a violent world. Josue and the students in his group took what fragments they could from the story and molded them into their own narratives.

Consistent with their fragmented picture of life in the Warsaw Ghetto, Josue and another group member, Delia, teamed up to write a story. Ironically, they even included me in their disjointed account of the war:

Jacob's Rescue

Jacob lived in a small and beautiful town named Warsaw, Poland. His favorite game was hide-and-seek. One day, eight-year-old Jacob was getting sleepy, because he was going to meet Alex Rosland, a wonderful young man in the woods.

When Alex arrived, they talked and talked. They heard a shot fired in the sky. It was the start of World War III. They prepared for the war by calling the emergency trucks to send three young men to call the Marines and the Air Force to fight Germany.

They went to go save the ghettoes. Germany was taking control of the world. The Marines and the Air Force weren't afraid of Germany. They weren't afraid, because they had already fought against Argentina.

The Marines and the Air Force were on the way to Germany to save a lot of people in the ghettoes. The Marines knocked at the door. Their allies opened the door. The Marines said that they were already prepared. Alex and Jacob were checking the planes and the trucks when they heard Marines coming and they got in the truck to hide. 30,000 people were on the way to Germany.

When Jacob got out of the truck, he looked and saw a lot of dead people. Germany was killing the ghettoes and the Warsaw, Poland people too. Alex and Jacob had no choice but to fight with Germany for one reason. Germany ran to hide from Jacob. When he got back to Warsaw, Poland, they all treated him like a hero.

When he woke up, he heard a man screaming, "Help me, please!"

Jacob got scared, because it was just a dream. He asked the man, "Who are you?"

The man responded, "I am Mr. Paul Boyd-Batstone."

Jacob helped Mr. Paul Boyd-Batstone get up. He saw more people on the floor, but they were already dead. Then a lot of Germans surrounded them.

(To be continued)

The ubiquitous "to be continued" left much of Josue's writing unfinished. Later, when I asked him how Jacob was going to save me, Josue shrugged his shoulders and said, "I don't know, they got away somehow." (I think my fate in the story was more important to me than it was to the author.) The fragmented images of battle, including a reference to the United States complicity in the Falkland Islands war between Argentina and England, did leave me wondering what connection there was between the book and an imaginary account of the start of WWIII. The logic of the events was not of particular importance to Josue. His use of a dream made the scattered references more acceptable, but what stayed consistent was the theme of a hero placed in a life-and-death scenario.

A third book that Josue studied was *Be a Perfect Person in Just Three Days!* by Stephen Manes (1982). Milo, the protagonist, catches a book that falls off a library shelf. The fallen book, written by the eccentric-looking Dr. Silverfish, was about becoming perfect. An obsession with perfection captures Milo's imagination and changes his life.

Josue began responding to this book in much the same way he wrote in response to the others. His writing on this occasion left the reader wondering what kind of heroic intervention would save the unwitting protagonist from being arrested by the police. The difference was that with *this* story, Josue used first person, putting himself in the hero's role:

Perfect Boy

I don't like to visit the library a lot; but one time I went to look for some biographies of Abraham Lincoln. I was talking to my friend when a book fell on my head. The title of the book was *The Perfect Boy*.

I got Abe's books and I took it [sic] home, but somehow that *Perfect Boy* book was in my backpack. I asked my friend why that book was in my backpack, but he didn't answer.

The next day, the cops came for me.

End of Part 1

This story fragment implied a heroic intervention. Josue's self-deprecation in writing a first person account may explain the lack of detail in the story. The subsequent discussion of the book, however, revealed Josue's abiding interest in the heroics of soccer. As we discussed the book, we talked about the notion of wanting to be perfect like the boy in the story. I asked him to write about the perfect person, or a person he knew who was as close to being perfect as possible. Josue wrote a free-verse poem about a fellow soccer player named Vicente:

My Perfect Soccer Player is Vicente

Vicente is the best player to me.
He was the best player on my team.
When he scored for the first time,
he was as happy as a monkey playing with its son.

One time he told us
that he was moving to San Diego,
so he could not play on our team anymore.

We gave him a party.
We lost a perfect player.

But then we got a good player named Efrain.
He scored goals almost like Vicente.

For Josue, perfection seemed to revolve around playing soccer. He loved soccer and led his team to third place in the league championship. Soccer challenged him to seek perfection and also reflected the role of the hero in conflict against an opponent. As I stood on the edge of the soccer field, watched him risk exposing his goal, and saw him sacrifice his body to save the game for his team, I saw a hero at play. This hero was, as we have seen, vividly expressed in his writing.

Josue's responses at times were fragmented and incomplete—but the themes of spirituality, family, sports, friends, and conflict were evident.

Conclusions

As Josue read, he told his *own* story. He used the text of the literary works he read to serve his own designs. He demonstrated the reading process as a lived-through experience that was mediated by a variety of sociocultural factors, and he applied his funds of knowledge to both his reading and writing. The shared experience was a mediated and literate relationship between student and the teacher.

The classroom instruction, however, needed to be structured to invite this kind of relational learning. It required a range of instructional approaches that encouraged students to respond authentically to their reading. Literature study (Cox, 2002) was a central instructional component, and students were asked to participate in self-selected reading (Krashen, 1993; Schon, Hopkins, & Davis, 1983) and literature study circles.

Oral and written responses to reading were analyzed (Cox, 1994; Dyson, 1997) for traces of cultural funds of knowledge (Greenberg, 1989; Moll &

Gonzalez, 1994). Attending to issues of culture resulted in the development, in collaboration with the students, of a culturally responsive curriculum (Au, 1980, 1993; Heath, 1983). Aesthetic response (Rosenblatt, 1986) and dialogue (Bakhtin, 1981) undergirded instruction and interpretation of the reading experience.

Reading instruction is much more than defining the author's intent or identifying the elements of story structure. It means reading with children to determine their perceptions and facilitating their expressions in response to literature; it means uncovering their funds of knowledge. Excellent readers freely make connections between the text and their lives. In a culturally and linguistically diverse instructional setting, it is crucial to collaborate with students to form "mediated and literate relationships" (Moll & Gonzalez, 1994). For me, reading with a hero became a mediated and literate experience.

REFERENCES

Au, K.H. (1980). Participation structures in a reading lesson with Hawaiian children: Analysis of a culturally appropriate instructional event. *Anthropology and Education Quarterly, 11*(2), 91–115.

Au, K.H. (1993). *Literacy instruction in multicultural settings.* Fort Worth, TX: Harcourt, Brace, Jovanovich.

Bakhtin, M. (1981). *The dialogic imagination: Four essays.* Austin, TX: University of Texas Press.

Bakhtin, M. (1983). *Problems of Dostoevsky's poetics.* Minneapolis: University of Minnesota Press.

Benton, M.G. (1983). Response to literature. In J.R. Squire (Ed.), *Response to literature* (pp. 3–10). Urbana, IL: National Council of Teachers of English.

Boyd-Batstone, P. (1996). Learning to walk together in a third grade bilingual classroom: From transmission to transactional instruction with literature. In N. Karolides (Ed.), *Reader response in elementary classrooms: Quest and discovery* (pp. 187–212). Mahwah, NJ: Erlbaum.

Britton, J.N. (1982). *Prospect and retrospect.* Montclair, NJ: Boynton/Cook.

Britton, J.N. (1984). Viewpoints: The distinction between participant and spectator role in language in research and practice. *Research in the Teaching of English, 18*, 320–331.

Clay, M.M. (1985). *The early detection of reading difficulties: A diagnostic survey with recovery procedures* (3rd ed.). Auckland, New Zealand: Heinemann.

Cole, M. (1971). *The cultural context of learning and thinking: An exploration in experimental anthropology.* New York: Basic Books.

Cox, C. (1992). Introduction. In J. Many & C. Cox (Eds.), *Reader stance and literary understanding: Exploring the theories, research, and practice* (pp. i–xi). Norwood, NJ: Ablex.

Cox, C. (1994). *Challenging the text: Case studies of young children responding to literature.* Paper presented at the 1994 National Reading Conference, San Diego.

Cox, C. (2002). *Teaching language arts: A student- and response-centered classroom.* Boston: Allyn & Bacon.

Cox, C., & Boyd-Batstone, P. (1997). *Crossroads: Literature and language in linguistically and culturally diverse classrooms*. Columbus, OH: Merril/Prentice Hall.

Daniels, H. (1994). *Literature circles: Voice and choice in the student-centered classroom*. York, ME: Stenhouse.

Dewey, J. (1987). Art as experience. In S.D. Ross (Ed.), *Art and its significance: An anthology of aesthetic theory* (2nd ed., pp. 205–223). Albany, NY: State University of New York Press.

Díaz, S., Moll, L.C., & Mehan, H. (1986). Sociocultural resources in instruction: A context-specific approach. In California State Department of Education (Ed.), *Beyond language: Social and cultural factors in schooling language minority children* (pp. 187–230). Los Angeles: Evaluation, Dissemination and Assessment Center, California State University.

Dyson, A.H. (1997). *Writing the super heroes: Contemporary childhood, popular culture and classroom literacy*. New York: Teachers College Press.

Fish, S.F. (1980). *Is there a text in this class?* Cambridge, MA: Harvard University Press.

Fish, S.F. (1987). Change. *South Atlantic Quarterly, 86,* 423–442.

Gonzalez, N.E. (1995). The funds of knowledge for teaching product. *Practicing Anthropology, 17*(3), 3–22.

Greenberg, J.B. (1989, April). *Funds of knowledge: Historical constitution, social distribution, and transmission*. Paper presented at the annual meetings of the Society for Applied Anthropology, Santa Fe, NM.

Harding, D.W. (1937). The role of the onlooker. *Scrutiny, 6*(3), 247–258.

Heath, S.B. (1983). *Ways with words: Language, life, and work in communities and classrooms*. Cambridge, UK: Cambridge University Press.

Iser, W. (1978). *The act of reading: A theory of aesthetic response*. Baltimore: Johns Hopkins University Press.

Iser, W. (1980). The reading process: A phenomenlogical approach. In J.P. Tompkins (Ed.), *Reader-response criticism* (pp. 50–69). Baltimore: Johns Hopkins University Press.

James, W. (1890). *Principles of psychology* (Vols. 1 & 2). New York: Holt.

Krashen, S. (1993). *The power of reading*. Englewood, CO: Libraries Unlimited.

McCarty, T.L., Wallace, S., Lynch, R.H., & Benally, A. (1991). Classroom inquiry and Navajo learning styles: A call for reassessment. *Anthropology and Education Quarterly, 22*(1), 42–59.

McMahon, S.I. (1992). *Book club discussions: A case study of five students constructing themes from literary texts* (Report #72). East Lansing, MI: Michigan State University, Center for the Learning and Teaching of Elementary Subjects.

Moll, L.C. (1992). Bilingual classroom studies and community analysis: Some recent trends. *Educational Researcher, 21*(2), 20–24.

Moll, L.C., & Gonzalez, N. (1994). Lessons from research with language minority children. *Journal of Reading Behavior, 26*(4), 439–456.

Moll, L.C., & Greenberg, J.B. (1990). *Community knowledge and classroom practice: Combining resources for literacy instruction* (OBEMLA Contract No. 300-87-0131). Tucson, AZ: University of Arizona, College of Education and Bureau of Applied Research in Anthropology.

Moll, L.C., & Greenberg, J.B. (1990). Creating zones of possibilities: Combining social contexts for instruction. In L.C. Moll (Ed.), *Vygotsky and education: Instructional implications and applications of sociohistorical psychology*. New York: Cambridge University Press.

Renzulli, J.S. (1977). *The enrichment triad model: A guide for developing defensible programs for the gifted and talented.* Wethersfield, CT: Creative Learning Press.

Rosenblatt, L. (1978). *The reader, the text, the poem: The transactional theory of the literary work.* Carbondale, IL: Southern Illinois University Press.

Rosenblatt, L. (1983). *Literature as exploration* (4th ed.). New York: Modern Language Association.

Rosenblatt, L. (1986). The aesthetic transaction. *Journal of Aesthetic Education, 20,* 122–128.

Samway, K.D., Whang, G., Cade, C., Gamil, M., Lubandina, M.A., & Phommachanh, K. (1991). Reading the skeleton, the heart, and the brain of a book: Students' perspectives on literature study circles. *The Reading Teacher, 45,* 196–205.

Schon, I., Hopkins, K., & Davis, A. (1983). The effects of books in Spanish and free reading time on Hispanic students' reading abilities and attitudes. *NABE Journal, 7,* 13–20.

Warren, B., Rosebery, A., & Conant, F. (1989). *Cheche Konnen: Science and literacy in language minority classrooms* (Report No. 7305). Cambridge, MA: Bolt, Beranek & Newman.

Wertsch, J.V. (1990). The voice of rationality in a sociocultural approach to mind. In L.C. Moll (Ed.), *Vygotsky and education: Instructional implications and applications of sociohistorical psychology* (pp. 111–126). New York: Cambridge University Press.

LITERATURE CITED

Dostoevsky, F. (1957). *The Brothers Karamazov* (Constance Garner, Trans.). New York: Simon & Schuster.

Drucker, M., & Halperin, M. (1993). *Jacob's rescue: A Holocaust story.* New York: Bantam Skylark.

Hermes, P. (1984). *You shouldn't have to say good bye.* New York: Scholastic.

Manes, S. (1982). *Be a perfect person in just three days!* Ill. T. Huffman. Boston: Houghton Mifflin.

CHAPTER 15

Access to Books and Beyond: Creating and Learning From a Book Lending Program for Latino Families in the Inner City

David B. Yaden, Jr., Patricia Madrigal, and Anamarie Tam

Introduction and Background

In general, emergent literacy research in the last decade is consistent in showing that parent-child reading interactions, supported by the presence of a wide range of literacy materials in the home, help contribute to a motivation to read and to growth in literacy ability in later schooling (e.g., Baker, Afflerbach, & Reinking, 1996; Bus, van IJzendoorn, & Pellegrini, 1995; Purcell-Gates, 1996; Sonnenschein, Brody, & Munsterman, 1996; Taylor & Dorsey-Gaines, 1988; Whitehurst & Lonigan, 1998; Yaden, Rowe, & MacGillivray, 2000). Unfortunately, limited access to a range of reading and writing materials—and, subsequently, fewer opportunities to engage adults in frequent literacy events—is more likely to exist in the homes of children whose heritage language is other than English and who live in urban, high-poverty areas (August & Hakuta, 1997; Goldenberg, Reese, & Gallimore, 1992; Snow, Burns, & Griffin, 1998).

Nonetheless, a substantial amount of extant family literacy research (e.g., Delgado-Gaitan, 1990, 1996; Hidalgo, 1997; Paratore & Gallagher, 2001; Reese, Garnier, Gallimore, & Goldenberg, 2000; Sosa, 1993, 1997; Yaden, Tam, et al., 2000), conducted with Latino families living at or below U.S. federal poverty standards, has demonstrated that despite high-stress living conditions, parents are more than capable of contributing at home and at school to their children's educational success: by communicating with teachers and school administration and by mobilizing other families within the community to provide a supportive environment for learning. This chapter reports on one such group of parents.

In the following discussion, we describe findings from a three-year implementation of a book lending program (also known as the book loan program) for Spanish-speaking parents and their children at an inner-city preschool in Los Angeles, California, USA. The program constituted one facet of a larger, emergent literacy intervention (see Yaden & Brassell, 2002; Yaden, Tam, et al., 2000, for details)—the Emergent Literacy Project (ELP), a study conducted under the auspices of the federally funded Center for the Improvement of Early Reading Achievement (CIERA). The investigation's primary purpose was to provide multiple opportunities for Spanish-speaking 3- and 4-year-old children to engage in a variety of reading and writing activities within the preschool center and at home. Further, because of the financial, transportation, and time constraints affecting the working families of this community (cf. also Sosa, 1997), an on-site lending library for parents was established with the overall goal of increasing access to books for families who were otherwise unable to visit the local library—and of providing opportunities for more interaction with literacy materials between parents and children at home. The program has experienced a growing level of parental involvement each year in addition to increased academic achievement on standardized tests of English reading and language when children entered elementary school.

In addition, because several studies (e.g., Baker, Allen, et al., 1996; Delgado-Gaitan, 1990, 1996; Heath, 1983; Purcell-Gates, 1995, 1996; Taylor & Dorsey-Gaines, 1988; Teale, 1986, 1987) have shown that literacy interactions of considerable variety occur even within low-income families, another goal of the book lending program was to discover the nature of these incidents within the children's home literacy environment. The premise of the study was that understanding the types of literacy interactions occurring at these homes and learning about the beliefs of these children's parents would make both the book lending program and the larger ELP more responsive to the indigenous resources, needs, and expectations of the community (cf. Moll, Amanti, Neff, & Gonzalez, 1992; Moll & Greenberg, 1990). Therefore, the central purpose of the following discussion will be to describe the nature and growth of the book lending program over three years and its role in facilitating collaborative interactions with parents—which, in turn, have been critical in furthering the overall goals of the study. First, however, we will review some of the demographic characteristics of the immediate region where the study has taken place and the specific principles that have guided implementation.

Changing Demographics and Educational Challenges

U.S. NATIONAL CHALLENGES.   At the time of this writing, the continued rapid growth of peoples identifying themselves as having a Hispanic origin has been documented recently by the U.S. Census Bureau (2000); described in detail in academic literature (e.g., Darder, Torres, & Gutiérrez, 1997; Fuentes, 1997; Gonzalez, 2000; Guerra, 1998; Gutierrez, 1995; Ruiz, 2000; Sanchez, 1993); and impressed repeatedly upon the public consciousness by the major print media (e.g., see Gibbs, 2001; King, 2001; Yeoman, 2000). The most recent census data (U.S. Census Bureau, 2000) indicate that the general Latino population in the 50 states now constitutes the largest minority group in the United States (12.5%), slightly surpassing African Americans (12.3%). Future estimates, according to Gonzalez (2000), are that by mid-century, one out of every four persons in the United States will claim a Latino heritage.

REGIONAL CHALLENGES IN SOUTHERN CALIFORNIA.   According to recent studies by the Southern California Studies Center and the Brookings Institution Center on Urban and Metropolitan Policy (2001), in metropolitan Los Angeles the Latino population has doubled and the Asian community has tripled during the last two decades, while the Anglo population has remained the same. Conversely, in the five-county area making up the Southern California region (Los Angeles, Orange, Riverside, San Bernadino, and Ventura), while the average yearly income level for Anglos has increased steadily over the past 10 years, that of Latinos and African Americans has actually decreased.

Additionally disturbing is the finding that the number of "working poor" in metropolitan Los Angeles is increasing much more rapidly than the population at large. For example, between 1990 and 1998, while the region's general population grew by 16%, the population of persons in working households (where at least one person works full time) increased 51%. Given that housing prices are increasing faster than household income in the area, statistics provided by the U.S. Department of Housing and Urban Development show that "48 percent of poor renters in the region must pay either more than half of their income for rent or live in an extremely inadequate housing unit" (cited in Southern California Studies Center and Brookings Institution Center on Urban and Metropolitan Policy, 2001, p. 22).

THE CHALLENGES OF PUBLIC EDUCATION IN SOUTHERN CALIFORNIA.   Despite both federal and state initiatives specifically intended to improve preschool and primary academic achievement in particular, the challenges for educators in Southern California are daunting. For example, using data from the October

1999 *Current Population Survey* (CPS), a monthly, nationally representative survey of 50,000 U.S. households conducted by the Census Bureau for the Bureau of Labor Statistics, the major risk factors, both "personal" and "familial," for students between the ages of 5 and 17 are (a) lack of English proficiency, (b) the presence of a personal disability, (c) school retention, (d) the absence of either or both parents in the home, (e) at least one foreign-born parent of recent immigration, (f) low family income, and (g) the absence of any employed parent or guardian in the household (Kominski, Jamieson, & Martinez, 2001, p. 4). In the particular area of the city of Los Angeles where the majority of the sample population for the present study reside, most of these seven risk factors loom large.

According to data collected by United Way of Greater Los Angeles in 1998–1999, 100% of the children's families in the area had an income below 75% of the state median income, with 40% of the population classified as living in extreme poverty. In addition, 30% of the school-aged children in L.A. County schools are classified as "limited English proficient," with over 50% of the entering kindergartners classified as "English learners" (Los Angeles County Children and Families First Proposition 10 Commission, 2000). Other estimates suggest that over 30% of the children live in single-parent households, that adult unemployment runs as high as 14%, and that approximately one out of every two adults in a household is a recent immigrant (Southern California Studies Center and Brookings Institution Center on Urban and Metropolitan Policy, 2001). Thus, the population from which the present sample is drawn is plagued by most, if not all, of the major risk factors identified as contributing to both inadequate living standards and underachievement in school.

Guiding Principles of the Book Loan Program

The long-term school performance of Latino youth in general lags consistently behind that of other ethnic groups (August & Hakuta, 1997; Galindo & Escamilla, 1995; Snow et al., 1998). The disparity, according to Delgado-Gaitan (1996), is frequently due to the fact that "many attempts to promote literacy and family-school relationships [in Latino communities] have limited effectiveness because they are driven by modernistic, capitalistic premises void of cultural affirmation and engagement of the local communities" (p. 2). Elsewhere, Delgado-Gaitan and Ruiz (1992) have also noted that "while the notion of home-school partnerships suggests an equal power base…, we find meager evidence to support the notion that the home influences the school" (p. 47).

In the present book lending program and within the larger ELP intervention, we have attempted to adhere to principles of collaboration such as those outlined in programs like the Carpinteria Family Literacy Project (Delgado-Gaitan, 1990, 1993, 1996), the "funds of knowledge" approach (Moll, 1998; Moll & Greenberg, 1990; Moll et al., 1992), and other types of reciprocal home-school partnerships (see also Baker, Allen, et al., 1996; Wells, 1999; Wells & Chang-Wells, 1992). These types of programs, alternatively called "cooperative systems" models (Delgado-Gaitan, 1990, 1993) or "partnership" models (Swap, 1993), are committed to the viewpoint that all partners in the educational process—teachers, children, parents, family—have indispensable and positive contributions to make in ensuring academic success. Thus, three of the major guiding principles of the program were (1) having easy access to books, (2) respecting cultural variations and beliefs, and (3) encouraging parent choice. (See Coppola, chapter 8; García & Beltrán, chapter 9; Chang, chapter 11; George et al., chapter 13; and Gallego et al., chapter 16, in this volume.)

EASY ACCESS TO BOOKS.   Early on, an effort was made to facilitate quick access to books for parents who, because of long hours at work and transportation problems, would otherwise not be able to visit the local library. For example, many parents juggle two or three bus schedules to and from work, and missing one bus may mean an hour's delay added to a workday of nine or more hours. Others have a ride waiting outside school and a long commute ahead. For these reasons, the on-site library was placed in the main entrance corridor directly adjacent to the children's classrooms. In this location, parents could quickly peruse the titles arranged along the counter, pick out one with their child, be signed out in the logbook, and be on their way home within as little as five minutes if need be. The placement of the book loan area also encouraged the preschool children themselves to initiate the process by pulling their parents over to the display of books and selecting one or two they wanted to take home. Overall, the arrangement allowed the program to maintain high visibility throughout the year and facilitated interaction with the researchers on an informal and personal basis.

CULTURAL AND CONTEXT SENSITIVITY.   In order to address the needs and expectations of the parents and children, it was crucial to recognize issues such as language use and economic condition as well as the nature of the home and school environment as factors that influence parents' interactions with the educational system. Our belief was that parents' perceived failure, in the view of some educators, to participate in school functions seldom indicated a lack of interest, but rather misunderstandings owing to cultural beliefs, language barriers, and/or a lack of familiarity with school policies and operating procedures. In order to help overcome language barriers and encourage collaboration and communication, two bilingual Latinas on the university research team staffed the program on a regular basis. Furthermore, books available in the loan library as well as duplicate copies in classrooms included numerous titles in Spanish as well as English, and many books addressed culturally relevant topics.

PARENT CHOICE. Although exact information on levels of parent education could only be collected slowly and over time, the research team designed both written and oral surveys to gather parent input with respect to the types of books (in terms of both content and genre) they would like to have available in the library. In addition to informal conversations, other opportunities such as short surveys and questionnaires were created so that parents could express what they wanted to know about early literacy practices and their children's learning; these suggestions were then incorporated into the topics presented at the parent literacy workshops. The workshops were conducted twice a year and consciously built on the families' primary language, literacy, and storytelling knowledge.

The Book Loan Program

Participants and Setting

Located just east of downtown Los Angeles in an area known as "Skid Row" (Rivera, 1999), Para Los Niños (PLN) is a Comprehensive Child Care and Family Support Services Center whose stated mission is "raising children out of poverty, into a brighter future." The agency's target Service Planning Areas (SPAs) are home to approximately 300,000 people in some of the poorest areas in the central city, where annual median household income for a family of four ranges from $9,134 to $27,000, with 36% of the families served making under $15,000. While 73% of the SPA population is Latino, currently over 90% of the children in day care are of Hispanic origin. The percentage in the particular child-care center discussed in this chapter was even higher, with 98% of the 136 children, from infants to 4-year-olds, identified as Latino (Thurlough Associates, 2001).

The majority of the parents of these children worked in the nearby wholesale garment and toy districts, where economic conditions are increasingly harsh. We have found, however, that the level of education of particularly the mothers is somewhat higher than reported by others doing work in Los Angeles (see, for example, Goldenberg, 1989, 1990), in that the average years of schooling for a sample of 76 families surveyed over the last two years who have children at PLN was approximately eight years in their home countries (Mexico, Guatemala, and El Salvador).

Design and Operation

As explained earlier, the loan program was operated from a walkway directly across from the two 4-year-old children's classrooms, thus providing access to the books by both parents and children when walking to the classrooms or leaving the building. During the hours of operation, books were set up on book holders and shelf boxes and displayed on the counter; afterward, they were stored in a cabinet until the next day of operation.

The book lending program began operation the last week of June 1998, at which time a preschool staff member assisted parents with book checkout. Owing to other duties, however, the staff member was not always available to assist with checkout or return or with choosing books. In only a few weeks, it became evident to the research team that in order for the program to function effectively, the on-site presence of a research team member during the hours of operation was essential. Therefore, since mid-July 1998, two members of the research team have staffed the library during the two days per week that parents could check out books.

The 2-, 3- and 4-year-old children were allowed to check out a maximum of two books per visit with their parents. A log was carefully maintained in which the parents signed in and out for the books, and the children were provided with a plastic bag to carry and store their books. An "incentive card" was provided that indicated the total number of titles a child had checked out; once a child had checked out 20 books, he or she was awarded a free book of his or her choice and "showcased" on the library's bulletin board. This involved the child getting his or her picture taken and documenting brief information about the child's particular interests.

The book lending library operated without penalties for late returns or damaged books. Knowing that many low-income parents could not afford to purchase library books that had been lost or damaged beyond repair, the research team decided that imposing fines would exacerbate the parents' already stressed financial condition and might discourage them from checking out books. Over the three years of the program, the good faith shown by the parents was such that, with the encouragement of the library staff and the teachers to return overdue books, the program's losses have been minimal (less than 10%). In fact, in several cases in which books have been lost or damaged, parents have replenished the supply, often with books of greater value than the ones that were lost.

The Loan Library Inventory

The book lending program has attempted to provide both easy, readable texts for emergent readers and a variety of multicultural picture storybooks, wordless picture books, and informational, counting, and alphabet books in Spanish and English—along with, when possible, bilingual texts. The program has been confronted, however, with recurring problems in purchasing books in the primary language, aside from the expense—especially the frequent existence of poor translations from English to Spanish, and the scarcity of alphabet, counting, and other informational books for young children written in Spanish. With the passage of Proposition 227, which has eliminated most bilingual programs in California, some publishers have greatly reduced or eliminated their offerings of children's literature in Spanish. Parents also requested books that teach how to form words, like the texts used in their native countries; however, these have been nearly impossible to obtain from commercial publishers in the United States.

Data Collection

In addition to keeping the logbook as a record of checkout frequency, most popular book titles, and student participation over the past three years, the researchers have taken field notes (see Emerson, Fretz, & Shaw, 1995, for a description of the exact format), recording incidences of parent-child interaction surrounding books and informal conversations with parents over a wide range of topics. Six parent book loan receptions have also been held (one each fall and spring), at which parents were invited to participate in half-hour literacy workshops on encouraging book reading at home. Subsequently, during these workshops and shared meals afterward, field notes of conversations, photographs, and video recordings were made to further document both parents' and children's responses to the program.

In order to obtain more systematic information from parents, an open-ended questionnaire in Spanish was developed inquiring into the families' perceptions of the on-site book lending program, the characteristics and services of the program that promoted access to books, and aspects of the literacy knowledge and at-home practices of these families. For those parents who might have difficulty reading the questionnaire, a semistructured oral interview based on the questionnaire was offered. In addition, after a year of working to build relationships and trust among the families in the program, several families were selected for further case studies involving home visits.

In addition to the three-year data regarding frequency of checkout and overall participation previously mentioned, we will draw from case study data collected over a five-month period from three families—primarily during the evening hours, when homework and literacy activities were typically performed. The goal was to better understand home literacy activities, parental involvement, and the pressures and barriers that affect the lives of Latino immigrant families. Ethnographic observations and interviews were used, along with audio recordings made during storybook reading. Parent interviews consisted of questions related to demographic information, the types of informational networks they drew from, their experiences with literacy during childhood, their beliefs about literacy in the home, and their involvement with their children's schooling.

Data Analysis

From the archival data recorded in the book loan log, descriptive frequencies have been computed for the daily rate of checkout and the monthly rate of child participation. Although outcome measures from early literacy assessments (e.g., Escamilla, Andrade, Basurto, Ruiz, & Clay, 1996) and subsequent elementary school records have been collected (see Brassell, 2001; Yaden, Tam, et al., 2000), the focus of the present analysis will be on the participation and checkout data, responses to questionnaires returned by parents, and field notes describing informal conversations with parents and observations at the loan program and elsewhere when relevant.

Results of the Program

The findings from this study will be presented in the succeeding sections. The first two sections depict the descriptive frequencies of book checkout and child participation over the three years of the lending program's operation. The third section is based on parent questionnaires as well as field-note observations, interviews, and conversations conducted with parents and children during book loan checkout regarding their perceptions and attitudes toward the presence and operation of the lending library and the value of books in general.

Next we discuss findings from the home visits, which probe more deeply into some of the language barriers that immigrant parents face in seeking an education for their children and uncover examples of home literacy practices and beliefs; and the following section describes styles of parent-child reading and what selected parents felt was important to focus on during literacy interactions with books. Data presented in the sixth section are taken from classroom observations and focus on the influence of the book lending program and home literacy activities as they were manifested in children's behaviors and comments during the school day.

Finally, we describe the important social function that the book loan parent receptions and literacy workshops served, as well as how we attempted to capture parents' oral stories in print. In all sections, parents' and children's names are pseudonyms.

Book Loan Program Rates of Checkout and Child Participation

RATE OF CHECKOUT.   In Figure 15.1, the rates of checkout for the three years of program operation are shown over 10-month periods from September to June for Years 1, 2, and 3. As charted, each year since September 1998 the daily mean of books being checked out per day increased, from an initial average of only four books per day in September 1998 to 56 books per day in June 2001. The substantial increase in the number of books checked out in Year 3 is partially because each child was allowed to check out two books per visit rather than only one, as in Years 1 and 2. It is important to note, however, that despite the extra book that could be checked out, the average number of books checked out per child per month by the end of Year 3 had increased nearly 370% from the program's inception (1.30, 1.33, and 3.67, respectively, over the three years of operation), as compared with a 19% increase in total participation over that same period.

RATE OF PARTICIPATION.   Initially, the book lending program was open only to the parents of the two classes of 4-year-old children. In only a few weeks, however, after the parents of the 3-year-olds had expressed interest in participating, the two classes of 3-year-olds also began to check out books. At the

FIGURE 15.1 Daily average of books checked out over three years

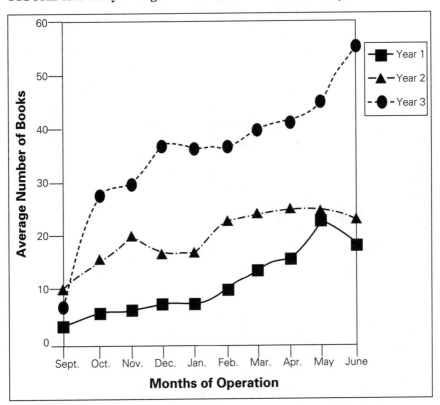

beginning of the new academic year in September 1999, the parents of the 2-year-old children were included as well. Figure 15.2 shows that the number of children participating in the book loan program rose steadily each month in each year of operation. In the final year of the program (2000–2001), of the 125 children in the 2-, 3-, and 4-year-old classes, 83% (10/12) of the 2-year-olds, 67% (39/58) of the 3-year-olds, and 98% (54/55) of the 4-year-old children were checking out books with their parents. Overall, of the children eligible to check out books, 83% (104/125) were making use of the book loan program.

By the third year of the program, several parents who were participating actively were also encouraging new enrollees to begin using the library as soon as possible. Hence, we attribute the steady growth of the program primarily to many of the parents themselves, who served as the primary catalysts for creating an atmosphere of enthusiasm and respect for the place of

FIGURE 15.2 Number of children participating monthly in the lending program over three years

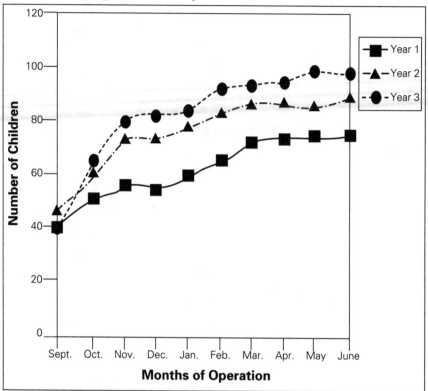

books—not only in the center, but in their homes as well. This topic is addressed in more detail in the following section.

Parents' and Children's Attitudes Toward the Library, Home Read-Alouds, and the Value of Books

Over the past three years, as the research team built friendships as well as trust with the parents and children, we learned just how important having quick and easy access to books was to these families. Parents frequently stated that their children now showed considerable interest in being read to at home, which, in turn, created additional opportunities to interact with them. As one parent wrote in the questionnaire, "Teniendo estos libros para leer, me permite más tiempo para estar con mi hija. [Having these books to read allows me to spend more time with my daughter.]" The following anecdote from field notes particularly attests to the value parents place on spending time with their children even when grueling work schedules do not allow for much, if any, leisure time for reading:

> Ms. Alvarez (a single mother of two) ran into the preschool at 10 minutes after 5:00 p.m. to pick up her children; she stopped to check out a book and as she was signing the book, I (the graduate research assistant) asked how she was doing. Her response was that she had been ironing for the last nine hours and that she was exhausted, but still had to hurry home on the bus, cook dinner for her two children, bathe them, and prepare everything for the next day. As she was leaving, she looked up and said, "Gracias maestra por haberme esperado y por hacer todo esto más fácil para nosotros. [Thank you teacher, for waiting for me and making this easier for us.]"

Such an example is only one of many in our field notes that indicated that immigrant parents, though often mistakenly portrayed as uninterested (e.g., Farkas, Johnson, Duffet, Aulicino, & McHugh, 1999) in their children's school progress (see also Delgado-Gaitan, 1996, and Yaden & Paratore, 2002, for a refutation of this view), frequently overcome considerable personal obstacles to ensure that their children have books. The convenience of the book loan program, therefore, served a very real purpose, as expressed plainly by another parent:

> Los papás siempre están cansados y tienen problemas de dinero y transportación y por eso no siempre pueden ir a la biblioteca pública. [The parents are always very tired and have both financial as well as transportation problems and therefore cannot always go to the public library.]

Furthermore, the children looked forward to the two days a week the lending library was open and expressed dismay when events intervened that kept them from their weekly visits. For example, one day as the book loan coordinator was walking into the preschool, a child yelled out, "Look! It's the book lady!" His mother then explained that he had been waiting with great anticipation that afternoon for the loan program to finally open. Another parent rushed into the center early in the morning prior to going to work and told the teacher that her daughter was very sick and needed to stay home; she added that her daughter was crying because she wanted to come to school to make sure she checked out a book. The mother said she had to promise her daughter that she would visit the lending library and check out a book for her. A final example of this enthusiastic and serious attitude toward books noted in field notes was of a child who accidentally left her book on the public bus en route to the preschool with her mother. This 4-year-old was embarrassed when she admitted to the book loan coordinator that she had lost the book. When the coordinator told her that it was okay because it was an accident, and that she was allowed to check out another book, Blanca said, "Y esta vez te prometo que no lo voy a dejar…te lo prometo! [This time I promise that I will not leave it (on the bus)…I promise!]"

We have also been struck with the high personal value that parents place on books themselves and how they should be treated. This conscientious attitude toward books is expressed earnestly by Ms. Hidalgo during a conversation about the importance of books in the home and community:

> A nuestros hijos les enseñamos que a los libros se les debe tener respeto…les digo que si le rompen la página al libro le duele y es como romperle el brazo a una persona—duele. Les enseñamos que deben cuidar las cosas y libros porque no tenemos dinero para comprarles más o reemplazarlos…eso es lo que quiero decir con respeto a los libros. [We teach our children to respect the books…I tell them that if they tear the page out of a book it hurts the book and it is like tearing off a person's arm—it hurts. We teach them to take care of things and books because we do not have the money to buy more or replace them…that is what I mean by respect for books.]

Valuing Both English and Spanish Literacy Activities

Despite the pressures, economic hardships, and language barriers that these families have endured, most parents have decided that they will not return to their native country (see Hondagneu-Sotelo, 1994, for extensive discussion of this issue). For most, this decision was based on their children's future. Several parents emphasized that they wanted their children not to suffer the way that they had, but rather experience greater opportunities. As expressed by one parent,

> En sus carreras, quiero que ellos sean lo que decidan…quiero que escojan su futuro y que puedan realizar sus metas. [I want them to be whatever they decide to be.… I want them to choose their future and be able to fulfill those goals.]

And a mother who worked long hours in the garment district was adamant about her children choosing a different vocation than her own:

> A veces me dicen que quieren trabajar como yo…me dicen, 'Quiero planchar como tú.' Yo les digo que no quiero que trabajen como yo…y si mi hija quiere ser una maestra, pues que sea una maestra…pero menos que trabajen en una

fábrica…no, eso no para mis hijos. [They will sometimes tell me that they want to work like I do…they will say, "I am going to iron." I tell them that I do not want them to work this way…and if my daughter wants to become a teacher, then she will…but not work in a factory…no, not for my children.]

Like Delgado-Gaitan (1990), we found that parents realized that becoming literate in English was vital to their children's participation in society. For example, Ms. Mari avowed that as a non-English speaker most of her activity was limited to within the Latino community only because of the language barrier. She further admitted that when spoken to in English she normally responded by smiling or nodding her head even though she did not understand what was being communicated to her—and added that she felt

muy ignorante…y más cuando mi niña de cinco años me tiene que traducir, pero también me siento orgullosa de ella porque ha aprendido inglés. [very ignorant…. I am especially embarrassed when my 5-year-old translates for me…but also proud of her because she has learned English.]

According to many parents, although storybooks were scarce in their native countries because of financial hardships, their childhood memories were filled with rich oral histories, as told to them by their parents and grandparents. Thus, along with storybook reading, oral folklore and storytelling have become significant parts of their children's home literacy activities. Therefore, Ms. Soco shares stories of her childhood with her 5-year-old son, but also takes advantage of the researcher's weekly visits to her home as an opportunity for her son to be read to in English. As the majority of families were not literate in English, the children tended to select Spanish-language books from the loan program. As an example, Elsita (age 4) always asked for books in Spanish because her mother told her that she was not able to read to her in English, but she did want to be able to read stories to her. Elsita, therefore, would point to a book, inquire if it was in Spanish, and if it was not, move on to another book until she found one in Spanish.

Still, despite the language barrier, some families came up with creative ways of compensating for their own lack of being able to speak or read in English. For instance, Ms. Mari used a tape recorder provided by the elementary school's library to listen to storybooks in English. She first read to the children using the Spanish version of the book, and then they sat together with the book in English and listened to the audio. For the mother, "La tomo como una oportunidad para que se les pueda leer en inglés. [I see it as an opportunity so that my children can be read to in English.]" Ms. Mari and her children also sit at the kitchen table and do homework together every evening after dinner and bathing. Even though Ms. Mari uses a Spanish-English dictionary to translate, particularly when the children forget the teacher's instructions, she is not always successful at deciphering the task. When she noticed that her children were beginning to mix Spanish and English words because they did not know certain words in Spanish and she did not understand what they were saying, she enrolled in English classes in order to "ayudarles a mis hijos a seguir adelante. [help my children move forward in life.]"

In another home, Ms. Lupita is becoming literate in English alongside her children (ages 5, 9, and 11). Her desire to become more involved in her children's education led her, too, to enroll in English classes. According to Ms. Lupita, her increased language skills in English have enabled her to "compartir más tiempo con mis hijos durante la hora de hacer la tarea. [spend more time with my children during homework.]" Additionally, during storybook reading, as Ms. Lupita reads books in English, she knows that she often mispronounces words. Although she worries that she will confuse her daughter, she adds, "No quiero que el miedo que tengo me vaya influir en ayudarles con sus actividades en inglés. [I don't want my fear (of mispronunciation) to affect my commitment to helping with activities in English.]" For Ms. Lupita, the risk of rendering some words in English with a nonstandard pronunciation does not outweigh the value of these home literacy activities with her daughter, which allow both of them to learn the English language together.

Parents' Reading Styles and Attitudes Toward Reading

Earlier findings by Goldenberg (1990) with respect to a population with similar demographics indicated that a large portion of Latino parents used books to teach skills directly. In our sample, however, of those surveyed, only 11.5% of parents (3 out of 26) used books to specifically teach letter-sound correspondence. Ms. Estrada, for instance, mentioned that she used the books to teach her children the sounds of the words as well as how to form them. She further shared that when she reads she has her daughter repeat the lines after her. Additionally, this small group of parents stated that they were interested in having access to more "instructional books"—in other words, books that show letter-sound relationships and teach phonemic and phonological awareness as well as vocabulary words. As one parent elaborated,

> Necesitamos más libros que enseñen la letra con el sonido que le corresponde y el dibujo...o si no, libros que les enseñen a los niños como pueden ellos remedar el movimiento de la boca que les corresponde al sonido de cada letra. [We need books that show the letter with the sound it makes and a pic-

ture of it…or books that show how the children can imitate what mouth movement corresponds to each letter sound.]

These parents in particular mentioned that they were drawing from how they were taught to read in their own countries as well as on "el método de 'phonics' del cual nos han dicho los maestros. [the phonics method that we have heard about from teachers.]"

A more common finding in our survey sample, however, was a focus on describing the illustrations and interpreting the *meanings* of stories. When asked what strategies she used to read, Ms. Feliz admitted that although she had difficulty reading, "Uso los dibujos…primero le describo los dibujos y después le invento un cuento. [I use the pictures…. I first describe the pictures and then make up a story.]" The majority of parents ($n = 23$) also indicated that they attempted to make the stories "come alive" for their children—not just for enjoyment's sake, but because they believed that their children's understanding of the relevant concepts would be increased. When asked what she was thinking while reading a book to her daughter, one mother reported that she pretends to be a character in the story and acts out the character to make the story seem more animated; she believed that this activity facilitated her child's comprehension of the story. In fact, all parents affirmed the value of reading aloud to their children:

> Cuando le leo a mi hija creo que está aprendiendo algo nuevo y le beneficia y le motiva para seguir adelante con sus estudios. [When I read to my daughter I think that she is learning something new and that it benefits her and motivates her to continue her studies.]

Effects of the Book Loan Program in the Classroom

We have further observed that the influence of the book lending program extended not only into the homes of the 4-year-olds, but also back into their classrooms. Based on classroom observations of the students as well as feedback from teachers and parents, we have seen how the program has helped to promote both early literacy and more positive parent-student-teacher relationships.

Teachers and assistants in both classrooms shared examples of how the book loan program influenced student behavior in their classrooms. According to an early survey given to each of the eight teachers and assistants toward the end of the first year (May 1999), all agreed that students who checked out books from the lending library were the same students who most enjoyed reading in the classroom, and who spent much of their independent play time with a book. In addition, all the teachers and assistants agreed that because students had more access to reading and writing activities, even parents who had limited time and resources to seek books from bookstores or public libraries were themselves more involved in literacy activities. The ELP, as we have mentioned, provided duplicate titles for the classroom and the book loan program, and the teachers mentioned students' excitement when they saw a book available for checkout that had been previously read aloud in class—or, vice versa, a book in the classroom library that they had previously checked out and read with their parents.

The children themselves provided many examples of the influence of the lending library. For example, when one child was asked by a researcher to read a book in the classroom, she responded by saying that she could not read it because her mother had not checked it out and read it to her before. Another student, who had consistently checked out books from the lending library for two years and who read regularly with her parents, demonstrated her "sense of story" during a circle time activity. The teacher was retelling in Spanish a story that was written in English. As he neared the conclusion of the story, he suddenly changed the plot and inserted a different ending. Immediately, Tita protested. When the teacher asked her what was wrong, she said that the story did not sound right: "Tienes que leerlo para saber que pasa en el final. [You have to read it to find out what happens in the end.]" The teacher then retold the story with the correct ending.

Social Effects of the Book Loan Program: Building Stronger Home-School Connections and Reinforcing Folklore

The preceding comments emphasized the role of the book lending program in promoting early literacy development in the classroom, but we also observed how the program and related activities have functioned as regular social gatherings for parents, teachers, and researchers. The unexpected result, we found, was to improve relationships among all the stakeholders in the child care agency.

Though it was not part of the original research design, we decided during the first year to organize a parent reception and workshop as a celebration of the teacher-parent-researcher collaborative efforts on behalf of the children that the program represented, and as a way to address some of the questions asked by parents about book reading activities at home. In organizing this and subsequent such events, we tried to accommodate parents' schedules and the need for additional child care. Because many parents used public transportation, for example, the receptions were scheduled in the late afternoon (usually 4:00 p.m. to 6:00 p.m.), thus allowing parents to attend the workshops and still ride the bus home before dark. Similarly, agency staff volunteered to provide additional child care so that parents could focus their attention during workshops and not worry about supervising their children at the same time. Finally, both family members and friends of the research team served the meal and assisted the parents during the workshops. The families were pleased to meet our own families and were encouraged to know that others also were interested in the welfare of their children. In the six receptions combined, approximately 300 parents attended the miniworkshops on various aspects of book reading and other related home literacy activities.

In order to make the workshops more culturally and context sensitive, presentations were made in Spanish, with individual translations provided in English for parents who were not bilingual. Handouts were also provided in both languages, and topics were selected based on comments and questions made by parents during book loans or on parent questionnaires. During the three years of the program's operation, the topics discussed at workshops included (a) using illustrations to help tell a story, so that students know that the words and pictures on the same page are related and meaningful; (b) developing an understanding of how print functions (in terms of, for example, the parts of a book, the direction of print [left to right; top to bottom], and tracking printed words on the page); (c) developing print awareness in their surrounding environment; (d) understanding that print performs different functions—in signs, labels, or calendars, for example, as well as books; (e) teaching sounds and letters within a meaningful context (for example, within a student's name, in a word or sentence, or while reading a story); (f) building on the strength of primary language use to develop vocabulary, to engage in more enriched communication and language play, and to develop awareness of sounds; (g) finding opportunities to read and write together with their children; and (h) how to prepare their children for kindergarten. The workshops also focused on building parents' awareness of how the routines and practices already established in their homes could help promote literacy development, thus allowing their children to define literacy development in broader terms and not only in terms of storybook reading.

As mentioned earlier, one goal of the project was to capture in written form some of the oral folklore extant in this community. Therefore, in one workshop activity, we invited (we did not require) parents to record on paper a poem, a rhyme, a song, or a special wish that they shared as a family. We anticipated that some parents might have difficulty with writing, and therefore offered to take dictation as well. The result was that parents worked with their children to create a page that would later be incorporated into a book that could be checked out from the lending library. The final product comprised pages ranging from the scribbled markings of a 2-year-old to "rondas" (children's rhymes to accompany a circle game) to several variations of the traditional song "Pimpón" (cf. Goody, 1987, on different story renderings within and between oral communities). In addition to this book, which became one of the most popular in the library's collection, several more of the songs and rhymes that the families shared were charted and became a part of the classrooms' collection of reading materials.

Parents' feedback regarding the receptions exceeded our expectations. One parent commented on an evaluation form,

> Yo en lo personal estoy muy agradecida por la atención que tienen con nosotros como con nuestros hijos y les digo mil gracas por ser como son. Nunca cambien. [I for one am very grateful for the attention shown to us and our children and I thank you very much for being the persons that you are. Do not change.]

Another observed,

> Es muy importante que hayan programas como este, porque nos enseña a nosotros como padres a tener ideas de como comportarnos con nuestros hijos y poder ayudarlos. Gracias por todo. [It is very important to have programs such as this one, because it shows us as parents ideas of how we can interact with our children and how we can help them. Thanks for everything.]

And a third parent remarked on the importance of the parent-child interaction during the book-making activity:

> A mi me gustó mucho porque pienso que a los niños les ayuda como tener confianza en ellos mismos haciendo los trabajos junto a sus padres, ellos se sienten más seguros y les encantan que sus papás les ayuden como deben pintar y hacer dibujos. [I enjoyed it very much, because I think that children gain more confidence when they work with their parents. They feel more secure and enjoy that their parents help them in drawing and making pictures.]

Other parents, too, mentioned the influence of the workshop presentations on their subsequent interactions with their children. One mother said she learned how tener paciencia cuando leo con mis hijos…y también que es importante enseñarles las ilustraciones o casos dentro del cuento que quizás sean insignificantes, pero que le puedan ayudar a saber más sobre el cuento. [to have patience when reading with my children…and how it is important to point out illustrations or issues in the story that may seem insignificant, but that help him know more about the story.]

Another parent noted, interestingly, that family reading time had become so important to her children that simply saying that she would not read to them if they did not behave was enough to bring about quick obedience.

As researchers we discovered from the families that reading was much more than just a skill to be developed; it created "tiempo para compartir juntos como familia. [time to spend together as a family.]" Ms. Mari used one word to describe this activity with her children—*solidaridad* (solidarity).

Touchstones of the Book Loan Program

As part of a comprehensive emergent literacy intervention program in an urban, high-poverty, bilingual preschool setting, the book loan program evolved dynamically into an important strand linking home and school, research team and families, agency (PLN), and parents. Interacting with the parents regularly and gaining their *confianza* (cf. Delgado-Gaitan, 1990; Moll & Greenberg, 1990) has helped us better understand how the program has been successful in achieving its primary goal of increasing families' access to books. The lending library also served its secondary purpose of enabling us to develop deeper insights about the nature of home and community literacy environments, the types of literacy knowledge that the children already possess as well as those they are developing, and the individuals with whom they interact during book reading at home.

In reviewing the functioning of the book loan program within the larger ELP, we have identified several facets that we believe are central to its implementation: (a) providing access to culturally sensitive and language-sensitive books, (b) providing access to extended information networks, (c) adhering to the importance of parental choice, (d) actively seeking to understand home literacy practices, (e) building on the literacy interactions that exist in the home, and (f) understanding the societal, economic, and political pressures shaping daily life, especially as they relate to language use. During the following discussion, we expand briefly on each of these.

Access to Culturally Sensitive and Language-Sensitive Books

In addition to books that were widely popular with young children, such as books about cartoon characters or childrens' television characters, books that celebrated cultural and linguistic diversity were highly valued by the parents. One example is *El Camino De Amelia* (*Amelia's Road*) (Altman, 1994), a story about a young girl struggling to understand her parents' migrant lifestyle. Another favorite was *Cuadros de Familia/Family Pictures* (Garza, 1993), which has a bilingual text and discusses daily life in a Hispanic community in Texas. Some parents have recognized these efforts to create a bilingual book lending program as an attempt by the research team to connect to students' background experiences while reinforcing a sense of cultural pride as well.

Providing Access to Extended Information Networks

Parents of the children participating in book lending consistently shared their appreciation for the convenient location and set-up and the availability of books that appealed to their children. But we expanded our view of information access to include not only books, but also an ongoing sharing of information with parents. Parent conversations with the research team, for example, included not only requests about the titles of instructional materials and children's books, but also requests for assistance with job searches, enrolling in ESL classes, interpreting utility bills, translating school bulletins, accessing the Internet, and understanding other written materials encountered in daily living. As a result of facilitating access to these resources, the research team unexpectedly found itself playing a role in the community's own information networks (see Moll & Greenberg, 1990).

Adhering to the Importance of Parental Choice

As reflected in the steady increases in the number of participants and in checkout frequency, the program expanded because of both parent and child interest. Parents openly shared their appreciation for our efforts to provide books related to the topics they requested. We also believe that the impact of book reading at home was stronger as a result of the parents' freedom to interpret suggestions from the researchers regarding how to interact with their child around books as opposed to being given a predetermined, scripted reading sequence (see Whitehurst, Arnold, et al., 1994; Whitehurst, Epstein, et al., 1994) or being told what books should be sent home with their children (see Mason, Kerr, Sinha, & McCormick, 1990). As we observed, parents demonstrated a variety of strategies as they read with their children: talking about the illustrations, reading the text and having their child repeat, retelling or translating a story, dramatizing a story, and asking questions about the pages read. By not dictating how storybook reading should be done, we attempted to acknowledge the cultural capital that families draw from in order to promote the success of their children within the mainstream culture. Given that the extant research on reading styles is inconclusive (see Yaden, Rowe, et al., 2000) with respect to whether any particular style of reading is better than any other for fostering long-term gains in reading achievement, we emphasized to the parents that there was no "one best way" to share a book. Rather, taking time to interact with their children around books was the most critical component (see Bus et al., 1995, for a comprehensive meta-analysis of the benefits of home storybook reading).

The fact that many parents saw themselves as genuine partners in the research endeavor was a deeply heartening experience for the research team. As one parent stated, "Nos hace sentir bien la manera en que nos traten y respeten. [We feel good about the way we are treated and respected.]" In addition, the agency administration also noticed the positive impact of the program and encouraged parents to share their experiences with local news agencies (see Tawa, 2000; Yang, 1999).

Actively Seeking to Understand Families' Home Literacy Practices

Although an important goal of the study was to learn firsthand about the nature of the literacy environment and interactions in the homes of the children participating in the study, the process of learning about home literacy posed interesting methodological as well as epistemological questions for the research team. For example, we elected to develop rich descriptions of the practices and environments of a few families who volunteered to participate, rather than attempting to visit the majority of homes and collect data more widely. We realized, however, that by focusing on fewer homes we risked what has been called the threat of "elite bias" (Miles & Huberman, 1994) in qualitative research: over-relying on the information provided by a few people who were the most open to the presence of the research team and, therefore, failing to capture important variations within the community that might exist in the homes of other persons less willing, for a variety of reasons, to interact with the researchers.

One fundamental goal of the study, however, was to understand the *individual* experiences of immigrant families and how those unique experiences shaped parents' daily lives, their views of education, and their goals for their children. In our approach and reporting, therefore, we have adopted what has been called a "standpoint epistemology." As Denzin (1997) has written, "the starting point is experience—the experiences of women, persons of color...and persons who have been excluded from the dominant discourses" (p. 55). Because we have no illusions that the experiences of immigrant families are even similar within the same community, we have been less interested in the "transferability" of our findings than in how "this starting point [of experience]...will lead to the production of local...knowledge about the workings of the world" (Denzin, 1997, p. 56) for us as a research team, in particular, and hopefully for these families and their children as they continue living and working in the United States.

As a result of being able to spend more in-depth time in fewer homes, the research team members conducting the home visits were able to assist in some domestic duties and allow working mothers some brief relief. In addition, some families extended invitations to all the research team members to attend birthday parties or mealtimes. According to one mother, these periodic visits were viewed "con respeto, con honor, y con cariño, [with respect, honor, and affection,]" expressing appreciation for the program and the benefits that their children received. In turn, during the course of these visits the research team and the families shared stories, experiences, and individual viewpoints on a variety of topics. Thus, by limiting the number of families visited, the research team engendered a sense of reciprocity and an exchange of information that, in turn, was felt to be of benefit to all the children in the project.

Building on the Literacy Interactions That Exist in the Home

As parents shared information about their literacy interactions at home, we documented, as have others (e.g., Delgado-Gaitan, 1990; Purcell-Gates, 1996), that many literacy events are already embedded in the course of everyday activities: the reading of environmental print during the bus ride home from the preschool, reading labels in the kitchen, reading and sending letters to family members. Nevertheless, enabling these families to have a variety of children's books available influenced the nature of literacy interactions at their homes. As indicated by parent responses to questionnaires, home observations, and comments to the researchers and teachers, many parents made time to sit together with their children to talk about a book. The importance of this latter activity as a regular part of parent-child interaction has been discussed by many researchers over the years (see Bruner,1986; Purcell-Gates, 1996; Wells, 1986) as being the foundation for the development of "a concept of story"—a sense of narrative structure—which seems to have a high correlation with later school achievement.

Understanding the Societal, Economic, and Political Pressures Shaping Daily Life

Given the many stresses families experience from living in economically depressed areas, finding ways to foster positive parent-child interactions around books was a central goal of the book loan program. As we noted earlier, most of the parents in this community worked long hours in the garment industry for minimum wage or less, and yet, despite the physical exhaustion of work and the ongoing financial burdens of raising a family on a small income, parents consistently expressed a strong desire for a better future for their children. For some parents, this has meant sacrificing more professional careers in medicine, teaching, or banking in their home country in the hope of obtaining better educational opportunities for their children and, subsequently, more stable and higher paying employment for them. Over the course of the study, parents repeatedly asked researchers for advice in helping their children achieve in school and helping them become better readers. By facilitating access to and experiences with books, we hope that the project has been able to assist parents in achieving some of the educational goals they desire for their children.

Conclusions

Though the book loan program successfully increased the availability of books for these children and fostered more parent-child interaction around books, the serious challenge remains of shifting responsibility for the continuation of the program to the preschool's full-time staff. As of this writing, we remain hopeful, because discussion has begun with preschool administration, staff, and parents about how to keep the program operating without depending on the research team to staff the library. In addition, several local and state philanthropic foundations have expressed interest in supporting the program, and jointly written grant proposals (university and agency) already have been submitted.

Though we have been able to track only a small portion (approximately 25%) of the children into one nearby elementary school, at present it is difficult to determine the long-term impact of the book lending program and the larger ELP in subsequent academic environments. However, early indications (see Yaden, 2002; Yaden, Tam, et al., 2000) of performance in kindergarten and first grade by former PLN preschoolers who participated in the intervention and book loan program are that growth in English language ability and literacy skills exceed that of other children entering from different preschool environments. Plans for follow-up of approximately 200 children through at least fifth grade are in progress, and funding has been sought.

The success of the book lending program, finally, has not been limited to increasing access to books. The library program served as a vital link within the overall ELP in fostering a positive group spirit on the part of all who were involved: children, teachers, parents, administrators, and university personnel. It also allowed the research team to build collaborative relationships that were essential for receiving invitations into the homes of several families. In turn, we as researchers have valued these opportunities to expand our knowledge of the cultural capital of this community. Hence, we actively seek to promote the vast reservoir of intellectual resources and strengths that exist in this community—and in other Latino immigrant neighborhoods as well.

Author Note

This research was supported in part under the Educational Research and Development Centers Program, PR/Award Number R305R70004, as administered by the Office of Educational Research and Improvement, U.S. Department of Education. However, the comments do not necessarily represent the positions or policies of the National Institute of Student Achievement, Curriculum, and Assessment; the National Institute on Early Childhood Development; or the U.S. Department of Education. Readers should not assume endorsement by the U.S. government.

REFERENCES

August, D., & Hakuta, K. (Eds.). (1997). *Improving schooling for language-minority children: A research agenda*. Washington, DC: National Academy Press.

Baker, L., Afflerbach, P., & Reinking, D. (1996). *Developing engaged readers in school and home communities*. Mahwah, NJ: Erlbaum.

Baker, L., Allen, J., Shockley, B., Pellegrini, A.D., Galda, L., & Stahl, S. (1996). Connecting school and home: Constructing partnerships to foster reading development. In L. Baker, P.

Afflerbach, & D. Reinking (Eds.), *Developing engaged readers in school and home communities* (pp. 21–41). Mahwah, NJ: Erlbaum.

Brassell, D. (2001). *The relationship between Latino preschoolers' book access and their conceptualizations of reading.* Unpublished doctoral dissertation, University of Southern California, Los Angeles, CA.

Bruner, J. (1986). *Actual minds, possible worlds.* Cambridge, MA: Harvard University Press.

Bus, A.G., van IJzendoorn, M.H., & Pellegrini, A.D. (1995). Joint book reading makes for success in learning to read: A meta-analysis on intergenerational transmission of literacy. *Review of Educational Research, 65,* 1–21.

Darder, A., Torres, R.D., & Gutiérrez, H. (Eds.). (1997). *Latinos and education: A critical reader.* New York: Routledge.

Delgado-Gaitan, C. (1990). *Literacy for empowerment: The role of parents in children's education.* London: Falmer Press.

Delgado-Gaitan, C. (1993). Parenting in two generations of Mexican American families. *International Journal of Behavioral Development, 16*(3), 409–427.

Delgado-Gaitan, C. (1996). *Protean literacy: Extending the discourse on empowerment.* London: Falmer Press.

Delgado-Gaitan, C., & Ruiz, N.T. (1992). Parent mentorship: Socializing children to school culture. *Educational Foundations, 6*(2), 45–69.

Denzin, N.K. (1997). *Interpretive ethnography: Ethnographic practices for the 21st century.* Thousand Oaks, CA: Sage.

Emerson, R.M., Fretz, R.I., & Shaw, L.L. (1995). *Writing ethnographic fieldnotes.* Chicago: University of Chicago Press.

Escamilla, K., Andrade, A.M., Basurto, A.G.M., Ruiz, O.A., & Clay, M.M. (1996). *Instrumentos de observacion: De los logros de la lecto-escritura inicial.* Portsmouth, NH: Heinemann.

Farkas, S., Johnson, J., Duffet, A., Aulicino, C., & McHugh, J. (1999). *Playing their parts: Parents and teachers talk about involvement in public schools.* New York: Public Agenda.

Fuentes, C. (1997). *A new time for Mexico.* Berkeley, CA: University of California Press.

Galindo, R., & Escamilla, K. (1995). A biographical perspective on Chicano educational success. *The Urban Review, 27*(1), 1–29.

Gibbs, N. (2001, June 11). The new frontier/La nueva frontera: A whole new world. *Time, 157*(23), 36–50.

Goldenberg, C. (1989). Parent's effects on academic grouping for reading: Three case studies. *American Educational Research Journal, 26*(3), 329–352.

Goldenberg, C. (1990). Research directions: Beginning literacy instruction for Spanish-speaking children. *Language Arts, 67,* 590–598.

Goldenberg, C., Reese, L., & Gallimore, R. (1992). Effects of literacy materials from school on Latino children's home experiences and early reading achievement. *American Journal of Education, 100,* 497–536.

Gonzalez, J. (2000). *Harvest of empire: A history of Latinos in America.* New York: Viking.

Goody, J. (1987). *The interface between the written and the oral.* New York: Cambridge University Press.

Guerra, J.D. (1998). *Close to home: Oral and literate practices in a transnational Mexicano community.* New York: Teachers College Press.

Gutiérrez, D.G. (1995). *Walls and mirrors: Mexican Americans, Mexican immigrants and the politics of ethnicity.* Berkeley, CA: University of California Press.

Heath, S.B. (1983). *Ways with words: Language, life and work in communities and classrooms.* Cambridge, UK: Cambridge University Press.

Hidalgo, N.M. (1997). A layering of family and friends: Four Puerto Rican families' meaning of community. *Education and Urban Society, 30,* 20–40.

Hondagneu-Sotelo, P. (1994). *Gendered transitions: Mexican experiences of immigration.* Berkeley, CA: University of California Press.

King, P.H. (2001, July 19). The rhetoric, reality of illegal immigration. *Los Angeles Times,* pp. Bl, B12.

Kominski, R., Jamieson, A., & Martinez, G. (2001, June). *At-risk conditions of U.S. school-age children* (Working Paper Series No. 52) [Online]. Washington, DC: U.S. Bureau of the Census, Population Division. Available: http://www.census.gov/population/www/documentation/twps0052.html

Los Angeles County Children and Families First Proposition 10 Commission. (2000, December). *Strategic plan: FY 2001–2004.* Los Angeles: Author.

Madrigal, P., Cubillas, C., Yaden, D., Tam, A., & Brassell, D. (1999). *Creating a book loan program for inner-city Latino parents* (Tech. Rep. No. 2-003). Ann Arbor, MI: Center for the Improvement of Early Reading Achievement.

Mason, J.M., Kerr, B.M., Sinha, S., & McCormick, C.E. (1990). Shared-book reading in an Early Start program for at-risk children. In J. Zutel & S. McCormick (Eds.), *Literacy theory and research: Analyses from multiple paradigms* (39th yearbook of the National Reading Conference, pp. 189–198). Chicago: National Reading Conference.

Miles, M.B., & Huberman, A.M. (1994). *Qualitative data analysis: An expanded sourcebook* (2nd ed.). Thousand Oaks, CA: Sage.

Moll, L.C. (1998). Turning to the world: Bilingual schooling, literacy, and the cultural mediation of thinking. In T. Shanahan & F.V. Rodriguez-Brown (Eds.), *Forty-seventh yearbook of the National Reading Conference* (pp. 59–75). Chicago: National Reading Conference.

Moll, L.C., Amanti, C., Neff, D., & Gonzalez, N. (1992). Funds of knowledge for teaching: Using a qualitative approach to connect homes and classrooms. *Theory Into Practice, 31*(2), 141.

Moll, L.C., & Greenberg, J.B. (1990). Creating zones of possibilities: Combining social context for instruction. In L.C. Moll (Ed.), *Vygotsky and education: Instructional implications and applications of sociohistorical psychology* (pp. 319–348). Cambridge, UK: Cambridge University Press.

Paratore, J.R., & Gallagher, J.D. (2001). *Opening doors, opening opportunities: Family literacy in an urban community.* Boston: Allyn & Bacon.

Purcell-Gates, V. (1995). *Other people's words: The cycle of low literacy.* Cambridge, MA: Harvard University Press.

Purcell-Gates, V. (1996). Stories, coupons, and the *TV Guide*: Relationships between home literacy experiences and emergent literacy knowledge. *Reading Research Quarterly, 31,* 406–428.

Reese, L., Garnier, H., Gallimore, R., & Goldenberg, C. (2000). Longitudinal analysis of the antecedents of emergent Spanish literacy and middle-school reading achievement of Spanish-speaking students. *American Educational Research Journal, 37,* 633–662.

Rivera, C. (1999, April 28). Skid row's frustrated families. *The Los Angeles Times,* pp. A1, A26–27.

Ruiz, R.E. (2000). *On the rim of Mexico: Encounters of the rich and poor*. Boulder, CO: Westview Press.

Sánchez, G.J. (1993). *Becoming Mexican American: Ethnicity, culture and identity in Chicano Los Angeles, 1900–1945*. New York: Oxford University Press.

Snow, C.E., Burns, M.S., & Griffin, P. (Eds.). (1998). *Preventing reading difficulties in young children*. Washington, DC: National Academy Press.

Sonnenschein, S., Brody, G., & Munsterman, K. (1996). The influence of family beliefs and practices on children's early reading development. In L. Baker, P. Afflerbach, & D. Reinking (Eds.), *Developing engaged readers in school and home communities* (pp. 3–20). Mahwah, NJ: Erlbaum.

Sosa, A.S. (1993). *Thorough and fair. Creating routes to success for Mexican-American students*. Charleston, WV: ERIC Clearinghouse on Rural Education and Small Schools.

Sosa, A.S. (1997). Involving Hispanic parents in educational activities through collaborative relationships. *Bilingual Research Journal, 21*, 285–293.

Southern California Studies Center & Brookings Institution Center on Urban and Metropolitan Policy. (2001). *Sprawl hits the wall: Confronting the realities of metropolitan Los Angeles* (Atlas of Southern California, Vol. 4). Los Angeles: USC Southern California Studies Center; Washington, DC: The Brookings Institution Center on Urban and Metropolitan Policy.

Swap, S. (1993). *Developing home-school partnerships*. New York: Teachers College Press.

Taylor, D., & Dorsey-Gaines, C. (1988). *Growing up literate: Learning from inner-city families*. Portsmouth, NH: Heinemann.

Tawa, R. (2000, March 7). "Mom, read me a story." *Los Angeles Times*, pp. E1, E3.

Teale, W.H. (1986). Home background and young children's literacy development. In W.H. Teale & E. Sulzby (Eds.), *Emergent literacy: Writing and reading* (pp. 173–206). Norwood, NJ: Ablex.

Teale, W.H. (1987). Emergent literacy: Reading and writing development in early childhood. J. Readence & R.S. Baldwin (Eds.), *Research in literacy: Merging perspectives* (36th yearbook of the National Reading Conference, pp. 45–74). Rochester, NY: National Reading Conference.

Thurlough Associates. (2001, April). *Para Los Niños funding proposal to the Los Angeles County Children and Families First Proposition 10 Commission*. Los Angeles: Author.

U.S. Census Bureau. (2000). *Census 2000: Profile of general demographic characteristics for the United States, Table DP-1*. Washington, DC: Author.

Wells, G. (1986). *The meaning-makers*. Portsmouth, NH: Heinemann.

Wells, G. (1999). *Dialogic inquiry: Toward a socio-cultural practice and theory of education*. Cambridge, UK: Cambridge University Press.

Wells, G., & Chang-Wells, G.L. (1992). *Constructing knowledge together*. Portsmouth, NH: Heinemann.

Whitehurst, G.J., Arnold, D.S., Epstein, J.N., Angell, A.L., Smith, M., & Fischel, J.E. (1994). A picture book reading intervention in day care and home for children from low-income families. *Developmental Psychology, 30*(5), 679–689.

Whitehurst, G.J., Epstein, J.N., Angell, A.L., Payne, A.C., Crone, D.A., & Fischel, J.E. (1994). Outcomes of an emergent literacy intervention in Head Start. *Journal of Educational Psychology, 86*(4), 542–555.

Whitehurst, G.J., & Lonigan, C.J. (1998). Child development and emergent literacy. *Child Development, 69,* 848–872.

Yaden, D.B. (2002, May). *CIERA's work with preschools.* Paper presented at the 47th Annual Convention of the International Reading Association, San Francisco, CA.

Yaden, D.B., & Brassell, D. (2002). Enhancing emergent literacy with Spanish-speaking preschoolers in the inner city: Overcoming the odds. In C. Roller (Ed.), *Comprehensive reading instruction across the grade levels* (pp. 20–39). Newark, DE: International Reading Association.

Yaden, D.B., & Paratore, J.R. (2003). Family literacy at the turn of the millennium: The costly future of maintaining the status quo. In J. Flood, J. Jensen, D. Lapp, & J. Squire (Eds.), *The handbooks of research on teaching the English language arts* (pp. 532–545). Mahwah, NJ: Erlbaum.

Yaden, D.B., Rowe, D.W., & MacGillivray, L. (2000). Emergent literacy: A matter (polyphony) of perspectives. In M.L. Kamil, P.B. Mosenthal, P.D. Pearson, & R. Barr (Eds.), *Handbook of reading research* (Vol. 3, pp. 425–454). Mahwah, NJ: Erlbaum.

Yaden, D.B., & Tam. A. (2000). *Enhancing emergent literacy in a preschool program through teacher-researcher collaboration* (CIERA Report No. 2-011). Ann Arbor, MI: University of Michigan, Center for the Improvement of Early Reading Achievement.

Yaden, D.B., Tam, A., Madrigal, P., Brassell, D., Massa, J., Altamirano, L.S., & Armendariz, J. (2000). Early literacy for inner-city children: The effects of reading and writing interventions in English and Spanish during the preschool years. *The Reading Teacher, 54,* 186–189.

Yang, E. (1999, February 28). Getting an early start. *Los Angeles Times,* p. B2.

Yeoman, B. (2000, July/August). Hispanic disaspora. *Mother Jones,* 34–41.

CHILDREN'S LITERATURE CITED

Altman, L. (1994). *El camino de Amelia/Amelia's road.* New York: Lee and Low.

Garza, C.L. (1993). *Cuadros de familia/Family pictures.* New York: Children's Book Press.

CHAPTER 16

Mediating Language and Literacy: Lessons From an After-School Setting

Margaret A. Gallego, Robert Rueda, and Luis C. Moll

There has been a recent upsurge in attempts to understand and promote children's literacy and language development, with an accompanying increase in various school programs and interventions. However, school environments are not the exclusive setting for children's learning and development (Lave & Wenger, 1991; Rogoff, 1994; see also Chang, chapter 11, and Yaden et al., chapter 15, in this volume). Studies that contrast school-based learning with learning in other settings (home, community, churches) (see Panofsky, 1994) conclude that socially assembled situations outside of school are likely to differ significantly from situations typical at schools. And this differentiation is important, because research has shown that children's competence (or incompetence) is context bound—that is, highly related to the features and organization of specific physical environments and social settings (Rueda & Moll, 1994).

Unfortunately, for many children of diverse linguistic and cultural backgrounds, participation in traditional classroom settings leads to the underestimation of their abilities on the part of teachers (Heath, 1983; McDermott, 1993; Moll, 1992; Rueda & Mehan, 1986). When there is a pattern of low academic achievement, one common explanation is rooted in deficit theories that attribute this to intrinsic characteristics of the child such as low intelligence, lack of linguistic or higher order thinking ability, or poor motivation. Often these deficits are seen as characterizing entire cultural, linguistic, or economic groups (Trueba, 1987; Valencia, 1998).

Other work, however, has focused on characteristics of children's learning *environments*, rather than solely on children's own characteristics and hypothesized deficits. Schools may extract valuable lessons by attending to how learning occurs in places outside the traditional classroom.

Indeed, research conducted in nonschool settings is gaining appeal based on its implications for the instruction of a diverse student population and with respect to educational reform generally: After-school activities—free of typical constraints, such as mandatory curriculum and a highly structured work environment, in the manner of many current school reform and restructuring programs—have a novel opportunity to support and enhance students' school-based knowledge (Schauble & Glaser, 1996). The National Association of Elementary School Principals has recognized that "the time spent by a child outside school and away from parents may be greater than the time spent at school. These hours are too many and too precious to waste" (1993, p. 1). Resnick (1991) cautions, however, that simply physically removing a child from the classroom is insufficient, noting that the majority of supplemental learning environments outside schools only replicate the typical interaction and content provided in schools. The need for appropriate and self-enhancing learning environments, then, is clear—and support for the development, design, and evaluation of new learning environments is increasingly available (cf. California Department of Education, 1994).

In this chapter, we draw from our research, conducted in several after-school projects that were designed by linking local universities with community organizations, and we provide computer-mediated activities for children of diverse backgrounds. The consortium of projects involved is known collectively as the Distributed Literacy Consortium (DLC) or Fifth Dimension. Our long-term goal in studying several selected sites within the wider consortium has focused on describing and defining features of language and culture as they emerged in each site, with particular attention to children's language and literacy activities and development. We argue that a systematic and theoretically grounded approach to understanding specific learning environments and the subsequent competence attributed to children in these nonschool settings has much to offer with respect to the development of dual-language opportunities for children; the possibilities of individual children's language and literacy learning and achievement; and the reconceptualization of school cultures that tend to be organized in significantly different ways.

Background of the Fifth Dimension Project

The Fifth Dimension Project is a distributed literacy consortium comprising after-school programs located in settings such as boys and girls clubs, YMCA/YWCAs, recreation centers, and sometimes even public schools. Each of the four sites that we have studied is an after-school computer club aimed at improving the literacy of English- and Spanish-speaking elementary school children. The clubs provide an informal learning environment in which students must learn to use computers and communicate about many different types of educational tasks and activities. Each site is linked with a university that provides staffing at that site consisting of both regular staff members and undergraduate students who participate as part of their course requirements. The Fifth Dimension is in its eighth generation and currently operates at 10 sites in the United States, Mexico, and Russia, and at additional sites on each of the campuses of the University of California (Cole, 1996). As part of a larger DLC in which these projects are embedded, the Language and Culture Evaluation Team (the authors) is one of three evaluation teams that have investigated various aspects of the functioning of these sites. (The other teams focused on cognitive outcomes, through the evaluation of individual children and the products of their participation, and on the social processes and social organization involved in coordinating activities within and across different sites.)

Basic Properties of a Fifth Dimension Project

The Fifth Dimension can be seen as a cultural system embracing rules, artifacts, divisions of labor, and outcomes that together constitute individual, local Fifth Dimension cultures mixing play, education, and peer interaction. The three overarching goals of the Fifth Dimension are to

1. create sustainable activity systems in different institutional settings, such as boys and girls clubs, libraries, and community centers (the formation of these activity systems is motivated by cultural-historical activity theory, described below);
2. provide contexts in which children can master knowledge (content, language, literacy, and technology); and
3. afford university students opportunities to connect theory with practice while they deliver community services to children in their local area.

There are three systems that constitute the immediate external context in which each Fifth Dimension site operates. Each site is linked with a local university that provides various types of support, such as labor, in the form of undergraduates, or funding for the classes in which these undergraduates enroll as part of their learning experience. Each site also is embedded in a specific and local community, with its own unique history and characteristics. Finally, there is an extended project community, connected electronically, which is made up of participants in the larger DLC. These systems are mutually interactive, in ways that differ for each site; they, and the relationships between them, are also dynamic, reflecting changes over time.

There are various "routines"—patterned, regular sequences of activities and behaviors—that constitute day-to-day life in each site. There are also various participants at each site: students, undergraduates, site coordinators, evaluation team members, parents, and visitors. As previously noted, the undergraduates play a key role, teaming with the youngsters to assist them with activities and submitting field notes to document the children's progress. The site coordinators also play a key role in facilitating the site's functioning and solving problems that may occur during each session. But perhaps the most novel form of mediation is that provided by an imaginary wizard, who can be contacted only through e-mail and who helps monitor the functioning of the site by providing answers, making suggestions, and even settling disputes. The true identity (and gender) of the wizard at each site is a closely guarded secret, but the children usually suspect that the site coordinator or one of the university students is playing the role of the invisible, all-knowing wizard.

The wizard, then, is an important artifact for mediating relations between adults and children at the sites. When conflicts or problems arise at a site, participants can write to the wizard for a decision on how matters should proceed. This imaginary and playful relationship, as well as those social relationships formed by other project participants (notably those between undergraduate students and their younger peers), create multiple social situations for learning unlike those found in a typical classroom setting.

The participants' roles are also flexible, especially in comparison to classrooms. For example, undergraduates come and go every semester. Students' roles change as they become more experienced or more proficient in the games or spend more time at the project. The constellations of activities and people at different sites suggest what we have come to refer to as "themes" or generalized "personality" characteristics that differentiate the various sites we have studied. Examples of these themes are a focus on computer literacy at one site, emphasis on a service orientation at another, primary language maintenance at a third, and community involvement at another. Our analyses suggest that the thematic characterization of a site is heavily influenced by the interests of the principal investigator and the local circumstances and resources at each site. They are examples of the flexible adaptation of a core set of organizing principles, tailored to the unique context in which the site is located and serving each site's need for sustainability.

Fifth Dimension activities take place after school, a strategic socioecological choice that represents unsupervised or unproductive time for many of the students targeted by the project. Several properties of Fifth Dimension are shaped by this fundamental property: (a) children's participation is voluntary, (b) play is mixed with education, and (c) all systems are intergenerational in their constitution. Computers and telecommunications networks are central to Fifth Dimension activities, but by and large the level of technology is low, depending on microprocessors of the kind that communities are likely to provide through donations and on off-the-shelf software. Access to the Internet is also an important element of each site and serves as an important link to the DLC.

All Fifth Dimension sites also combine community institutions with university courses. The majority of adult participants in a Fifth Dimension program are college students taking a demanding laboratory course in developmental psychology, communication, or introduction to teaching. These courses provide undergraduates with opportunities to observe and test theories of learning, development, and instruction in practice and to ground abstract concepts presented in university courses in the everyday activities of children. A culture of collaboration underpins social interactions within the Fifth Dimension, characterizing not only relationships between peers working together but undergraduate-child activity as well.

From the point of view of children, the Fifth Dimension is an activity system that mixes play, education, peer interaction, and affiliation with others in ways that compel their voluntary attendance. A visit to a Fifth Dimension site will reveal children working individually and in small groups on a variety of activities, including computer and board games, drawing, and reading and writing tasks, and using a variety of multimedia software. A central artifact of the Fifth Dimension is "the maze," which provides participants a tool by which to organize their computer game play. Children travel through the maze, attaining different levels of mastery during computer play that dictates the range of choice or freedom with which they can travel throughout the maze. Involved in computer-based activities such as computer games and Internet searching, children study or practice reading, writing, mathematics, history, geography, health, problem solving, and technology skills.

The next section briefly describes our role in documenting the Fifth Dimension project and describes the sociocultural theoretical framework that underlies the creation of the Fifth Dimension and serves as the basis for much of our own work—Cultural Historical Activity Theory (CHAT). Later, we apply these principles to our analysis of the properties of the Fifth Dimension; for the purposes of this chapter, we are specifically interested in understanding how the roles of members of a community change in the "transformation of participation" (Rogoff, 1991). Last, we discuss the implications of this study for the development of learning environments that seek to support dual language and literacy development.

The Language and Culture Team

As part of the evaluative component of the overall project, the Language and Culture Evaluation Team (the authors) was one of three teams created to document learning in the Fifth Dimension. The work of our team was guided by the following questions: (a) Is there a unique recognizable Fifth Dimension culture? (b) How does one get acculturated into the Fifth Dimension? (c) What is considered success in the Fifth Dimension? and (d) What are the language and literacy outcomes associated with participation in the Fifth Dimension?

Our data sources included (a) university course syllabi, which provided a general overview of the nature of specific sites and the connections between specific sites and the local university; (b) university student surveys, wherein undergraduate participants recorded their academic background, their experience with children, their observations of the local community, and the amount and nature of their computer experience; (c) interviews with key undergraduate participants at each site, which documented general perceptions and experiences regarding site operations, goals, history, and the like; (d) field notes taken by university participants that documented and recounted their interactions with children (submitted twice a week, as required by the university course in which they were enrolled); and (e) research team field notes (based on biweekly visits to each of the four research sites), which documented various aspects of site operations and participants' activities. In addition, we evaluated children's performance on the Language Assessment Scales (LAS), a standardized measure of children's English and Spanish language proficiency.

Cultural Historical Activity Theory (CHAT)

The Fifth Dimension project, as well as our work and the analysis reported here, is motivated theoretically by cultural-historical psychology. The central thesis of the cultural-historical school is that of the social origins of human thinking (Vygotsky, 1978)—that is, that one's thinking develops through participation in culturally mediated activities. As Scribner (1990) suggests, the concept of the mediation of human actions (including thinking) is central to Vygotsky's theorizing and is perhaps its defining characteristic. The point is that people interact with their worlds through cultural artifacts—especially language in oral and written forms—and that this mediation of actions plays a crucial role in the formation and development of human intellectual capacities. Thus, human thinking must be understood in interaction with social contexts—in clear distinction from traditional American psychological orientations, wherein the individual is the exclusive focus of study.

Kozulin (1995) notes that Vygotsky's notion of mediation includes three large classes of mediators: signs and symbols, interpersonal relations, and individual activities. Vygotsky (1978, 1987) concentrated primarily on what he called "psychological tools"—the semiotic potential of systems of signs and symbols (most significantly language) in mediating thinking (see also Wertsch, 1985, 1991). Pontecorvo (1993) summarizes well this Vygotskian idea of tool mediation:

> Mediation tools include the semiotic systems pertaining to different languages and to various scientific fields; these are procedures, thought methodologies, and cultural objects that have to be appropriated, practices of discourse and reasoning that have to be developed, and play or study practices that have to be exercised. (p. 298)

Without entering into details, Vygotsky (1987) emphasized a double function of language: how it serves communication, enabling human beings to socially coordinate (or discoordinate) actions with others through exchanges of meaning, and how through the internalization of this communication, it comes to mediate intellectual activity through the discourse of inner speech. The development of this capacity for self-regulation through inner speech is what helps bring actions under the control of thought, a development to which Vygotsky assigned great importance (see also, e.g., Bakhurst, 1986; Berk & Winsler, 1995; Martí, 1996; Shotter, 1993a, 1993b; Wells, 1994).

Cultural-historical psychologists' notion of mediation as individual action is visually represented by the basic subject-mediating tools-object triangle at the top of Figure 16.1, which provides a graphic representation of the CHAT model. This is the level of mediated action through which a subject transforms an object in the process of acting on it, as illustrated by a triadic relationship that depicts the individual (subject) and the environment (object) with the artifacts or tools involved in their mediation. In this mediational triangle, subject and object are both directly and indirectly connected through a medium constituted of artifacts (i.e., culture) (Cole, 1996). There are multiple sources of mediation in an activity system; instruments, including symbols and representations of various kinds, mediate the subject and the object, or the actor and the environment. This triangle, however, is but the "tip of the iceberg."

Engeström (1998) notes that the less visible social mediators of activity—the community of practice, rules and procedures, and division of labor represented at the bottom of the triangle—always are implicated in the subject's action. The "community" means those who share the same general object(ive); the "rules" are the explicit norms and conventions that constrain actions within the activity system; and the "division of labor" refers to the division of

FIGURE 16.1 A graphical representation of the CHAT (Cultural Historical Activity Theory) Model

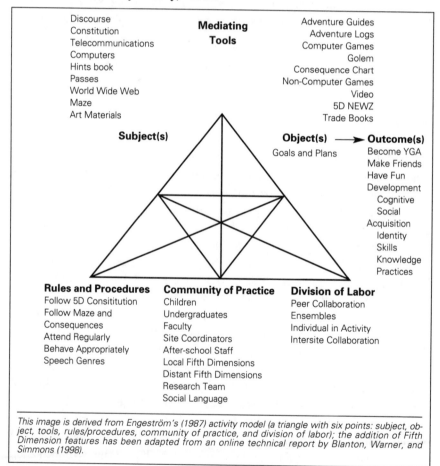

This image is derived from Engeström's (1987) activity model (a triangle with six points: subject, object, tools, rules/procedures, community of practice, and division of labor); the addition of Fifth Dimension features has been adapted from an online technical report by Blanton, Warner, and Simmons (1998).

object-oriented actions among members of the community. Engeström elaborates on the basic triangle, then, by incorporating it into a larger frame of interconnected relationships, as illustrated in the expanded triangle figure that makes up all of Figure 16.1. It is important to note that the various components of an activity system do not exist in isolation from one another; rather, they constantly are being constructed, renewed, and transformed. By including other people who must somehow be taken into account, the Engeström model enhances our understanding of the subject in activity.

The dynamic nature of these relationships can be illustrated by examining the different social arrangements and cognitive demands imposed on children that represent the multiple purposes operating in settings such as schools. From this perspective, Engeström (1987) revealed that a child's school day is filled with numerous activities only a portion of which are "learning" activities. Engeström explains that true learning activities are difficult to maintain because schools have multiple purposes, some of which may be in conflict or in competition with one another and therefore with learning (e.g., encouraging critique versus creating a compliant citizenry). Each school task objective or goal marks the subject's membership in the community that is the school/classroom; implicit and explicit rules guide students' behavior in ways appropriate for preserving community membership. In this way, teachers and students engaged in "schooling" may very well participate in different versions of the same activity, as defined by their distinct perceptions, motives, investment, and interest in the object(ive) of the task and based on their own histories and their status, or power, within the community.

Fifth Dimension sites are learning environments that, similar to schools, encompass multiple purposes. One aim is to provide children with educative experiences while retaining a balance of playful options (cf. the Fifth Dimension principles described above). Once "inside" the Fifth Dimension, children's participation is fluid, with multiple purposes (objectives) depending on the child's (or subject's) personal goal (for example, socialize with peers, partake of free snacks, gain access to the Internet, or attain the next mastery level with respect to a particular computer game). Indeed, choice is a cornerstone of the Fifth Dimension program, evident in children's very presence at the site because their attendance is voluntary. But although children's membership in the Fifth Dimension is voluntary and their choices with respect to participation are fluid, the Engeström triangle suggests that those choices, though numerous, are governed by a set of rules and a set of assumptions regarding product, outcomes, and division of labor among participants. In the following sections, we apply this framework to understanding the functioning of the Fifth Dimension sites we investigated.

Language and Literacy Learning in the Fifth Dimension

Guided by the theoretical framework just outlined, we realized that the key to understanding the Fifth Dimension as a cultural system was in the interactions. Our review of data collected across the Fifth Dimension sites we studied suggested that the relationship between the subject (child) and the community membership (undergraduate students, staff, peers) significantly influenced children's site experience; that is, their language and literacy learning. Even as sites provided tools, created shared experiences and histories, provided context, and engineered ways of praising participants, these features became the backdrop to the spontaneous interaction between dyads consisting of children and university students.

Nocon (1998) has discussed the importance of privileging community within the CHAT framework. He explains that the community is composed of individuals, past and present, who share with the subject an interest in the object of the activity (Engeström, 1991). However, those individuals occupy different roles with respect to the division of labor, as well as have their own histories, and they therefore have different relationships to the object, the subject, and the means of mediation. In this way, the resulting learning community can be viewed as a site of human diversity as well as commonality. And through social and productive activity the community is in continual development, as a dynamic composite of changing individuals. Relationships between those individuals participating in the activity change the rules, the division of labor, and orientations to the mediational means and object, and are part of the process of activity, not the product.

As Nocon argues, the transformation in the subject (the individual participant) is meaningful only when this change is communicated to the community, thus changing not only the subject's relationship to the object, but also that of the community.

Transformation of Participation

Rogoff (1997) also has elaborated sociocultural theory with respect to the notions of communities of learners and of learning as participation. She explains,

With an emphasis on participation, the emphasis for the central research question shifts from trying to understand the acquisition of capacities or skills or mental objects to understand the processes of participation. Individuals are seen as inherently changing through their lifetimes, through their involvement in necessarily changing events. Thus development is an aspect of participation. The focus is on questions of how people's actual involvement transforms in activities of particular interests, rather than on attempts to answer when or whether certain mental objects have or have not been acquired.... From a transformation of participation perspective, we examine how children actually participate in sociocultural activities to characterize how they contribute to those activities. The emphasis changes from trying to infer what children *can* think to interpreting what and how they *do* think. (p. 273)

As Rogoff suggests, evaluations of learning and development from the perspective of transformation of participation focus on

■ the roles that people within a community of learners play (including leadership and support of others' roles), and with what fidelity and responsibility; their changing purposes for being involved; their commitment to the endeavor; and their trust with respect to unknown aspects of it (including its future);

■ their flexibility, and their attitude toward change in their involvement (i.e., their interest in learning as opposed to rejecting new roles or protecting the status quo);

■ their understanding of the interrelationship of different contributions to the endeavor, and their readiness to switch to a complementary role (e.g., to fill in for others);

■ the relationship between participants' roles in this activity and their roles in other activities, including individuals extending themselves to other activities or switching to different modes of involvement as appropriate (such as skillfully generalizing or switching approaches—to participation in certain roles at school and at home or to involvement in several different ethnic communities); and

■ how their involvement—including their flexibility and vision in revising ongoing community practices—relates to changes in the community's practice.

In the following example, we examine an instance of the transformation of participation. Because transformation affects at minimum two individuals (that is, is social), we focus below on an interaction between one child and one university student, using a CHAT approach to understanding the dynamics of the encounter. Taken from one of the four sites we studied, this interaction represents two individuals with distinct experiences, motivations, and goals related to computers and to the specific teaching-learning activity to be described. The child is a fully bilingual/biliterate first grader who has been paired with an eager and willing but not so proficient (in Spanish) university student.

We believe this example is useful for two reasons. First, bilingual children paired with English-speaking undergraduate participants is the most frequently occurring arrangement encountered across the Fifth Dimension sites. (This arrangement is also the most often encountered in schools. That is, students are language proficient in their native, non-English language [e.g., Spanish] and their teachers less so. Conversely, teachers are proficient in *their* native language [e.g., English], and their students less so.) Second, this pairing allows for an analysis of how diversity—in this case, differences between child and adult in biliteracy proficiency—serves individual (subject) site success, in the form of increased biliteracy competence.

In playing the computer game *La Corrida de Toros* (1983) as shown in the following interaction (transcribed from videotape), the players, Cynthia (university student) and Claudia (child), are required to select alphabet letters to guess a secret word, as in the game hangman:

7:18   Cynthia comes over, says, "Aw right! There we go. La Corrida de Toros."

7:34   Cynthia picks up the task card and asks, "How old...?" "Seven?"

7:40   Cynthia asks, "Do you know how to play?"
       Claudia shakes head yes.

8:22   Cynthia sits down, says, "OK," and points to the screen.

8:32   Cynthia struggles with Spanish and asks if Claudia speaks English. Claudia responds "No."

8:43   Claudia nods toward the computer screen, saying, "They [the instructions] are not in English, they are in Spanish." Cynthia says, "You know how to play, right?" Cynthia continues pointing at the screen saying, "OK, OK."

9:28   As Yolanda [a staff coordinator] walks up, Cynthia says to her, "Hi, my Spanish is really being tested here. I don't know."

9:47   They start to use the task card. Cynthia tries to read in Spanish but goes slowly. They struggle.

10:23   Claudia looks at the task card. She looks at Cynthia and points to a spot on the task card and begins to read. Claudia translates for Cynthia.

11:15   Claudia reaches over and takes the mouse. Cynthia asks her to pay attention to the task card. Claudia reads aloud the task card in Spanish.

12:45   Claudia again grabs the mouse.

13:03   Cynthia puts her hand on top of Claudia's.

13:21   Cynthia, who is now manipulating the mouse, looks around the room. Claudia is now manipulating keys.

13:27   Cynthia reads from the screen in Spanish. She asks Claudia, "What do you think?" Pointing to the screen, Cynthia asks, "Do you think it's a day or a...time?" Claudia looks but answers by shaking her head. Later she says, "Time?" They keep working. Claudia continues manipulating the keys.

14:16   Cynthia says, "Oh, very good." Claudia gives her a knowing look. Cynthia says, "Give me five." They hit hands.

14:28   Cynthia gives the mouse to Claudia. Claudia continues working alone.

15:40   Cynthia asks Claudia if she got it [understood]. Claudia responds, "Yes."

15:46   Cynthia reacts, touches Claudia's hand on the mouse, and says, "Wait. Let's..." and then pulls up the task card. She grimaces, struggling with language. Claudia intervenes and takes over the mouse. Cynthia says, "We want...?" Claudia nods and affirms Cynthia's Spanish with "Uh huh." Claudia continues supporting Cynthia, with nodding and verbal affirmation. Cynthia suggests starting over. Claudia says, "OK."

19:14   Cynthia asks, "What are you thinking?" Cynthia groans. "I thin..." Cynthia puts her face in her hand and says, "Pardon, my Spanish is very bad." Claudia giggles and smiles and continues playing. Cynthia remarks, in English, "Oh, he's coming after you." She points at the screen.

20:48   Interaction continues with a mix of Spanish and English. Cynthia asks Claudia what a word on the computer means. Claudia tells her.

22:02   Cynthia gets up and leaves. Claudia continues working alone.

22:22   Cynthia comes back with a notebook. Cynthia asks Claudia, "What's your name?" (Como se llama?) Claudia responds very slowly and clearly, "La Corrida...de Toros." Cynthia recognizes the misunderstanding, this time pointing to *Claudia*, she asks, "Como se llama?" Claudia then gives *her* name and helps Cynthia to spell it. Claudia continues playing.

23:37   Cynthia asks, "What are the ones you got? Do you remember?" Claudia helps Cynthia with the proper articles: Cynthia asks, "*El* or *la* clase?" Claudia says, "la." They continue working, arms crossed, with Cynthia pointing to the screen and Claudia using the mouse.

24:27   Cynthia says, "What's this? Can you see it?" Claudia indicates that she does not know. Cynthia starts to lead Claudia through the words on the screen. Cynthia is now leading in terms of content while Claudia is still helping with linguistic form and pronunciation.

29:59   Cynthia initiates an interaction by pointing to the screen. Claudia maintains control of the mouse.

37:31   Cynthia explains what a journalist is with a mix of Spanish and English. Claudia indicates that she understands, rubbing her face and looking away.

39:53   Cynthia takes the mouse and becomes engaged. Cynthia says, "This person is on television. Do you know?" Claudia raises her finger in the air, nods yes, and smiles while starting to use the keys.

41:05   Cynthia points and says, "One more...think. Say the word *actriz*." After Claudia fills in one of the blanks with an appropriate letter, Cynthia says, "Very good." Cynthia holds up four fingers and says, "One more."

44:49   Cynthia asks Claudia if she has seen the answer in the notes. Claudia laughs and shakes her head yes.

45:38   Cynthia says, "Two more." She tries to explain in Spanish, then switches to English: "I'll give you a hint." "The people who..." They negotiate meaning without ever saying the word aloud.

48:25   Cynthia asks in Spanish if she wants help. Claudia hesitates and then shakes her head yes.

49:41   Cynthia says, "Very good." She gives Claudia the high-five and says, "All right!" She then picks up the task card and shows it to Claudia saying, "Finished...all."

Transformation of the Participant

As they were interdependent partners in the transcribed interaction, Cynthia was able to help Claudia with computer game play only to the degree to which Claudia helped with Cynthia's negotiation of the language (Spanish) of the game and guide sheet. The participants' dependence on each other's knowledge helped to define the most effective division of labor. During this episode, Cynthia was in charge of reading the task card and directing the interaction toward explicit goal attainment (namely, completion of the beginner level). Claudia, a veteran Fifth Dimension citizen, guided Cynthia through the Spanish instructions that guided their game play. Both drew from their language resources. Cynthia's field note written after the episode records her account of the interaction:

> This game was in Spanish, which was good because Claudia preferred Spanish over English. I can't really say the same, though, since my Spanish is so limited. The goal I set for her was to pass the beginner level, which the task card said was to get 5 words correct.... It (task card) said we could review all the words the game would use, which would help Claudia out.... Once we got started, it was interesting to see her strategies at guessing the word. In Spanish, a word is either masculine or feminine (*el* or *la*). Thus, the first letters she would always type would be *el* or *la* and then guess from there. Though my Spanish is equivalent to a first grader, she understood what I was saying, which did help her out a bit.

Survey data indicate that Cynthia's limited language skills and scant experience in bilingual situations were typical among the undergraduate participants. Indeed, the undergraduates often expressed concern about their usefulness to children. Cynthia summarizes these sentiments in her reflection notes:

> I don't know how much help we are to the children at site. I mean we can try and use our Spanish. Though I think it gets in the way sometimes. I tried, but you know I kept thinking this must be frustrating for the children, as it was for me. If this is a place to support Spanish language skills, how am I helping? I don't know, I really liked the kids and the experience. But maybe if you want to keep the Spanish the children have, you should have only really proficient

Spanish undergraduates go to that site. I thought my high school Spanish would be enough.... I mean if that is what it is all about, keeping Spanish, I don't think I helped much.

Clearly, Cynthia did not teach Claudia Spanish. However, Cynthia's notes suggest that she has underestimated her influence on Claudia's language and literacy development. The consequences of their language discoordination—namely, stalled progress in the game—provided a genuine opportunity for the participants to use multiple tools to mediate communication. For example, as Cynthia "runs out" of Spanish she points to the computer screen to "import" the Spanish texts available. To better understand the goal of the computer game, the child, Claudia, supports Cynthia through the local norms of the Fifth Dimension culture—the university student depends on the younger participant's specific and local Fifth Dimension experience. Both participants liberally shifted between and combined two languages (English and Spanish) (code-switching). Dual-language abilities were not only encouraged but essential, both for the completion of the task and for advancement within the local Fifth Dimension system of activities (progressing through the maze). Opportunities like this, to use all language resources freely and assert expertise (e.g., with respect to computer games) are commonplace within the Fifth Dimension culture.

Transformation of Community

Our focus on transformation of *community* implicates transformations in the rules that guide such interactions (e.g., with respect to language choice or what constitutes collaboration or "paired work") and indicates the division of labor that is most productive with respect to the objective of the joint activity.

In the Fifth Dimension, as in other settings, the features of community, rules, and division of labor influence the learning that the subjects (participants) gain. The social organization of the Fifth Dimension, which highlights the notion of play, contributes to an atmosphere in which risk and error are encouraged and seen as instrumental to learning. For instance, although students make errors, display incompetence, and engage in behavioral transgressions, these do not "mark" them in other than a temporary way. Instead, participants' attempts are "absorbed" by the social context in ways that work to reconstitute and encourage reconsideration of community rules and norms (transformation) rather than permanently defining their competence.

The changes that occurred in the episode between Cynthia and Claudia, and many like them that transpire across a relatively short time period (a 10-

week quarter in the university schedule), constitute incremental transformations, which build up and develop into changes that ripple influentially throughout the system: first within the dyad, then on the level of local site operations, and eventually reaching distant sites. As a result of these changes and exchanges, the community of learners continues to develop.

And although the voluntary nature of participants' involvement in the Fifth Dimension obviously differs from the compulsory nature of children's attendance in school, the ways the respective environments are organized for interaction are not necessarily bound to their setting. There is no reason why the excerpt we provided could not prompt a reconsideration both of the roles and responsibilities—the division of labor—typically ascribed to participants in a conventional classroom and of their underlying assumptions and purposes, or rules.

Implications for Conventional Learning Environments

We have identified themes or "personalities" that characterize each of our sites (Gallego, Rueda, & Moll, 1997). In turn, these personalities influence the goals of each site and affect how dual language and biliteracy are supported at each of the sites. The differences in goals or themes at each of the sites result in different opportunities for dual language and biliteracy development. The broad goals of each site influence participants' interactions, including the object(ive) of their activities. This is not different in principle from the variations seen at many schools. However, there are crucial differences.

Although there are differences across sites, two common observations are noteworthy. First, the features that appear to promote language and literacy development at these sites are rarely tolerated and almost never used as means for language and literacy development in more formal learning settings. In the typical school setting, language variation such as code-switching is perceived as nonstandard, deviant, and in some cases, a sign of semilingualism. Strict adherence to school-like rules, (language) tools, and division of labor (teachers teach, students learn) is particularly true in the remedial and special education programs in which low-achieving and minority students often are placed (Rueda & Mehan, 1986). Yet the code-switching by both children and university students routinely heard at many Fifth Dimension sites indicates that even partial proficiency can be a learning resource.

There is a danger in assuming that one can make do with the participation of less than bilingually proficient university students and still provide successful interactions. However, it is important to note that other fully bilingual resources (the site coordinator, the project director, other children, a few undergraduates) were available to children. The range and mix of language capacities combined to create an "additive" environment in which children's dual-language abilities were genuinely useful and practical. It is precisely this situation that drove learning in the example we examined.

Second, the analysis suggests that the deficit theories that commonly attribute low achievement primarily to intrinsic characteristics within the child are incomplete (Rueda, Gallego, & Moll, 2000). As others from a sociocultural bent have argued (e.g., McDermott & Vareene, 1995), constructs such as competence and success do not reside solely in the individual but rather in the interaction of the individual with others in specific activity settings. It follows that judgments about competence and success, as well as steps taken to promote them, should draw from this expanded view. What is being argued is not that individual differences do not exist, or that these differences are not important in ultimate academic achievement and later life success. Rather, the argument is that these differences interact with specific activity settings that mediate outcomes in significant ways.

In the case presented here, language and literacy development and competence are more accurately seen as resulting from the interaction of individual characteristics with the features of specific activity settings rather than as a function solely of the individual child. To suggest otherwise is to ignore the other critical components of the activity. Engeström's expanded triangle provides a means for gaining a more complete account of learning and development. In the analysis provided here, we have highlighted that the relationships (or community) that developed between the undergraduate and the child are a key element in the knowledge construction and language and literacy competence gained by both.

Conclusions

The fact that the Fifth Dimension operates in a nonschool setting raises the question of whether this fact is solely responsible for the patterns we have observed. Indeed, some research has indicated that some of the learning features described as instrumental for learning—intrinsic motivation, greater flexibility, a greater range of learning arrangements (Resnick, 1991; Schauble &

Glaser, 1996)—are, ironically, found most frequently in nonschool environments. This does not mean, however, that they could not be transposed to school settings.

An increase in the frequency of children's involvement in what Engeström (1987) has referred to as "learning activities," in after-school settings such as the Fifth Dimension as well as in school classrooms, requires more than simply adopting and implementing one or several of the features of the Fifth Dimension, however. Rather, what is required is the careful design of socioculturally relevant activities within a larger, supportive context. Understanding learning in complex activity settings requires an analysis of the variables represented in Engeström's expanded triangle, which guide the engagement of the participants and influence the potential outcomes of their interactions. Such an analysis in turn obligates one to consider the very definitions of community, rules, and division of labor that guide interactions in a given context, and to recognize their influence on learning.

As sociocultural theorists argue, learning is social and distributed, and research and interventions related to learning and development require a focus not only on the characteristics of the individual student, but on the student *in interaction*, within activity settings—and on the critical features and social organization that characterize those activities, and any given learning environment. The CHAT perspective used here to illustrate learning within the Fifth Dimension is one tool that provides such an analysis.

REFERENCES

Bakhurst, D. (1986). Thought, speech and the genesis of meaning: On the 50th anniversary of Vygotsky's Myslenie i Rec. *Studies in Soviet Thought, 31*, 103–129.

Berk, L., & Winsler, A. (1995). *Scaffolding children's learning: Vygotsky and early childhood education*. Washington, DC: National Association for the Education of Young Children.

Blanton, W.E., Warner, M., & Simmons, E. (1998). *The Fifth Dimension: Application of Cultural-Historical Activity Theory, inquiry-based learning, computers, and telecommunications to change prospective teachers' preconceptions*. [Online]. Available: http://129.171.53.1/ blantonw/5dClhse/publications/tech/effects/undergraduates.html

California Department of Education. (1994). *Organizing a successful parent center: A guide and a resource*. Sacramento, CA: Author.

Cole, M. (1996). *Cultural psychology: A once and future discipline*. Cambridge, MA: Belknap-Harvard University.

Engeström, Y. (1987). *Learning by expanding*. Helsinki, Finland: Orienta-Konsultit Oy.

Engeström, Y. (1991). Activity theory and individual and social transformation. *Activity Theory, 7/8*, 6–15.

Engeström, Y. (1998). *Expansive visibilization of work: An activity-theoretical perspective.* Draft manuscript, Laboratory of Comparative Human Cognition, University of California, San Diego & The Academy of Finland.

Gallego, M.A., Rueda, R., & Moll, L.C. (1997). *Language and culture team report, year three.* Laboratory of Comparative Human Cognition, University of California, San Diego.

Heath, S.B. (1983). *Ways with words: Language, life, and work in communities and classrooms.* Cambridge, UK: Cambridge University Press.

Kozulin, A. (1995). The learning process: Vygotsky's theory in the mirror of its interpretations. *School Psychology International* [Special Issue: Lev S. Vygotsky and contemporary school psychology], *16*(2), 117–129.

La Corrida de Toros. (1983). [Computer software]. New York: Gessler Publishing.

Lave, J., & Wenger, E. (1991). *Situated learning: Legitimate peripheral participation.* Cambridge, UK: Cambridge University Press.

Marti, E. (1996). Mechanisms of internalisation and externalisation of knowledge in Piaget's and Vygotsky's theories. In A. Tryphon & J. Voneche (Eds.), *Piaget-Vygotsky: The social genesis of thought* (pp. 57–83). Hove, England: Psychology Press.

McDermott, R.P. (1993). The acquisition of a child by a learning disability. In S. Chaiklin & J. Lave (Eds.), *Understanding practice: Perspectives on activity and context* (pp. 269–305). New York: Cambridge University Press.

McDermott, R.P., & Vareene, H. (1995). Culture as disability. *Anthropology & Education Quarterly*, *26*(3), 324–348.

Moll, L.C. (1992). Literacy research in communities and classrooms: A sociocultural approach. In R. Beach, J.L. Green, & T. Shanahan (Eds.), *Multidisciplinary perspectives on literacy* (pp. 179–207). Urbana, IL: National Council of Teachers of English.

National Association of Elementary School Principals. (1993). *Standards for quality school-age child care.* Alexandria, VA: Author.

Nocon, H. (1998). *Privileging community in activity theory.* Draft manuscript, Laboratory of Comparative Human Cognition, University of California, San Diego.

Panofsky, C.P. (1994). Developing the representational functions of language: The role of parent-child book-reading activity. In V. John-Steiner & C.P. Panofsky (Eds.), *Sociocultural approaches to language and literacy: An interactionist perspective* (pp. 223–242). New York: Cambridge University Press.

Pontecorvo, C. (1993). Social interaction in the acquisition of knowledge. *Educational Psychology Review* [Special Issue: European educational psychology], *5*(3), 293–310.

Resnick, L. (1991). Literacy in and out of school. In S.R. Graubard (Ed.), *Literacy: An overview of fourteen experts* (pp. 169–185). New York: Noonday Press.

Rogoff, B. (1994). Developing understanding of the idea of community of learners. *Mind, Culture, and Activity*, *1*(4), 209–229.

Rogoff, B. (1997). Evaluating development in the process of participation: Theory, methods and practice building on each other. In E. Amsel & K.A. Renninger (Eds.), *Change and development: Issues of theory, method, and application* (pp. 265–285). Mahwah, NJ: Erlbaum.

Rueda, R., Gallego, M.A., & Moll, L.C. (2000). The least restrictive environment: A place or a context? *Remedial and Special Education (RASE)*, *21*(2), 70–78.

Rueda, R., & Mehan, B. (1986). Metacognition and passing: Strategic interactions in the lives of students with learning disabilities. *Anthropology and Education Quarterly*, *17*(3), 145–165.

Rueda, R., & Moll, L.C. (1994). A sociocultural perspective on motivation. In H.F. O'Neil & M. Drillings (Eds.), *Motivation: Research and theory* (pp. 117–140). Hillsdale, NJ: Erlbaum.

Schauble, L., & Glaser, R. (1996). *Innovations in learning: New environments for education.* Hillsdale, NJ: Erlbaum.

Scribner, S. (1990). A sociocultural approach to the study of mind. In G. Greenberg & E. Tobach (Eds.), *Theories of the evolution of knowing* (pp. 107–120). Hillsdale, NJ: Erlbaum.

Shotter, J. (1993a). The social construction of remembering and forgetting. In D. Middleton & D. Edwards (Eds.), *Collective remembering: Inquiries in social construction* (pp. 120–138). Thousand Oaks, CA: Sage.

Shotter, J. (1993b). Getting in touch: The metamethodology of a postmodern science of mental life. *Humanistic Psychologist* [Special Issue: Psychology and postmodernity], *18*(1), 7–22.

Trueba, H.T. (1987). *Success or failure? Learning and the language minority student.* Cambridge, MA: Newbury House.

Valencia, R.R. (1998). *The evolution of deficit thinking: Educational thought and practice.* Bristol, PA: Falmer Press.

Vygotsky, L.S. (1978). *Mind in society: The development of higher psychological processes* (M. Cole, V. John-Steiner, S. Scribner, & E. Souberman, Eds. and Trans.). Cambridge, MA: Harvard University Press. (Original work published 1934)

Vygotsky, L.S. (1987). *The collected works of L.S. Vygotsky (Vol. 1: Problems of general psychology).* New York: Plenum.

Wells, G. (1994). *Dialogic inquiry: Towards a sociocultural practice and theory of education.* New York: Cambridge University Press.

Wertsch, J.V. (1985). *Vygotsky and the social formation of mind.* Cambridge, MA: Harvard University Press.

Wertsch, J.V. (1991). *Voices of the mind: A socio-historical approach to mediated action.* Cambridge, MA: Harvard University Press.

AUTHOR INDEX

A

ABOUZEID, M., 91
ABRAM, P.L., 249, 250
AEBERSOLD, J.A., 103, 107, 110
AFFLERBACH, P., 357
AGOR, B., 287
ALLEN, J., 74, 358, 361
ALLINGTON, R.L., 8, 14, 67, 185
ALMASI, J.E., 110
ALTAMIRANO, L.S., 357, 358, 365, 382
ALTMAN, L., 378
ALVERMANN, D.E., 110
AMANTI, C., 358, 361
ANDERSON, L.M., 97, 98
ANDERSON, R., 8, 9, 13, 26, 74, 85, 89, 176
ANDERSON-LEVITT, K.M., 324
ANDRADE, A.M., 365
ANGELL, A.L., 378
APPEL, G., 264
APPLEBEE, A.N., 98, 326
ARECCO, M.R., 75
ARMBRUSTER, B.B., 98
ARMENDARIZ, J., 358, 365, 382
ARNOLD, D.S., 378
ARREAGA-MAYER, C., 185, 210
ASATO, J., 3, 13
ASHER, J.J., 160, 166
AU, K.H., 8, 13, 243, 327, 329, 354
AUGUST, D., 57, 199, 239, 357, 360
AULICINO, C., 369
AZMITA, M., 265

B

BACHMAN, L.F., 221
BAKER, K., 67, 243, 250, 280, 296
BAKER, L., 357, 358, 361
BAKER, S., 126, 199, 200, 203, 210, 218

BAKHTIN, M., 334, 335, 336, 337, 354
BAKHURST, D., 393
BALDWIN, L.E., 4
BALL, E.W., 79
BANDURA, A., 129
BANKS, J., 327, 329
BARNHARDT, S., 27
BARRERA, R., 199
BARTOLOME, L., 186
BASURTO, A.G.M., 365
BEAN, T.W., 107, 110
BEAR, D.R., 71, 72, 74, 75, 76, 79, 80, 84, 86, 93
BECK, I.L., 107, 144, 218
BEEBE, L.M., 228
BEED, P.L., 98
BEERS, J., 74
BEIMILLER, A., 239
BENALLY, A., 338
BENTON, M.G., 334
BERK, L., 393
BERMAN, P., 167
BERNE, J.I., 310
BETTS, E., 99
BIBER, D., 58, 173
BIEMILLER, A., 26
BILLINGS, D.K., 202
BIRD, C., 265, 279
BLACHMAN, B., 79
BLAKEY, J., 172
BLOOR, M., 232, 234
BLOOR, T., 232, 234
BOSSER, B., 56, 57
BOURDIEU, P., 315
BOURHIS, R.Y., 228
BOYD-BATSONE, P., 335
BRANSFORD, J.D., 263
BRASSELL, D., 357, 358, 365, 382
BRISK, M., 186

BRITTON, J.N., 334
BRODY, G., 357
BROMLEY, K., 134
BROWN, A.L., 243, 263
BROWN, A.N., 98
BROWN, D.H., 232, 233, 244
BRUNER, J.S., 97, 153, 264, 316, 317, 319, 325, 326, 328, 381
BRUNSWICK, N., 94
BULLOCK, T., 143
BUNCH, G.C., 249, 250
BURNS, M.S., 98, 277, 357
BURT, M.K., 157
BUS, A.G., 357, 379
BUSH, L., 261, 276
BUTLER, G.Y., 220, 231
BYERS, B., 105
BYRNE, B., 45

C

CADE, C., 347
CALDERON, M., 57
CALFEE, R., 245, 250
CALIFORNIA DEPARTMENT OF EDUCATION, 7, 210, 231, 234, 246, 287, 388
CALIFORNIA READING AND LITERATURE PROJECT, 76
CALLAHAN, C., 293
CANADAY, D., 250
CANALE, M., 242
CANTRELL, R.J., 85
CARLE, E., 170
CARLO, M., 57, 239
CARR, J., 293
CARRASQUILLO, A., 184
CASHION, M., 14
CATHEY, S.S., 78
CAVEZ, R.C., 323
CAZDEN, C.B., 98
CELANO, D., 67
CENTER FOR APPLIED LINGUISTICS, 297

CENTER FOR RESEARCH ON EDUCATION, DIVERSITY & EXCELLENCE, 201, 203
CHALL, J.S., 4
CHAMBERS, J., 167
CHAMOT, A.U., 27, 157, 166
CHAN, J., 170
CHANG, J.M., 259, 260, 261, 262, 264, 265, 267, 268, 270, 271, 273, 274, 275, 276, 277, 279
CHANG-WELLS, G.L., 361
CHANOINE, V., 94
CHAPMAN, J.W., 8, 11
CHASTAIN, K., 153, 154
CHICAGO TEACHERS' UNION QUEST CENTER, 289, 292, 294
CHIPS, B., 170
CHO, G., 65, 66
CIBOROWSKI, J., 103, 107, 110
CLARK, K., 98
CLAY, M.M., 18, 341, 365
CLEMENTS, A., 114
CLOUD, N., 131, 132, 137
COADY, J., 26
COBO-LEWIS, A., 56, 58
COCKING, R.R., 263
COHEN, A.D., 221
COHEN, B., 320
COLE, M., 264, 319, 337, 389, 393
COLES, G., 8, 12, 22, 23
COLLIER, V.P., 4, 36, 159, 231
CONANT, F., 338
CONSORTIUM ON READING EXCELLENCE, 76
COOKE, C.L., 98
COOPER, C.R., 265
COOPER, M.L., 114
COPPOLA, J., 188
CORBIN, J., 188
CORREA, V.I., 200
CORSON, D., 24
COX, C., 334, 335, 353
COXHEAD, A., 24, 25
CRAWFORD, A.N., 163, 165, 173, 175, 176

CRONE, D.A., 378
CUETOS, F., 74
CUMMINS, J., 3, 4, 16, 18, 36, 56, 57,
    129, 139, 141, 159, 168, 173, 199,
    201–202, 220, 232, 296
CUNNINGHAM, A., 8, 11, 12
CUNNINGHAM, P., 209
CUSHNER, K.H., 323
CZIKO, C., 103, 107, 110

D

DALTON, S., 201, 263, 264
DAMICO, J.S., 222, 227
DANIELS, H., 347
DANZIGER, S., 311
DARDER, A., 359
DAVIS, A., 353
DE AVILA, E., 220
DELGADO-GAITAN, C., 357, 358, 360,
    361, 369, 371, 377, 380
DELPIT, L.D., 210, 238, 328
DEL VECCHIO, A., 221, 222
DEMONET, J.F., 75
DENZIN, N.K., 380
DETAR, J., 319
DEWEY, J., 315, 323, 327, 335
DIAMOND, B., 327, 329
DIAZ, S., 208, 249, 337
DILLARD, C.B., 329
DOHERTY, R.W., 265
DONOVAN, M.S., 263
DORRIS, M., 190
DORSEY-GAINES, C., 357, 358
DOSTOEVSKY, F., 335
DOUGHTY, C., 231, 244, 247
DOWELL, C., 208
DREHER, M.J., 74
DRESSLER, C., 239
DRUCKER, M., 349
DRUM, P.A., 74
DUFFET, A., 369
DULAY, H.C., 157
DUMAS, G., 157

DURGUNOGLU, A., 186
DUTRO, S., 202, 233, 234, 235, 237
DYSON, A.H., 336, 353

E

EAGAN, R., 14
ECHEVARRIA, J., 250
EGAN, K., 326
EHRI, L.C., 8, 72
EILERS, R., 56, 58
EL-DINARY, P.B., 27
ELLEY, W.B., 23, 63, 64, 67
ELLIOTT, G., 172
ELLIS, A., 11, 12
ELLIS, L.C., 72, 74
EMERSON, R.M., 364
ENGESTRÖM, Y., 394, 395, 396
EPALOOSE, G., 265, 279
EPSTEIN, J.N., 378
ERICKSON, F., 319, 325, 328, 329
ERNST, G., 185
ERVIN-TRIPP, S.M., 157, 159
ESCAMILLA, K., 56, 57, 360, 365
ESTES, T.H., 76
ESTRADA, P., 264, 265

F

FARKAS, S., 369
FARLEY, R., 311
FASHOLA, O.S., 74
FAZIO, F., 75
FEATHERS, M., 265, 279
FERREIRO, E., 72
FERROLI, L., 74, 76
FERRUGGIA, A., 174
FIELD, M.L., 103, 107
FIELDING, L.G., 27
FIELDING-BARNSLEY, R., 45
FIGUEROA, R.A., 200
FILLMORE, L.W., 27, 126, 199, 206,
    215, 218, 227, 231, 238, 254
FINOCCHIARO, M., 154
FISCHEL, J.E., 378

FISH, S.F., 334
FITZGERALD, J., 97, 99, 120, 177, 199
FLAKE, E., 172
FLEGE, J.E., 75
FLETCHER, J.M., 8, 13
FLOOD, J., 107, 110
FLORIO-RUANE, S., 308, 310, 315, 319, 324, 325, 329
FLOYD-TENERY, M., 283
FOORMAN, B.R., 8, 13
FOUNTAS, I.C., 99, 103, 107, 110
FOURNIER, D.N.E., 98
FRADD, S.H., 200
FRANCIS, D.J., 8, 13
FREEMAN, D.E., 46, 49
FREEMAN, Y.S., 46
FREIRE, P., 276, 328
FRETZ, R.I., 364
FRIENDS OF CHILDREN WITH SPECIAL NEEDS, 274
FUENTES, C., 359
FUNG, G., 262, 273

G

GALDA, L., 314, 358
GALINDO, R., 360
GALL, J., 143
GALL, M.D., 143
GALLAGHER, J.D., 357
GALLAGHER, M., 98
GALLEGO, M.A., 278, 403, 404
GALLIMORE, R., 264, 279, 357
GAMBRELL, L.B., 110
GAMIL, M., 347
GANDARA, P., 3, 13, 30, 167, 265
GANSKE, K., 76
GARCIA, E., 3, 13, 144, 264
GARCIA, G.E., 199
GARDNER, H., 275
GARDNER, R., 158
GARNIER, H., 357
GARZA, C.L., 315, 378
GAVELEK, J., 312

GEE, J.P., 155, 326
GEERTZ, C., 319, 324
GENESSE, F., 131, 132, 137
GENISHI, C., 29
GEORGE, M., 310, 325
GERSTEN, R., 126, 185, 199, 200, 203, 210, 218, 220, 243, 250, 280, 296
GEVA, E., 74
GIBBONS, P., 217
GIBBS, N., 359
GILL, C.E., 74, 91
GLASER, R., 388
GLAZIER, J., 329
GOLDENBERG, C., 18, 199, 202, 217, 357, 363
GONZALES, R., 283
GONZALEZ, J., 359
GONZALEZ, N., 283, 334, 339, 354, 358, 361
GOODMAN, K.S., 21, 23, 46, 47, 171
GOODY, J., 376
GRAVES, B.B., 97, 98, 107, 121
GRAVES, M.F., 97, 98, 107, 120
GREENBERG, J.B., 334, 337, 339, 353, 358, 361, 377, 378
GREENLEAF, C., 103, 107, 110
GRIFFIN, P., 98, 264, 277, 357
GROMOLL, E.W., 144
GUERRA, J.D., 359
GUERRERO, M., 221, 222
GUICE, S., 67
GUION, S.G., 75
GUTIÉRREZ, D.G., 359
GUTIÉRREZ, K., 3, 13, 198, 199

H

HACKETT, J.K., 115
HAKUTA, K., 199, 204, 205, 220, 221, 228, 231, 286, 296, 357, 360
HALLIDAY, M.A.K., 232, 233, 234
HALPERIN, M., 349
HAMAYAN, E.V., 131, 132, 137, 227
HAMILTON, R., 107, 218

HAMPSTON, J.M., 98
HARDING, D.W., 334
HARRINGTON, M., 186
HARRIS, D., 293
HASTY, N., 310, 325
HATCHER, P., 11, 12, 22
HAWAII DEPARTMENT OF EDUCATION, 291
HAWKINS, E.M., 98
HAYCOCK, K., 254, 255
HEALD-TAYLOR, G., 173
HEATH, S.B., 243, 250, 354, 358, 387
HELFAND, D., 261
HELLER, M.F., 174
HENDERSON, E., 72, 74, 76
HERMAN, P.A., 26, 176
HERMES, P., 347
HERNÁNDEZ, H., 250
HEWISON, J., 6
HIDALGO, N.M., 357
HIEBERT, E.H., 9
HIGHFIELD, K., 310, 325
HILBERG, R.S., 265, 279
HOEFNAGEL-HÖHLE, M., 158
HOLDAWAY, D., 153, 174
HOLLINGSWORTH, S., 278
HOLLINS, E.R., 327, 329
HOLT, D., 297
HOLZER, H.J., 311
HONDAGNEU-SOTELO, P., 370
HONIG, B., 43
HOPKINS, K., 66, 353
HUBERMAN, A.M., 188, 379
HUDELSON, S., 177, 250
HUDSON, A., 158
HULME, C., 11, 12
HUMMER, P., 74
HURWITZ, L., 103, 107, 110

I

INTERNATIONAL READING ASSOCIATION, 201
INVERNIZZI, M., 71, 76, 86, 91, 92

IRUJO, S., 287
IRWIN-DEVITIS, L., 134
ISER, W., 334
IVERSON, S., 8, 12

J

JACOBS, V.A., 4
JACOBSEN, D., 143
JAMES, W., 335
JAMIESON, A., 360
JENKINS, J.J., 99
JIMINEZ, F., 104
JIMINEZ, R.T., 199
JOHNSON, J., 369
JOHNSTON, F.R., 71, 76, 86
JONES, B.F., 143
JONES, M.B., 173
JORDAN, C., 327
JOYCE, B.R., 279
JOYCE, W., 316
JUEL, C., 10, 107

K

KAME'ENUI, E.J., 239
KANG, S., 74
KEHUS, M., 310, 325
KENDALL, J., 291
KERR, B.M., 378
KING, M.L., 108
KING, P.H., 359
KINSELLA, K., 248, 250
KLESMER, H., 4
KOMINSKI, R., 360
KONDO, K., 66
KORKEAMÄKI, R.L., 74
KOZULIN, A., 393
KRAJENTA, M., 74, 76
KRASHEN, S.D., 8, 9, 23, 35, 36, 55, 56, 58, 61, 62, 63, 65, 66, 67, 126, 131, 155, 156, 157, 159, 161, 163, 167, 170, 171, 173, 228, 244, 353
KUCAN, L., 107, 218
KWAN, A.B., 4, 17, 18

L

LAI, A., 262, 273
LAMBERT, W.E., 4, 16, 158
LANCE, K., 67
LANGER, J.L., 98
LANKSHEAR, C., 319
LANTOLF, J.P., 264
LAPP, D., 107, 110
LATCHAT, M.A., 289
LATZKE, M., 250
LAUFER, B., 26
LAVADENZ, M., 222
LAVE, J., 387
LEE, L.J., 78
LENNEBERG, E., 158
LEVY, C.M., 75
LI, S., 67
LIANG, L.A., 98
LIEBERMAN, P., 75
LIGHTBROWN, P.M., 244, 245, 246
LINDFORS, J., 46
LIU, P., 158
LIU, S.H., 75, 79
LLOYD, S., 17
LONG, M.A., 159
LONG, M.H., 228, 243, 247
LONIGAN, C.J., 357
LOS ANGELES COUNTY CHILDREN AND
    FAMILIES FIRST PROPOSITION 10
    COMMISSION, 360
LOS ANGELES UNIFIED SCHOOL
    DISTRICT, 169
LOTAN, R.A., 249, 250
LOXTERMAN, J.A., 144
LUBANDINA, M.A., 347
LYNCH, P., 174
LYNCH, R.H., 338

M

MACEDO, D., 276
MACGILLIVRAY, L., 357, 379
MADRIGAL, P., 357, 358, 365, 382
MALEN, B., 200

MANES, S., 352
MANGUBHAI, F., 23, 63
MARKS, S.U., 280, 296
MARTI, E., 393
MARTINEZ, G., 360
MARZANO, R.J., 243, 245, 291
MASON, J.M., 378
MASSA, J., 357, 358, 365, 382
MATHES, P.G., 8, 14, 28
MATSUDA, F., 79
MAXWELL-JOLLY, J., 3, 13
MAYER, R.E., 74
MCCARTY, T.L., 337
MCCLELLAND, A., 323
MCCLELLAND, J., 243
MCCORMICK, C.E., 378
MCCRORY, E., 94
MCDERMOTT, R.P., 387, 404
MCHUGH, J., 369
MCINTYRE, E., 277, 280
MCKEOWN, M.G., 107, 144, 218
MCLAUGHLIN, B., 167, 228, 239
MCMAHON, S.I., 347
MCNEIL, L., 3, 30
MCQUILLAN, J., 8, 21, 23, 45, 55, 65, 66
MCTIGHE, J., 289, 291, 292
MCVEE, M.B., 329
MEHAN, H., 250, 337, 387, 403
MEHTA, P., 13
MICHAELSON, N., 67
MILES, M., 188, 379
MINDEN-CUPP, C., 10
MINICUCCI, C., 167
MITCHELL, R., 289, 292, 294
MOATS, L.C., 238, 239
MODLO, M., 134
MOHAN, B., 128, 133
MOLL, L.C., 208, 249, 264, 283, 309,
    329, 334, 337, 338, 339, 353, 354,
    358, 361, 377, 378, 387, 403, 404
MOLNER, L.A., 250
MONZO, L., 264, 265
MOON, T., 293
MOORE, D.W., 103

MOORE, M., 327, 329
MORAN, C., 244, 245, 249
MORITA, A., 79
MORO, C., 73, 74
MORRIS, D., 78
MORRISON, S., 280
MORSE, J., 30
MOSS, M., 205
MOUSTAFA, M., 173
MOYER, R.H., 115
MUÑIZ-SWICEGOOD, M., 8
MUNSTERMAN, K., 357

N

NAGY, W., 26, 176
NATION, P., 25, 26
NATIONAL ASSOCIATION OF
    ELEMENTARY SCHOOL PRINCIPALS,
    388
NATIONAL CENTER FOR EDUCATION
    STATISTICS, 184
NATIONAL CLEARINGHOUSE FOR
    BILINGUAL EDUCATION, 228
NATIONAL COUNCIL FOR ACCREDITATION
    OF TEACHER EDUCATION, 185
NATIONAL INSTITUTE OF CHILD HEALTH
    AND HUMAN DEVELOPMENT, 63
NEFF, D., 358, 361
NELL, V., 67
NELSON, B., 167
NESSEL, D.D., 173
NEUMAN, S., 67
NEWMAN, D., 264
NGUYEN, A., 56
NIETO, S., 308, 319, 329
NOCON, H., 396
NUNES, S., 8

O

OBIAKOR, F.E., 223
O'DELL, S., 65
O'DONNELL, J., 323
OGAWA, R.T., 200

OGLE, D., 299, 318
OKETANI, H., 56
OLLER, D.K., 58
OLLER, J., Jr., 158, 222
O'MALLEY, J.M., 27, 223, 295, 297
OMANSON, R.C., 144
OPITZ, M., 51

P

PALINSCAR, A., 98, 243
PANOFSKY, C.P., 387
PARATORE, J.R., 357, 369
PARIS, S.G., 268
PASSERON, J.C., 315
PASTA, D.J., 67, 202
PAULESU, E., 75
PAYNE, A.C., 378
PEARSON, B., 56, 58, 153
PEARSON, P.D., 27, 98, 208, 278
PECK, J., 173
PELLEGRINI, A.D., 357, 358, 379
PELLEGRINO, J.W., 263
PENROSE, J., 173
PERDOMO-RIVERA, C., 185, 210
PÉREZ, B., 143
PERFETTI, C.A., 72, 74, 79
PHILIPS, S.U., 319
PHOMMACHANH, K., 347
PIAGET, J., 139
PINAL, A., 250
PINHEIRO, A.M.V., 74
PINNELL, G.S., 99, 103, 107, 110
POLACCO, P., 317, 318
PONTECORVO, C., 393
POPHAM, W.J., 268
POPLE, M.T., 144
PORPODAS, C.D., 74
POSTLETHWAITE, T.N., 6, 19, 20, 23, 27
POWER, M.A., 26
PRESSLEY, M., 98, 106, 208
PRESTRIDGE, K., 234, 235, 237
PUCCI, S., 67, 68
PUMA, M., 205

PURCELL-GATES, V., 357, 358, 380, 381
PURVES, A., 67

R

RAMEY, D.R., 67, 202
RAMIREZ, D., 67
RAMIREZ, J.D., 202, 210
RAMNARAIN, R., 245
RAMOS, F., 67
RAND READING STUDY GROUP, 99
RANDSDELL, S., 75
RAPHAEL, T., 8, 13, 98, 278, 310, 312, 315, 325, 329
RASINSKI, T., 51
READ, C., 78
READENCE, J.E., 97, 99, 103
REESE, L., 357
REIMAN, A.J., 279
REINKING, D., 357
RENDON, P., 283
RENZULLI, J.S., 339
RESNICK, L., 388, 404
REYES, M.L., 15, 16, 245, 250
RICHARD-AMATO, P.A., 169
RICHARDSON, J.S., 107
RICKELMAN, R.J., 103
RIEBEN, L., 73, 74
RIGG, P., 172
RIVERA, A., 283
RIVERA, C., 362
ROBBINS, J., 27
RODRIGO, V., 66
RODRIGUEZ, T.A., 215
RODRIGUEZ, V., 184
ROGERS, T., 316, 317
ROGOFF, B., 262, 263, 264, 266, 267, 269, 319, 387, 396, 397
ROLLER, C.M., 98
ROSEBERRY, A., 338
ROSEN, H., 326
ROSENBLATT, L., 334, 335, 337, 354
ROSENBLATT, R.A., 261
ROSS, G., 97

ROSS, K.N., 6, 19, 20, 23, 27
ROUSSEAU, M.K., 245
ROUTMAN, R., 98
ROWE, D.W., 357, 379
RUEDA, R., 264, 265, 277, 280, 387, 403, 404
RUIZ, O.A., 365
RUIZ, R.E., 359
RUMELHART, D., 243
RUSSELL, W., 76
RUTHERFORD, W., 167

S

SAADA-ROBERT, M., 73, 74
SACHAR, L., 64
SAFFORD, P., 323
SAMWAY, K.D., 287, 347
SANCHEZ, G.J., 359
SAVILLE-TROIKE, M., 56, 57, 158
SAWICKI, F., 172
SAY, A., 320
SCARCELLA, R.C., 159, 231, 244, 245
SCHATSCHNEIDER, C.S., 8, 13
SCHAUBLE, L., 388, 404
SCHIFINI, A., 169, 171
SCHLAGAL, R.C., 76
SCHMECK, R.R., 143
SCHMIDA, M., 228
SCHMITT, N., 75
SCHOENBACH, R., 103, 107, 110
SCHOFIELD, W.N., 6
SCHON, L., 66, 353
SCHREIBER, P., 78
SCHWAB, J., 319, 328
SCOTT, J.A., 9
SCRIBNER, S., 392
SELINKER, L., 157
SHANY, M., 74
SHARE, D., 9
SHARWOOD-SMITH, M., 167
SHAW, L.L., 364
SHEN, H., 74, 75, 76, 80, 86
SHIMIZU, W., 262, 273

SHIN, F., 56, 64
SHOCKLEY, B., 358
SHORT, D.J., 170, 250
SHOTTER, J., 393
SHOWERS, B., 279
SHU, H., 74, 85, 89
SIMMONS, D.C., 239
SIMON S., 106
SINATRA, G.M., 144
SINHA, S., 378
SMAGORINSKY, P., 216
SMALLWOOD, B., 287
SMITH, F., 51, 171, 175, 176
SMITH, M., 357, 378
SNOW, C.E., 98, 126, 199, 206, 215, 218, 227, 231, 238, 239, 254, 277, 357
SNOW, M.A., 158, 169, 287
SOLDIER, L.M., 316
SONNENSCHEIN, S., 357
SOSA, A.S., 357
SOTER, A.O., 316, 317
SOUTHERN CALIFORNIA STUDIES CENTER AND THE BROOKINGS INSTITUTION, 359
SOWELL, J., 26
SPADA, N., 244, 245, 246
SPENCER, K., 329
SPINELLI, J., 89
SPINKS, J.A., 79
SPIVEY, E.M., 78
SPRINTHALL, N.A., 279
STAHL, S., 8, 239, 358
STANOVICH, K.E., 8, 9, 10, 12, 176, 251
STANOVICH, P.J., 8, 10, 12
STAUFFER, R.G., 99
STEVENS, L., 107, 110
STODDART, T., 250
STRAUSS, A., 188
STRICKLAND, D., 29
STRITIKUS, T., 3, 13
SUGRUE, T.J., 310
SWAIN, M., 157, 229, 242
SWAP, S., 361

T

TAM, A., 357, 358, 365, 382
TAM, B.K.Y., 245
TAN, L.H., 79
TAWA, R., 379
TAYLOR, B.M., 8, 13, 98, 208
TAYLOR, D., 357, 358
TEALE, W.H., 358
TEBEROSKY, A., 75
TEMPLE, C.A., 74
TEMPLETON, S., 71, 72, 76, 78, 84, 86
TERRELL, T.D., 109, 157, 161, 162, 163, 164, 166, 167, 171, 172, 173, 228
THARP, R.G., 199, 262, 263, 264, 265, 279
THIES-SPRINTHALL, L., 279
THOMAS, W.P., 4
THURLOUGH ASSOCIATES, 362
TIERNEY, R.J., 97, 99
TIZARD, J., 6
TOLCHINSKY, L., 75
TOMLINSON, C., 288
TORGESON, J.K., 8, 14, 28, 45
TORRES, R.D., 359
TORRES-GÚZMAN, M., 143
TRACHTENBURG, P., 174
TREADWAY, J., 21, 22
TREGAR, B., 56, 57
TREIMAN, R., 78
TRUEBA, H.T., 387
TSE, L., 65, 66
TUCKER, G.R., 4, 16
TUNMER, W.E., 8, 11, 12
TURNBULL, A., 270

U

ULANOFF, S., 67, 68
UMBEL, V., 56, 58
U.S. CENSUS BUREAU, 359

V

VALDÉS, G., 185, 205, 208, 249, 250
VALDEZ-PIERCE, L., 223, 295, 297

VALENCIA, R.R., 387
VALERIO, P.C., 107, 110
VAN IJZENDOORN, M.H., 357, 379
VAREENE, H., 387, 404
VEATCH, J., 172
VERHOEVEN, L., 186
VERNON, S.A., 72
VOGT, M.E., 250
VOJIR, C., 66
VON SPRECKEN, D., 67
VYGOTSKY, L.S., 19, 98, 131, 153, 263, 264, 392, 393

W

WADE-WOODLEY, L., 74
WALLACE, S., 329, 338
WALMSLEY, S., 185
WALPOLE, S., 98
WALQUI, A., 206, 210
WARREN, B., 338
WARTON-MCDONALD, R., 98
WEAVER, C., 43
WELLS, G., 361, 393
WENGER, E., 387
WERTSCH, J.V., 264, 337
WHANG, G., 347
WHITE, C., 239
WHITE, S., 26
WHITE, T.G., 26
WHITEHURST, G.J., 357, 378
WIGGINS, G., 289, 291, 292

WILKINSON, I.A.G., 9
WILLIAMS, J., 231, 244, 247
WILLIS, M., 289, 292, 294
WILLOWS, D., 4, 8, 17, 18
WIMMER, H., 74
WINSLER, A., 393
WITT, D., 220, 231
WONG, B.F., 56, 57
WOOD, D.J., 97, 107, 110
WOODSIDE-JIRON, H., 8, 14
WOODWARD, J., 220

Y

YADEN, D.B., 357, 358, 365, 369, 379, 382
YAMAUCHI, L.A., 264
YANAGIHARA, A., 26
YANG, E., 379
YENI-KOMISHIAN, G.H., 75
YEOMAN, B, 359
YIN, R., 188
YOPP, H.K., 103, 107, 110
YOPP, R.H., 103, 107, 110
YUEN, S., 67, 202

Z

ZEICHNER, K., 186
ZHANG, S., 74
ZUKOWSKI, A., 78
ZUTELL, J., 74

Note: Page numbers followed by *f* indicate figures; those followed by *t* indicate tables.

A

ACADEMIC LANGUAGE, 25, 230–242; functions of, 231–236
ACADEMIC LANGUAGE PROFICIENCY, 5–6; vs. decoding skills, 5–6
ACCOUNTABILITY, 34–35; in ELD programs, 219–223. *See also* standardized testing; standards-based instruction
ACCURACY, 242
ACQUISITION-LEARNING HYPOTHESIS, 126, 155
AFFECTIVE FILTER HYPOTHESIS, 156, 244
AFFIXES: orthographic meanings and, 89–90; orthographic patterns and, 86–87
AFTER-SCHOOL PROGRAMS: book lending, 357–382; Fifth Dimension Project, 388–405
AGE: language acquisition and, 158–160
ALL-ENGLISH INSTRUCTION. *See* English-only instruction
ALLOPHONES, 44
ALPHABETIC LAYER: orthographic, 77
AMELIA'S ROAD (ALTMAN), 378
ANGLO-SAXON LEXICON, 23–25
APPROXIMATION, 153
ARITHMETIC: cognitive development in, 140–141, 142*f*
ARIZONA: reading instruction policy in, 14
ART ACTIVITIES: in scaffolding reading experience, 112
ASIAN AMERICAN STUDENTS: multilevel collaboration for, 259–281. *See also* multilevel collaboration; in special education, 260, 274
ASSESSMENT: in ELD programs, 219–223. *See also* standardized testing
AUDIOLINGUAL APPROACH: in L2 acquisition, 154
AUTOBIOGRAPHIES, 314–316, 325–326; critical, 186–195

B

BACKWARD PLANNING/MAPPING, 289, 290*f*
BALANCED APPROACH, 10–11, 22–23, 278–279; benefits of, 29–30
BASIC INTERPERSONAL COMMUNICATION SKILLS, 231
BE A PERFECT PERSON IN THREE DAYS (MANES), 352
BEHAVIORISM: vs. Vygotskian approach, 28–30
BIG BOOKS, 174–175

BILINGUAL INSTRUCTION: Common Underlying Proficiency model for, 202; English introduction in, 17–18; gifted-and-talented program in, 339–353; literacy transfer from L1 to L2 in, 55–62; orthography in, 75–91; policy context for, 2–3

BILITERACY: devaluation of, 16; spontaneous, 15

BOOK CLUB *PLUS*, 310–329

BOOK LENDING PROGRAM, 357–382; book inventory in, 364, 371–372, 378; changing demographics and, 359; children's attitudes toward, 368–370; classroom carryover from, 373–374; cultural and context sensitivity in, 361–362; data analysis for, 365; data collection for, 364–365; design and operation of, 363–364; easy access to books in, 361; educational challenges and, 359–360; extended information networks in, 378; guiding principles of, 360–362; home literacy practices and, 379–381; home-school connections and, 374–377; language barriers and, 370–372; long-term impact of, 382; oral folklore and, 371, 375–376; parental aspirations and, 370–372, 381; parental attitudes toward, 368–370; parental attitudes toward reading and, 372–373; parental choice in, 378–379; parental input in, 362; parental reading styles and, 372–373; participants in, 362–363; participation rates in, 366–368; results of, 365–377, 381–382; setting for, 362–363; social effects of, 374–377; touchstones of, 377–381

BOOKS. *See under* texts

BRICK AND MORTAR WORDS, 239–241, 241*f*

THE BROTHERS KARAMAZOV (DOSTOEVSKY), 335

C

CALIFORNIA: bilingual education in, 359–360; Hispanic students in, 359–360; reading instruction policy in, 3–4, 13, 30, 204–205, 207, 244

CALIFORNIA DEPARTMENT OF EDUCATION: ELD Standards of, 287

CHARTING ACTIVITIES, 87–89, 88*f*

CHICKEN SUNDAY (POLACCO), 317

CHILDREN'S LITERATURE: vs. decodable texts, 28–29

CHINESE: orthography in, 79–80, 85–86

CHINESE AMERICANS. *See* Asian American students

THE CIRCUIT: STORIES FROM THE LIFE OF A MIGRANT CHILD (JIMINEZ), 104

COGNATES, 90, 91*f*

COGNITIVE ACADEMIC LANGUAGE PROFICIENCY, 139, 232, 233*f;* age and, 159

COGNITIVE DEVELOPMENT, 139–142; in mathematics, 140–141, 142*f*

COGNITIVE INVOLVEMENT, 141

COLLABORATIVE TEACHING, 182–195; critical autobiography in, 186–195; observational study of, 187–195

COMMON UNDERLYING PROFICIENCY MODEL, 202

COMMUNICATION OF MEANING, 126–132

COMMUNICATIVE APPROACHES, 152–178; access to core curriculum and, 167–171; acquisition-learning hypothesis for, 155; affective filter hypothesis for, 156, 244; approximation and, 153; constructivist model and, 152–153, 171–172, 177; grammar in, 166–167; historical perspective on, 153–155; input hypothesis for, 156; key-vocabulary approach and, 172–173, 174; Krashen's hypotheses for, 155–156; L2 literacy and, 171–177; language experience approach and, 172–174; monitor hypothesis for, 156; natural approach, 161–165; natural order hypothesis for, 155–156; scaffolding and, 153, 167–171; sheltered English instruction and, 167–171, 250–251; thematic teaching units in, 170; topical curricula in, 165–166; total physical response method, 160–161; vocabulary in, 172–174, 176–177; writing and, 177

COMMUNITY: culturally literate, 339; of learners, 396–397; privileging, 396; transformation of, 402–403

COMMUNITY-SCHOOL PARTNERSHIPS: in Fifth Dimension Project, 388–405; reconceptualization of, 262–269. *See also* multilevel collaboration

COMMUNITY SUPPORT, 207–209, 272–274; cultural diversity and, 316

COMPARISONS, 240–241

COMPREHENSIBLE INPUT, 36

COMPREHENSION. *See* reading comprehension

CONCEPTS: preteaching of, 105

CONSONANT-VOWEL-CONSONANT PATTERN, 84

CONSTRUCTION OF MEANING, 47–49

CONSTRUCTIVIST MODEL, 152–153; communicative approach and, 171–172, 177; writing and, 177

CONTENT AREA INSTRUCTION: academic language in, 231–242; communication of meaning and, 126–132; comprehension skills in, 134–137, 136*f;* content-based interaction and, 132–138; coteaching in, 182–195; front-loading language in, 229*t,* 230, 249–252; general skills goals in, 132; goals in, 132; instructional approaches in, 132–134, 139–140; instructional materials in, 144–147; interdisciplinary activities in, 139; in L1, 170–171; language goals in, 132; modeling in, 131–132; sample lesson plan for, 140*f;* scaffolding reading experience in, 114–120; sheltered instruction and, 126, 127–128, 167–171, 168*f,* 250–251, 261; student-student interaction and, 128–130; study skills in, 142–144; teacher-student interaction and, 131–132; text comprehensibility in, 144–147; vocabulary in, 137–138, 138*f,* 216–217

CONTENT-BASED INSTRUCTION, 132–138; expository approach in, 133; graphic organizers in, 134; instructional approaches in, 132–134; knowledge framework in, 133; student-centered activities in, 133; visual aids in, 133–134

CONTENT-COMPATIBLE LANGUAGE, 138

CONTENT KNOWLEDGE: A COMPENDIUM OF STANDARDS AND BENCHMARKS FOR K-12 EDUCATION (KENDALL & MARZANO), 291

CONTENT-OBLIGATORY LANGUAGE, 138

CONTENT VOCABULARY, 137–138, 216–217

CONTEXT-BOUND COMPETENCIES, 387

CONVERSATIONAL FLUENCY, 4–5

COOPERATIVE ACTIVITIES: in content area instruction, 128–130; in ELD programs, 216–217, 244; shared reading as, 63–64, 174–176

CORRECTION: in language acquisition, 157–158

CREDE STANDARDS, 203, 210, 262–265, 266*f;* multilevel collaboration and, 262–265

CRITICAL AUTOBIOGRAPHY, 186–195

CRITICAL PERIOD HYPOTHESIS, 158–159

CUADROS DE FAMILIA/FAMILY PICTURES (GARZA), 378

CUEING SYSTEMS: in psycholinguistic approach, 47–51; in word recognition approach, 47–51, 50

CULTURAL DIVERSITY, 275–276, 278, 308–329; autobiographies and, 313–316; book lending program and, 357–382; case study in, 341–353; cultural knowledge and, 243, 323–329, 337–339; deficit model and, 338, 387, 404; dialogical relationships and, 335–337, 350–351; family stories and, 317–318, 320–321, 340; gifted-and-talented program and, 339–353; home-school connections and, 316; literacy curriculum, instruction, and assessment and, 309–329; literacy materials and, 314–322, 325–327; mediated and literate relationships and, 338–339; mediation and, 392–396, 394*f;* multicultural/multilingual consciousness and, 336–337; oral folklore and, 371, 375–376; principles of, 323–328; reader response and, 334–337; shared narratives and, 315; stories of culture and, 318–323; TLC literacy curriculum framework and, 309–329; Vygotskian approach and, 337–339

CULTURAL HISTORICAL ACTIVITY THEORY (CHAT), 391, 392–396, 394*f*

CULTURAL KNOWLEDGE, 243, 337–339; acquisition of, 323–325; sharing of, 313–323, 325–329

CULTURALLY LITERATE COMMUNITIES, 339

CULTURALLY MEDIATED ACTIVITIES, 392–396, 394*f*

CULTURAL STORIES, 318–323

CULTURAL SYSTEM: Fifth Dimension Project as, 396

CULTURE: meaning of, 319–320, 322–323

CURRICULUM FRAMEWORKS: for L2 instruction, 203–205

D

DANCE: in scaffolding reading experience, 112

DECODABLE TEXTS, 7, 14, 28–29; vs. nondecodable texts, 28–29; overreliance on, 19

DECODING SKILLS, 7–19; vs. academic language proficiency, 5–6; phonemic awareness and, 21–22; in second language, 16–18

DEEP ORTHOGRAPHY, 73

DEFICIT MODEL, 338, 387, 404

DERIVATIONAL RELATIONS, 90

DIALOGICAL RELATIONSHIPS, 335–337, 350–351

DICTATING: in language experience approach, 173–174

DIRECT INSTRUCTION MODELS, 152

DISCRETE LANGUAGE SKILLS, 5

DISCUSSION: in scaffolding reading experience, 111

DISTRIBUTED LITERACY CONSORTIUM, 388

DRAMA: in ELD programs, 218; in scaffolding reading experience, 112

E

EARTHQUAKES (SIMON), 106

EL CAMINO DE AMELIA/AMELIA'S ROAD (ALTMAN), 378

ELD PROGRAMS, 218; academic language instruction in, 231; accountability and assessment in, 219–223; accuracy in, 242; architectural approach for, 227–255; bottom-up approach in, 19; clear goals in, 244; components of, 211–219; content area instruction and, 230, 231; cooperative activities in, 216–217, 244; curriculum framework for, 203–205, 212; dedicated instructional time for, 209–211; drama in, 218; essential elements of, 242–246; explicit language instruction in, 228–246; family/community support for, 207–209; feedback in, 218, 219, 244, 245; fluency in, 232, 233*f,* 242; front-loading language in, 229*f,* 230, 248–252; importance of, 209–211; increasing need for, 227–228; instructional guidelines for, 18–19; instructional strategies in, 213; L1 resources in, 214–215; L1 use in, 201–203, 214–215; language forms and, 232, 233*f,* 236–241, 247; language functions and, 232–236, 233*f;* language learning vs. language acquisition in, 35–36; listening skills in, 218–219; literature-based instruction in, 211–212, 217–218; meaningful contexts in, 243; modeling in, 218, 243–244; modulating cognitive and language demands in, 245; multimedia resources in, 214; vs. New Literacy, 198–200; physical activities in, 214; policy context for, 2–3; practice and application in, 244; preschool/kindergarten, 199; prior knowledge in, 243; problems in, 246; progression in, 247–248; psycholinguistic approach in, 36–37, 47–52; research basis for, 200–203; safe learning environment in, 244; scaffolding in, 213, 218; schema in, 214; special education and, 250, 262, 274, 279–281; standards for, 203–205, 210, 221–222; systematic approach to, 246–255; teachable moments in, 229*f,* 230, 252–254; teacher training for, 205–207, 277–279; texts for, 211–212, 217–218; top-down approach in, 19, 30; vocabulary development in, 216–217; word recognition approach in, 36–47; writing in, 219. *See also* ESL instruction

ENGLISH. *See also* L2

ENGLISH LANGUAGE DEVELOPMENT. *See* ELD programs; ESL instruction

ENGLISH LANGUAGE LEARNERS: increasing number of, 34; standards-based instruction for, 294–305

ENGLISH LANGUAGE PROFICIENCY: assessment of, 219–223

ENGLISH-ONLY INSTRUCTION: lack of empirical data on, 200; limitations of, 198–224; literacy transfer from L1 to L2 in, 55–62; standardized testing and, 271–272

ESL INSTRUCTION: critical autobiography in, 186–195; explicit, 209–219, 227–255; family/community support for, 207–209; importance of L1 in, 201–203; increasing need for, 194; in kindergarten, 199; lack of empirical data on, 200; in preschool, 199; pull-out programs in, 195; shortcomings of, 195; standards for, 204–206; teacher training in, 194–195, 205–206. *See also* ELD programs; L1; L2

EXPANSION, 158

EXPLICIT LANGUAGE, 137

EXPOSITORY APPROACH: in content-based instruction, 133

F

FAMILY INVOLVEMENT: book-lending program and, 357–382

FAMILY PICTURES (GARZA), 315, 378

FAMILY STORIES: cultural bases for, 317–318, 320–321, 340

FAMILY SUPPORT, 207–209, 272–274; cultural diversity and, 316

FEEDBACK, 218, 219, 244, 245

FIFTH DIMENSION PROJECT, 388–405; background of, 388–392; basic properties of, 389–392; community transformation in, 403–404; computers in, 391; vs. conventional learning environments, 403–404; Cultural Historical Activity Theory in, 391, 392–396, 394*f;* as cultural system, 396; flexibility in, 390; goals of, 389–390, 395; imaginary wizard in, 390; Language and Culture Team in, 389, 392; language and literacy learning in, 396–401; maze in, 391; participants in, 390; participant transformation in, 396–403; privileging community in, 396; routines in, 390; themes in, 390; undergraduates in, 390, 391

FIRST LANGUAGE. *See* L1

FIVE STANDARDS FOR EFFECTIVE PEDAGOGY, 201–203

FLUENCY, 232, 233*f,* 242; conversational, 4–5

FOLKLORE, 371, 375–376

FREE READING, 23–27, 51–52; in L1, 65–66; in L2, 62–66

FRINDLE (CLEMENT), 114, 115

FUNCTION CHARTS, 234*f*–237*f*

FUNCTIONS-FORMS-FLUENCY BLUEPRINT, 232–255

G

GAMES: in natural approach to L2 acquisition, 164

GENERAL ACADEMIC VOCABULARY, 25

GEORGE, MARIANNE, 310–329

GIFTED-AND-TALENTED PROGRAM, 339–353

GRADE 4 SLUMP, 4

GRAMMAR: in communicative approaches, 166–167; teaching of, 236–241

GRAMMAR-TRANSLATION APPROACH: in L2 acquisition, 153–154
GRANDFATHER'S JOURNEY (COHEN), 320
GRAPHIC ARTS: in scaffolding reading experience, 112
GRAPHIC ORGANIZERS: in content-based instruction, 134; in ELD instruction, 217
GRAPHOPHONICS, 49–50; acquisition of knowledge of, 46; vs. phonics, 50, 50*t;* in psycholinguistic approach, 47–50; in word recognition approach, 50
GRECO-LATIN LEXICON, 23–25
GROUP ACTIVITIES. *See* cooperative activities
GUESTS (DORRIS), 190–192
GUIDED READING: in scaffolding reading experience, 108

H

HERITAGE LANGUAGE. *See* L1
HIGH-FREQUENCY WORDS, 25
HISPANICS. *See* Latino students
HOLES (SACHAR), 64
HOLISTIC LEARNING, 10–11, 22–23; benefits of, 29–30
HOME ENVIRONMENT, 14–16
HOME-SCHOOL-COMMUNITY PARTNERSHIPS: in book lending program, 357–382; cultural diversity and, 316; in Fifth Dimension Project, 388–405; reconceptualization of, 262–269. *See also* multilevel collaboration

I

IDENTITY NEGOTIATION, 16
IMMERSION INSTRUCTION. *See* English-only instruction
IMPLICIT LANGUAGE, 137
INDIAN SCHOOL: TEACHING THE WHITE MAN'S WAY (COOPER), 114
INPUT HYPOTHESIS, 131, 156
IN-SCHOOL FREE READING, 23–27, 51–52; in L1, 65–66; in L2, 62–65
INSTRUCTIONAL MATERIALS: in content area instruction, 144–147
INTERESTING WORD ACTIVITIES, 89
INTERLANGUAGE, 157
ISLAND OF THE BLUE DOLPHINS (O'DELL), 65

J

JACOB'S RESCUE (DRUCKER & HALPERIN), 348–349
JOLLY PHONICS PROGRAM, 17–18, 19
JOSUE (CASE STUDY), 341–353

K

KEY-VOCABULARY APPROACH, 172–173, 174
KINDERGARTEN: English language development in, 199

L

L1: in content area instruction, 170–171; instructional utility of, 201–203, 214–216; in scaffolding reading experience, 105–106

L1 ACQUISITION: age and, 158–160; vs. L2 acquisition, 156–157; vs. language learning, 35–36, 47–52

L1 LITERACY: continuing development in, 65–66, 66*t;* importance of in L2 acquisition, 201–203; predictors of, 65–66, 66*t;* transfer of to L2, 55–68, 56*t*

L1 TEXTS: availability of, 67–68

L2: decoding skills in, 16–18; reading comprehension in, 16–18. *See also* English language learning

L2 ACQUISITION, 35–36; access to core curriculum in, 167–171; affective factors in, 156, 158, 244; age and, 158–160; audiolingual approach in, 154; communicative approaches in, 152–178. *See also* communicative approaches; constructivist model and, 152–153, 171–172, 177; correction in, 157–158; critical period hypothesis and, 158–159; curriculum frameworks for, 203–205; expansion in, 158; family/community support and, 207–209; free reading and, 62–66; grammar-translation approach in, 153–154; importance of L1 in, 201–203; interlanguage in, 157; key-vocabulary approach and, 172–173, 174; vs. L1 acquisition, 156–157; L1 literacy and, 55–68, 56*t;* language experience approach and, 172–174; vs. language learning, 35–36, 47–52; role of reading in, 55–68; scaffolding in, 167–171; shared reading and, 174–176; sheltered English instruction and, 167–171; syntax development in, 157; teaching expertise and, 205–207; vocabulary in, 172–174, 176–177; writing and, 177. *See also* EDL programs; ESL instruction

LANGUAGE: academic, 231–242; content-compatible, 137–138; content-obligatory, 137–138; explicit, 137; forms of, 236–241; functions of, 232–236; implicit, 137. *See also* L1; L2; vocabulary

LANGUAGE ACQUISITION: age and, 158–160; critical period hypothesis and, 158–159; vs. language learning, 35–36, 35*t,* 47–52, 228. *See also* L2 acquisition

LANGUAGE AND CULTURE TEAM, 389, 392

LANGUAGE DEVELOPMENT: cognitive development and, 139

LANGUAGE EXPERIENCE APPROACH, 172–174

LANGUAGE INSTRUCTION. *See* ELD programs; ESL instruction

LANGUAGE LEARNING: vs. L1 acquisition, 35–36, 35*t,* 47–52

LANGUAGE PROFICIENCY: academic, 5–6; dimensions of, 3–6; time needed to acquire, 4

LATINO STUDENTS: *See* book lending program; case study of, 341–353; increasing population of, 359; mediated and literate relationships and, 338–339, 353–354, 387–405; poverty among, 359, 360; risk factors for, 359

LEARNING: behaviorist vs. Vygotskian approach to, 28–30; as participation, 396–397; relational, 338–339, 353–354

LEARNING DISABILITIES, 262, 279–281; Asian American views of, 274

LEARNING ENVIRONMENTS, 387–388

LESSON FRAMEWORK, 99

LESSON PLAN: for content area instruction, 140*f*

LESSON PLANNING: in content-based instruction, 132–133

LETTER-NAME STRATEGIES, 79–80, 81

LIBRARIES: book lending program and, 357–382; L1 texts in, 67–68

LIMITED ENGLISH PROFICIENCY: definition of, 34; among Latino children, 350

LISTENING SKILLS, 143; in ELD programs, 218–219

LITERACY: continuing development of in L1, 64*t,* 65–66; as cultural practice, 309; vs. reading, 277–278; transfer of from L1 to L2, 55–62, 56*t*

LITERACY DEVELOPMENT: identity negotiation in, 16

LITERACY LEARNING: phases of dominance in, 73–74

LITERATE HOME ENVIRONMENT, 14–16

LOW-FREQUENCY WORDS, 25

M

MAROO OF THE WINTER CAVES (TURNBULL), 270

MATHEMATICS: cognitive development in, 140–141, 142*f*

MATTHEW EFFECT, 176

MEANING CONSTRUCTION, 47–49

MEANING LAYER: orthographic, 72–74, 89–90

MEDIATED AND LITERATE RELATIONSHIPS, 338–339, 353–354; in after-school setting, 387–405; case study of, 333–354

MEDIATION, 392–393

METACOGNITIVE APPROACH, 10–11

METACOGNITIVE PROCESSES, 143

METALINGUISTIC REFLECTION, 245–246

MEXICAN AMERICANS. *See* Latino students

MODELING, 243–244; in content area instruction, 131–132; in ELD programs, 218

MOLLY'S PILGRIM (COHEN), 320, 321–322, 326

MONITOR HYPOTHESIS, 156

MULTICULTURALISM. *See* cultural diversity

MULTILEVEL COLLABORATION, 259–281; administration support for, 270–272; challenges and opportunities in, 274–281; community plane in, 267–268; community support for, 272–274; CREDE standards and, 262–265; cultural diversity and, 275–276, 278; definition and, 262–269; family support for, 272–274; home-school-community partnerships and, 262–274; learning disabilities and, 262, 279–281; multiple learning sites and, 275–276, 275*f;* new partnerships in, 269–274; personal plane in, 268–269; planes of analysis and, 263, 266–269; prior knowledge and, 276–277; professional development and, 277–279; special education programs and, 262, 279–281; standardized testing and, 267–268, 271–272; teacher support for, 270–272; theoretical framework for, 262–269; within-school factors in, 267–269, 270–272

MULTIMEDIA ACTIVITIES: in scaffolding reading experience, 112

MULTIPLE LEARNING SITES, 275–276
MUSIC: in scaffolding reading experience, 112

N

NARRATIVES: cultural, 318–323; family, 317–318, 320–321; personal, 314–316, 325–326
NATIONAL ASSESSMENT OF EDUCATIONAL PROGRESS (NAEP), 21
NATIONAL ASSOCIATION OF ELEMENTARY SCHOOL PRINCIPLES, 388
NATIONAL BOARD FOR PROFESSIONAL TEACHING STANDARDS, 206
NATIONAL BOARD TEACHER CERTIFICATION, 206
NATIONAL READING PANEL, 63
NATURAL APPROACH: to L2 acquisition, 161–165
NATURAL ORDER HYPOTHESIS, 155–156
NEGOTIATION OF MEANING, 131
NESTING COMMANDS: in TPR approach, 161
NEW LITERACY, 198–224. *See also* English-only instruction
NONDECODABLE TEXTS: vs. decodable texts, 28–29

O

OPAQUE ORTHOGRAPHY, 73
ORAL FOLKLORE, 371, 375–376
ORAL READING, 46–47; in scaffolding reading experience, 108–109
ORTHOGRAPHY, 71–92; advanced reading and, 90; affixes and, 87–88, 89–90; alphabetic layer in, 77; beginning reading and, 79–83, 84; in bilingual instruction, 75, 76–77; Chinese, 79–80, 85–86; cognates and, 90; consonant-vowel-consonant pattern in, 84; deep, 72–73; emergent-phase, 77–79; emergent spelling/reading and, 77–80; graphic similarities in, 83–84; intermediate spelling/reading and, 86–90; learning progression in, 73–75, 77–90; letter-name strategies and, 79–80, 81; meaning layer in, 72–74, 73f, 89–90; opaque, 72; pattern layer in, 72–74, 73f, 83–89; pronunciation and, 85; relative complexity of, 75; semitranslucent, 73; semitransparent, 73; shallow, 72; sound layer in, 72–74, 73f, 77–83; sound-symbol correspondence in, 72–73; Spanish, 73, 79, 80–83, 85; spelling inventories for, 76–77; stages of, 73–74, 77–90; tracking and, 79; transitional reading and, 84–86; translucent, 72; transparent, 72; word derivations and, 90; word-study activities and, 71–72, 76–90
OUTREACH ACTIVITIES: in scaffolding reading experience, 112–113

P

PARTNERSHIPS: in content area instruction, 128–130; negotiation of meaning in, 131; in shared reading, 63–64
PATTERN LAYER: orthographic, 72–74

PERSONAL NARRATIVES, 314–316, 325–326

PERSONAL VIGNETTES, 316

PHASES OF DOMINANCE, 73–74

PHONEMIC AWARENESS, 7–8; decoding skills and, 21–22; definition of, 7; instruction in, 11; reading comprehension and, 21–22; in word recognition approach, 43–46

PHONICS: in balanced approach, 10–11, 22–23, 278–279; decodable texts and, 7, 14, 19, 28–29; direct instruction in, 18, 29–30, 42–46; vs. graphophonics, 50, 50*t;* integrated with reading, 11–19; in isolation, 11, 13, 18, 29–30, 42–46; in psycholinguistic approach, 49–50; in second language, 16–18; vs. whole language approach, 11–19, 22; in word recognition approach, 42–43

PHONOLOGICAL SENSITIVITY, 8–9

PHOTO JOURNAL, 345–347, 346*t*–347*t*

PHYSICAL ACTIVITIES, 214; in ELD programs, 215–216

PIAGET'S COGNITIVE DEVELOPMENT THEORY, 139

PICNIC AT MUDSOCK MEADOW (POLACCO), 317

PINYIN, 80

PLANES OF ANALYSIS, 263, 266–269

POVERTY, 261, 359–360

PREFIXES: orthographic meanings and, 89–90; orthographic patterns and, 86–87; in word recognition approach, 41–42

PRESCHOOL: English language development in, 199

PRIMARY LANGUAGE. *See* L1

PRIOR KNOWLEDGE: building on, 243

PRIVILEGING COMMUNITY, 396

PROFESSIONAL DEVELOPMENT, 205–207, 277–279

PRONUNCIATION, 85

PROPOSITION 227, 13

PSYCHOLINGUISTIC APPROACH, 36–37, 47–52; construction of meaning in, 47–49; goals of, 42–43; graphophonics in, 47–50; phonics in, 49–50; reading proficiency in, 52; silent reading in, 51–52; vocabulary in, 48–49; word parts in, 49; vs. word recognition approach, 36–37, 37*t,* 47–52, 52*t*

R

REACH OUT AND READ, 276

READABILITY: vocabulary and, 26

READER RESPONSE THEORY, 334–337

READERS THEATRE, 218

READING: as aesthetic experience, 335–336, 337; as dialogical relationship, 335–337; emergent, 78–79; guided, 108; in L1, 55–62; in L2, 62–65; vs. literacy, 277–278; oral, 46–47, 108–109; reading comprehension and, 8; shared, 63–64, 174–175; silent, 23–27, 51, 62–66; as sociocultural experience, 335–337

READING ABILITY: transfer of from L1 to L2, 55–62

READING ALOUD: in scaffolding reading experience, 107–108

READING COMPREHENSION, 19–27; construction of meaning in, 47–49; in content learning, 134–137, 136*f;* vs. decoding skills, 5–29; enhancement strategies for, 130*f,* 136*f;* extensive reading and, 19, 23–27; phonemic awareness and, 45–46; phonics and, 19–20; predictors of, 20, 20*t;* in second language, 16–18; text cues in, 47–49; variables in, 20

READING DEVELOPMENT: identity negotiation in, 16

READING FREQUENCY: comprehension and, 19, 23–27; vocabulary knowledge and, 23–27

READING INSTRUCTION: acquisition vs. learning in, 36–52; balanced approach in, 10–11, 22–23; home environment and, 14–16; metacognitive approach in, 10–11; phonics in, 7–14. *See also* phonics; psycholinguistic approach in, 36–37, 47–52; word recognition approach in, 36–47. *See also* literacy learning

READING PROFICIENCY: in psycholinguistic approach, 52, 52*t;* in word recognition approach, 52, 52*t*

RELATIONAL LEARNING, 338–339, 353–354

RETEACHING: in scaffolding reading experience, 113

RETELLING: in language experience approach, 173–174

ROGOFF'S PLANES OF ANALYSIS, 263, 266–269

ROOTS: in word recognition approach, 41–42

ROSENBLATT'S READER RESPONSE THEORY, 334–337

ROUND-ROBIN READING, 46

S

"SAM'S STORM" (BYERS), 105

SCAFFOLDING, 97–98, 121, 153, 213, 218; extent of, 121; sheltered English instruction and, 126, 127–128, 167–171

SCAFFOLDING READING EXPERIENCE, 98–121; amount of scaffolding in, 121; benefits of, 121; definition of, 99; differentiated, 115–120, 117*f;* during-reading activities in, 101–103, 102*f,* 107–110; for easy narrative, 113–114; examples of, 113–120; implementation phase of, 99–101, 100*f,* 117*f;* as lesson framework, 99; planning phase of, 99–100, 100*f,* 117*f;* postreading activities in, 101–103, 102*f,* 110–113; prereading activities in, 100–102, 102*f,* 103–107; for science text, 115–120; for social studies text, 114–115; support for, 98; underlying principles of, 97–98

SCHEMA, 139, 214

SCHOOL LIBRARIES: L1 texts in, 67–68

SCHOOLS: as cultural institutions, 327–328; home/community partnerships with. *See* home-school-community partnerships

SCIENCE-LANGUAGE INTEGRATION RUBRIC, 250

SECOND LANGUAGE. *See* L2

SEMANTIC MAPPING, 177

SEMANTICS: in construction of meaning, 48

SEMITRANSLUCENT ORTHOGRAPHY, 73

SEMITRANSPARENT ORTHOGRAPHY, 73

SHALLOW ORTHOGRAPHY, 73

SHARED NARRATIVES, 315

SHARED READING, 63–64, 174–175

SHELTERED INSTRUCTION, 126, 127–128, 167–171, 168*f,* 261; collaborative, 261; vs. front-loading for language, 250–251

SHELTERED INSTRUCTION OBSERVATION PROTOCOL, 250

SIGHT WORDS: in word recognition approach, 42–43

SILENT READING, 23–27, 51; in L1, 65–66; in L2, 62–65; in scaffolding reading experience, 107

SKILL-AND-DRILL PROGRAMS, 11

SMITH-GOODMAN HYPOTHESIS, 55

SOCIOCULTURAL THEORIES: vs. behaviorism, 28–30; multilevel collaboration and, 262–264

SOCIOECONOMIC FACTORS, 261, 359–360

SOCIOPSYCHOLINGUISTIC APPROACH. *See* psycholinguistic approach

SORTING ACTIVITIES, 87

SPANISH: consonants in, 80; orthography in, 73, 79, 80–83, 85; vowels in, 81

SPANISH-SPEAKING FAMILIES. *See* Latino students

SPECIAL EDUCATION PROGRAMS, 250, 262, 279–281; Asian American views of, 274; home and community support for, 274; as placement vs. service, 260

SPECIALIZED VOCABULARY, 25

SPEECH: telegraphic, 157

SPELLING: emergent, 78–80. *See also* Orthography

SPELLING INVENTORIES, 76–77

SPONTANEOUS BILITERACY, 15

STANDARDIZED TESTING, 3, 13, 219–223; English-only instruction and, 271–272; multilevel collaboration and, 267–268, 271–272

STANDARDS-BASED INSTRUCTION, 286–305; accommodations and modifications in, 295–297, 296*f,* 297*f;* vs. activity-based instruction, 293; assessment methods in, 292–293; benchmarks in, 286; benefits of, 288; California's ELD Standards in, 287; concepts, skills, and knowledge in, 291; content standards in, 286; culminating tasks in, 292–293; designing instructional units for, 288–294; determining acceptable evidence for, 291–293; ELD programs and, 219–223; for English language learners, 294–305; exemplars in, 292–293; identifying desired results for, 289–291; performance standards in, 286; planning learning experiences and instruction for, 293–294; published standards and, 291; sample units for, 298–305, 298*f*–304*f;* teacher practices in, 287–289, 288*f;* TESOL's ESL Standards and, 287

STANDARDS MOVEMENT, 204–205

STANDARDS PERFORMANCE CONTINUUM, 265

STORIES OF CULTURE, 318–323

STUDENT PARTNERSHIPS: in content area instruction, 128–130; negotiation of meaning in, 131

STUDY SKILLS: instruction in, 142–144, 145*f,* 146*f*

SUFFIXES: orthographic meanings and, 89–90; orthographic patterns and, 86–87; in word recognition approach, 41–42

SUSTAINED SILENT READING, 23–27, 51; in L2, 62–65

SYLLABLES AND AFFIXES SPELLING STAGE, 86–87, 89–90

SYNTAX: in construction of meaning, 48

T

TEACHABLE MOMENTS, 229*f,* 230, 252–254

TEACHERS: expectations of, 254; linguistic knowledge of, 227, 238–239, 254; shortage of, 267; training of, 205–207, 277–279

TEACHERS' LEARNING COLLABORATIVE: literacy curriculum framework of, 309–329

TEACHERS OF ENGLISH TO SPEAKERS OF OTHER LANGUAGES (TESOL), 204, 287; ESL Standards of, 287

TEACHER TRAINING: in ESL instruction, 194–195, 205–206

TEACHING: collaborative, 68, 182–195. *See also* Collaborative teaching

TEACHING TO THE TEST, 3, 13

TECHNICAL VOCABULARY, 25

TELEGRAPHIC SPEECH, 157

TESOL STANDARDS, 204

TEXAS: reading instruction policy in, 14, 30

TEXTBOOKS: content area, 144–147

TEXT COMPREHENSIBILITY: in content area instruction, 144–147

TEXT CUES, 47–48; in word recognition approach, 50

TEXT MODIFICATION: in scaffolding reading experience, 109–110

TEXTS: decodable, 7, 14, 19, 28–29; L1, 67–68; multicultural, 314–322, 325–327; nondecodable, 28–29

TOOTER PEPPERDAY (Spinelli), 89–90

TOP-DOWN APPROACH, 19, 30

TOPICAL CURRICULUM: in communicative approaches, 166–167

TPR METHOD, 160–161

TRANSFER EFFECT, 55–62

TRANSFORMATION OF PARTICIPATION, 396–403

TRANSLUCENT ORTHOGRAPHY, 73

TRANSPARENT ORTHOGRAPHY, 73

U

UNDER ATTACK (Krashen), 62

USAGE: teaching of, 236–241

V

The Very Hungry Caterpillar (Carle), 170

VIRTUAL TEXT, 335

VISUAL AIDS: in content-based instruction, 133–134; in ELD programs, 214; in natural approach to L2 acquisition, 163

VOCABULARY: academic, 5–6, 25, 231–242; Anglo-Saxon lexicon in, 23–25; classification of, 23–26; in communicative approach, 172–174, 176–177; content, 137–138, 138*f*, 216–217; contextual acquisition of, 26–27; in ELD programs, 216–217; explicit instruction in, 24, 239–240; extensive reading and, 23–27; general academic, 25; Greco-Roman lexicon in, 23–25; high-frequency words in, 25; isolated study of, 24; low-frequency words in, 25–26; preteaching of, 39–41, 49–50, 105, 245; readability and, 26; technical/specialized, 25; in word recognition approach, 39–41

VYGOTSKIAN APPROACH: vs. behaviorism, 28–30; cultural diversity and, 337; double function of language in, 393; mediation in, 392–396, 394*f*; in multilevel collaboration, 262–264

W

WHOLE LANGUAGE APPROACH, 8; vs. phonics, 11–19, 22

WITHIN-WORD PATTERNS, 84–85

WORD CHARTS, 87–89, 88*f*

WORD DERIVATIONS, 90

WORD PARTS: in word recognition approach, 41–42

WORD RECOGNITION APPROACH, 36–47; goals of, 39; phonemic awareness in, 43–46; phonics in, 42–43; vs. psycholinguistic approach, 36–37, 37*t*, 47–52, 52*t*; reading proficiency in, 52, 52*t*; round robin reading in, 46–47; sight words in, 42–43; vocabulary learning in, 39–41; word parts in, 41–42

WORDS: brick and mortar, 239–241, 241*f*; high-frequency, 25; low-frequency, 25. *See also* vocabulary

WORD-STUDY ACTIVITIES, 71–72, 76–90; meaning-layer, 90–91, 91*f*; pattern-layer, 83–90; sound-layer, 76–83

WORD USAGE: teaching of, 236–241

The World of William Joyce Scrapbook (Joyce), 316

WRITING: communicative approaches and, 177; in ELD programs, 219; in scaffolding reading experience, 111–112

Y

You Shouldn't Have to Say Goodbye (Hermes), 347–348

Z

ZONE OF PROXIMAL DEVELOPMENT, 19, 29, 53, 99, 131–132, 264; CREDE standards and, 265